The Author

Alfred F. Kuen is a professor at the State Teacher's Training College in Strasbourgh, France. He attended the Emmaus Bible School in Switzerland, where Rene Pache is president. His outstanding work *I Will Build My Church* was translated from French by Miss Ruby Lindblad, French teacher at Trinity College in Deerfield, Illinois.

I WILL BUILD
MY CHURCH

I WILL BUILD
MY CHURCH

by

ALFRED KUEN

Translated by

RUBY LINDBLAD

MOODY PRESS • Chicago

The New Berkeley Bible has been used for both the New and Old Testament references, except where otherwise noted.

The use of selected references from various versions of the Bible in this publication does not necessarily imply publisher endorsement of the versions in their entirety.

The free churches are the churches of professing believers, the churches in which conversion is required for membership.

The multitudinist churches are sometimes called churches of the masses, state churches, national churches, and in them people are enrolled at the time of birth.

ENGLISH EDITION

© 1971 by
THE MOODY BIBLE INSTITUTE
OF CHICAGO

Translated from the original
French edition, *Je bâtirai mon Eglise*

Library of Congress Catalog Card Number: 70-163443

Printed in the United States of America

Contents

Foreword

It is said that the twentieth century is the century of the church. Actually, from all sides one hears talk of elucidation, of reform of the structure, of the church community, of liturgical renewal, of involvement of the laity, of interecclesiastical dialogue. The church's task and nature, her mission and her relationship to the world are proposed to Christians for their consideration.

Now those who are preoccupied with these problems, and rightfully so, often let themselves be guided by traditional opinions or by a revolutionary desire to adapt themselves to contemporary thought.

The author prepared for this writing by studying in only one school, the school of Holy Scripture. It is in the directives given by Jesus to His apostles, in the teachings given in the book of Acts and in the epistles that he sought the norm to which the churches of our times, as well as all times, must conform. What does the Bible say concerning the structure of Christian assemblies, their organization, conditions for membership, their ministries, their worship services, baptism and the holy communion? That is what is important; we must abide by that alone.

It is always difficult to rid oneself of preconceived ideas. To be on the right path, we must submit our thoughts and deeds to the Word of God. Certain readers will possibly not be in entire accord with the author's conclusions, but they cannot deny that he has given himself honestly to the study of the New Testament message in order to present it in all of its purity.

Moreover, he has not done it as one would who repudiates the twenty centuries of Christian history. He clings unreservedly to the Bible, but he is careful not to despise that which the most diverse believers through the ages have been able to say, write, or do. The numerous quotations from the church Fathers, the Reformers, and the contemporary theologians are not the least of the riches of the book. Even if Alfred Kuen shows himself to be a resolute supporter of the principle of the free churches, one cannot accuse him of having ignored the position of the

7

multitudinists. He has put into practice the exhortation of the apostle: "Test everything; hold fast what is good." The extensive bibliography would encourage the reader to pursue a personal research by consulting the most diverse works, in agreement with or contrary to the ideas of the author.

We hope that believers in nonconformist groups will read this exposition and be kept from accepting the practices of their assemblies without reflecting. Thus they will acquire convictions based on a solid foundation. This reading will be profitable also to members of institutional churches. It will give them information on the position, so often misunderstood, of their brothers in the free churches and will prompt them to see what changes might be desirable in their own communities.

In brief, this well-documented, well-balanced, definitely evangelical volume merits a place of honor in the abundant literature consecrated to the subject of the church.

J. M. NICOLE

Introduction

TO GOD

> "I also tell you that you are Peter, and on this rock I will build My church, and the gates of hades shall not prevail against her" (Mt 16:18).

THESE WELL-KNOWN WORDS of Jesus bring us face to face with the importance of the church. Jesus Christ Himself, the very Son of God, of whom it is said "all things were created . . . through Him and for Him" is the one who wishes to build this church, His church. He knew that its construction would not be completed without difficulties and that all the powers of hell would form a league against it. Nevertheless, the triumph of the church is as certain as is the final victory of its Head.

Other passages in the New Testament emphasize the great interest which God has in the church. "Christ loved the church and gave Himself for her" (Eph 5:25). Would He have loved it if it had not been of such great value in His eyes? Would He have sacrificed Himself for it if it had not been of such great value to Him?

"And not alone for the nation [Jesus was to die], but to gather into one all the scattered children of God" (Jn 11:52). The final objective of the death of Christ on the cross was therefore not only the salvation of the individual but also the building of this body whose calling is recorded in a plan of cosmic dimensions: ". . . the many-sided wisdom of God may now be made known through the church to the rulers and the authorities in the heavenly spheres" (Eph 3:10)—by this "church of the living God, the pillar and bulwark of the truth" (1 Ti 3:15).

If God attributes to the church such an important role, can we exclude it from our concerns? Several hundred passages in the Bible speak of it: the book of the Acts relates how the churches were founded; the epistles, all addressed to churches or to their leaders, give a great deal of consideration to problems of the church; and it is still to the churches that the Spirit of God, in the Apocalypse, addresses His final revelations. If the church

9

occupies so great a place in divine revelation, dare we consider it of secondary importance?

FOR US

Moreover, who among us would claim to be able to do without her? Is it not through the church, according to the degree to which she has remained faithful, that the gospel is transmitted to us? Is it not the church—that is, the body of Christ, the whole body composed of the true children of God—which has nourished us, educated and corrected us from the first days of our new life, because God instituted it to help us to grow normally and harmoniously (Eph 4:11-15)? Is it not within the church that we find the possibilities for action and testimony which enable us to develop fully?

The Christian of the first century would never have conceived of his Christian life other than in communion with his brothers and sisters in the church.

"Primitive Christianity lives in the thought of the Church."[1] The Robinson Crusoe Christian does not exist.[2] During the first centuries of Christianity, the church became progressively so important that one finally thought: "Outside of the Church—no salvation." The Catholic overvaluation of the church was followed by the Protestant overemphasis of individual salvation. The church has little place in the Protestant theological research from the sixteenth to the nineteenth century.[3]

THE CENTURY OF THE CHURCH

However, although the peak of the individualistic tendency was reached in the nineteenth century, in the twentieth we have recognized the error of this trend. In 1926 Bishop O. Dibelius prophesied: "The twentieth century will be the century of the church."[4] The same year E. Thurneysen wrote: "This revival of research concerning the Church seems to me significant for the historical hour in which we live. I believe that this research will continue to engage our attention in the course of the years and decades to come."[5]

These predictions were to be revealed as correct. In 1935 Drobnitsky affirmed: "The time for individualism in Christianity is past . . . today the great search for the Church is before us."[6] We speak of the "rediscovery of the Church,"[7] of a "new love for the old Church,"[8] and even of "panecclesiology."

The Catholics themselves state: "In the heart of Protestant Christendom, the matter being considered is the total rediscovery of the Church."[9] Thus in 1943 Professor Ehrenstrom could write: "It is not necessary to be a great prophet to predict that, in the decades to come, the problem of the Church will be predominant in all Christendom." And Karl Barth affirms: "The Church has been talked about more in the thirty years that followed the first World War than during the eighteenth and nineteenth centuries combined."[10]

Other voices, however, are less optimistic. Emil Brunner speaks of a "groping research for a new form of the Church," of "the era of the crisis of the Church which some thirty years ago was announced to be the century of the Church."[11]

Today everybody is talking about the church, but what do we mean by "the church"? Do we agree, at least, on the same concept which this term represents? Far from it. On the contrary, all thorough research seems to have brought to light only more clearly the profound confusion of Protestantism concerning this problem.[12] In 1965, after half a century of theological research on the church, Pastor J. P. Benoît repeated, "To our knowledge, no one has ever defined what the Church is."[13]

"I WILL BUILD MY CHURCH"

"I will build My church." When the Christians of the first century heard that word, they knew of what the Lord was speaking; they saw that church being built before their very eyes; they were forming it; they were the living church. The Christian of the twentieth century no longer knows to what the Lord was referring, because the word *church* contains for him a multitude of different notions.

The Word of the Lord stresses for us the importance and the unity of the church; it tells us clearly who will be its Head and its Builder, what will be its future. But on the other hand, it presents as many problems as it solves and, to these problems, each fractional part of present-day Christianity gives a different answer.

The most important differences among the historical branches of Christianity assume a definite form in their answer to this question. Upon whom or upon what did Jesus Christ plan to build His church? Upon Peter, upon Peter's confession, or upon Himself?

Following what plan did He wish to construct it? Following the one that He transmitted to the apostles, once for all, or following a plan which He would communicate to the builders as the work proceeded?

What materials would He use? All men, all the baptized, or only those who, like Peter, would confess that He is the Christ, the Son of the living God?

In what form would this church be presented? Are we to look for a visible church or be content with the invisible church?

To what church is this promise addressed: "The gates of hell shall not prevail against it"? To the one that gathers together the greatest number of the faithful? To the one which claims to be the lawful one by continuous historical succession from the first to the twentieth century? Or, to the one which, abandoning the succession, returns to the apostolic model and perseveres in "the teaching of the apostles"?

WHAT IS THE CHURCH? WHERE IS THE CHURCH?

At present some three hundred religious groups claim, often for themselves alone, this appellation. Certain groups even go so far as to anathematize all the others which, according to them, are usurping this title. They alone are the church!

Who then has the right to bear this name? What community can affirm that it answers to the definition which God gave of it? Where is the church according to God's plan? These are questions which are asked from the very beginning of the Christian life. Need for fellowship in the life of a church is one of the first manifestations of the new life. What church, among all those which are open to the young believer, will bring him the elements which he needs for growth and development? Evidently, that one which corresponds the most closely to God's plan, for "if the Church does not correspond to the will of God, it has every chance to turn us from the Gospel instead of leading us into it," asserts J. de Senarclens.[14] But how can one discern the divine plan concerning the church? Who will guide the young convert, often still hesitant, in the study of the Bible? Evangelical literature written in French, still very scant in the field of evangelization and personal edification, scarcely has an answer for the one who asks to be guided in his study of what the Bible teaches concerning the church.

I still remember my own confusion during the first years of my Christian life while seeking the answers to the ecclesiastical propositions which I faced. Each argument seemed plausible and each interpretation could be defended. Which one was true?

HOW THIS BOOK CAME TO BE

One day I resolutely put aside all my books, I took my New Testament and there underlined all that concerned the church; then I picked out and classified on cards what I had found. What a joy it was to see roughly outlined and gradually taking shape a living picture of the primitive church. Each day my convictions became stronger: Yes, there was the church according to the plan of God!

In this way, some twenty years ago, the first data of this book was gathered. Progressively, as problems arose from the experience of community life, the answers were sought in the same manner: the whole New Testament was reread to find the answer to the question which had been raised; then all of the interesting elements were picked out and classified. In this way a firsthand documentation of this controversial subject was gradually formed. What assurance when one knows that his convictions are not based upon reflections or experiences of men, no matter how valuable they may be, but on the Word of God!

That does not mean that we are to ignore what others have thought, experienced, or written, because they could offer us nothing! How much useful enlightenment and valuable advice we have gleaned from books and from interviews with the elders of the most diverse ecclesiastical milieux! Would it not be pure presumption to seek truth in the Bible without concerning oneself with what generations of Christians have already discovered? Does one have the right to neglect the thoughts of all those who with us constitute the church of all times and all places? Would it even be honest to discard the arguments of certain churches without even examining them?

All these reasons have obliged us to read what has been written on the question—in French, German, and English—and to constantly compare our discoveries in the Bible with the thoughts of others. However, the present work does not claim to enter into theological dispute. Writing as a layman for laymen, the author would like in all simplicity to bring them the fruit of the discoveries he made in the Bible and introduce them to a personal study of what the Word of God teaches us concerning the church.

"The Church does not live by the work of theologians [this is a theologian affirming it], but by the Word of God. God be praised, this Word is accessible even to those who cannot follow the theologians in the development of their ideas."[15]

Having no personal authority to cast into the balance to accredit his affirmations, the author had to be all the more careful to base all that he put forward on the sole authority of the Word of God. So he certainly does not expect that his conclusions will be accepted immediately, but rather that the readers will follow the example of the Bereans who "searched the Scriptures daily, whether those things were so" (Ac 17:11, KJV).

Indeed, it is only in the measure that the Word of God effectively and practically finds its rightful place among us that the problem of the church will find its solution.

Notes

1. O. Scheel, *Zum urchristlichen Kirchen—und Verfassungsproblem*, p. 409.
2. "Not to come to the assembly is to commit an act of pride and to exclude oneself, for it is written: 'God resists the proud'" (Ignatius of Antioch, *To the Ephesians* 5:2).
   "The Bible knows nothing of a religion of hermits" (John Wesley). "The true Church is a part of the true Christian faith; Christian faith is an impossibility without the Church and leads only to the Church" (Emil Brunner, "Eglise et Révélation," *Revue de Théologie et de Philosophie* [Jan.-Mar. 1930], p. 7). "We know that it is not possible for a living Christianity to endure long if it is not expressed in an ecclesiastical and community form" (Brunner, *La Situation de l'Eglise*, p. 4). "The Christian at the end of the first century is no more an isolated being than is the one in the apostolic age; such is the first observation which we must accept. . . . The Christian is by very nature, by definition, one might say, a man who has brothers. . . . Every Christian is a member of a Church and by this word should first of all represent to us a local community" (Canon G. Bardy, *La Théologie de l'Eglise de Saint Clément de Rome à Saint Irénée*, pp. 7, 8, 19). "An 'individual' Christianity which exists far from the Church and separate from it is unthinkable in the primitive Church" (R. Schnackenburg, *Die Kirche im N.T.*, p. 14). "No writer of the New Testament would ever have supposed that a man could be 'in Christ' and not 'in the Church'; to him that would have seemed a practical impossibility" (Geddes MacGregor, *Corpus Christi*, p. 4).
3. "In the consciousness of Christians and in the theology up until the first world war, the Church played only a secondary role" (U. Valeske, *Votum ecclesiae*, p. 1). "The doctrine of the Church and that of the Holy Spirit which are bound together are the forgotten realms of the Christian tradition" (Theodore Wedel, *The Coming Great Church*, p. 56).
4. Otto Dibelius, *Das Jahrhundert der Kirche*.
5. E. Thurneysen, "Die Frage nach der Kirche," *Zwischen den Zeiten* 4 (1926).
6. W. Drobnitzky, "Die ewige Kirche," *Eine heilige Kirche*, no. 17 (1935), p. 285.
7. Plachte, *Die Wiederentdeckung der Kirche*.
8. H. W. Wolff, *Neue Liebe zur alten Kirche*.
9. "Autour du renouveau de l'ecclésiologie," *La Vie intellectuelle* 51 (1939): 9.
10. Karl Barth, *L'Eglise*, p. 57.
11. Brunner, *Evang. Théologie* (1959), p. 147.
12. "What is the Church? This question has never been resolved by Protestantism. Never since the Reformation has light been shed on the relationship between the Church in the confessional sense of the community of Jesus Christ and the institution or institutions which are called the Churches" (Brunner, *Le Malentendu de l'Eglise*, p. 5).
13. J. P. Benoît, *Dénominations et Sectes*, p. 7.
14. J. de Senarclens, *De la Vraie Eglise selon Calvin*, p. 9.
15. Brunner, *Les églises, les groupes et l'Eglise de Jésus-Christ*, p. 11.

Outline of This Study

B. The Human Body: Type of the Church
    1) The body an indivisible unit
    2) The body a complete unit in itself
    3) The body a diversified unit
    4) The body a unit of relationships
    5) The body an organized unit
    6) The body a unit in growth
    7) The body a unit of life
C. The Three "Bodies of Christ" in the Bible
    1) The physical body and the "mystical body of Christ"
    2) Holy communion and the body of Christ
D. The Teaching of These Images Concerning the Church
    1) The relationship between the church and Christ
    2) The nature of the members

PART IV: LAYING THE FIRST STONE

8. You Are Peter, and on This Rock . . .
  A. First Mention of the Church
  B. "You Are Peter . . ." What sure deduction can we make from this word?
  C. "And on This Rock" Who is this rock?
    1) The rock is the apostle Peter.
    2) The rock is Jesus Christ.
    3) The rock is Peter's confession.
  D. Upon Whom Is This Church Built?

PART V: BEGINNING OF THE CONSTRUCTION

9. The Birth of the Church
  A. The Role of the Apostle Peter
  B. The Schema-Type for the Founding of the Church
  C. Exceptional and Temporary Factors in Pentecost

PART VI: THE MATERIALS

10. The Members of the Church
The two groups
  A. The Local Church: An Open or Closed Society?
  B. How Did They Become Church Members?
  C. Must One Be Born Again to Be a Church Member?
    1) The teaching of Jesus and the apostles concerning the church

D. From the Seventeenth to the Twentieth Century
  1) Seventeenth century—Pietism
  2) Eighteenth century
  3) Nineteenth century—France, Switzerland
  4) Twentieth century—churches outside the institutional churches

PART VIII: "LET EACH MAN TAKE CARE HOW HE BUILDS . . ."

13. Multitudinist Church or Free Church
  A. Nature of the Church According to the Bible
    1) The name of the church
      a) The name *ekklesia*
      b) The historical background
      c) The Jewish *ekklesia*
    2) The local church and the universal church in the Bible
      a) First mention of the church
      b) Second mention of the church
      c) Composition of the universal church
      d) Community of believers and not an institution
    3) The church and salvation
      a) Salvation an individual matter
      b) Salvation a conditional matter
      c) Two responses: two camps
      d) Human liberty and personal decision
      e) Conversion in the epistles
      f) Designating names of church members
    4) The types of the church
      a) Relationship between Christ and the member
      b) Identity of the nature of the members
      c) No members who are not in Christ
    5) The symbolic acts of the church
      a) Baptism of believers constitutes a free church
      b) Testimonies in favor of this baptism
      c) The significance of baptism
      d) The multitudinist church and baptismal regeneration
      e) Conscious engagement in baptism
      f) The biblical observance of holy communion
  B. The Church in History
    1) The churches of the first three centuries

Part I

THE FOUNDATION

1

Return to the Origin: The Plan of God

"See to it," He said, "that you make everything according to the pattern that was shown you on the mountain."

Hebrews 8:5

THE REQUIREMENTS OF GOD

GOD ASKS THAT WE CONFORM to His directives. When Moses constructed the tabernacle in the wilderness, God told him to make it exactly according to the pattern revealed to him on the mountain (Ex 25:9, 40; 26:30; 27:8; Heb 8:5). And Moses obeyed the Lord God.

When Jesus Christ began to build His church, He also had a plan. He certainly could not condone building haphazardly, especially since He is the great master Architect. This plan was communicated orally to the builders; that is, to the apostles while here on earth and, after His departure, by directives transmitted through the Holy Spirit (Jn 16:13; Ac 13:2; 15:28) and which the apostles followed faithfully. The churches which we discern through the writings of the apostles (Acts and the epistles) are therefore churches built according to God's plan, churches which conform to His idea, to His will. Religious groups born of the historical evolution of these primitive or early churches toward a different type will no longer be able to claim this conformity to God's plan. The idea that the church should evolve during the course of the centuries under the leading of the Holy Spirit is unknown to the apostles. It was, moreover, introduced into the Catholic Church only at the beginning of the nineteenth century by J. A. Moehler.[1] On the contrary, the apostles speak of "the faith which was once for all delivered to the saints" (Jude 3) and ask Christians "that you may not support one teacher against the other" (1 Co 4:6).

God had spoken by Moses to His people of the old covenant: "You are neither to add to the word that I command you, nor take from it; these commands which I enjoin upon you are of the LORD your God" (Deu 4:2; cf. 12:32). In the book of the Proverbs it is written: "Add not to His words, lest He reprove you, and you be found a liar" (30:6). The preacher said: "I know that everything that God does shall remain forever; nothing can be added to it" nor can anything be taken from it" (Ec 3:14). Would this no longer be true in the time of the new covenant?

This Holy Scripture "is inspired by God and is profitable for teaching, for reproof, for correction, for training in righteousness, so that the man of God may be well-fitted and adequately equipped for all good work" (2 Ti 3:16-17). Would these Scriptures no longer suffice when we pass from the individual plan to the collective plan, from that of the "man of God" to that of the "church of the living God"? Had the Lord not promised the apostles that the Holy Spirit would guide them "into all truth" (Jn 16:13)?

This gospel, announced by the apostle Paul, which, unless one has believed in vain, must be held fast (1 Co 15:1-2), these curses uttered against whoever might announce another gospel than that which had been preached (be he an angel or the apostle Paul himself), do these dangers concern only the individual aspect of salvation (Gal 1:7-9)? Do we not call the canonical writings of the new covenant in their entirety the New Testament? And have we forgotten one of the most elementary rules of law which the apostle Paul reminds us: "Speaking in terms of human relationships, brothers, no one sets aside or adds to a person's last will when it has been ratified" (Gal 3:15)? Will we permit ourselves this liberty with regard to the testament of God? Do we not fear that some day Jesus will rebuke us as He rebuked the Pharisees: "You let go of God's commandments to cling to human tradition. . . . How well you frustrate the law of God to observe your own tradition" (Mk 7:8-9)! And do not all the fine systems which we have constructed risk falling under the implacable verdict of which the Lord reminds them: "Uselessly, they worship Me with their teaching of human commands" (Mt 15:9, citing Is 29:13)?

Yes, let us fear lest all these human structures fall one day under the judgment of the word of the Master: "He who rejects Me and does not receive My teachings has his judge: My spoken word will judge him on the last day" (Jn 12:48).

Must one believe that God would not have been capable of building from the very beginning the church the way He wanted it? If His ideal had been the organized, hierarchical, clerical system which we find after several centuries under the name of church, would He not have established it thus from the very beginning? Would the present-day church correspond better to the will of God and to the needs of men than did the primitive church? If so, one would have to admit that men with their artifices and their clever management of affairs are more competent to arrange the affairs of God than He is Himself!

Superiority of God's Plan

Moreover, why would it have been necessary to change anything whatsoever in the initial plan of God? God does not change. Man remains the same before Him throughout the centuries and the different civilizations: a sinner, having come short of the glory of God (Ro 3:21-23), incapable in himself of doing good and of saving himself.

Salvation is accorded him on the same conditions: by faith laying hold of the justification which the grace of God offers him. The factors of progress in the new life remain the same: prayer, faith, communion of the brethren. Thus, all of the essential elements of the spiritual life remain unchanged. Why then should the church have changed?

Has not the history of twenty centuries of Christianity proved that the plan of the primitive church is the only one which is suitable for all times and places, is most flexible in its adaptation to the most diverse conditions,[2] is the best able to resist and stand against persecutions,[3] and offers the maximum of possibilities for the full development of the spiritual life?

Each time that man has believed himself to be more intelligent than God, that he has painstakingly developed a religious system "better adapted to the psychology of man,"[4] more conformable to the spirit of our times, instead of simply following the neotestamentary model, his attempt has been short-lived because of failure due to some unforeseen difficulty.

All heresies and deviations in the church spring from the abandonment of the Scriptures and of the model for the church which they present. Clement of Alexandria, even in his time, used to say, "One becomes heretic when one does not submit to the Scriptures. Those who undertake great things must necessarily fall to great depths if they do not cling to the rule of truth which they have received from the Truth Himself." According to J. H. Merle d'Aubigné, "As we advance through the centuries, light and life begin to decrease in the Church. Why? Because the torch of the Scripture begins to grow dim and because the deceitful light of human authorities begins to replace it."[5]

Various Attempts to Return to the Source

IN THE SIXTEENTH CENTURY

The humanist Renaissance of the sixteenth century exhumed the Bible. The religious Reformation was born of the rediscovery of the Word of God, the only norm of faith and of the church. *Sola scriptura* (the Scripture alone) was one of the guiding principles of the whole Reformation.

Luther. Often affirming this supreme authority of the Word of God, Luther said, "All the articles of faith are sufficiently established in the Holy Scriptures so that one should establish no other."[6] That is why "one

cannot constrain anyone to believe something if it is not by the Holy
Scriptures which are properly of divine authority."[7] The revolutionary
act of Luther was that of placing the authority of the Scripture above that
of the church. "The Word of God is incomparably above the Church,"
he said.[8]

Facing Tetzel, who proclaimed that "one must teach Christians that
the Church holds, as definite articles of Catholic truth, several points
which are not found in the collection of the Holy Scriptures" (17th thesis
against Luther), Luther affirmed:

> One must not in anything concern himself with human laws, rights, ear-
> liest beginnings, traditions, and customs: whether they have been insti-
> tuted by pope or emperor, prince or bishop, whether half or all of the
> world has respected them, whether they have lasted a year or a thousand
> years! Because the human soul is an eternal thing above all that is tem-
> poral, it ought to be governed by and concerned with the eternal Word
> alone. For it is an abominable thing to govern consciences before God by
> human laws and ancient traditions, That is why one must act in these
> matters according to the Scripture and the Word of God.[9]

He also said, "It is the Word of God which lays down the articles of
faith, and no one has the right to impose others upon us, not even the
angels."[10] The authority of the Word of God is as valid for the questions
of the church as for those which concern personal salvation. "Primitive
Christianity alone is the true Church," Luther affirmed.[11] "The true
Church must be the one which tenaciously holds to the Word of God. . . .
That is why you should not say to us: 'Church, Church, Church!' You
ought to convince us that you are the Church."[12]

> One must contradict pope and councils to save the Holy Scriptures. The
> Church judged and condemned the heretics by the Word of God . . . she
> was not master of the Word; she submitted herself to the Word of God
> in order that she might hear Christ alone and do the will of Him who sent
> her, that she might be a disciple of this Man, of His Word, and of His
> teaching. Because of that, she will be in authority over all things, and it
> was according to that Word that she decided this doctrine to be right,
> that one false, and this man to be a heretic. . . .[13]

Zwingli. Having been lost in the labyrinth of philosophy for eight
years, Zwingli said, "Finally, led by the Holy Scriptures and the Word of
God, I have come to say to myself: 'You must drop all that and learn God's
thought in all its purity in His Word alone.' "[14]

Calvin. Calvin also wanted them to "examine by the rule of the Scriptures the point in question . . . at all times the Scripture would be preeminent and all would be subject to it. . . . The Word of God remains the
rule to which are subject not only men, but also angels."[15]

"We submit our judgment and intelligence to it as to something far beyond the province of human judgment," he said.[16] "Every agreement made apart from the Word of God is entered into not by consent of believers, but unbelievers."[17]

> It is these principles which the confessions of faith of the Reformation have established. We believe that the Word which is contained in these books has God for origin and that it retains its authority from God alone and not from men. This Word is the rule of all truth and contains all that is necessary for the service of God and for our salvation; therefore neither men, nor angels are permitted to add to it, subtract from it, or change anything in it. It follows then that neither antiquity, nor customs, nor number of adherents, nor human wisdom, nor judgments, nor laws, nor decrees, nor councils, nor visions, nor miracles can oppose these Holy Scriptures, but, on the contrary, all things are to be examined and amended according to it.[18]
>
> We reject wholeheartedly all that is not in accord with this infallible rule.[19]

As for the Anglican Reformation, it specified in the sixth of the "39 articles of religion" which constitute the charter of Anglicanism: "Holy Scripture containeth all things necessary to salvation, so that whatsoever is not read therein nor may be proved thereby, is not to be required of any man, that it should be believed as an article of Faith, or be thought requisite or necessary to salvation."

Thus the Reformation movement as a whole affirms its desire to return to the source of faith, to the Word of God, where the water is still clear and pure. "The profound and permanent movement of the Reformation is the reversion or return to this divine authority . . . the sovereign, absolute, and infallible authority of the Holy Scriptures," says P. Courthial.[20]

According to Brunner, "The Reformers were conscious of the fact that the neo-testamentary form of the Ekklesia was the normative form of the Church."[21] Unfortunately, the successors of the Reformers, instead of continuing the work begun by the Reformation, often sought above everything else to remain faithful to the thought of Luther, of Calvin, or of Zwingli, at the risk of forgetting that the principle of the Reformers themselves—primacy of God's thought over that of men—repudiated them.

IN MORE RECENT TIMES

In the nineteenth century a reaction took place. "Protestants according to Luther, Protestants according to Calvin,—these are a sorry group of Protestants. The only Protestants worthy of that name are the Protestants according to the Bible," wrote Count A. de Gasparin.[22] The men of the

Revival want to return to the apostolic model to which they are led by the Word of God.[23]

In the twentieth century the greatest theologians of the church reaffirm the sovereign authority of the Word of God.[24] However, since the sixteenth century, the movement for the return to the source has also continued outside of the "official" church. By means of men such as Wesley, Darby, G. Müller, Spurgeon, etc., through movements of the Spirit such as the revivals (Moravian Awakening, revivals of Geneva, of France and of Wales) the outlines of the primitive church reappear more and more distinctly.

More recently two Eastern movements have proved the extraordinary dynamic and vitality of the truly biblical church. After a few years of ministry, the Indian evangelist Bakht Singh saw several hundred churches formed in India and in Pakistan. In China, the "Little Flock," born from the ministry of Watchman Nee, gave rise to six hundred churches of the apostolic type and—what is more important—it is these churches which have most firmly withstood persecution.[25]

Again consider the evangelical assemblies, of which more than a hundred are born annually, in Catholic Italy, and the Mykiokai movement which has spread considerably in Japan. Brunner writes that its initiator, Kanzo Utchimura, "recognized in the Ecclesia of the New Testament a community of believers fundamentally different from all that he had come to know in the West under the name of Church. . . . He eagerly desired to see established a Christian community of believers which would be brought together only by faith in Christ and maintained by the Holy Spirit. . . . It is very significant that Utchimura's faith corresponds exactly to that which Paul taught. . . . This movement indicates clearly the direction which the Protestant church ought to take in the future."[26]

As Christianity disengages itself from Christendom,[27] there appears among the children of God everywhere an increasingly intense desire to rediscover the church according to God's plan. In all countries Christians sigh for a church liberated from the bondage which centuries of error have imposed on it; groups of unnamed believers are born outside of confessional and denominational boundaries, sustained by the sole desire to realize the divine will in this plan for the assembling of believers.

Even within many assemblies and historical churches one senses a new need to find again the mind of God. Behind the mountains of human traditions which have come between the church as God intended it and the institutions bearing today the name of churches, the Christian would like to rediscover the divine thought which presided at the founding of the

2

Return to the Source: Bible or Tradition?

THE "APOSTOLICITY" OF THE CHURCH

"THE BIBLE is the sovereign authority in matters of faith and doctrine." Such is the essential and first principle of the Reformation and of Protestantism. This principle guarantees in fact "apostolicity," one of the most important signs of the church, the one upon which they lay the greatest stress in the Roman Church. The term *apostolic church* appeared for the first time in 381 at the Council of Constantinople in the context of the anti-Arian struggles; in the West, "apostolicity" will be spoken of only several centuries later, according to Professor Michel Réveillaud.

Very early, however, two concepts of apostolicity appeared in the church:

1. A sacramentalist concept which sees the guarantee of apostolicity in the uninterrupted and visible transmission of ecclesiastical charges from the apostles to the present day.

2. A spiritual concept which holds that apostolicity consists in the faithfulness to the teachings of the apostles.

The Roman Church, the Greek Church, the Anglican Church, the *Old Catholics*, and others claim to be apostolic by relying on this supposedly continuous chain made by the laying on of hands of the apostles up to the present-day dignitaries of these churches. This notion does not come from the Bible, but from the Roman legal notion which makes legitimate succession in office the mark of legal continuity.

We do not stress here the precarious character of this concept,[1] nor the internal contradictions of the system.[2] We simply point out that the apostles had an entirely different idea of apostolicity.

When the apostle Paul affirms that the church is "constructed on the foundation of the apostles and prophets" (Eph 2:20), he is thinking above all of the message which the apostles and the prophets of the New Testament proclaimed, the message which brought the heathen to the faith and, in so doing, founded the church.[3] It is by persevering in the gospel announced by the apostles that the church continues to be "apostolic," that

33

is, in continuity with the foundation. The thought that a man who has received the laying on of hands of an apostle can no longer err, nor cause the church for which he is responsible to turn aside, is not only foreign to the New Testament, but it is contradicted by numerous clear teachings of the apostles. Why are there so many exhortations to persevere in sound doctrine, to hold fast to the gospel as it was proclaimed, and not to imitate those who have departed from the faith and from the sound Word?

Why this mention of so many "false workmen" and even "false apostles"? Does not the apostle Paul seem to envisage even the eventuality that one day he himself might deviate and announce "another gospel" (Gal 1:8-9)? According to the Catholic concept, the guarantee of the continuity and apostolicity is the apostle himself—or his successor—led by the Holy Spirit which was conferred upon him by the laying on of hands. According to the apostle Paul, it is the gospel which they had preached which must remain invariable even if the apostle who had preached it were later to change; "let him be accursed," and let the original message be kept intact.

Luther had this idea of apostolicity in view when he wrote, "We belong to the early church and stand with her, for those who believe as did the early church and who hold the same truths are the early church. . . . You [papists] have indeed come from the early churches, but you are no longer of those churches, neither members of those churches."[4]

Calvin also understood apostolicity in this way. "The Church is apostolic because it preaches and teaches what the apostles preached and taught," he said. "How can they act on the authority of a succession of bishops from the time of saint Peter when they have altered his testimony in order to teach innovations?"[5]

THE CATHOLIC IDEA OF TRADITION

THE ORAL TRADITION

The Catholic Church insists upon the *oral tradition* which conveys an apostolic teaching which we do not find in the Bible.[6] It is probable that such an oral catechism did exist. The church Fathers (Papias, Irenaeus, etc.) speak of this to us, but various remarks on this subject command consideration.

To begin with, the gospel is not a religion of mysticism. In the great religions of mysticism, esoteric teaching was transmitted orally only to the initiated. All the Gnostics of the second and third centuries seek to accredit their systems by claiming to have received them by oral transmission directly from the apostles, and we know what fantastic and contradictory deviations they have tried to pass off under this label! On the contrary, Jesus Christ and the apostles insisted that their teaching be done in public. To the high priest who questioned Him concerning His doctrine, Jesus said, "I have spoken openly to the world; I have been teaching right along in the synagogue and in the temple, where all the Jews gather, and I said nothing in secret" (Jn 18:20).

After the death of the Lord, the apostles "never stopped for a single day to teach and to preach Christ Jesus in the temple and at home" (Ac 5:42). Paul said to the elders of Ephesus, "I never failed to tell you what was for your benefit and to teach you publicly and in homes; how I bore testimony to both Jews and Greeks that they should repent before God and have faith in our Lord Jesus" (Ac 20:20-21). He said, "We have renounced underhanded ways of which one should be ashamed" (2 Co 4:2).

If, then, their message was delivered publicly, there can be no question of secret teachings reserved for the initiated alone. The content of this message was known by everybody. Its echo is found in the Acts and the epistles also set it forth. Paul writes, after having presented the summary of this message, "So, whether I or they, so is our preaching and such is what you believed" (1 Co 15:11). "For I determined to know nothing among you except Jesus Christ and Him crucified" (1 Co 2:2).

Oral tradition was strictly parallel to written tradition, and the latter gives an account of that which is essential in what the apostles were preaching. Moreover, the written tradition of the New Testament contains all that God judged to be "profitable for teaching, for reproof, for correction, for training in righteousness, so that the man of God may be well-fitted and adequately equipped for all good work" (2 Ti 3:16-17).

As O. Cullmann indicates, the church of the second century recognized that the direct revelation of the New Testament covered a span of time from the birth of Christ to the death of the last apostle.[7] He wrote, "The establishing of the Canon signifies that the Church itself drew a clear and distinct line of demarcation between the times of the apostles and the times of the Church."[8] "The new-born Church itself made a distinction between apostolic tradition and ecclesiastical tradition by definitely subjecting the latter to the former."[9] "Through their writings in the New Testament the apostles have given the church of all ages the benefit of their teachings."[10] To establish a canon is to say that our tradition needs to be controlled; it is to renounce all other traditions as norms, *even if they were apostolic* and authentic; it is to declare that "we consider as apostolic norm only that which is written in these books. . . . To say that the writings gathered together in a Canon were to be considered as a *norm* was to say that they were to be considered as *adequate.*"[11]

By this fact, then, the church renounced being its own norm. Consequently, if new doctrines (such as the infallibility of the pope or the ascension of the virgin) appear in the church, claiming to rest on the oral tradition of the early church, we can be sure that this claim is without foundation.

WRITTEN TRADITION

As for the tradition found in the writings of the apostolic Fathers and the church Fathers, it is too multiform and contradictory to constitute a sure foundation for a doctrine.[12] He who has even a slight knowledge of patristic literature knows that one can justify anything by citations from the Fathers. Too often—and very early—the Fathers welcomed all sorts of thoughts foreign to the apostolic message and combined them with the Revelation so that, far from furnishing us a criterion for biblical truth, their doctrine must itself be subjected to examination by the New Testament. Chrysostom had already recognized it when he wrote that "those who wish to know which is the true Church can determine this only through the Scriptures."[13] Moreover, the Fathers themselves employ the word *tradition* in a sense different from the one which the Roman Church gives to it today. Often this word designates the Scripture itself.

Irenaeus (125–202) writes: "We have not known the economy of our salvation through others than those who brought us the Gospel. This [gospel] they first preached. Then, by the will of God, they committed it to us in the Scriptures so that it should become 'the base and pillar' of our faith." G. Bardy translates: "By the will of God, they committed everything to the Scriptures."[14]

Cyprian (200–258) affirms: "God Himself attests that one is obliged to practice what is written. So if we find something ordained in the Gospels or contained in the Epistles or in the Acts of the Apostles, let us then observe that divine and holy tradition."[15]

The Fathers place the Holy Scriptures above all other sources of revelation.

Athanasius (298–373) says, "There [in the Scriptures] are the sources of salvation; it is by them alone that we can learn the evangelical discipline of piety. Let no one add anything to them; let no one take anything from them."[16]

"The holy and divinely inspired Scriptures alone suffice to enable us to know the truth."[17]

"If you wish to cite extra-Scriptural authority, if you wish to affirm as truth something not found in Scripture, why do you dispute with us who are resolved to listen to nothing and to say nothing beyond that which is written?" "These texts have been inspired of God and written by men who speak to us from God; and we have received them from these divinely inspired masters and give them to you since you have a desire for knowledge."[18]

"To neglect anything of that which is written or to introduce something which is *not* written is evidence of falling from the faith and of a great presumption."[19]

"That which is written, believe it; that which is not written do not seek it!"[20]

Cyril of Jerusalem (315–386): "Concerning divine and holy mysteries of the faith, one must not advance anything without the authority of the divine Scriptures. . . . Nor should you believe my word, what I say to you, without having seen my teachings incontestably proved by divine Scripture. For the security of our faith depends, not on the artifice of language, but on the testimony of divine Scripture."[21]

Chrysostom (347–407): "When we accept money, we do not accept it blindly; we want to count it for ourselves. And when it is a question of divine matters, would it not be folly to recklessly fall headlong into the opinions of others, we who have a rule by which we can examine everything, I mean, the divine laws? That is why I beseech you not to rely on the opinions of others, but that you consult the Scriptures."[22]

"I beg you and entreat you that, closing your ears to every other voice, you follow as your guide the canon of the Holy Scriptures."[23]

Augustine (354–430), writes: "He who knows only the canonical Holy Scriptures is confined within well-determined limits and must place them above all the letters which bishops may have written later. For, as for the Scriptures, there could be no doubt nor discussion possible concerning the truth or the justice of what is incontestably written therein."[24] Moreover, this infallible authority is set in opposition to the fallible authority of human reasoning of bishops and councils.

If there is one point on which the Fathers are in agreement, it is the recognition of the supreme authority of the Holy Scriptures. The proof?

Jerome, the scholarly translator of the Bible, writes on this subject:

"It is the doctrine of the Spirit which is transmitted to us in the canonical books; if the councils establish something contrary to it, I regard that as blasphemy" (Epistle to the Galatians). "If one speaks without the authority of the Scriptures, it is nothing but empty talk which merits no faith."[25] "All that which does not have Scripture for its authority can as well be rejected as proved."[26] "It is not the error of parents or ancestors that must be followed, but the authority of the Scriptures and the will of the Master, who is God."[27]

Augustine concludes, "Let us take away from the midst of us all of our

papers and books, and let the Book of God alone take priority. Does someone ask me why? —Because I do not want anything whatever to be proved
by human documents but by the oracles of God."[28] "One must not follow
Catholic bishops who may hold views contrary to the canonical Scriptures
of God."[29]

"It is only the books of the Scriptures, also called the canon, for which
I have learned to have this high regard and firm belief: not one of their
authors has committed any error in writing them."[30]

And we could cite many more testimonies to the same effect.[31]

What the Catholics call "Tradition" is a collection of rites and customs
of various origins which have constituted, over the course of the centuries,
the "Roman Catholic religion." This "Tradition" has been established by
writings in the Codes of Roman Canonical Law, which have completely
rejected the authority of the Bible in the church.

TRADITION IN THE PRESENT-DAY CATHOLIC CHURCH FROM THE TIME OF THE
REFORMATION

"When we deal with the problem of the Scriptures and of Tradition,"
says G. Millon, "we are dealing with the very foundation of that which divides these churches [the Roman and the Evangelical], the root of our
evangelical faith."[32]

The whole Reformation depends on two events: (1) the public act by
which Luther burned the books of canon law, and (2) his translation of
the Bible. By the first act he removed the obstacle to the Reformation in
the church; by his second act, that of giving back the Bible to Christian
people, he gave them the basis for the reconstruction of the church. In
contrast to this, the Roman Church became even more entrenched in its
fallacies, elaborating on its tradition, thereby gradually freeing itself completely from the authority of the Bible.

In *The Misunderstanding of the Church* Emil Brunner has retraced the
steps by which, through the course of six centuries, the church has attained this complete independence from biblical revelation.

The most important stages in the process are:

1. The Tridentine Council when the *sine scripto traditiones* were placed
on the same level of importance as Holy Scripture itself and therewith
Scripture—the testimony of the apostles—not only completed by a new
source of knowledge, but effectively eliminated as a final court of appeal.

2. The Vatican Council in which tradition, in turn, is supplanted in
favor of the final authority of the Pope to decide matters of dogma. . . .

3. The last step in this direction is taken by the completed *Codex juris
Canonici* of 1918 in which all matters connected with the Church, both

faith and morals, are subordinated to the authority of the Pope, and dogma as a whole becomes part of the papal *potestas jurisdictionis.* The Pope
is no longer bound to what has always been the rule in the life of the
Church; he can make new departures. . . . It is now *de jure* exactly as
Pope Pius IX declared: *"La tradizione son Io."* I, the Pope, am tradition.
What the Pope declares to be tradition, that is tradition and every Catholic Christian must profess his belief that it is tradition, even though no
trace of such a tradition exists . . . the process which began with the
institution of the episcopate as the guarantee of original apostolic truth
has here reached its logical conclusion. The formal institution has triumphed over living tradition. . . . Since the Council of Trent every appeal
to Scripture is rendered null and void by the conception of the tradition
which completes—and eventually, in point of fact, eliminates—Scripture.
Since the Vatican Council every appeal to real tradition also is made in-
efficacious through the theory that the Pope alone has authoritative knowledge of tradition. The Pope has not only the right but also the sacred
canonical duty of repudiating and disallowing every critical further in-
quiry based upon an appeal to Scripture or tradition and of excommunicating anyone who persists in such an attitude.[33]

And he adds:

From these considerations it may be seen how hopeless it is for Protestants, non-Roman and Roman Catholics to discuss the rights and the
wrongs of tradition, since all three mean by tradition something quite
different. . . . By their system of Canon Law and ecclesiastical jurisdiction
they reject the idea of any need to test received authoritative doctrine by
the touchstone of apostolic teaching. No one is warranted in applying this
test except him who is least fitted to do so, the official representative or
rather creator of the now accepted doctrine.

It is one of the almost insurmountable difficulties which also the Protestant observers at the Vatican Council II emphasize: How can people
validly hold a dialogue if they do not succeed at the beginning in coming
to an agreement on the basis of authority: the Bible alone or the Bible
and tradition.[34]

TRADITION IN PROTESTANTISM

The notion of tradition is not confined to Roman Catholicism. There
are Protestant traditions just as tenacious and dangerous as those of the
Catholics when they come between the Bible and the church. The words
of a great man, whether it be Luther, Calvin, Zwingli, Wesley, or Darby,
and the decisions of such and such a synod or conference often dispute
the authority of the Bible. A certain spiritual guidebook by a highly
esteemed leader, a certain experience common to a great number of
Christians, a certain practice which is venerable because of its antiquity
and the number of its followers—these easily become the norms of a whole

Christian circle. It is one of the most dangerous tendencies of Protestantism, and certainly the greatest obstacle to the unity of real Christians.

Instead of having one infallible pope, we have an infinite number of
those who are semi-infallible but whose authority is nonetheless absolute
over their circle of followers where they rule. Many theologians, pastors
and evangelists have their groups of disciples who see only through their
leaders' eyes and who consider all of their affirmations as gospel truth.

To recognize a norm superior to that of the written Word is to open the
door to Illuminism, to mysticism, and to all the deviations to which these
tendencies have given rise over the centuries. It is to rejoin, by another
route, the Roman Catholic position.[35]

However, if there is a lesson to draw from the history of the church, it
is indeed that of the danger into which every community which blindly
follows a man is certain to fall. Did not the Lord forewarn of this danger
by putting His disciples on guard against the practice of the scribes and
the Pharisees who liked "to be called Rabbi by men. 'But you must not be
called Rabbi, for one is your teacher and you are all brothers . . . neither
be called teachers, for you have one teacher—the Christ' " (Mt 23:7-10).

What is the platform of salvation? Constantly verifying by the Scriptures everything that is taught, and accepting only that which receives
the approval of the entire body of Christians—these are the only means of
being preserved from error. If we wish to remain in the line of the Reformation, we must also:

1. Burn tradition, or at least shake off its yoke in the measure that it
tries to impose itself as a norm of faith next to the Scripture or above it.
It is a matter of resolutely putting aside all authority which would practically supplant that of the Word of God, whether that authority be that
of man, of a council, of a synod, or simply that of the antiquity of the
ecclesiastical practice.

2. Reestablish the effective authority of the Bible against those who
undermine its foundation by denying its plenary inspiration, against those
who tear it into shreds by contesting the authenticity of large portions,
against those who devaluate it by a subjective or too allegorical interpretation.

As Luther said toward the end of his life, "It is a matter of believing all
of the Scripture or none of it. For the Holy Spirit is indivisible; He does
not teach truth and falsehood. . . ; by meddling with one single point of
the faith, heretics produce at the same time doubt and denial of all the
others, just as the least defect makes a link in the chain unserviceable and
the least crack makes a bell of no value."[36]

The Bible is not a book sealed with seven seals which only the initiated are able to understand. "All prophetic and evangelical Scripture can clearly and without ambiguity be understood by all men. One must be satisfied with the testimony of God which is clearly put forth," said Irenaeus. There are, of course, "some statements in them which are hard to understand" (2 Pe 3:16), but "all the things necessary are clear," said Chrysostom,[37] and, according to Augustine, "among the things which are clearly taught are found all those which concern both faith and practice." Among these clear things are also found, fortunately, the essential truths concerning the church.

Let us then begin with the principle that all that is necessary for the life of a Christian and for the church is found clearly taught in the Scripture. Since the passages which speak of it are numerous, it will be possible to arrive at a clear conviction on these questions, and at an agreement among all Christians accepting the authority of the Word of God. As for the other points on which the Bible does not furnish precise evidence and which, because the texts are obscure or not very numerous, are susceptible to varied interpretations, why not allow each Christian the liberty of personally working out for himself a conviction, without forcing him to adopt our point of view?

If God had deemed it necessary for His children to be of one mind on these questions, why would He not have given them all the useful and precise details in this Scripture which is capable of making "the man of God . . . well-fitted and adequately equipped for all good work" (2 Ti 3:17)?

With all those who thus accept the authority of the Bible and who are groping to find God's plan concerning the church, we should like to set out to discover it through the pages of the New Testament. "To the Law and to the testimony! Whoever will not speak according to this word, there shall surely be no dawn for him. He shall wander through [the land] distressed and hungry" (Is 8:20-21).

Notes

1. Does not one missing link suffice to cause the collapse of a whole scaffolding? And does not history relate the case of several popes and antipopes fighting among themselves before all of them were excommunicated by a new pope named by a council? In such cases, along what line does the legitimate chain of succession pass? See on this subject J. Blocher, *Le Catholicisme*, pp. 33-36.
2. Would not the fact that at least three important communions can exercise the right of this "apostolic succession" without agreeing on the doctrine suffice to demonstrate the inanity of this theory?
3. The mention of "prophets" could also refer to the prophets of the Old Testament. The church is built on the work of Christ as prophesied in the Old Testament, on His expiatory work as was predicted by the Levitical sacrifices and the major prophets.

4. Martin Luther, W.A. 51, 482, 5-6; 51, 501, 7-8. "Of what value is apostolic succession which leads to error? The true apostolic succession should be manifested
   in teaching which conforms to that of the apostles. Otherwise it is only historical
   continuity, a succession of persons" (J. de Senarclens, *De la Vraie Église selon
   Calvin*, pp. 29-30).

5. de Senarclens, p. 34. A confirmation of this way of understanding apostolicity of
   the church is given in a rather unexpected way by one of the most eminent
   Catholic theologians of the present day, Father Hans Küng: "True, only that
   Church which is essentially and in its innermost core in conformity with the
   apostles through succession in the apostolic spirit is truly an apostolic Church.
   True, only that Church which is in conformity with the attestation that the
   apostles have handed down to us is truly an apostolic Church, through succession
   in the apostolic faith and confession" (Hans Küng, *Structures of the Church*,
   p. 119).

   "Unity, holiness, and catholicity are the unity, holiness, and catholicity of the
   Church of Jesus Christ only if it is founded on the same grounds on which Jesus
   Christ willed to found the Church; it is the ground of the apostles. . . . It is only
   in the testimony of the apostles that we perceive the glorified Lord. This is why
   the attestation of the apostles occupies a unique, lasting—and unrepeatable—
   normative position within the Church and vis-a-vis the Church. That is why . . .
   it requires a succession that is not only historical in character but also one which
   is objectively understood as such, in the spirit of the apostles, in the faith in their
   Gospel, and in obedience to their binding example" (Ibid, p. 111).

6. "Tradition is the Word of God not recorded in the holy books but preached by
   the apostles and transmitted from generation to generation by the Church.
   Catholic tradition is therefore as much the Word of God as are the Holy Scriptures. Jesus Christ did not give to the apostles the mission of writing but of
   preaching" (Haas, *Grand Catéchisme*). One must not forget, however, that even
   in Catholicism this definition is debated.

7. O. Cullman, *La Tradition* (1953).

8. Ibid., p. 43.

9. Ibid., p. 41.

10. Ibid., p. 36.

11. Ibid., p. 45. The Catholics themselves seem to adhere to this norm, at least
    theoretically: "Neither Catholics nor Protestants can consider themselves exempt
    from making a continuous effort to model themselves upon the apostolic Church.
    Neither do appeals to Catholic tradition or to the Protestant Reformation release
    them from the obligation to embody the constantly new which is the crucial
    factor, if one desires the designation "apostolic": namely, *essential agreement
    with the apostolic message*" (Küng, p. 110).

12. That is, the oral tradition of which we find at least a trace written in the works
    of writers subsequent to the apostles as opposed to that which would have re-
    mained purely oral, even during the postapostolic period.

13. Chrysostom, *Homily on Matthew 24.*

14. Irenaeus, *Advers. Haer III*, 1. Also see G. Bardy, *La Théologie de l'Eglise de
    Saint Clément de Rome à Saint-Irénée*, p. 188.

15. Cyprian in Migne, *Epist.* 24, *Patrol. lat.*, 3:294

16. Athanasius, *Epist. Fest. 39, Corpus Scriptorum christianorum orientalum* (Lou-
    vain, 1955), 151:37.

17. Athanasius, *Orat. contra gent.*, Coll. Sources chrétiennes (Paris: Cerf, 1946),
    p. 107.

18. Athanasius, *De Incarn.* (*De l'Incarnation du Verbe.*) Coll. Sources chrétiennes
    (Paris, 1946), p. 315.

19. Athanasius, *De vera Fide.* Oper., 2:386.

20. Athanasius in Migne, *Homil. De Trin.* 29, 28:1603-9.

21. Cyril of Jerusalem in Migne, *Catech.* IV, 33:453-504.

22. Chrysostom in Migne, *Homil 13 in II Cor.*, 61:490-96.

23. Chrysostom in Migne, *Homil 13 in Genesim*, 53:105-8.

24. Augustine, *Contra Donatist.*, lib. 2, c. 3.

25. Jerome, *Ep. ad Titum.*

26. Jerome, *In Matt. 22.*

27. Jerome, *In Jer. 9:12.*
28. Augustine, *In Psalm 57.*
29. Augustine, *De Unitate Eccl.,* c. 10.
30. Augustine, *Ep. ad Hieronymus,* vol. 2.
31. See citations from Tertullian, Irenaeus, Clement of Alexandria, Origen, Cyprian, etc., in Halldane, *De l'authenticité et de la divine inspiration des Saintes Ecritures,* pp. 25-44; and *Dieu a parlé.*
32. G. Millon, "Ecriture sainte et Tradition in Cahier," *Le Vent Souffle,* no. 2-3, p. 53.
33. Emil Brunner, *The Misunderstanding of the Church,* pp. 43-45.
    "The attitude of Pius IX appears to us to be a manifestation of pure 'illuminism' (in the sense that the reformers gave to this term)" (R. Stauffer, *Le Premier Concile du Vatican,* p. 5).
    "The Pope is the only person who is authoritatively inspired by the Holy Spirit; everything in this tremendous structure of the institution of sacred Church law depends on his inspiration, his ex cathedra infallible spoken word" (Brunner, *Dogmatics,* 3:72).
    Luther had already said, "The pope claims that all the laws are in the jewel-case of his heart . . . and all that he orders and decides in his Church must be considered to be just, even if that is contrary to the Scripture or to the oral Word" (*Livres symboliques,* p. 274).
    It is claimed that the pope would not have pronounced the quoted words, "La Tradizione son Io." Professor Stauffer states that it was in a fit of anger that Pius IX pronounced them, in response to a proposition of Cardinal Guidi suggesting replacing the words, "the infallibility of the sovereign pontiff" by "the infallibility of his doctrinal definitions" in order to win over those opposed to infallibility (Stauffer, p. 40).
    In 1866, Pius IX had already expressed himself thus: "I alone am the successor of of the apostles, the vicar of Jesus Christ; I alone have the mission of conducting and directing Peter's boat; I am the way, the truth, and the life. Those who are with me are with the Church; those who are not with me are outside of the Church; they are outside of the way, the truth, and the life." At least, it was clear! (Quoted by J. Friedrich, *Geschichte des Vatikanischen Konzils* 1:498.) At the council (at least at Vatican I), the bishops had to swear to "maintain, defend, spread, and promote the rights, honorary privileges, and the authority of their lord, the pope." (Cited by Canon I de Doellinger, *La Papauté,* p. 254.) In the definition of the doctrine of infallibility, we read, "Such is the doctrine of catholic truth, from which none can deviate without losing the Faith and Salvation" (French translation in J. Sambin, *Hist. du Concile oecuménique et général du Vatican,* p. 165).
    This evolution had, moreover, been prepared a long time before by the Jesuits. "In 1847 the Jesuit Perrone explained that neither the Bible nor Tradition was necessary to define an article of faith. All that was needed was to admit a secret tradition retained in the preaching of the church and in the general consciousness of believers until finally, at some moment, it would be expressed publicly. 'Without which,' Perronne adds, 'one would have to consider many dogmas to be of recent origin . . .' Pius IX proceeded according to the suggestion of Perrone . . . he alone made the Immaculate Conception of Mary an article of faith, without the Episcopate" (Doellinger, pp. 223-24).
    Bishop Malou, in his book on the immaculate conception which he wrote at the order of Pius IX, states, "As soon as a thing is generally accepted in the Church, this general testimony of the living Church is infallible proof that this truth is contained in tradition and that independent of any monument of antiquity" (cited by Doellinger, p. 227).
    The Catholic Church tends increasingly to abandon the fabrication of tradition: "In justification of the dogma proclaimed in 1950, the Church is not slow to give a Scriptural base to it, but she relies on the concensus of the Church" (O. Cullmann, p. 40).
34. All things considered, this council brought nothing new to this chapter except that it allows to exist and continues to aggravate the misunderstanding concerning the place and authority of tradition. The next to the last session maintains side by side two propositions which are logically incompatible: the Bible alone

is the source of revelation, and tradition also reveals to us God's thought. This is not the only ambiguity of the council.

35. "The Catholic Church, gnosticism, illuminism, ancient and modern sects, in spite of the profound abyss which separates them in other respects, do they not agree in their common refusal to consider the Scripture as a superior norm destined to control the present action of the Holy Spirit in the domain of truth?" (Cullmann, p. 37).

36. Luther, *Kurzes Bekenntnis vom heiligen Sakrament*, quoted by K. Barth from F. Gonin, *Alliance évang.* (Oct., 1964), p. 8.

37. Chrysostom, *Homil. 3 in II Thess.*

3

The Meaning of the Word "Church"

MORE THAN A HUNDRED TIMES the word *church* is used in the New Testament from the pen of almost all the inspired authors. In order to understand a reality, one must begin by inquiring into the meaning of the word which expresses it. "For decades and even centuries they have openly called church something which is not the church, and it has been so for the sole reason that they were not clear as to the meaning of the word and as to its content."[1]

WHAT DOES THE WORD "CHURCH" MEAN?

The French word *église* (church) is the result of a double transliteration of the Greek word *ekklesia* first in Latin: *ecclesia,* then into French: *ecclésiastique* and *église.* Thus there has not been any translation from the Greek word, but Latinization and then Frenchifying of the original word.[2] The Romans could have expressed the Greek word by *contio* or *comitia* or literally by *convocation;* the French, by the word *assemblée* (assembly), as the Darby Version puts it. But they preferred to keep the original word, doubtlessly considering that it alone was capable of expressing the particular idea to which it was linked.[3] The Italians and Spaniards followed the same practice (*chiesa, iglesia*) while the Germans, the English, and the Flemish abandoned at one and the same time the transliteration and the translation in order to link the name of the Christian community with that of the Lord to whom it belongs (*Kirche, Church, Kerk* are derived from the Greek word *Kurios,* the Lord).

ETYMOLOGICAL MEANING

What is the etymological meaning of the word *ekklesia*?[4] The word is composed of the prefix *ek,* signifying "out of" (found in words derived from the Greek, such as eclectic and ecchymosis, and corresponding to the Latin prefix *ex,* found in extract, exclude, etc.), and the radical *klesia,* which is the passive form of the verb *kaleō,* "I call." (In the New Testament, *kaleō* is used in the sense of "to call" or "to invite" in Mt 2:7; 20:8;

22:3; to bid or invite the guests to the wedding, Mt 22:8-9; 25:14; Mk 3:31; Lk 7:36; 14:7-10.) This verb itself is derived from the old Indo-European root *kel* which contains the idea of "to cry out," or "to call out" (in Sanskrit *usakalah*, it is the rooster, the one who calls out the dawn. This root has given in the Latin the verb *calare*, to call, and the noun *concilium*; in German the words *hallen, schallen*: to ring or resound; in French, *clamer, proclamer*: to cry out). Therefore, etymologically speaking, the word *ekklesia* signifies "one who has been called out of."[5]

HISTORICAL MEANING

The word *ekklesia* had a political meaning, never a religious meaning, in Greece. In Athens, for example, the *ekklesia* was the regularly summoned assembly of all the citizens of the city, that is, of those who had the freedom of the city. All the inhabitants of the city did not have this right; full citizens formed only a small minority.

The word gives a vivid picture. At the call of a herald the citizens came out of their homes, separated themselves from the rest of the inhabitants of the city, and assembled in a place agreed upon (the *Pnyx*) to discuss city affairs, such as the nomination of magistrates, officers, governors of the city, military operations, etc. Each convocation began with prayer and a sacrifice.[6] The word *ekklesia* is used by Luke in this sense: "in the legal assembly" (Ac 19:39).

JEWISH MEANING

To the Greek meaning there came to be added a religious sense by the fact that the Septuagint used almost a hundred times the word *ekklesia* to convey the meaning of the Hebrew word *qâhâl*, which designates assemblies of all kinds and, principally, the assembly of the chosen people of God (see Num 19:20; Deu 23:2, 3, 8), the great convocations of Israel (Num 27:17, 22; 28:18, 25).[7]

"The word has the same general meaning of assembly as it had in the Greco-Roman world, but it takes on a religious significance since the One who calls is God. The Old Testament uses the term 'assembly (*ekklesia*) of God' for the chosen people instituted by the call which God addressed to them. In the same manner, the Church in the New Testament is the assembly of believers formed by the call of God through Jesus Christ . . . the gathering of those who obey God's call."[8]

So in secular Greek writings and in Jewish writings this word *ekklesia* designates assemblies "called out as a body" from a given human context. The word places the emphasis on the one who calls. However, one must emphasize, as does E. Lewis, that "there was no Church before Christ had accomplished His work."[9]

CHRISTIAN MEANING

Out of 114 uses of the word *ekklesia* in the New Testament, only six have any bearing on the Greek meaning (Ac 19:39) or the Jewish meaning (Ac 7:38; Heb 2:12). In all other cases it has a specific meaning which is peculiar to the authors of the New Testament. This meaning embodies and is more inclusive than all previous meanings, as Emil Brunner says: "The New Testament . . . has filled both the Old Testament concept and the secular Greek concept of Ekklesia with entirely new Christological content."[10] So there is found in the Christian sense:

The etymological meaning. This means "called out of."

1. *Vocation (keleo: I call).* Who is calling?
   ". . . whom he called, them he also justified . . ." (Ro 8:30, KJV).
   ". . . for this [salvation] He called you through our gospel . . ." (2 Th 2:14, NASB). So it is God who calls.

2. *Separation (ek: out from).* God calls out from what?
   "Be saved from this crooked generation" (Ac 2:40).
   "Come out from their midst, and be separate, says the Lord" (2 Co 6:17).
   "Who gave Himself for our sins, to rescue us out of this present evil world (Gal 1:4).
   ". . . Him who called you out of darkness into His marvelous light" (1 Pe 2:9).
   ". . . their turning from darkness to light and from the authority of Satan to God" (Ac 26:18).

3. *Gathering (ekklesia: assembly).*
   "After being enlightened, you endured . . . partly by being partners with those so treated" (Heb 10:32-33, NASB).
   "When you meet together . . . everything should be constructive" (1 Co 14:26).
   "A large number had gathered and were praying" (Ac 12:12).
   ". . . the secret of His purpose . . . to bring everything together in Christ" (Eph 1:9-10).

God calls men to leave the world of darkness, the kingdom of Satan, to pass into His marvelous kingdom of light.

The historical Greek meaning. This is also embodied in the Christian meaning. As Greek citizens separated themselves from the rest of the city's inhabitants at the call of the herald to assemble in a place apart and discuss public affairs, so Christians, at the call of their God, gather together to speak of the things which concern the kingdom of God and to attend to matters of their city which is in heaven (Phil 3:20). The church, as Mgr. Cerfaux says, is "the community of the summoned." "The first or main idea which the word ekklesia suggests to us is that of separation much more than union," says A. Nicole.[11]

The Jewish meaning. Also embodied in the Christian meaning is the Jewish meaning. According to the prophecies of Isaiah, Jeremiah and Daniel, only a remnant of the Israelites would subsist and enjoy the divine promises. The people of the new covenant who considered themselves to be this remnant, the Israel of God (Ro 9:8; 11:1-5; Gal 3:29; 6:16), considered themselves rightfully entitled to the term used in the Greek version of the Old Testament as applying to the Messianic community: the people of "the saints of the Most High" (Dan 7:13-27) gathered about the Son of Man. "The Ekklesia of the New Testament which is the heir of the chosen people of the Old Covenant is also its fulfillment," says Brunner.[12]

WHAT THEN IS THE CHURCH?

Some attempts at definitions of the church have been made by theologians. Emil Brunner distinguishes three definitions of the church, each of which contains a part of the truth. He says the church is:

1. *Coetus electorum* (the company of the elect). "The Ekklesia . . . knows itself as a chosen people of God; in itself, the little flock of Christ's redeemed, it recognizes the vanguard of the Kingdom of God, of the new humanity united with God and in God."

2. *Corpus Christi* (the body of Christ). This definition stresses the fact that it is Christ who has called and united the chosen ones in the unity of the body of Christ.

3. *Communio sanctorum* (the communion of saints).

> The ground of the Ekklesia [is] in the faith of individual Christians. . . . The election, the transcendent ground, becomes immanent in the individual's experience of faith. . . . The Holy Spirit, who apprehends and creates anew the individual when the Word of Christ is heard, makes the eternal decree of God a present experience. The living Christ builds His body for Himself by taking possession of the hearts of men and "adds them" as saints called to the community of disciples. The Ekklesia is the community of the *sancti*, of those who have been called out of the world and into the service of Christ. It is the community of believers. . . . By believing we became capable of fellowship and willing for it.
>
> Each of the three definitions of the Ekklesia shows us a special aspect of its basis: the transcendent (*electio*), the historical-objective (*corpus Christi*), and the spiritual-subjective (*sanctorum communio*). Each of them taken by itself would necessarily lead to a one-sided conception: either to an abstract spiritual intellectualism (the number of the pre-

destined, *numerus praedestinatorum*), or to a sacramental hierarchism (the Body of Christ, *corpus Christi*), or to an emotional or pietistic individualism (the communion of the faithful, *communio fidelium*). Only in their unity do they reproduce the reality of the Ekklesia. It is at once the company of the elect, the Body of Christ, and the communion of the saints.[13]

The first definition is preferred by the Calvinists. "The Church is the company of those whom God has chosen for salvation," said John Calvin. According to W. Zoellner, "The Church is the assembly of the elect, of those who have been predestined to faithfulness by Jesus Christ, of those who believe in Him, of those who have been sealed by the Holy Spirit of promise."[14]

The second definition is especially favored by Catholic and Catholicizing theologians. It contains, however, an important part of truth. "The Church is the temporal form of the body of Christ and of its members" says Karl Barth.[15]

Evidently the third definition is preferred by evangelical Christians because it places the emphasis on the necessity of personal faith as a response to God's call and on the walk in holiness as evidence of faith— without neglecting the other aspects of the truth (the body of Christ and the company of the elect).

Calvin also had already defined the truth as the communion of the saints: "If now you are willing to accept a definition of the church which is more agreeable to the truth, say, that it is a community of all saints, extending over the whole world, and through all ages, but that, being united by the doctrine of Christ and by one spirit, it desires unity and brotherly concord."[16]

Luther said, "A seven-year-old child knows what the Church is: holy believers and lambs who hear the voice of their shepherd (John 10:3)."[17]

Let us again call attention to these *definitions from Reformation days:*

"The Christian Church is the mass or gathering of all those who believe in Christ, who live in the unity of the Spirit, of faith, hope, and love; that is why it is called a communion of the saints."[18]

Confession of La Rochelle (1559): "It is the company of the faithful who agree to follow this Word and the pure religion which depends on it, and who grow and become stronger in it all the days of their lives, growing and being established in the fear of God" (art. 27).

Confession of the Netherlands (1571): "It is a holy congregation and assembly of true, faithful Christians, awaiting their complete redemption in Jesus Christ, being washed by His blood, and sanctified and sealed by the Holy Spirit; this holy assembly and congregation is the assembly of the saved" (art. 27, 28).

The men of the Revival of the nineteenth century also have defined it: "The Church is the assembly of those who walk by faith and live by the Spirit," said Vinet.

"The Church is a holy community, a confederation of believers, a society of Christians," according to E. de Pressensé.

Some modern theologians define it thus:

Brunner writes: "The Church is the community of those who have been pardoned and given new life in Jesus Christ."[19] "In the New Testament the Church is never anything other than the people of God, the community of the saints, of the elect, the assembling of believers, believers gathered together. It is never anything but the ensemble of men who, by communion with Christ, the living Lord, are united one with another in a living community."[20]

H. Venske states, "The *ekklesia*—the Church—is the ensemble of those who have been begotten by the vital power of God, have been baptized by the Spirit through Christ, and who thus constitute and remain a foreign body in this world."[21]

Bishop Newbigin writes: "The divine society into which He invited all men was more than a school of good theology; it was a fraternal community formed of all those who believed in Him."[22]

According to the Scandinavian theologian N. A. Dahl, "The Church is nothing else than justified men."[23]

Some may be astonished at this assent of theologians from all over the world concerning the biblical description of the church when the churches that they represent correspond so poorly to the definition which they give of it. Brunner's explanation puts the finger on the sore:

> It is however a well-known fact that dogmatists and Church leaders often pay but small attention to the results of New Testament research, and are only too ready to bridge the gulf between then and now by a handy formula such as that of development or by appealing to the distinction between the visible and invisible Church, and thus to give a false solution to this grave and distressing problem. But while many theologians and Church leaders are able to quieten their consciences by such formulae, others are so much the more painfully aware of the disparity between the Christian fellowship of the apostolic age and our own "churches," and cannot escape the impression that there may perhaps be something wrong with what we now call the Church.[24]

WHAT IS THE MEANING OF THE WORD "CHURCH" AS USED IN THE NEW TESTAMENT?

The two first uses of the word *church* come from the lips of Jesus:

1. *Matthew 16:18:* "On this rock I will build My church, and the gates of hades shall not prevail against her."

The church of Jesus Christ includes believers of all times and places, beginning at Pentecost. (I *will* build: Without the baptism of the Holy Spirit, there is no body of Christ; now, in Acts 1:5 this baptism was still in the future. It took place on the day of Pentecost. See also Ac 2:1; 11:15-16.) It is what was sometimes called the universal or general church, the one that is written conventionally with a capital, even in our Bibles. (It is evidently a modern practice, since we know that our oldest manuscripts of the New Testament are written entirely in capitals.)

2. *Matthew 18:17:* "If he refuses to listen to them, tell the church; and if he will not listen to the church, treat him like a pagan and a tax gatherer."

This church is connected with a precise time and place: one can assemble it, speak to it; it can express itself. It is what they have agreed to call "the local church," comprised of believers of a given time and place. In the writings of the apostles the church appears to us under two forms.[25] They are the universal church and the local church.[26]

UNIVERSAL CHURCH

Example: "God has placed everything under His feet and has given Him as head over everything for the church, which is His body, the completeness of Him who fills the universe at all points" (Eph 1:22-23).

"Christ also is Head of the church" (Eph 5:23).

"Christ loved the church and gave Himself for her, in order that by cleansing her by means of the washing in water He may sanctify her through His word (Eph 5:25; cf. 5:27, 30, 33; Col 1:18, 24; 1 Co 15:9).

"The church enjoyed peace *all over* Judea, Galilee and Samaria" (not the church *of* Judea) (Ac 9:31).

LOCAL CHURCH

It is the second meaning which is the most frequent: out of 108 uses of the word, about 90 refer to the local church (Ac 8:1; 13:1; 15:41; 14:23; Ro 16:5; Col 4:16; 1 Pe 5:13, KJV).

"Where there are two or three people, even laymen, there is a church," says Tertullian.[27]

IN WHAT IMMEDIATE CONTEXT DO WE FIND THE WORD "CHURCH" IN THE NEW TESTAMENT?

The word is frequently found associated with others which complement it. The study of the names of the church or of the churches permits us to make several interesting and important observations.

1. The same word designates at one and the same time the universal

church and the local assembly. Even broader expressions like "the church of God" or "the temple of God" refer sometimes to one, sometimes to the other (1 Co 15:9 and 1 Ti 3:5; 2 Co 6:16 and 1 Co 3:16). The local church is only a small part, a fraction, of the universal church. In the ancient world when each group of Roman citizens gathered, wherever it might be, it was a *Conventus Civium Romanorum*, a voice of Rome. This group had no meaning apart from Rome and her various functions. Each Roman citizen arriving in a city where such a group existed, automatically and without ceremony, became a member of that assembly. Geographically these groups could be several thousands of miles from Rome; in spirit they were a part of Rome. "That is the true idea of the Church; each local church is only a part, a miniature of the great general Church."[28]

The different local churches are only "particular manifestations of the community in its entirety," says R. Sohm.[29]

2. The apostle frequently associates with the church the name of her leader: the church of the living God (1 Ti 3:15, KJV); God's building (1 Co 3:9); the church of the Lord (Ac 20:28, RSV); the churches of Christ (Ro 16:16); the church of God (2 Co 1:1); or "the church . . . in God our Father and the Lord Jesus Christ" (2 Th 1:1).

3. Other times the churches are named with reference to their members: churches of the saints (1 Co 14:33); of the Gentiles (Ro 16:4); of the first-born (Heb 12:23); of the chosen (1 Pe 5:13); of the Laodiceans (Col 4:16); of the Thessalonians (1 Th 1:1; 2 Th 1:1).

4. Frequently the word *church* is associated with a geographical term: the church of Jerusalem, the church of Antioch, the churches of Macedonia (2 Co 8:1); of Asia (1 Co 16:19); of Galatia (Gal 1:2); in Judea (1 Th 2:14); or simply the church that meets in their house (1 Co 16:19; Phile 2; Col 4:15; Ro 16:5). The word *church* never designates a building; the first Christians did not possess one.

We never find the expressions: the churches of Rome, of Jerusalem, nor the church of Macedonia, of Judea, of Galatia.[30] We do not read of any church of Paul, of John, or of Peter—although Paul, John, and Peter founded churches[31]—nor "Congregational church" nor "Presbyterian"—although these forms of churches existed. No name, either of an apostle, or of a form, or of an ecclesiastic symbol is linked with the word *church*. The only names which matter are, on the one hand, those of God and of Jesus Christ who do the calling, and on the other hand, those of the people who are called (elders, Gentiles, elect of God, those born again, declared to be saints) who meet in houses in Jerusalem, in Corinth, in Colosse, and in Rome, to praise God, to be mutually edified, and to spread the Word of God.

In this term *ekklesia* are two aspects: the objective and the subjective. The objective is the will of Him who calls; the subjective, the will of the one receiving and accepting the call. We examine these two aspects successively: the call of God (chap. 4) and the response of man to that call (chap. 6).

Notes

1. Emil Brunner, *Le Renouveau de l'Eglise*, p. 10. Barth says, "The more one speaks of the Church and the more one delves into this problem in our times, the more one realizes that it is necessary to render an account of what one thinks and what one means by this term unless one wishes to make of it only an empty notion" (Karl Barth, *L'Eglise*, p. 58).
2. Several authors have drawn our attention to the fact that the term *ekklesia* was not translated by the Latin people. See G. A. Deissmann, *Licht vom Osten*, p. 90; K. L. Schmidt, *Die Kirche des Urchristentums*, p. 265. Either the Romans saw no need to translate the word or they had no means to do it. Tertullian tried to substitute the word *curia;* Augustine, the expression *Civitas dei* (The City of God), while others used *contio* or *comitia*, but none of these terms seemed appropriate.
   For the history of the term *ekklesia*, see Otto Michel, *Das Zeugnis des N.T. von der Gemeinde*, pp. 5-10.
3. "The choice of this word preserved Christianity from compromises with the world of pagan religious associations" (Mgr. Cerfaux, *La Théologie de l'Eglise suivant Saint Paul*, p. 155).
4. For more details on the semantics of the word *ekklesia*, see ibid., pp. 143-57.
5. Consult de Hauterives, *Dict. des Racines européennes* (Larousse) and *Indogermanisches etymologisches Wörterbuch*, 1:548.
   See also Schmidt's article, "Ekklesia," in G. Kittel, ed., *Theol. Wörterbuch zum N.T. . . .*, 3:502-39; and the article, "Kaleo," 3:488.
   Geddes MacGregor, *Corpus Christi*, pp. 110-27. J. Y. Campbell, "The Origin and Meaning of the Christian Use of the Word Ekklesia," *Journal of Theological Studies* (1948), pp. 133 ff. For the relationship between *kaleo* and words of the same family used in the N.T., see Kittel's *L'Eglise dans la Bible*, p. 67.
6. "*Ekklesia* in classical Greek (Thucydide 2, 22; Platon, Gorgias 456b) means 'an assembly of the people regularly summoned,' in contradistinction to the word *syllogos* which means a fortuitous or occasional meeting. The idea of convocation plays an essential part in the Christian conception of the Church since the Church is established by the call of Christ on men's obedience" (M. Goguel, *The Primitive Church*, 3:24).
   "The etymology is as simple as it is full of meaning: the citizens are the *ekkletoi;* that is, those who have been 'called out' and assembled by the call of a herald. From that one can deduct the biblical Christian use of the word; God in Christ calls men out of the world" (Schmidt in Kittel, *Theol. Wörterbuch zum N.T.*, 3:516).
   "Let us imagine citizens called by the trumpet and coming hastily from every direction. They are present; they form a company, the company of the faithful, of those who, called by the faithfulness of God, have responded with faithfulness" (Barth, *La Confession de Foi de l'Eglise*, p. 75).
7. See O. Cullmann, *Peter:Disciple–Apostle–Martyr*, p. 166. We know that the Septuagint Version was the Bible of the first Christians of Greek origin. More than half of the quotations from the Old Testament which we find in the New Testament are taken from this version.
8. P. Menoud, "Eglise" in *Vocabulaire biblique;* see also H. S. Bender, *These Are My People*, pp. 5-6.
9. Edwin Lewis, *The Ministry and the Sacraments*, p. 478. The most complete coverage of the notion of *qâhâl* is found in Kittle, *L'Eglise dans la Bible*, pp. 9-18. For the relationship between *qâhâl* and *ekklesia*, see Gloege, *Reich Gottes und Kirche im N.T.*, pp. 206-9.

10. Brunner, *Dogmatics,* 3:32.
11. A. Nicole, *La Notion biblique de l'Eglise et nos Devoirs actuels,* p. 5.
12. Brunner, "Eglise et Révélation" in *Revue de Théologie et de Philosophie* (Jan.-Mar. 1930), p. 10. For an analysis of recent research on the word *ekklesia,* see Olof Linton, *Das Problem der Urkirche in der neueren Forschung.* For a list of books and articles dealing with the term *ekklesia,* see Kittel, *L'Eglise dans la Bible,* p. 172, and Kittel, *Theologisches Wörterbuch zum N.T.,* 3:502-3.
13. Brunner, *Dogmatics,* 3:24-27.
14. W. Zoellner, "Die Kirche nach dem Epheserbrief" in *Die Kirche im N.T.*
15. Barth, *La Confession . . . ,* p. 77.
16. Calvin, "Epître à Sadolet," and *Trois traités,* p. 52.
17. Luther, "Articles de Smalkalde," *Die Bekenntnis-Schriften* (1537), p. 459.
18. *Ansbacher evangelischer Ratschlag* (Sept. 30, 1524).
19. Brunner, *Dogmatics,* 3:21.
20. Brunner, *Wahrheit als Begegnung,* p. 168.
21. H. Venske, *Vollendete Reformation,* p. 27.
22. Lesslie Newbigin, *L'Eglise,* p. 96.
23. Nils Alstrup Dahl, *Das Volk Gottes,* p. 248.
24. Brunner, *The Misunderstanding of the Church,* pp. 5-6.
25. For various meanings of the word *church,* see Paul Jalaguier, *De l'Eglise,* pp. 5-12.
26. "The idea of the universal Church seems to have forced itself upon man's mind long before that of local churches" (G. Bardy, *La Théologie de l'Eglise de Saint Clément de Rome à Saint Irénée,* p. 59). "Where Christ Jesus is, there is the Church universal" (Ignatius of Antioch, *Aux Smyrniotes*). "All those who live in Him are united in *one* spirit, *one* synagogue, *one* Church which is formed in His name, for we are all called Christians" (Justin Martyr, *Dialog. LXIII,* p. g). Calvin called it the "universum electorum numerum" (the universal number of the elect). Lutheran orthodoxy named it "the synthetic Church": "We call the Church which is made up of all believers synthetic, those who teach and those who listen, those from present, past, and future" (Quenstedt, *Theologia didactice-polemica* 4 (1961): 478.
27. "The Church is composed of all the believers in a place because they are united by the Spirit of God to form the body of Christ" (W. Hildebrandt, *Das Gemeindeprinzip der christlichen Kirche,* p. 33).
28. William Barclay, *New Testament Wordbook.*
29. R. Sohm, *Kirchenrecht,* 1:13. See Hildebrandt, p. 35; and Scheuerl, "Die geistliche und die rechtliche Kirche" in *Sammlung Kirchenrechtlicher Abhandlungen.*
30. "The Church of God has been divided into churches of God on the basis of the difference of locality, the only Scriptural basis for the division of the Church into churches. The church is neither more restricted nor more inclusive than the locality. Each separate locality must have its own independent church" (Watchman Nee, *The Normal Christian Church Life,* pp. 46-57).
"The New Testament knows nothing of an organized Church or of one to be organized, or one still only an idea in the mind, of which particular communities would be only parts" (Barth, *Connaître Dieu et le servir*).
The only verse which indicates an exception to the rule is Acts 9:31: "The church enjoyed peace all over Judea, Galilee and Samaria." It is true that in most English versions and in certain German versions are the words, "the churches," but the best manuscripts put "church" in the singular. Is it a question of a generic singular or of the church of Jerusalem dispersed in Galilee, Samaria, and Judea? It seems more natural to see in it a mention of the universal church, as in Acts 20:28, "Feed the church of God" (KJV). "Luke, by using the singular here, has for the first time sought to make one feel the beauty and holy unity of all the disciples of the Saviour in all the countries which he names. They form only one Church" (L. Bonnet, *N.T. annoté,* 2:379). See also the development by O. Dibelius in *Die werdende Kirche,* pp. 131-37. In any case, Luke does not speak of the church of Judea, of Samaria, or of Galilee.
31. Luther said, "I do not like to have the doctrine and people called Lutheran and thus, because of my name, subject the Word of God to ridicule."

"I beg you to drop my name and take the name Christian. Who is Luther? My doctrine is not mine. I was not crucified for anyone. Saint Paul did not want anyone to be named after Paul or Peter or Christ. How then would it be fitting for me, a wretched sack of dust and ashes, to give my name to the children of God? Stop, my dear friends, stop taking these names of parties and making these distinctions; leave all that and let yourselves be called only Christians after the One from whom our doctrine comes" (Luther as quoted by T. Stork, *The Life of Luther*, p. 289).

"We confess that the word 'Lutheran' next to the word church is a *contradictio in adjecto* [a contradiction in itself]" (W. Löhe, theologian of the Lutheran Confessional Revival of the 19th century).

Part II

THE EXTRACTION OF MATERIALS

4

The Call of God

THE FATAL ERROR which seems to have contributed most to the establishment of this politico-religious system that is called Christendom seems to
be the confusion between the new ond old covenants. Under the old
covenant, Israel in its entirety was the "people of God." All the Hebrews
born of Hebrews and circumcised according to the law were automatically
a part of this people. All of them together had the advantages of the
promises and privileges given to these people.[1]

Those who directed the churches in the second and third centuries were
not sufficiently attentive to the radical change that the coming of Jesus
Christ had brought. Following the natural inclination toward ease, Christianity fell back imperceptibly to the level of the religion of the old covenant. The Old Testament served the church Fathers (and consequently
the Reformed theologians) to justify, a posteriori, the status quo. However, there is between the two alliances an essential difference: the people
of the new covenant are no longer recruited "biologically," that is, by
birth, but individually on the basis of a personal acceptance of the offer
of salvation in Jesus Christ. It is the issue of a line begun under the old
covenant.

"God proceeds by the method of concentration. His promises will remain valid, but only for those who are truly His people. From now on
there will be a distinction between nominal Israel and the true people of
God, the remnant in Israel. At the time of Sinai, all the people had been
the Church. Henceforth these two entities will no longer completely
overlap. . . . Belonging to the people of God is not a matter of flesh and
blood. Thus there is a progressive "reduction" in the plan of God. The
circle of salvation is becoming more restricted. God began His work with
humanity; He continued it with just one people from among the peoples
of the earth. Now He operates through a remnant, a faithful minority of
this people. . . . He concentrates on some in order to reach a great many
. . . God says: 'I will be their God and they shall be my people,' but He

also says: 'come out from among them and be ye separate' (II Cor. 6:16-17)," says Dr. W. A. Visser't Hooft.[2]

According to F. Godet, "By its official representatives, the nation, as such, refused to receive Jesus; from that moment faith took on a purely individual character and, as it were, sporadic."[3]

In fact, as we are going to see, the call to salvation, from the mouth of Jesus Christ and of His disciples, takes on a character which is individual,[4] conditional and selective.

INDIVIDUAL CHARACTER OF THE CALL

The law and the prophets of the old covenant say: "You shall observe . . . you shall hear." Jesus Christ no longer addresses Himself to people en masse; He speaks to the individuals He has before Him, saying, "Follow me" and "If you will believe you will see the glory of God."

This individual character is found constantly emphasized by expressions like "he who," "those who" and "they who," which appear about 130 times in the gospels (not including synoptic parallels, of course: 70 in Matthew, 30 more in Mark and Luke, 30 in John). Almost 200 times in the gospels Jesus uses these expressions to emphasize that the call is essentially personal:

"whoever" (about 30 times in the gospels, 20 in the synoptics, 10 in John); "if anyone" (13 times); "if a man," "every man who," "let each one," "not one," "several," etc.

An investigation through the rest of the New Testament will reveal that the apostles strictly maintained this individual character of salvation in their teaching with the words "he who" and "whoever" which appear 40 times in the Acts; 160 times in the epistles of Paul (and Hebrews); and 140 times in the other epistles and the Revelation. "If anyone" is used 60 times, not including the gospels; and "each one," "some," "not one," and several" are used 80 times.

Thus, almost 500 times in the apostles' teaching are found expressions which speak of individual salvation. Almost 700 are in the entire New Testament.

These little words constitute, as it were, the thread of neotestamentary thought. Better than many verses, they prove that from then on it would be the individual who personally would have to take up his position before God. As Professor Kellerhals says, "We are called upon to make a personal decision: to believe and obey."[5]

This individualism is something rather new in religion. "For the first time in the Hellenic world, religion becomes an individual matter," comments E. D. Faye. "One is concerned with individual salvation. In the classic religions the individual was completely forgotten."[6]

From this individual character of the call springs a new form of "people of God" of the new covenant. "God created the Church through Christ, calling the individual by means of the proclaimed Word," says N. A. Dahl. "By this Word, men as individuals are faced with a decision, and the Church is formed when by faith men respond to the Word."[7]

"Only a fellowship of men which rests on the foundation of personal commitment of life to Christ can be called Christian—whatever its form may be," comments Brunner.[8]

All medieval Christianity, which is reflected in different forms of Catholicism, has deliberately set aside the individual aspect of the call to salvation, falling back into the economy of the old covenant. Schleiermacher compares the two means of access to salvation in a famous statement: "The contrast can be perceived in the following manner: protestantism teaches that the relationship of the individual to the Church depends on his relationship to Christ, while catholicism declares that the relationship of the individual to Christ depends on his relationship to the Church."[9] In the light of this definition, are all present-day Protestants really protestant?

According to the Augsburg Confession, the true church is "the congregation of saints in which the Gospel is rightly taught and the sacraments rightly administered." According to the Bible, says Brunner, "The Church is not necessarily there where the Gospel is preached even in its purity but where there is faith,—faith which is not merely pure orthodoxy,— conformity to the teaching of the Church—but which results in a new creation, a new birth—there is the Church."[10]

If "the assembly gathered to hear the preaching (*Predigtgemeinde*) is composed of those who are faced with the personal choice of accepting or rejecting the Gift of God,"[11] the true church is made up of only those who accept the offer of salvation. The individual's profession of faith will manifest his response.

"Only profession of faith in Christ made one a member of the Apostolic Church. This profession must always be the requirement for membership," says A. de Gasparin. "It is the profession of individual faith, a faith which exists in man only when he believes that he has been individually lost because of his sins, that Christ died for him personally and is now his personal Savior."[12] And the best way to confess one's faith is the one Jesus Christ instituted: baptism. "Baptism stresses the individual character of the call of Grace while uniting the believer to the Church," according to Aug. Lemaître.[13]

CONDITIONAL CHARACTER OF SALVATION

Following each of the expressions mentioned above is the statement of a condition to be met in order to claim the promises of God:

He who hungers and thirsts after righteousness

He who seeks, who knocks

He who is weary and heavy laden

If anyone wishes to do the will of God

If anyone hears His Word and does His will

Those who obey God

Those who repent and *believe*

At least fifty times the statement of this condition is used for salvation: "Whoever believes in Him should not perish . . . he who believes in the Son has eternal life."

That salvation is conditional is also stressed by the little word *if* which is found at least forty-two times followed by a precise condition to be met:

"Unless you repent you will all likewise perish."

"Unless you turn and become like children, you will never enter the kingdom of heaven."

"If you believe not. . . ."

"If . . . you believe in your heart. . . ."

"If you keep My commandments. . . ."

"If you continue in My word. . . ."

Or again by imperatives: "You must be born anew," "Believe in the Lord Jesus, and you will be saved."

Christ accomplished perfectly and totally the work of salvation which the Father committed to Him. On the cross He cried out, "It is finished." But this word is only for the man who accepts it personally by an act of faith.

"Only on the basis of an individual decision is faith produced," says Brunner. "He who dares to stand alone before God and remain in the quiet of his room with his Maker, he it is who believes. The Church can be composed only of such isolated individuals, each one bearing before God the full responsibility for his faith."[14]

According to Mgr. Cerfaux, "Faith occurs especially in response to the Christian message: I Cor. 15:11; Rom. 10:14."[15]

"It is the Holy Spirit Who binds us one to another in the love with which Christ has loved us," says L. Newbigin, "on the human side, it is faith which is fundamental: it consists in casting oneself totally upon this love and in opening one's heart, spirit, and soul to its influence."[16] Let us note that salvation was obtained under the old alliance only by faith, even as in the New Testament. Thus is manifested the continuity of God's plan through various alliances.

By faith Abraham was justified (Ro 4) and likewise "it is those who are of faith that are the sons of Abraham" (Gal 3:7, NASB). Hebrews 11 is a magnificent illustration of this truth: "By faith Abel . . . Enoch . . . Noah . . . Abraham . . . Jacob . . . Joseph . . . Moses . . . were saved." "In the past, all those who were saved were saved by faith, not by belonging to an ethnic group," says Harold Bender.[17]

Inversely, the apostles show us that "by no means all who descend from Israel belong to Israel . . . it is not his physical descendants who make up the children of God" (Ro 9:6-8).

"Neither is one a Jew from his looks, nor is circumcision what shows in the body" (Ro 2:28; see also 1 Co 10:1-5; Heb 3:10-11, 16, 19; 1 Ki 19:18; Is 8:5-20; 29:13; Joel 2:13).

John the Baptist warned the Jews: "Do not think you can excuse yourselves by saying, 'Abraham is our father'" (Mt 3:9, TEV), and Jesus said to them, "If you were Abraham's children, you would do what Abraham did" (Jn 8:39).[18]

So it is with all the spiritual blessings in Christ. They are all available to us, but to appropriate them the child of God must meet a number of conditions of which the Word of God reminds him:

"He who keeps His Word . . . His commandments. . . ."
"Those who obey Him, who love Him, who call upon Him. . . ."
"He who confesses that Jesus is the Son of God. . . ."
"He who loves his brother. . . ."
"He who is awake, keeping his garments. . . ."
"He who endures to the end. . . ."
"Those who draw near to God through him. . . ."
"You [who] do justice. . . ."
"He who hates his life in this world. . . ."
"Who walk . . . according to the Spirit. . . ."

To affirm that man has no role to play in effecting his salvation is contrary, then, to biblical teaching.[19]

His participation, limited to the voluntary appropriation of blessings acquired by Christ, in no way detracts from the work of Christ, and it safeguards the most precious gift that God has given man: his liberty.

SELECTIVE CHARACTER OF PREACHING IN THE NEW TESTAMENT

The selective character of preaching of necessity follows the two preceding considerations: if the call is addressed to the individual, if one asks him to meet certain conditions, this call will automatically necessitate a choice among the listeners; there will be those who will be ready to meet the required conditions and those who will refuse to do so. The call of Jesus Christ anticipates these two possible choices:

"*He who believes* in the Son has eternal life, but *he who disobeys* the Son will not see life but God's wrath remains upon him" (Jn 3:36).

"Unless a person is born from above he cannot see the kingdom of God . . . everyone who is born of the Spirit . . ." (Jn 3:3, 8).

"One who practices the truth wants light on it (Jn 3:21).

"Every one who practices evil . . . keeps away from the light" (Jn 3:20).

The gospel relates to us that immediately after the messages of Jesus Christ the boundary was clearly defined between those who believed on Him and those who persisted in unbelief.

"Many . . . believed in His name" (Jn 2:23; cf. 7:31; 8:30; 10:42; 11:45).

"Many more believed" (Jn 4:41).

"The man believed" (Jn 4:50).

"You do not believe . . . you do not want to come to Me in order to have life" (5:38-40; cf. 5:43; 8:45; 10:25).

"You do not receive Me" (5:43).

"But there are some of you who fail to believe" (6:64).[20]

Does not Jesus Himself say that He has come "to bring . . . discord; for from now on five will be at odds in one home, three against two and two against three—father against son and son against father; mother against daughter and daughter against mother; mother-in-law against daughter-in-law and daughter-in-law against mother-in-law" (Lk 12:51-53).

This same choice is made after the preaching of the apostles. At the time of Pentecost the apostle Peter issued the call: "Repent and be baptized, each of you in the name of Jesus Christ. . . . With many other words he charged them earnestly and warned them: 'Be saved from this crooked generation.' Then those who welcomed his message were baptized, and there were added that day about three thousand souls" (Ac 2:38-41).

All through the book of the Acts, after the preaching of the gospel, we read that several believed, or many, few, a certain number, a great number of people, a great multitude, or some believed; a great number believed, the company of those who believed (in all, 23 times). It is a question of "the number of those who had believed," "many thousand . . . among the Jews . . . have believed." These expressions show us that in the crowd of listeners a boundary line was unconsciously drawn. Some crossed the line; others remained where they were.

"Some, indeed, were convinced . . . but others did not believe" (Ac 28:24).[21] The presentation of the gospel divides men into two opposing camps. By it God offers man an opportunity to cross, by his own free choice, from one camp to the other.

Notes

1. "The ruinous and fateful confusion which was very early produced here only to be constantly repeated, consists in the fact that the Christian Church has begun again to consider itself and to conduct itself as if it were a sort of continuation or new edition of the people of Israel" (Karl Barth, *Church Dogmatics*, 3, 2, 2, p. 280). "But the difference between the church of the new age and ethnic Israel is that entrance into the people of God is by a personal decision of the individual" (H. S. Bender, *These Are My People*, p. 18).
"The Old Covenant was contracted with a people; one belonged to it by blood; it was an ethnic alliance; the present Alliance has been established with the Church; one becomes a part of it by faith; it is a spiritual alliance. Birth ushered one into the first; the new birth gives access to the second" (G. Francus, *Il n'y a pas de Protestants*, chap. 4).
"For this is the new thing in the Ekklesia in contrast with Israel that one does not enter the people of God by being born but by being born again, i.e., through faith" (Emil Brunner, *Dogmatics*, 3:56).
"State religions belong to the first period of the religious history of humanity. This first period came to an end eighteen centuries ago; one seeks to prolong it only by failing to distinguish between the two covenants and by upsetting the divine plan" (E. de Pressensé, *Discours religieux*, p. 29).
2. W. A. Visser't Hooft, *Misère et Grandeur de l'Eglise*, pp. 13-15. See on this subject the prophecies of the O.T. concerning the remnant: Is 4:3; 10:21; 11:11; 11:16; 37:32; 49:6; Jer 23:3; 50:20; Eze 14:22; Mic 2:12; Zeph 3:13; as well as Ro 2:17-29.
3. F. Godet, *Commentaire sur l'Evangile de Jean*, 2:62.
4. In the Old Testament "it is the nation as a whole that is summoned to repent. It is a corporate conversion, a revival of the nation, that is spoken of." One example is in Ezekiel 36. "The sins to be repented of are essentially national sins. . . . But do we also read in the pages of the O.T. of individual conversions in the sense made familiar to us by later usage? . . . All children were brought up within the Covenant and taught to think of themselves as being within it, so that no later experience of a critical kind was required of them" (John Baillie, *Baptism and Conversion*, pp. 58-61).
5. E. Kellerhals, *Bekehrung und Wiedergeburt*, p. 7.
6. E. de Faye, *Esquisse de la Pensée d'Origène*, p. 110.
7. Nils Alstrup Dahl, *Das Volk Gottes*, p. 248.
8. Brunner, 3:117.
9. Friedrich Schleiermacher, *Der Christliche Glaube*, pp. 137-38.
10. Brunner, *Le Renouveau de l'Eglise*, p. 16.
11. Dietrich Bonhoeffer, *Sanctorum communio*, p. 186.
12. A. deGasparin, *Les Ecoles du Doute et l'Ecole de la Foi*, p. 390.
13. A. Lemaître, *Foi et Vérité*, p. 468.
14. Brunner, *Le Renouveau de l'Eglise*, p. 18.
15. Mgr. Cerfaux, *La Théologie de l'Eglise suivant Saint Paul*, p. 123.
16. L. Newbigin, *L'Eglise*, p. 18.
17. Bender, p. 9.
18. See ibid., pp. 5-13 and Alan Stibbs, *God's Church*, pp. 16-23, 51-59.
19. "Throughout the whole of the Old Testament there is maintained a continuous and clear correlation between divine revelation and human responsibility, God's faithfulness and human trust, God's claim and human obedience" (Brunner, *Dogmatics*, 3:276).
20. "Here we come to the decision: I or Thou—either I am my own master or Thou art my master. This decision is faith" (Ibid., p. 286).
21. "Let Christianity again become what it always was: a sect . . . on this condition only it will be able to meet the demands of this age" (A. Vinet).
"To be a real man you must first of all be a dissenter" (Emerson).

5

Two Opposing Camps

The essential, unique, and most profound theme in the history of the world and of humanity, the one to which all others are subordinate, remains the conflict between unbelief and faith.

GOETHE (*Notizen zum westöstlichen Divan*)

RUNNING THROUGH all of the teaching of Jesus Christ and of His apostles there appears a *frontier* separating men into two opposing camps. The Scriptures use the most diverse images and expressions to characterize these two camps.

CONTRASTS JESUS USES IN THE GOSPELS

light	darkness (Jn 1:4-5)
wheat	chaff (Mt 3:12)
sons of the kingdom	sons of the evil one (Mt 13:38)
sons of light	sons of this world (Lk 16:8)
sons of the Father, freed from sin	children of the devil, slaves of sin (Jn 8:32-44)
those who are of God	those not of God (Jn 8:47)
that which is born of the Spirit	that which is born of the flesh (Jn 3:6-8)
he who believes in Him	he who does not believe (Jn 3:18)
he who is with Me, who gathers with Me	he who is against Me, who scatters (Mt 12:30)
My sheep whom I know and who know Me, follow Me	not My sheep, strangers, hireling, wolves (Jn 10)
servants	unfaithful servants (Lk 12:46)
servants of a future king	citizens who hated him, enemies who did not want him to reign over them (Lk 19:13-14, 27)
ten wise maidens	ten foolish maidens (Mt 25:1-13)
the sheep	the goats (Mt 25:31-33)

66

Contrasts in the Epistles

This same line of demarcation is found again in the letters of the apostles which distinguish:

those inside	those outside (1 Co 5:12)
fellow citizens with the saints, members of the household of God	strangers and sojourners (Eph 2:19)
you who believe	those who do not believe (1 Pe 2:7)
children of God	a crooked and perverse generation (Phil 2:14-15)
the saints	the unrighteous (1 Co 6:1)
a believer, a brother	unbelievers (1 Co 6:6; 2 Co 6:15)
brothers	false brethren, enemies (2 Th 3:15; 2 Co 11:26; Gal 2:4)
the household of faith	all men (Gal 6:10)
of us	not of us (1 Jn 2:19)
those who are being saved	those who are perishing (1 Co 1:18; 2 Co 2:15)
the believers	the world, the unbelievers (1 Co 7:14)
the spiritual man	the unspiritual man (1 Co 2:14-15)
men in whom Jesus Christ lives	the unregenerate (2 Co 13:5)
he who was born according to the Spirit	he who was born according to the flesh (Gal 4:29)
sons of light and sons of the day	sons of the night or of darkness (1 Th 5:5)
his saints, all who have believed	those who do not know God and who do not obey the gospel of our Lord Jesus (2 Th 1:8, 10)
those who have faith and keep their souls	those who shrink back and are destroyed (Heb 10:39)
the righteous man	the impious, the sinner (1 Pe 4:18)
he who confesses the Son	he who denies the Son (1 Jn 2:23)
he who is born of God, knows God, loves God, believes on the Son, has the Son and life	he who is not born of God, does not know God, does not love Him, does not believe in the Son, has not the Son, has not life (1 Jn 5:12)
he who is righteous and holy	he who is filthy (Rev 22:11)

Frequently, in contrast to the "you" by which recipients of the letters were addressed, the apostles call those of the other camp these names:

the Gentiles, the pagans, the heathen (1 Pe 2:12; 1 Co 5:1; 1 Th 4:5; Eph 4:17-20)

outsiders and unbelievers (1 Co 14:23)

those who are least esteemed by the church (1 Co 6:4)

lawless men (2 Pe 3:17)

children of wrath (Eph 2:3)

those who are to perish, those who refuse to love the truth (2 Th 2:10-12)

Characteristics of the Members of These Two Camps

Jesus Christ and the apostles describe the members of these two groups of humanity by numerous characteristics.

In His teaching, Jesus Christ portrays the benefits peculiar *to the one who follows Him:* he will live because of Him, abide in Christ as Christ abides in him, may have eternal life, shall never perish, does not come into judgment, will come forth to the resurrection of life, will never thirst but will find in him a spring of water welling up to eternal life, enters into the kingdom, worships in spirit and in truth, possesses the light of life, will not walk in darkness, is truly free, belongs to Christ, follows Him, knows His voice, will do the works that Christ has done, will never see death.[1]

The apostles say of Christians that they have been snatched from this present evil world; have become sons of God by faith, have put on Christ; belong to Him; Christ is formed in them and makes of them new creatures; they have received Christ because they have known the truth; they have been begotten by the word of truth and have become participants of the divine nature; they have been ransomed from the futile ways inherited from their fathers. They are risen in Christ, new men, chosen of God, holy and beloved of God; they share in Christ, are sons of God, fellow heirs with Christ; they have the liberty to draw near to God; they lead a life hidden with Christ in God, are led by the Spirit of God, love God, are called in Christ to eternal glory, to share the glory and inheritance of Jesus Christ.

To those of the other camp Jesus says:

You do not receive our testimony; you do not believe; you refuse to come to Me that you might have life; you have not the love of God within you; you do not receive Me; you do not seek the glory that comes from the only God; you are slaves of sin; your guilt remains; you will die in your sins; My word finds no place in you; you are not of God; you are of your father the devil; you know neither Me nor My Father; you have not known Him; you are all liars; you do not belong to My sheep.

The apostles speak of men who love darkness rather than light, reject the Word, oppose the name of Jesus, are a rebellious people, unbelieving, far from God, without God, without hope in the world, who are living under the power of Satan as enemies of the cross of Christ, whose end is destruction.[2]

The two camps are completely separated with no neutral area between! Everywhere is the uncompromising choice: "the one or the other."

"He who has the Son has that life; he who does not have the Son of God does not have life" (1 Jn 5:12); such is the teaching of Jesus Christ and His apostles.[3]

Notes

1. "Then came Jesus with His mighty and inexorable: 'either-or' (*Entweder-Oder*). . . . He went through the nation and divided it into two groups: those who heard Him unto salvation and those who were offended in Him and were thus lost. In like manner Jesus has passed through mankind down through the centuries and has divided men into two classes: those who chose to follow Him and those who chose to reject Him . . . He is the rock in the midst of the stream of life by which the human race is to be divided into two classes" (O. Hallesby, *Why I Am a Christian*, pp. 148-49).
2. "The New Testament writers used the strongest words which their language possessed to designate the difference between a Christian and a non-Christian. It is, they say, a difference as between life and death" (Ibid., p. 80).
3. "Each frontier is both defensive and offensive . . . this gives to their relationship the positive and the negative, clarity and assurance" (Karl Müller, *Kirche, Gemeinde und Obrigkeit*, p. 625).

6

Crossing from One Camp to the Other

Repent (Mt 3:2; 4:17; Ac 2:38).
Unless you are converted and become as little children, you will certainly not enter the kingdom of heaven (Mt 18:3).
He who believes in the Son has eternal life (Jn 3:36).
Unless a person is born from above he cannot see the kingdom of God (Jn 3:3).

ACCORDING TO THE TEACHING of Jesus and the apostles, humanity is divided into two opposing camps. By Jesus Christ—and in Him—God calls men "out of the world." He invites them to cross over from the camp of "the children of this world" to that of the "children of God," from the generation of "those who are lost" to the people of "those who are saved."

How does one cross the frontier? In other words: *What must one do to be saved?*

Within Christianity itself replies vary from one religious persuasion to another; for some, one is saved by baptism; others add to this obedience to God and to the commandments of the church; "evangelical Christians" insist on the necessity of a personal conversion.

What do the Scriptures say? The natural tendency of man is "to work for his salvation." All religions testify to this. The Bible is radically opposed to such a presumptuous assertion. Man, it affirms, can do nothing to merit eternal life; all are sinners (Job 15:14-16; Ec 7:20; Ro 3:9-19; Eph 2:1-3) and unable to achieve what God demands of them. A man is not justified by works of the law (Ro 3:20; Gal 2:16; Eph 2:9).

"But God . . . loved us" (Eph 2:4). "But God proves His own love for us by Christ's dying for us when we were still sinners" (Ro 5:8; cf. 1 Jn 4:9-10).

So the initiative belongs to God alone. God sent His own Son, He reconciled us, and justified us. When Jesus bowed His head and gave up His spirit, He said, "It is finished," thereby indicating that He had accomplished the perfect work of God and of His Son. Does that mean all men are now automatically saved? Would God save humanity "against man's will"?

The Lutheran and Reformed theologies have a tendency at present to lay stress on the work of God so much so that they render the part of man almost of no account.[1] This reaction against the theology of the will and experience of the nineteenth century is no closer now to the truth than it was then. In the Bible "God never acts mechanically and without laying down a condition for salvation."[2]

Emil Brunner said,

> Regeneration is the new creature through faith, and this faith in Christ demands our active participation. . . . It is just as necessary to empha- size this active side as the passive side, regeneration and the active side of one and the same faith is conversion, both in the negative sense of a turning away and in the positive sense of a turning to. . . . In the Word of God both aspects are included. Only in the apprehension of both move- ments, that of claim and that of promise (*Anspruch und Zuspruch*), is the Word of Christ completely apprehended.[3]

And P. Valloton comments,

> It is indeed a certain fact that the Bible speaks constantly of *man's* faith, and the apostle Paul especially stresses this (Phil. 2:17; Col. 4:2-5; I Thess. 1:3, 5, 6, 7, 10); of a faith in which man is the conspicuously ac- tive participant; "Do not fear, only believe" (Mark 5:36). "He who be- lieves in him is not condemned" (John 3:18). "I believed" (II Cor. 4: 13). "Telling the people to believe in the one who was to come" (Acts 19:4). "Your faith has saved you" (Luke 7:50). "Your faith in God has gone forth everywhere" (I Thess. 1:8). "The faith which our father Abraham had" (Rom. 4:12). "Your faith" (II Pet. 1:5). "Our faith" (I John 5:4).[4]

God does not want to rob man of the free will which He Himself gave him. God respects man's free will. Jesus said, "If anyone wills to do His [the Father's] will . . ." (Jn 7:17), and His call is heard to the very end of the Revelation: "He who desires it, let him take freely the water of life" (Rev 22:17). But, unfortunately, this will also possesses the formid- able power to say no to God. "Yet you do not want to come to Me in order to have life" (Jn 5:40).

Throughout the history of salvation, God requires certain things of man, not that he should achieve his salvation, but that he should prove that he wishes to be saved.

Everywhere in the Bible are found commandments, counsel and recom- mendations. The New Testament alone contains more than a thousand imperatives and several thousand exhortations of various kinds.[5] It is useless to deny that God expects something from man. What does He want? What must man do to be saved?

MAN'S PART

REPENT (Mt 3:2; Ac 2:38)

The word *metanoïa*, translated by *repentance* (*keen regret* or *penitence* in certain Catholic versions) signifies: changing one's mind, manner of thinking, attitude. He who repents critically examines his past; he is sorry for his mistakes and decides to change his conduct. Before repentance, which is, above all, a meeting with God, the self is the center of our lives. Before divine holiness, man discovers he has sinned in neglecting to give God the place which belongs to Him. From then on values change: "Everything that was gain for me I have considered loss for Christ's sake" (Phil 3:7).

The story of the prodigal son is the most forceful biblical illustration of repentance. It shows us that thought, feeling, and will all unite their efforts in a man who repents to bring him to definite action: the return to God. Repentance is the door to salvation.

TURN ABOUT (Ac 3:19)

The verb for "to be converted" (*epistrephein*) is found forty times in the New Testament. It signifies to turn toward, to turn to God, to turn to the Lord (Ac 9:35; 11:21; 15:19; 1 Th 1:9). It is "after having recognized his error and the dangers of a false situation, to pledge oneself wholeheartedly to a new position, a true one," says J. P. Ramseyer.[6] "Man turns away from his own way and toward the will and way of God," Brunner comments, and G. Berguer says, "Conversion is not the main goal of the Christian life; it is only one stage; it is the moment when man realizes the unity of his will with God's."[7]

Conversion is the decisive turning point in a life, slow or sudden, it matters little, but it must take place for "man is not born a Christian; he becomes one," says Tertullian.

BELIEVE

The Hebrew words translated *believe* signify to put one's trust in, to count on, to trust. The Greek word *pistis* (used 235 times in the New Testament) indicates also that burst of confidence which leads man to speak to God or His Son, Jesus Christ. To meet Jesus Christ is to become acquainted with Him, to trust Him and to love Him, to receive Him and give oneself to Him. To follow Him is to obey Him and remain faithful to Him; that is true faith. It is a promise as total and final as the one that binds a man to a woman by marriage. Confidence is central in the act of faith. To believe in Jesus is to put one's trust in His power, in His person, and in His testimony. Paul uses Abraham as an example of faith, justified by God because he trusts in Him.

Faith produces a radical change in man; he is led to self-surrender. The human *I* is dethroned and Jesus becomes Lord, says Brunner. "God reigns in that man by His Spirit. Faith is participating in the life of the living, present God."[8]

Far from being a simple mental assent, it is an about-face which involves the whole life. The word *pistis* says the same as the words *metanoïa* and *epistrephein*; it evokes this same complete change of attitude toward God, toward oneself and the life which is now ours through Jesus Christ.

Unfortunately, beginning with the second century, adherence to the creed of the church is called faith. The biblical view, like that of the Reformers, makes faith a new attitude, personal and conscious, toward God; to believe is to put one's trust in the atonement accomplished by Jesus Christ on the cross for one's salvation.

Thus, repentance, conversion, and faith are three very closely related words. They express one and the same reality, but each word stresses only one aspect. Repentance places the emphasis on renunciation of the past and a change in direction; faith defines one's new relationship to God; conversion embraces the total change, visible and invisible. It concerns a transformation of one's inner attitude toward life and God more than it does one's visible experiences. In the first centuries he who repented was converted, and believed, and was baptized. By this act he testified that he considered himself dead to his old life and resurrected to a new life.

GOD'S WORK IN MAN

THE BAPTISM OF THE HOLY SPIRIT

The Holy Spirit acts in men's hearts even before their conversion (see Jn 15:26; 16:8; 6:44; 2 Co 3:15; 4:3).

Death. John the Baptist prophesied that the Messiah would baptize with the Holy Spirit. He said that his baptism in the river Jordan was only symbolic of what Christ would do in man. The Jews who came confessing their sins were buried by the Baptist in a virtual tomb, the water; they accepted the judgment of God and died symbolically.

If we go to Christ prompted by a state of mind comparable to that of those Jews, He puts to death and causes to disappear before the eyes of God the "old man," the sinner from whom we would like to be free. By the power of His Spirit, He places us where we profit by His death; He makes us His very own; thus we are identified by God with His Son in His death on the cross. This is what the apostle Paul is speaking about in Romans 6:3-7. (See also 1 Co 11:31; Jn 5:24; Col 2:11; 1 Pe 3:20.) "One died for all, so that they all died" (2 Co 5:14).

The results of this death: pardon and justification. The death of a guilty man stops a lawsuit against him and removes all condemnation. God pardons the sinner who reckons himself dead with Christ (Lk 24:47; Ac 2:38; 5:31; Heb 9:22; 10:18; Eph 4:32). He goes even further: He justifies him; that is, He declares him righteous.

Resurrection. The apostle Paul speaks also of the second aspect of the baptism of the Holy Spirit (Ro 6:4-11). Since man who has chosen to die with Christ to his old life is considered by God Himself to be righteous, nothing henceforth hinders the Spirit of God from dwelling in him. Henceforth Christ, by His Spirit, dwells with him (Jn 14:17, 20, 23). This is what Jesus calls the "new birth."

THE NEW BIRTH

The biblical teaching. The Old Testament foretold individual and radical transformations with the coming of the Messiah (Jer 31:29-34; Eze 11:19-21; 36:26-27).

Jesus, speaking to Nicodemus, stressed the necessity of a new birth if one would enter into the kingdom of God (Jn 3:3, 5, 7), for "what is born of the flesh is flesh" (v. 6). Now "flesh and blood cannot inherit the kingdom of God" (1 Co 15:50). In the teachings of Jesus we find many other allusions to the new birth (Mt 9:17; 10:38; 16:26; 18:3; Mk 8:34; Lk 9:23; Jn 5:24, 26; 12:24).

The writers of the New Testament use about ten different expressions to evoke the varied aspects of the new birth. Some of them stress its unique aspect, once for all; others present it as a continuous process of renewal. In the first group we find the noun "regeneration" (*palingenesia*), and the verbs "to beget" (*gennaō, apokueō*), "to cause to be born again" (*anagennaō*), and the adjective "newborn" (*artigennetos*), all used symbolically. But a birth is followed by a new life; that is why a whole series of words describes the work of regeneration which goes on in the one who is born from above: "to change," "to renew" (*anakainoō, ananeoō*); "the renewing" (*anakainosis*); "newness" (of mind, of life) (*kainotes*); and the adjectives "new" (*kainos*) and "recent" (*neos*).

The apostles present the new birth under the image of a new creation, a new life, a spiritual resurrection, a new man that is clothed upon, as the circumcision of the heart. It is the work of God which makes us "sharers of the divine nature" (2 Pe 1:4).

The consequences of our regeneration. We are reconciled to God, brought near to Him, adopted as His children, sealed by the Holy Spirit;

we become the dwelling place of this Spirit. Brunner says that "all these expressions are images, parables which, as it were, surround the spiritual reality, like the spokes of a wheel, leading toward an identical center but without ever touching it."[9]

The fruits of the new life. Believers receive these things as they trust in Christ:

1. the assurance of salvation (1 Jn 5:10-13; 3:14; Ro 8:10)
2. a progressive walk in the way of sanctification (1 Jn 5:18; 3:6; 2:9; 1:8)
3. a spirit of prayer (Ro 8:26)
4. hunger for the Word of God (Jn 10:3; 1 Jn 4:6; 1 Pe 2:2)
5. love for God and for Christ (Lk 7:36-50; Ro 5:5; 1 Jn 4:18-19; Jn 21:17; 1 Pe 1:8; Eph 6:24)
6. the desire to serve Christ (Jn 1:40-45; 1 Jn 4:2-3, 15; Ro 10:9-10)
7. the love for the brethren and the search for Christian fellowship (Jn 13:35; 1 Jn 3:14; 4:7; 5:1; 2:11)

HOW TO APPLY THESE CRITERIA

One would have to be careful, of course, not to apply these criteria rigidly, concluding from the absence of one or two of the fruits that there is no new life. Certain fruits bear later than others and there is nothing stereotyped about the development of the fruit in the life of each Christian. Nevertheless, if there is no discernible change in the one who says he is converted, if he has no assurance of his salvation, no desire to witness for Christ or to meet other Christians, one can rightfully doubt the reality of his new birth. To express such a doubt is not judging in the wrong sense of the word, since the Word of God itself gives us the identifying marks of the new life and tells us to judge those who are "within the church" (1 Co 5:12).

If, as we shall try to show, the true members of the church as God planned it should be only those who have been born again, it is indeed necessary that those who have the responsibility of "guarding the entrance" have some criteria which will permit them to grant or refuse entrance into the local church. The most important indication will be, of course, the profession of faith from the candidate for membership himself, but this profession must be confirmed by the testimony of a changed life.[10] That the appraisal of life always should be made in love, "by the judgment of love," as Calvin says, is evident from the very spirit of the gospel. Yet, if we wish to remain faithful to biblical truth, we will not find it possible to reduce the new birth to an imperceptible event of the inner life or even to a formality on the spiritual level without any repercussion on the moral level.

"The new birth is the central event of Christianity for the writers of the New Testament," says A. Harnack.[11] It is the central event of the human life, the passage from spiritual death to eternal life. "The whole Gospel is summed up in the second birth," comments Vinet. But, he adds, "it is this very thought which frightens and repels. That is what people would like to remove. Everything except regeneration is accepted; that is, everything but that which is essential, everything except everything."[12]

The new birth remains, even today, "the greatest scandal of Christianity," as Professor Hallesby puts it, "the stumbling block which causes the greatest number of people to trip up." He says it is an established fact that you can speak of everything, tell people they should be more religious, pray more, attend church services more often, contribute more effectively to God's work of missions, etc.

> But when we tell them that they must be born again, they balk exactly as Nicodemus did nineteen hundred years ago. They become irritated and even offended. . . . People like those pastors who speak sternly and appealingly, best of all perhaps when the tears trickle down the cheeks of both the speaker and the listeners. Note well that this is the case only as long as the pastor speaks sternly and yet avoids mentioning conversion and the new birth, avoids making the Biblical distinction between regenerate and unregenerate men.[13]

THE BAPTISM OF THE HOLY SPIRIT AND INCORPORATION INTO THE CHURCH

"For by one Spirit we were all baptized into one body" (1 Co 12:13). The baptism of the Holy Spirit, by which we die to ourselves and are born from above, unites us at the same time to the church of Jesus Christ.

WE HAVE ALL BEEN BAPTIZED

We: The apostle Paul and Sosthenes wrote the first letter addressed to the Corinthians. These Corinthians are called "those made holy in Christ Jesus and called to be saints," they "invoke the name of our Lord Jesus Christ," (1:2), they are "saved" (1:18), "bought" (7:23), "born again" (4:15), "washed," "made holy," "made righteous" (6:11). Their new birth divides their lives into two parts: formerly and now (6:9-11).

all: All those who have experienced the new birth, all those who are saved and justified, have also been baptized by the Holy Spirit.[14]

have been: As in all passages from the epistles which refer to the baptism of the Holy Spirit, the apostle Paul here speaks of this event in the past. Nowhere in the letters does he exhort new converts to seek the baptism of the Holy Spirit. Judging from appearances, however, if ever a group of Christians had need of this baptism of the Spirit as it is taught today in certain circles, it was the Corinthians.[15] The apostle, without any hesitation, could write to them that they had all been baptized by the Holy Spirit, for he knew that the local church admitted only those who had experienced the new birth.

BAPTISM IN ONE SPIRIT—OR BY JUST ONE SPIRIT

The Spirit plunges the believer into the death of Christ and keeps his old nature there.[16] We are "all the while bearing about in the body the dying of Jesus, so that by our bodies the life of Jesus may also be shown" (2 Co 4:10). The Spirit into whom the believer is plunged permeates him as water permeates a sponge.

Only *one* Spirit is of God, but other spirits also exist which are at work in the world. There are spirits which claim that Jesus is cursed (1 Co 12:3), spirits which do not confess that Jesus came in the flesh (1 Jn 4:1-3), and spirits which come to lead Christians astray. These spirits are fully prepared to grant "spiritual baptism" in order to bring souls into subjection and have them at their mercy. The history of the Christian church confirms only too well the reality of these dangers.

Corinth was full of idols and occult religions. The apostle does not want the Christians to be in communion with demons (1 Co 10:20); he wants to keep them under the direction of the one Spirit who unites them with the Lord Jesus in His death and resurrection. The apostle speaks especially of *one* Spirit because the Spirit seeks to gather together in *one* body all regenerated men.

If an alleged baptism of the Spirit separates us from other children of God, can we truly attribute the source of the baptism to the Spirit of Christ, who has no other goal than to unite Christians? Indeed, if this one and only Spirit dwells in my brother and in me, will it not draw us together? For the supreme objective of the Spirit, in baptizing believers, is to form *one* body. Fourteen times in these few verses the apostle uses the words "one," "one only," and "the same," because the entire theme of this chapter is the unity of the body of Christ, though there is a diversity of gifts, ministries, and vocations.

BAPTISM RESULTS IN THE FORMING OF ONE BODY

Literally, the Spirit works within believers with a view to forming just one body. The ultimate objective of the Spirit in baptizing believers is to form one body: the body of Christ on earth. When a child is born, he immediately becomes a member of a family. The very moment the believer is born again he enters the great family of the children of God. God does not want us to continue as wandering sheep, each one turning to his own way (Is 53:6), strangers, sojourners, people far off. He welcomes us into His family; we become "fellow citizens with the saints and members of God's household" (Eph 2:19); we "are Christ's body and individually members of it" (1 Co 12:27).

Only the baptism of the Holy Spirit can make one a member of the body of Christ; neither water baptism, nor joining the church of one's free will, nor confession of faith can replace it. Therefore, only those who have received the baptism of the Spirit are members of this body, and all who are baptized by the Spirit are a part of the body of Christ. Scripture recognizes neither a mixed body of regenerate and unregenerate men, nor a body of those "baptized by the Spirit" separated from those who are "only saved," nor isolated believers living outside of the body. God's plan for His children works through the church and results in the church.

Nowhere in the New Testament do we see a believer living his life as a Christian apart from his brothers and sisters. Still today, if the Lord baptizes with His Spirit, it is always "with the purpose of forming a body"; if He instills divine life in believers, it is not so that they may be isolated living cells. Today, as in the first century, God wants to "form *one* body," the body of Christ, "an instrument of the will of God among men," "the completeness of Him who fills the universe at all points" (Eph 1:23).

Notes

1. "One of the characteristics of the present theological stress consists in rendering Biblical truths objective. Baptismal regeneration, the Church, 'the Word,' faith, worship are presented as objective values; the subjective relationship is relegated to the background or it is to a great extent theologically suspect" (Otto Riecker, *Erweckung heute*, p. 66).
2. F. Heitmüller, *Die Krisis des Gemeinschaftsbewegung*, p. 40.
3. Emil Brunner, *Dogmatics*, 3:281.
4. P. Valloton, *Christ et la Foi*, p. 129.
5. "If one counts the passages in the New Testament that speak of faith or in a similar sense of repentance, conversion, love to God, turning toward God, and what otherwise expresses the response of man, one recognizes how the meaning and truth of everything depends upon both sides and their correspondence" (Brunner, *Wahrheit als Begegnung*, p. 160).
6. J. P. Ramseyer, *Vocabulaire biblique*, p. 248.
7. G. Berguer, *Traité de Psychologie de la Religion*, p. 247.
8. Brunner, *Wahrheit* . . . , pp. 105-59.
9. Brunner, *Der Mittler*, p. 411.
10. We are not able to express a final opionion here. However, one must know with whom one can work. Although the church is never perfect, she is nevertheless a team of brethren. But who are these brethren? "We must recognize as members of the Church all those who by confession of faith, exemplary lives, and

partaking of the sacraments, confess with us the same God and Christ" (John Calvin, *Institutes* 4, 1:8). "Therefore, not just any member of the official church is a member of the Church, the Body of Christ, but only he who confesses the true faith. This principle is at the foundation of church discipline; it is the condition for the effectiveness of the Church and also the test of its unity" (Jacques de Senarclens, *De la Vraie Eglise, selon Calvin*, p. 28).

11. A. Harnack, *What Is Christianity?*, p. 113.
12. A. de Gasparin, *Les Ecoles du Doute et l'Ecole de la Foi*, p. 390.
13. O. Hallesby, *Why I Am a Christian*, p. 88.
14. The recent doctrine which disassociates the new birth from baptism of the Holy Spirit cannot withstand a close examination of New Testament verses which speak of the baptism of the Spirit. It leads to arbitrary discriminations, unwholesome expectations, complexes of frustration, and false conclusions like the following: "Even if being born again is sufficient for salvation, being baptized by the Holy Spirit is indispensable if one is to become a part of the Body of Christ. . . . A child of God who has not experienced the baptism of the Holy Spirit who partakes in the Lord's Supper with his brethren, will not therefore be a part of the Body of Christ, but only in the life of his Savior" (E. A. Hofer, *Eglise où es-tu?*, pp. 17, 21). By "the baptism of the Holy Spirit" the author means a "spiritual overflowing which moves the spirit, soul, and body of the believer" (p. 17) and of which speaking in tongues is "the initial evidence" (p. 146).
15. "One who is baptized by the Holy Spirit is recognized by his speaking in tongues, his spiritual radiance, his boldness in speaking of the Lord, his love for souls, his love for and increased comprehension of the Word of God" (Ibid., p. 152). Where do we find these signs or fruits of the baptism of the Holy Spirit among the Corinthians?
16. "The Greek preposition *en* often denotes the means." See F. Godet, *Commentaire sur I Cor.*, p. 217.

For Further Reading

Hallesby, O. *Why I Am a Christian*, pp. 71, 100, 119.
Pohlmann, H. *Die Metanoïa als Zentralbegriff christlicher Frömmigkeit.* Leipzig: Hinrichs, 1938.
Rienecker, F. Wiedergeburt und Bekehrung als enge Pforte zur Gemeinde *Praktischer Handkommentar zum Epheserbrief.* Neumunster: Ihloff, 1934, pp. 443 ff.

Part III

DESIGNS AND WORKING PLANS

7

Images and Parables of the Church

IN GLANCING THROUGH the gospels, we notice only two occasions where Jesus uses the word *church*. Does that mean He spoke of it only twice and placed little value on it? On the contrary, all of His teaching was directed toward the community which would bring His disciples together after His departure. Jesus never intended to form hermits. The picture of a normal Christian life, as seen in the gospels, is inseparable from its normal setting: the Christian community. Each time Jesus speaks of the relationship among the brethren, He is addressing Himself to the church.

When Jesus wished to reveal to His disciples truths which they were still unable to comprehend, He frequently used images and parables. These were implanted in their memories and would crop up again when the Spirit would lead them into all truth. Before approaching the study of the church of the apostolic period, it is fitting to examine the principal figures and parables of the church which we find in the gospels and epistles, then see what teachings are thus given to us concerning the church and the nature of its members.

PRINCIPAL FIGURES AND PARABLES OF THE CHURCH

We shall set aside the allegorical details which one can ascribe to the church (e.g., the inn where the good Samaritan takes the man he has befriended, the importunate widow, the pearl) to study seven figures of speech which are better developed and each one of which illustrates one aspect:[1]

the kingdom	the organized community
the flock	the relationship between the community and Christ
the plant which grows	the laws of growth
the vine	dependence upon Christ
the building	the construction
the bride	the affectionate relationship with Christ
the body	the different functions of the church

THE KINGDOM

The gospels often speak of the kingdom. Certainly one cannot apply only to the church all that Jesus says of it, but these two ideas have as many points in common as two concentric circles. The kingdom extends beyond the church, but at present Jesus exercises His kingship in the church, which is composed of those who here and now accept His lordship.[2]

In the parable of the talents the two phases of the history of the kingdom appear clearly: kingdom contested—kingdom established. During the first phase, that of the church, the kingdom is represented by the entire group of servants who are called to make the most of their talents in the midst of the hostility of their fellow countrymen. This is the present condition of the church. All the other "parables of the kingdom," or those which concern a king, illustrate the privileges and duties of the king's subjects (see Mt 18:23-35; 22:1-14; 25:14-30).[3]

THE FLOCK

The flock is also a community, grouped this time about the shepherd. Jesus' allusions to the flock (Lk 12:32; Jn 10:16; Mt 26:31) bring out clearly the role of the shepherd, which is more apparent than that of the king in the kingdom.[4]

The good Shepherd is Jesus Christ (Jn 10:11, 16). "He calls His own sheep by name and leads them out" (v. 3; remember that the name *church* is born of this call of Christ). "He walks ahead of them" (v. 4); He protects them, knows them (v. 14), adds them to the sheep of His other folds in *one* flock (v. 16). All *that* Jesus Christ does for His church. "He will feed His flock like a shepherd; He will gather the lambs in His arms, carrying them in His bosom and gently leading those that are with young" (Is 40:11). He goes to seek the lost sheep and "when he has found it, he lays it on his shoulders, rejoicing" (Lk 15:5-7). "I, even I, will search for My flock and seek them out. As a shepherd seeks out his sheep . . . so will I seek out My sheep and rescue them from all the places where they have been scattered. . . . In good pastures will I feed them . . . they will lie down in a good fold. . . . I will seek the lost and bring back the strayed; I will bind up the wounded; I will strengthen the sick" (Eze 34:11-16).

The epistle to the Hebrews calls Jesus "that great Shepherd of the sheep" (Heb 13:20), and the apostle Peter speaks of Him as "the Chief Shepherd," "the Shepherd and Guardian of your souls" (1 Pe 5:4; 2:25).

That does not exclude the ministry of other shepherds. The apostle Paul says that Christ established certain ones as "pastors and teachers" in the church (Eph 4:11). He enjoins the elders of the church of Ephesus to "be on guard for yourselves and for the entire flock over which the Holy Spirit has appointed you overseers; shepherd the church of God, which He has bought with His own blood" (Ac 20:28).

Thus, it seems that when the Word of God uses the image of the flock, it seeks to draw attention especially to the role of the shepherd, whether it is to remind believers of their privilege in having Jesus as their good Shepherd, or to exhort human shepherds to carry out their duties in the midst of the flock as the chief Shepherd would have done.[5]

The Christian church has especially adopted the image of the flock by taking the name *congregation* (from the Latin *grex:* flock), and in speaking of pastors (shepherds), of little sheep (lambs), of the shepherd's crook and the bishop's crook, etc. The danger of this image is that it gives the sheep a passive or lesser role with respect to the human shepherds, which does not correspond in any way to biblical teaching or to what is suggested by the other images. So it is not surprising if in the clerical forms in the church they have retained, so to speak, this one image (neglecting to lay stress on the fact that the Bible teaches that it is especially Jesus Christ who is the Shepherd).

THE GROWING PLANT

The growing plant often appears in the teaching of Jesus to illustrate the laws of the growth of the church. In Matthew 13:31, the grain of mustard seed which becomes a bush illustrates the disproportion between the diminutive seed and the important result. Some interpreters think that in this parable Jesus is trying prophetically to call our attention to certain anomalies in the development of His church. The mustard seed normally produces small plants growing close together in a field, but it can happen that, due to some alteration in a living cell, a plant may be subjected to abnormal growth and take the form of a bush in whose branches the birds can make their nests (Mt 13:32). The normal state of the church is not the gigantic system but the small community.[6]

The short parable of the seed which sprouts and grows (Mk 4:26) speaks to us of the slow, silent and progressive development of the church; this follows the rules and steps of organic growth.

The parable of the weeds (Mt 13:24-30, 36-43) does not teach that unbelievers are to be kept in the church, since the Lord Himself says "the field is the world" (v. 38), but rather that the church will have to share this field to the end of time with systems which, though sown by the adversary, resemble the church. In fact, in their first stages of development, wheat and darnel are so similar that even specialists are incapable of telling them apart. By the time the difference is apparent, it is too late to weed out the darnel without endangering the wheat. In this parable the church is represented by the wheat, the good grain sown by the owner of the field. The apostle Paul says in 1 Corinthians 3:9, "You are God's fields." In this verse the fields represent the church.

Shortly before His death, Jesus again used the image of the wheat. A delegation of Greeks had asked for an interview. What did they want of Him? Had they had wind of a plot being hatched against Him so that they were suggesting that He follow them to the Hellenic Diaspora where He could safely continue to teach? The gospel does not say, but from the reply given by Jesus this assumption is not untenable. "The hour has come for the Son of Man to be glorified. Truly I assure you, unless a grain of wheat drops into the earth and dies, it remains single, but if it dies, it produces a rich yield. . . . Now My soul is disturbed, and what shall I say? Father, save Me from this hour? But for this reason I came to this hour. Father, glorify Thy name" (Jn 12:23-28).

While stating the reason for His refusal of an easy solution, Jesus reveals to us one of the most profound laws of the vegetable and spiritual world: through death to life. This law has been scientifically verified for the grain of wheat: the phenomena of necrosis has literally been produced within the seed which has been sown. If this necrosis does not take place, there is no plant development and "the grain remains alone." This law is true in many other situations.[7]

But if the grain dies, if it is buried in the earth, a new life will soon spring forth from its tomb, a plant will reach upward toward heaven, really in defiance of the laws of mechanics and gravity; it will blossom, will become fertilized, and bear fruit. Several months later, in the very place where the seed died, numerous seeds identical to the first one appear pressed closely together in perfect unity and order. The dead seed remains invisible, but the ear of grain is there to show what it was like, where it was, and why it died.

To those who come to God today, saying, "We wish to see Jesus," He answers by pointing to the church. Is she not the entire group of those whom He "appointed beforehand to share the likeness of His Son" (Ro 8:29)? He whom God prophetically called the Branch (Is 4:2; Jer 23:5; 33:15; Zech 3:8; 6:12) died. The world believed it was rid of Him. Less than two months later there was the harvest: numerous grains closely pressed together, organically united, reproduced the image of Christ in three thousand copies (Ac 4:13, 32). These grains were scattered throughout the entire ancient world; they, in turn, willingly "died with

Christ" in various ways indicated by their Master (Ac 4; 5:41; 7; 8:1-4; 16:22; 18:17; 23:14; Ro 6; Gal 2:20; 1 Pe 4:4).

New plants and heads of grain are produced; death has made way for life. After several decades the Greco-Roman world is strewn with heads of grain—that is, the local churches—each kernel of which is both an image of the original grain and a new powerful head.

THE VINE AND THE VINEYARD

The vine and vineyard were, for those who heard Jesus, familiar symbols of the people of God. The prophets of the Old Testament had already used these symbols (Ps 80:9; Is 3:14; 5:1-7; Jer 2:21; 12:10; Eze 15:2; Ho 10; Joel 1:7).

The parables of the laborers hired at different hours (Mt 20:1-16) and of the two sons (21:28) present the church as a field of labor where each one finds work and a chance to earn wages. These will be distributed, however, according to the law of grace, not of merit. The parable of the wicked tenants (Mt 21:33-44) prophesies the replacement of the people of Israel by the church in this vineyard which the Lord lets out to tenants.

Like the church, a vineyard is a collection of plants of the same kind, belonging to the same owner, benefiting from the same care, and mingling the individual fragrances of their fruits to give the agreeable fragrance characteristic of the wine of the vineyard.

In the metaphor of the vine and the branches (Jn 15), where it is a question not of the whole vine but only of the base of the vine, the emphasis is on the unity between Christ and the church and on the necessity of a vital and permanent relationship between the living Christ (as opposed to the dead grain of wheat) and the members of the church. Apart from the vine the branches remain unfruitful, destined only for death (v. 4). They are joined to the trunk, not by a series of branches graduated in size as in most trees, but directly with no connecting link. On the other hand, the vine can bear fruit only through the branches. Vine and branches must act interdependently if they are to fulfill their purpose. Fruit can be produced only by close collaboration: sap is drawn up through the roots, enriched in the leaves, and transported by the ducts. So, its nourishment is drawn as much from the soil into which the roots go as from the air that the leaves of branches breathe; both are indispensable to the plant's normal development.

All the teachings of the vine reveal laws of prime importance to the life and growth of the believer as well as to the church. Useless branches must be removed if the vine is to bear much fruit, said the Lord; this is also the secret of a fruitful spiritual life, and is the principle of church discipline which the Lord Himself exercised. A detailed study of this passage in its context shows that it is speaking of the church rather than the individual believer.

THE BUILDING AND THE TEMPLE

A building. Jesus as well as His disciples used the building and the temple as images of the church. We remember that Jesus was a carpenter, or mason or architect, which amounted to the same thing in Palestine in those days. He knew the principles of construction well enough to draw spiritual applications from them. We shall not repeat here what we have already said concerning the institution of the church: Jesus Christ, the foundation; the apostle Peter, the first stone laid on the rock; the other disciples, then the 120 disciples, then the 3,000 converted at Pentecost building on the foundation already laid.[8]

Believers are the building of God. The image of the building offers a wealth of teaching to the Christian. The apostles used it: "You are the building which God is constructing" (1 Co 3:9). "You are . . . members of God's household; you are constructed on the foundation of the apostles and prophets of which the cornerstone is Christ Jesus. The whole building, framed together in Him, rises into a temple that is holy in the Lord, in whom you also are built up together for a dwelling of God in the Spirit" (Eph 2:19-22).

"Be built up as living stones into a spiritual house" (1 Pe 2:5); "We are his house" (Heb 3:6, RSV); "God's household, which is the church of the living God" (1 Ti 3:15). Each believer must be extracted from the quarry of the world before he can be used in the construction of the house of God. The divine engraver will have to smooth many rough and irregular places to make us serviceable in the place assigned us on the architect's plan so that we fit perfectly into our places and in relationship to the other stones around us. God does not shape us all in the same form; but, like a good master-builder, He assigns and places the stones which He utilizes where their form, solidity, and grain best fit in.

However, a pile of stones, even perfectly hewn, is not yet a house. The task of the divine builder is to place each stone in the church and fasten it securely to the others. "God has appointed in the church first apostles, next prophets, third teachers, then miracle workers, then gifts of healing, helpers, administering" (1 Co 12:28). It is not a question here of hierarchy, but of a plan to put the various construction materials in their proper places. "But crown it all with love, which is the perfect bond of union" (Col 3:14). The quality of love given us by the Holy Spirit is perfect (Ro 5:5); God does not use human materials.

Moreover, in this building we are "God's fellow workers" (1 Co 3:9). That is why the apostle Paul says, "Let each one look out how he does the building . . . each one's work will become evident . . . it will be revealed by fire. Of whatever quality each one's work may be, the fire will test it. In case one's construction survives, he will receive his pay" (1 Co 3:10-14).

Though the construction of a building may be important, it is only a means, one step. The purpose is to give man a home, a shelter against cold and rain, protection against danger, a peaceful and safe place where he can be refreshed, where he can find rest and love. This is the purpose of the local church as well. In the midst of a "faithless and perverse generation," the child of God needs a haven of peace where he can renew his strength, find shelter, participate in communion with God and the brethren, and find the needed warmth and affection necessary for life, which the world cannot give him.

The temple. The Scriptures also liken the church to a particular building: "We are the temple of the living God" (2 Co 6:16; cf. 1 Co 3:16-17). "The cornerstone is Christ Jesus. The whole building, framed together in Him, rises into a temple that is holy in the Lord" (Eph 2:21). ". . . God's household, which is the church of the living God" (1 Ti 3:15). The temple is "My Father's house" (Jn 2:16), "a house of prayer" (Mk 11:17) where one worships, offers praise, and brings intercession; it is the place where offerings are made: burnt offerings, sacrifices of thanksgiving, of atonement, and sin offerings.[9]

THE FIANCÉE AND THE BRIDE

Christ, the Bridegroom of the church. The fiancée and the bride also symbolize the church in the New Testament. Here the emphasis is on the affectionate relationship between Christ and the church.

IN THE OLD TESTAMENT. This figure had already been used by writers of the Old Testament to illustrate the relationship between God and His chosen people (Is 54:4-5; 62:5; Eze 16:8; Ho 2:18-21). The Song of Solomon, which was read publicly at each Passover feast, described the young Shulammite's conflict of soul between her love for the poor shepherd and the charms of the powerful monarch of Jerusalem.[10] Thus the faithful community of the old as well as that of the new covenant is engaged in a constant conflict between the love for God and the enticements of the world. It is the same figure of marriage, a symbol of the normal relationship between the chosen people and their God, which furnishes the severe expressions of *adulterous* and *prostitute* with which the prophets brand the faithlessness of Israel.

IN THE GOSPELS. So it is not surprising that John the Baptist designated Jesus as the Bridegroom (Jn 3:29), that Jesus Himself compared His followers to the joyous wedding guests (Mt 9:15), and frequently represented the kingdom of God as a wedding feast. The image is implicit in several parables. In the parable of the unrighteous judge, the church, exposed to the hostility of the world, is compared to a widow. In the parable of the lost coin, it is possible that the lost coin belonged in the necklace of coins which each Jewish fiancée collected before her marriage.[11] Each member of the body of Christ who goes astray delays the hour for the wedding of the Lamb. In the parable of the ten virgins, there is indeed a bridegroom for whom they are impatiently waiting, and a room for the wedding feast. But where is the bride? Is she represented by the group of virgins who enter with the bridegroom? This interpretation, which is far from a normal situation, would be strangely like the application which the apostles later make of this image.

IN THE EPISTLES. "I gave you in marriage to one Husband to present you as a pure virgin to Christ" (2 Co 11:2). "Husbands, love your wives, even as Christ loved the church and gave Himself for her, in order that by cleansing her by means of the washing in water He may sanctify her through His word, so that He might present the church to Himself gloriously, having no spot or wrinkle or any of such thing, but holy and blameless" (Eph 5:25-27). "There is a great, hidden meaning in this, but I am speaking about Christ and the church" (Eph 5:32), of which the human relationship is only a symbol.

" 'Let us be joyful, and let us celebrate, and let us ascribe glory to Him because the wedding banquet of the Lamb has come and His Bride has gotten herself ready. It has been granted to her to be dressed in pure, resplendent linen.' For the fine linen is the righteous deeds of the saints" (Rev 19:7-8).

"I also saw the holy city, the new Jerusalem, descending out of heaven from God, made ready as a bride adorned for her husband" (Rev 21:2). " 'Come this way. I will show you the bride, the Lamb's wife.' He then . . . showed me Jerusalem, the holy city" (Rev 21:9-10).

"The Spirit and the bride say, 'Come!' " (Rev 22:17). The mystics of all ages have taken the image of marriage and have applied it to the relationship between the individual soul and Christ, the divine Bridegroom. But the Word of God does not warrant such an application. The fiancée or bride is always the church, never the soul of the believer. Let us note, moreover, that the only passage which develops this image (Eph 5:22-32) presents an interesting peculiarity. The apostle does not use human marriage as an example to clarify the relationship of Christ to the church, but rather he makes the union of Christ with the church the model for normal marriage relationships: "As the church is submissive to Christ, so wives must in every respect be submissive to their husbands. Husbands, love your wives, even as Christ loved the church" (vv. 24-25). So his readers were familiar with the image and accepted it, but it is evident also that we can, from human marriage, draw many teachings concerning Christ's relationship with His church.

The application of this image to the church. What conclusions can we draw from this image? Christ loves the church as He does His own body. He nourishes it, protects it, and cares for it as He does His own body. So the church can expect the Lord to meet all her spiritual and material needs: He will nourish her through the various ministries of the Word. He will defend her against those who would attack her person, her honor, or her possessions. Like a loving husband, He considers the desires of those who fear Him (Ps 6:9; Is 65:24). As a church, have we always this confidence in our divine Bridegroom?

On the day of their marriage, the bride and groom promise to remain faithful to each other "for better and for worse," to share all that life will bring them. The wife will share in all the advantages and honors which her husband will receive as well as in his financial reverses and disgrace. The church shares in the victory of her heavenly Bridegroom over "all government and authority" and in the power that was given Him over all things. She is spiritually seated beside Him in heavenly spheres on the throne (Eph 2:6), but on the human level she shares with the Lord the reproach (Mt 10:24-25; Heb 12:3), the mockery (Mt 9:24; 27:41; Ac 17:32; 2 Pe 3:3), and the persecution (Mt 5:10, 12; Jn 15:20; 2 Ti 3:12) which were His on earth.

However, what the wife especially expects from her husband, more than money, privileges and honors—that which will enable her in the evil days to bear disrepute and misfortune with him—is his affection. What do the scorn and hatred of others matter as long as he loves her? She is no longer alone in bearing the trials of life, alone in the face of a selfish and hostile world. Someone has noticed her, chosen her, and has consented to share his whole life with her. Someone appreciates her, thinks of her, seeks to please her; someone is ready to make any sacrifice for her sake. "Because you are precious in My eyes, you are honored and I love you. . . . Fear not, therefore, for I am with you" (Is 43:4-5). "Christ loved the church and gave Himself for her" (Eph 5:25). Is not the greatest source of joy for the church that of remembering the great love of which she is the object? Is not that her supreme consolation when facing the slights of the world?

But privilege implies responsibility. What does the husband expect of the wife? That she respond to his love, that she remain faithful to him, that she share his preoccupations, his interests, and his cares. That is what the Lord also expects from His church.

The church is in submission to Christ. The submission of the wife does not imply that she is being placed under constant watch; it is a necessity for order and harmony in the home. In the church, order and harmony are maintained as long as she submits to the Word of God as authority just as a beloved and loving wife submits to her husband.

Vocation of the church. How do a husband and wife fully realize their calling? How do they achieve and come to the fullest realization of this calling? By bringing children into the world and rearing them. Childbirth is the miracle of creation by which God seeks to exalt not only the collaboration of the Creator and those He creates, but also that of two beings who love each other so much that they are now "one."

Spiritual birth also is a miracle resulting from the intimate collaboration of God with man, a mystery which cannot be conceived of apart from perfect unity between the Spirit of God and that of man. If, on the one hand, the children of God "owe their birth neither to human blood, nor to physical urge, nor to human design, but of God" (Jn 1:13), then, on the other hand, the apostle Paul speaks of being "in travail," suffering pain for the Galatians until Christ is formed in them (Gal 4:19); he speaks of Onesimus as "my son . . . who became my son during my imprisonment" (Phile 10; cf. 1 Co 4:15). Thus, man, that is, the church, also has a role to play in this new birth. This image, so familiar to the family, also represents the church. The Scripture calls us "children of God." We have become "members of God's household," the family of God (Eph 2:19; 1 Jn 3:2; Eph 3:15).[12]

As in a family, the church is called upon not only to bring children into the world, but also to rear them, to watch over their growth, and to bring them to full maturity. Many times the Word of God brings out the various stages in this development (Heb 5:11-14; 1 Co 3:1-2; 1 Pe 2:2; 1 Jn 2:12-14). God has chosen the local church to watch over this growth "until we all may arrive at the unity of faith and that understanding of that Son of God that brings completeness of personality, tending toward the measure of the stature of the fullness of Christ" (Eph 4:13). God has given various gifts and ministries "to equip the saints" (Eph 4:12) so that "we should no longer be babes, swung back and forth and carried here and there with every wind of teaching that springs from human craftiness . . . but we should grow up in every way toward Him who is the Head— Christ" (Eph 4:14-15).[13]

The body. The type of the church, both the most frequently used and the best developed, is unquestionably that of the body, so much so that the church is often designated as "the body of Christ" without further reference to the original analogy. The Lord Himself never explicitly uses this image.[14] On the other hand, the apostle Pàul uses it in several of his letters. He tells us that Christians are:

all baptized into one body (1 Co 12:13)
one body (1 Co 10:17)
one body in Christ (Ro 12:5)
the body of Christ (1 Co 12:27)
members of the body of Christ (Eph 5:30; 1 Co 6:15)
members one of another (Ro 12:5; Eph 4:25)
called in the one body (Col 3:15)
members of the same body with the Jews (Eph 2:16; 3:6)

The church is the body of Christ (Col 1:24; 1 Co 12:4-27; Eph 4:1-16). Christ is the head of the body (Col 1:18; Eph 1:22-23; 5:22-23; Col 2:19; Eph 4:15-16).[15]

We shall not make a theological study of the Pauline idea of the body of Christ but shall limit ourselves to a few elementary and practical considerations which we can deduce from the image.

THE HUMAN BODY: TYPE OF THE CHURCH

What conclusions can be drawn from this image?

THE BODY IS AN INDIVISIBLE UNIT

In the other types the indissoluble union between Christ and the church is not so clearly seen: the king and his subjects, and the shepherd and his flock could be dissociated; even in a plant one can cut off the branches without doing very great harm to the whole. But as soon as one touches an organ of the body, the general health is compromised; if one amputates a member, the body is mutilated, and if the head is separated from the body or if an essential organ is damaged, death results.

Thus a church lives only as long as she maintains a living relationship with Christ, the Head of the church, and protects the essential unity of her members. Any attack on that unity, no matter what it is, endangers the life of the church.

THE BODY IS A COMPLETE UNIT IN ITSELF

The body is a self-governing entity which is sufficient unto itself. God has provided in the body all that is necessary for life. It can nourish itself, move, work, procure food, think, feel, and will. And for all of its functions, all it needs is a little air, water, and food. It does not require the aid and care of others, except in the early stage of its existence and in the event of sickness.

The Word of God uses the body sometimes as the type of the universal church, sometimes of the local church (Eph 1:23; 1 Co 12). The local church is a complete entity in itself which really needs the help of no other local bodies except at its beginning or in case of a crisis. The apostle Paul writes to the Corinthian church, "In Him you have in every respect been enriched with full power of expression and full knowledge. In this way our witnessing of Christ has been confirmed in you, so that you are falling behind in no spiritual gift" (1 Co 1:5-7).

Certainly, relationship with other churches is a precious source of enrichment and spiritual renewal for the local group; but even if a church is cut off from all others and isolated from the rest of the Christian world, she subsists and grows by the Word and by prayer. History has proved this many times. Moreover, the universal church possesses "every requisite for life and godliness" (2 Pe 1:3), thanks to the various gifts and ministries which the Lord has bestowed upon her. She can very well manage without the help of philosophy, science, or politics, which some believe she needs. A sound church has no need of the world's help. A major church will refuse to be directed by any other head than Christ Himself.

THE BODY IS A DIVERSIFIED UNIT

The apostle often speaks of this diversity: In the body, which is the church, there is a diversity of nationalities (Jews and Greeks, 1 Co 12:13; Eph 2:11; 3:6), of social classes (slaves and freemen, 1 Co 12:13), of spiritual gifts (1 Co 12; Ro 12:6-8; Eph 4:11). But in these spiritual gifts there is unity of origin (1 Co 12:4-7; Eph 4:7, 11); unity of heritage (Eph 3:6), of redemption (Eph 2:16), of Spirit (1 Co 12:13), of access to God (Eph 2:18), unity of hope, of calling, of faith, etc. (Eph 4:3-6).

Paul says, "The body consists not of one but of many members. If the foot should say, 'Because I am not a hand, I do not belong to the body,' it would nevertheless remain part of the body" (1 Co 12:14-15).

"If the entire body were an eye, where would the hearing come in? Or if all were hearing, what of the smelling? If they were all one member, where would the body be?" (1 Co 12:17, 19). Unity does not mean uniformity. Each member, each organ, has its specific and indispensable function; the body enjoys good health only if each organ performs its own function and not that of another. So it is with the church. "There are distinctive gifts of grace, but the same Spirit, and there are distinctive ministries, yet the same Lord. There are also varieties of things accomplished, but the same God does all the energizing in them all" (1 Co 12:4-6).

In the church each member has received a gift, a particular ministry from the Holy Spirit, and the church functions normally when each one fulfills that ministry. There is also a diversity of temperaments, of thoughts, of opinions in a normal church; such diversity is not at all incompatible with unity.[16]

Although 1 Corinthians 12 deals more particularly with the local church problems, this diversity applies as fully to the universal church. Each local assembly has its own characteristics and divine call, and contact with several assemblies certainly gives a more exact idea of the body of Christ than observing just one church. However, one must guard against hasty conclusions which the Word of God does not support. There can be no question of one church being the hand and another the head. This diversity should lead the believer to accept the place and task which God has given him in the body and to accomplish his task without envy or complex.

THE BODY IS A UNIT OF RELATIONSHIPS

If the body is to live and develop, the connective elements must function without interruptions and hindrances. A sound condition of the nervous and circulatory systems is essential for health; a limb through which the blood does not flow as it should becomes gangrenous; an organ cut off from the nerve centers becomes paralyzed.

So it is in the church; only constant interaction among the members maintains life. It is from the head that the whole body draws cohesion and unity; it is by remaining dependent upon the head that the whole body, well joined and knit together by the various joints, muscles and ligaments, forms a harmonious structure—on the condition that each organ fulfill its office according to its assigned function and the strength and capacities adapted to its needs. In this manner all members contribute, in a spirit of love, to the organic growth of the body (Eph 4:16).

THE BODY IS AN ORGANIZED UNIT

Without organization, diversity leads to anarchy. In the body the various members are commanded by only one organ: the brain; the different functions are coordinated by nerve centers. Only in this way is the unity of the body maintained. "The head—Christ, from whom the entire body is fitted together and united by every contributing ligament, with proportionate power for each single part to effect the development of the body"

(Eph 4:15-16). "For just as the body is one and has many members, while all the numerous parts of the body compose one body, so it is with Christ" (1 Co 12:12).

Christ Himself is, of course, the Head of the body (Eph 1:22; Col 1:18). And in the measure that the different assemblies in the universal church remain united to Him, listening to His will in the Word, they will be kept united among themselves in spirit and in works. The independence of the different local churches does not preclude, perhaps, certain coordinating centers for specific activities common to several of them, on condition that these centers never usurp the prerogatives reserved for the Head alone.

In the local church as well it is important that each member be joined not only to the other members of the body, but directly to the Head. This point must be emphasized since some people ascribe excessive importance to the church and to certain of her ministries and functions. According to them, a relationship with Christ can be enjoyed, and life and grace received, only in the bosom of the church and by placing oneself under the benefit of the ministry of certain men who transmit Christ and His grace to the entire body.[17]

Some believe that the image of the head in 1 Corinthians 12:21 does not refer to Christ but to those who have received the gift of administration (v. 28), of ruling (1 Ti 5:17); that is, to the leaders (Heb 13:17) or bishops (1 Ti 3:1-5). In any case, two things are essential if the local church is to remain a harmonious and united body: a minimum amount of organization, and the recognition by all its members of the authority of those who govern.

THE BODY IS A UNIT IN GROWTH

In a normal body all the members grow together, each one contributing to the growth of all the other organs as well as to its own. If a member or an organ ceases to grow, the body remains crippled, malformed or invalid, and other members are obliged to compensate for the deficiencies of the imperfect members. If the left arm is atrophied, the right arm will have twice as much work to do.

It is no different in the local church. If she wishes to accomplish her mission in a normal fashion, it is important that all her members grow together and reach maturity, "mature manhood." The retarded growth of one member has repercussions on the collective testimony and gives added work to the other members. If each organ performs its duty according to its assigned function, its strength, and the capacities adapted to its needs, all the members contribute to the organic growth of the body in a spirit of love. It is from the head that the whole body, by its joints and ligaments, receives both coordination and strength that it may continue to grow to the stature that God desires (see Col 2:19).

"The Church is a living organism," says Workman, "which, like every living organism, has its laws of growth and its laws of recession, only vaster, richer, and fuller, since it is animated by divine life and possesses a superior soul where the work of the Holy Spirit Himself is perceived."[18]

There are strong churches, and there are those which have remained weak (1 Co 3:1-2; Heb 5:11-14). Let us remember that the growth of the body depends on each one of us.

THE BODY IS A UNIT OF LIFE

The relationships, the growth, the organization, and the specialization of functions are only different manifestations of this mystery: life. This life of the body is one. One cannot speak of the life of the hand as one life, the life of the ear another, and the life of the eye yet another. The different members share the life of the body and contribute to it. Not one of them lives by itself or for itself.

The Three "Bodies of Christ" in the Bible

It is not by chance that in the Bible this expression "body of Christ" designates things which at first glance are very different: (1) the physical body of the Lord (Mt 26:12, 26; Jn 2:21; Ro 7:4; 1 Pe 2:24); (2) His "mystical" body, the church (Ro 12:5; 1 Co 12; Eph 4); and (3) the bread of communion (1 Co 10:16). This authorizes us to establish analogies between these different realities and to apply to the church certain characteristics of the body of Jesus and of the bread of communion.

THE PHYSICAL BODY AND THE "MYSTICAL BODY OF CHRIST"

How did Jesus use His body? He "traversed the land doing good" (Ac 10:38). His eyes rested on the unfortunate, the maimed, and the sick; His hands healed, helped, and blessed; they broke the bread and multiplied it for the hungry; they opened the eyes of the blind and the ears of the deaf. By His mouth He proclaimed the grace of God and showed sinners the way of salvation, but He also reproved the Pharisees and Sadducees, uncovering their hypocrisy and unbelief. So His enemies tried to get rid of Him.

But, as He had prophesied, three days after they destroyed the temple of His body, He rebuilt it more glorious than before. However, this resurrected body, filled with heavenly power, remained strangely inoperative: no more miracles or healings, no more messages of grace addressed to the crowds; ended also were the severe words, the public humiliations. Could the salt possibly have lost its flavor and its penetrating power? Could this resurrected body be nothing but a vague, amorphous apparition? After the world had waited a few days it began to realize that another body of Christ was existing, a body just as active but in a new diversified, multiplied and expanded form that would remain thus through the centuries and carry the divine Word and acts to the uttermost parts of the world.

It is upon this new body, the church, that Christ conferred full power to continue His mission on earth. Had he not promised His disciples: "The one who believes in Me will himself do the works I do, and do greater works than these, for I go to the Father" (Jn 14:12)?

The book of the Acts presents the beginning of the realization of this promise. Through the ministry of the different members of the body, the sick are healed, the physically and spiritually infirm are restored, the word of salvation is preached to the multitudes, and—a miracle which Jesus did not perform—in response to that word, lives are effectively and radically transformed. But the religious world of that day heard again that courageous voice which they thought they had silenced permanently, that voice which fearlessly and bluntly denounced hypocrisy and formalism. "They . . . recognized them as having been with Jesus" (Ac 4:13). They had rid themselves of *one* Jesus; they then found three thousand, and later five thousand of them, preaching, healing, and spreading the new doctrine everywhere.

The body shares in the honors as well as in the disgraces of the head. If the head is gifted, the hands are skillful; if the head is active, the body is honored; the church as the body of Christ sees herself as having been entrusted with the gifts which characterized the ministry of Christ (Mt 25:14-30; Eph 4:7-8). It is through her that He works in the world, even as the head works through the members of its body. It is true that if members fail or if obstacles are insurmountable, at times other means are used by Him "who makes . . . His ministers flames of fire" (Heb 1:7; e.g., the gust of wind which one day carried a Bible verse to the feet of a soul in distress). He can act through the unconverted, or even animals like Elijah's raven or Balaam's ass (e.g., the dog which carried a page of the Bible into a camp closed to the gospel). However, the normal way in which the Lord transmits the gospel message and accomplishes the will of God is by using His members. As H. S. Bender puts it, "The Spirit chooses to work usually through the Church as a body and not through individuals separately."[19] But the church as the body of Christ is also subject to the hatred, scorn and persecution with which the world pursued the Master (Mt 5:10; Lk 21:12; Jn 15:20; 1 Co 4:12; 2 Co 4:9; 2 Ti 3:12).

HOLY COMMUNION AND THE BODY OF CHRIST

In his first epistle to the Corinthians, the apostle Paul uses the expression "body of Christ" in speaking of the Last Supper: "Is not the bread which we break a fellowship in the body of Christ?" (1 Co 10:16); "Whoever eats and drinks without due appreciation of the body of Christ eats and drinks to his own condemnation" (1 Co 11:29). Of what body is he speaking? Of the physical body of Christ, or of His mystical body, the church? Each of these interpretations encounters great difficulties. Recalling the words of the Lord, "This is My body," one may think that the apostle saw beyond the symbol to one or the other of the realities that it represents and which, moreover, are designated by this name—perhaps even to both of them. That justifies us in drawing a parallel between the bread of the communion and the church. The first Christians did this: "The many of us are one bread, one body, since we all participate in the one bread" (1 Co 10:17).

"As this broken bread at one time scattered on the mountains has been gathered together to become a whole, so let your Church be reassembled from the extremities of the earth into your kingdom," reads *The Didaché* (11:4-5).

Believers are as grain from different lands, soils, and ears of grain; but the individual flavors combine in the bread so that it no longer carries the taste of a certain grain or a certain flour, but a totally new and different flavor: that of good bread. To accomplish this, these different grains must cease to be distinct, must be crushed and the flour separated from their outer coverings, then mixed and kneaded with an outside element from heaven: water. The dough must pass through the test of fire which will transform it completely and permanently. Then only will we have good, nourishing bread.

Does not all that speak to us in a striking way of the church? Have we not an even more precise prefiguration at the same time of Christ and of His body in these offering cakes made with fine flour, mixed with oil and spread with oil—cakes without leaven, baked in an oven or on a grill (Lev 2)? And these Passover loaves waved before the Lord "made of two tenths of an ephah; they shall be of fine flour, they shall be baked with leaven." Are they not an image of the true church begun on the day of Pentecost and in which, in spite of the presence of the Holy Spirit, sin continues to exist? However, these loaves of bread also, like the church, are "firstfruits to the LORD" (Lev 23:17).

There is no doubt that all these details were given to present to us symbolically conditions in a life—individual or collective—of which the offering would be a fragrant odor to the Lord: death to self, a life filled, permeated with the Holy Spirit, without malice and evil (Mt 16:6; 1 Co 5:7-8), ready for sacrifice and suffering for Christ.

What riches there are in this image of the body, a constantly new source of teachings of which we have barely skimmed the surface! The striking similarity between these two organisms cannot be chance. It can be explained only by the fact that both come from the hand of the same Creator, that they reflect but one thought of "the one who works out everything in agreement with the design of His own will," who has created us "in His image," and who desires to lead us into a perfect resemblance, in "the likeness of His Son."[20]

The Teaching of These Images Concerning the Church

All of these images contain numerous teachings concerning the nature and calling of the church. We shall try to draw out here those which concern

1. the relationships between the church and Christ
2. the nature of its members

THE RELATIONSHIPS OF THE CHURCH WITH CHRIST

An analysis of these figures shows us that Christ is always the essential party without whom there could be no reality. Christ is the center or heart of gravity in the image. In the same way, the church exists only through Christ and in relation to Him, and she can live and subsist only if she maintains a constant and living relationship with Him.

Through Christ. Without a king there is no longer a kingdom; there are only dispersed subjects. Without a shepherd, there is no flock, but only scattered sheep, each one going his own way. Without the vine that nourishes, the branches are condemned to become dead wood. The construction of a house begins with the foundation; if it gives way, the building immediately collapses. Woman was made from man (1 Co 11:8, 12). It is the man who has the initiative in founding a home, and without a husband the wife becomes a powerless widow.

Even in the secret embryonic growth of the human body the head is formed first and, from that time on, will command the rest of the body. Without the head the body is nothing more than an inanimate corpse.

For Christ. The king commands, but his subjects are there to execute his plans. In the old monarchies the king was the only person who mattered; the whole country was in his service. The flock is the shepherd's wealth and, in reality, the shepherd does not exist for the benefit of the sheep, but the sheep for the shepherd. "The woman is the man's glory" (1 Co 11:7); she was created for man (v. 9) to be "a suitable helper" (Gen 2:18). The body serves the head, executing its ideas and the plans it has conceived.

Christ needs the church. Many of these images also bring out the dependence of Christ on the church, a position in which He willingly placed Himself for the accomplishment of His will here below. The king without his subjects is powerless to carry out any of his plans; without sheep we cannot speak of a shepherd; without branches the vine can bear no fruit; without healthy members the head can do nothing.

Christ needs the church and the church needs Christ.[21] If the king is wounded, the people weep; if the people suffer a misfortune, the king comes to their defense. If the shepherd is sick, the whole flock suffers from it; if one of the sheep suffers, the shepherd carries it and looks after it. The root and the branches of a plant are interdependent; if the vine or the branches be injured, the fruit does not develop. The building serves its purpose only if the foundation and superstructure remain undamaged. And what shall we say of the home or of the body where interdependence is vital? Is it not significant that in all of these images the part which represents Christ is the least vulnerable? Is not the king the best-guarded man in the kingdom, the shepherd more intelligent than the sheep, the foundation well anchored in the ground, the vine deeply rooted and better able to offer resistance than the branches, the husband stronger than the wife, and the brain the best-protected organ under the cranium? Christ is in heaven and His members are on earth; but if a member suffers, Christ suffers with him nonetheless. As for us—His members, His bride— are we sensitive to all that affects and touches Him? Are we ready to suffer with Him in all His afflictions within His body and outside of it?

A living, constant relationship. The kingdom prospers only if the king knows all that is taking place in his country and if his people know and execute the will of their sovereign. A constant interaction is indispensable. All revolutions and tyrannies have their origin in the breakdown of communications.

As long as the flock remains close to the shepherd, within the sound of his voice, all goes well. "If you adhere to My teaching, you will truly be My disciples"; "The sheep listen to his voice . . . and . . . follow him; for they know his voice" (Jn 8:31; 10:3-4). If the sheep stay at a distance, they go astray and become the prey of wild beasts. Constant exchange is established between the vine and the branches; if for any reason this relationship is interrupted, the plant withers and dies. The foundation and the superstructure are very dependent upon one another: if the mortar crumbles, if the beams disintegrate, the building loses its stability. There is no harmony in a home without communication, no unity without sincerity.

Are we conscious of the necessity of this communication and this vital relationship with Christ, or do we think that, once started, the church herself can provide for her needs, finding in herself the resources necessary for her life and development?

THE NATURE OF THE MEMBERS

What do these images teach us about the nature of the members of the church? An identical nature in all members of the church stands out in all these images. In a kingdom all of the inhabitants are subjects of the same king.[22] The flock is not a zoo. In a head of grain all the kernels are of one kind only.[23] The vine bears *vine* branches, and even if one were to graft on branches of pear or peach trees, no fruit would come from this abnormal association.

If another woman contrives to steal into the home, and if she is accepted as an equal to the wife, it would mean the destruction of the home. Any foreign element entering the human body must be either assimilated or eliminated; otherwise, the whole body will suffer from it.[24]

The thorough study of a living organism reveals a deep chemical and biological unity of all the cells of which it is composed. Does not the Creator of these marvels have in them a lesson for us concerning the body of Christ—"the fulness of Him who fills all in all" (Eph 1:23, NASB)?

However, although the image can suggest and confirm reality, it cannot serve as proof; so, to establish indubitably the nature of the members of the church according to God's plan, we shall have to abandon the use of symbols and return to the clear texts of the Acts and the epistles. The study of these figures and parables of the church has taught us, however, many precious lessons about the nature and calling of the church. It has shown us that although the Lord seldom spoke of the church, she occupied His thoughts constantly, which is clearly shown through numerous symbols and parables. The apostles, enlightened by the Holy Spirit, developed these images and drew from them applications as circumstances arose. They did not exhaust the meaning of these symbols; nor have we. If we understood that the whole material creation is only an immense parable of the spiritual world, we would know, under the guidance of the Spirit, how to enrich again and again our vision of Christ and His church.

Notes

1. Paul S. Minear has pointed out more than eighty figures and analogies of the church in the New Testament in *Images of the Church in the New Testament*.

2. "The members of the Church know that Christ reigns, so they are consciously members of His kingdom. It is this more than anything else which distinguishes them, as a Church, from all other members of the Kingdom of Christ . . . they know what their own position is, that of men who believe they are redeemed by the death of Christ, who believe in His sovereignty and in His Church, the Body of Christ which they themselves form" (O. Cullmann, *La Royauté du Christ et l'Eglise dans le Nouveau Testament*, pp. 37-39).

3. One of the great controversies between the Catholic Church and the Protestant churches is this: Is the church the kingdom of God or is it not? The Catholic Church answers in the affirmative. "The Church is precisely this kingdom of Christ destined to cover the entire world" (Encyclical Quas Primas, 1925).
On this subject see Mgr. Besson, *L'Eglise et le Royaume de Dieu* and F. J. Leenhardt's reply under the same title. But in the Bible, the kingdom seems to be a future reality: "The Church announces the kingdom of God; she is not the kingdom of God. Her only reason for existence is to do this in this intermediate time when the victory of God has been declared but not yet gloriously manifested" (Karl Barth, *La Confession de Foi de l'Eglise*, p. 77). "This people lives in this world as if in a foreign country, for its members belong to the Kingdom of God which is to come" (K. L. Schmidt, article in G. Kittel, *Theol. Wörterbuch zum N. T.*, 5:850.
There is, on the other hand, a reality which extends beyond the church in time. See G. Gloege, *Reich Gottes und Kirche im N.T.* (Gütersloh, 1929), pp. 352-61. "All the doctrinal errors of the Church of Rome stem from a direct identification of the Church as an organic institution, participant in the process of history, with the Kingdom of God" (William Temple as quoted by F. A. Iremonger, *William Temple*, p. 420). W. A. Visser't Hooft, who cites this quotation, adds that it also applies to churches other than the Roman Catholic.
The Reformation maintains first and foremost this erroneous identification of the church with the kingdom of God (see Bucer and Bèze). See on this subject F. Hübner, *Weltreich und Gottesreich in Prophetie und Erfüllung*, especially pp. 16-21, 101; Gloege's book; C. H. Dodd, *The Parables of the Kingdom*; Cullmann, *Königsherrschaft Christi und Kirche im N.T.*

4. However, one should not stress too much the difference between the king and the shepherd. For the Oriental these ideas are much more closely associated than they are for others.

5. In New Testament writings other than the synoptic gospels, the terms *flock, shepherd, sheep* and *pasture* almost always refer to the church (Jn 10:11 ff.; 21:16 ff.; 1 Co 9:7; Ac 20:28) (Cullmann, *Peter: Disciple–Apostle–Martyr*, p. 197).

6. See A. Lüscher, *Der Triumph der Hl. Geistes über das Selbst*, pp. 49-56.

7. See Lilias Trotter, *Parables of the Cross*, and Henry Drummond, *Natural Laws in the Spiritual World*.

8. Roland de Pury in *La Maison de Dieu* shows how the three Persons of the Trinity are associated in the construction of this building. The house is built *on* the foundation, God the Son; *by* the Founder, God the Holy Spirit; *for* God, the Father.

9. A detailed study of the teachings of the tabernacle concerning the church would be too lengthy. Those who wish to study this question thoroughly will profit from a study of J. Ritchie, *The Tabernacle in the Desert*; G. R. Brinke, *Die Symbolik der Stiftshütte* (Bern: Aerenleseverlag); A. J. Flack, *According to the Pattern* (London: Witness and Testimony Publishers); Bakht Singh, *God's Dwelling Place* (Bombay: Gospel Literature Service); C. H. Mackintosh, *Notes on the Book of Leviticus* (New York: Loiseaux); R. Pache, *Notes sur le Lévitique* (Vennes-Lausanne: Emmaüs).

10. F. Godet, *Etudes bibliques sur l'Ancien Testament*.

11. William Barclay, *And Jesus Said*, pp. 173 ff.

12. The apostle Peter describes the church also as "the brotherhood" (1 Pe 2:17; 5:9). This expression was taken up later by Clement of Rome, Polycarp and Hermas (G. Bardy, *Théologie de l'Eglise de Saint Clément de Rome à Saint Irénée*, pp. 19, 36).

13. See Charles G. Finney, *Lectures to Professing Christians*, lecture 25: "Christ, the Husband of the Church," pp. 453 ff.

14. For the origin of the use of the body as a type see Wilkenhauser, *Die Kirche als der mystische Leib Christi nach dem Apostel Paulus*, pp. 130-43, and his bibliography, p. 130; and the article by L. Oulette in *L'Eglise dans la Bible*, pp. 85-93. For the body of Christ, see "the Body of Christi" in G. MacGregor, *Corpus Christi*, pp. 157-75. For Augustine's teaching about this image, see ibid., pp. 251-58 (in Latin). For a bibliography of the idea of the "mystical body of Christ" see U. Valeske, *Votum ecclesiae*, pp. 196-212. See also E. Brunner's note in *The Misunderstanding of the Church*, p. 127.
15. The use of the body as a type was not originated by the apostle Paul; in fact, "from the end of the fifth century B.C. the comparison of the state with the human body and, consequently, the idea that the state is an organism, had become current in Greek philosophy. For example, Plato and Aristotle used the image. Hellenic philosophy continued this concept and, conforming to its cosmopolitan tendencies applied it to humanity as a whole, indeed to the cosmos which included men and gods. The best-known example is furnished by Tite-Live in Roman history, who relates the fable in which Meninius Agrippa, in 494 B.C. is supposed to have quelled a seditious movement in Rome" (Werner Goosens, *L'Eglise, Corps du Christ d'après Saint Paul*, p. 81).
16. See A. Kuen, *Que tous soient un*, pp. 72-78.
17. Alan Stibbs, *God's Church*, p. 40.
18. Workman, *Foi et Constitution*, p. 166.
19. H. S. Bender, *These Are My People*, p. 64.
20. For a bibliography concerning the expression "Body of Christ" refer to *L'Eglise dans la Bible*, pp. 185-88, which lists some sixty works and articles which appeared betwen 1940 and 1961 on this question. Also see L. S. Thornton, *The Common Life in the Body of Christ*.
21. There is no parallelism between our need for Christ and His need for us. We are dependent on Him whether we wish to be or not. He is willing to need us, as He needed an ass on Palm Sunday, but by grace, not because there is any lack in Him (J. M. Nicole).
22. Calvin said, "It is essential that they recognize only one king, their liberator, Christ, and that they be governed by the law of Christ alone; that is, by the sacred truth of the Gospel."
23. "One can claim that the elect children of the invisible church belong not only by priority to the visible church, but they *alone* belong there. The others are only weeds in the wheat field. The same people belong to both the invisible and visible church; the two are one" (Wilhelm Löhe, "Drei Bücher von der Kirche," *Gesammelte Werke* 5 [1954]: 116). Löhe (1808-1872) was one of the theologians of the confessional Lutheran revival of the nineteenth century.
24. Luther never recognized unbelievers as members of the church; he said that the heretics and the wicked are in the Church as dandruff and vermin . . . are on the body, but they are not normal and good members" (Luther, *Sermon on John 7:38-42*, W. A. 33, 456, 40 ff.). "Christ is indeed Master of all things, the godly and the ungodly, angels and devils, virgins and prostitutes; but He is the head of only godly, believing Christians gathered together in the Spirit, because a head must be a part of the body, and the members must depend on the head, draw from it their life and movement. That is why Christ cannot be the head of a wicked community, even if the latter is submitted to Him as to its Lord" (Luther, *Vom Papsttum in Rom*, W. A. 6, 297, 36).

For Further Reading

Finney, Charles G. *Lectures to Professing Christians*. Lecture 25: "Christ, the Husband of the Church."

Nee, Watchman. *The Normal Christian Church Life*. Chap. 11: "One Body in Christ."

Nelson, J. R. "Many Images of the Church." *The Ecumenical Review* (1959), pp. 105 ff.

Schultz, H. "Vier biblische Bilder von der Kirche." *Monatschrift für Pastoraltheologie* (1941), pp. 76 ff.; 108 ff.

Valeske, U. *Volum ecclesia*. For the kingdom, 2:62-66 (116 titles); and for the body, pp. 41-47 (198 titles).

Vinet, A. "L'union du Christ avec l'Eglise." *Premières méditations évangéliques*. Lausanne, 1941. P. 278.

Part IV

LAYING THE FIRST STONE

8

"You Are Peter, and on This Rock . . ."

FIRST MENTION OF THE CHURCH

THE FIRST TIME that Jesus spoke of the church was on a road in Caesarea Philippi (Mt 16:13-20). It was a decisive moment in His ministry. Until that moment He had continued to conceal from His disciples the fact of His Messiahship. He did not wish to impose this thought on them, but was patiently waiting until the Father, through the Holy Spirit, did His work in them. The moment had come for Christ to find out what His disciples believed. "Who do people say the Son of Man is?" (v. 14). Various opinions came to light. But what interested Him was what the disciples themselves believed: "But you, who do you say I am?" (v. 15). Then it was that Peter, in an impulsive outburst, gave this magnificent confession: "You are the Christ [which is the Greek word for Messiah], the Son of the living God" (v. 16).

It is with great difficulty that we today grasp the staggering, revolutionary character of that confession. The Messiah! He whose advent all the prophets had been foretelling for millenniums, He for whom Israel had been waiting for many generations, He who was to fulfill all the prophecies concerning Him, to redeem Israel from her sins (Is 53), to usher her into the new covenant (Eze 36). This Messiah was there before them in flesh and blood, and a man had just recognized Him as such. The principal moment in the life of the Lord—nay more—of history and of all humanity!

Until then the purpose of the work of Jesus had been to manifest the signs of His Messiahship (teaching, miracles, etc.); now that His Messiahship had been recognized, Jesus could speak of the Messiah's future work. It was comprised of two essential aspects: His redeeming death followed by His resurrection (He would speak of it almost immediately, vv. 21-23) and the establishing of the Messianic community, the church (vv. 18-19).

Jesus began with this last plan, for it was the final result of His redemptive work, and His gaze took in at a glance the history of this church from its inception to the end of time. However, before speaking of the church, Jesus was going to speak to Peter who had just made this inestimable con-

107

fession: "Blessed are you, Simon, son of John, because it was not flesh and blood that revealed this to you" (v. 17*a*). To recognize Jesus to be the Messiah was not within the province of human power, "but My heavenly Father [has revealed it]" (v. 17*b*). A direct intervention of God, a revelation, was necessary in order for Peter to have this conviction (see Jn 6:44; cf. Eph 1:18).

Jesus found Himself face to face with the first fruit of His ministry; there was the first stone for the building He wished to construct. "I also tell you that you are Peter, and on this rock I will build My church, and the gates of hades shall not prevail against her" (Mt 16:18). This is one of Christ's most famous words, the one which Catholics quote the most often in controversies to support their dogmas concerning the apostolic succession and the infallibility of the pope. They are inscribed in letters of gold around the cupola of the Vatican. Voluminous treatises have been written on these words; research and discussions on the meaning of the words have been going on for centuries. From the earliest days of Christianity, opinions have been manifold; even today, differences of interpretation of this verse are one of the greatest obstacles to the establishing of closer relations between the Roman Catholic Church and the other branches of historical Christianity. It is impossible to determine within the framework of this study the exact point at which this controversy stands.[1] Let us be content with drawing these conclusions: (1) what we can deduce with certainty from these words, (2) what has given rise to these various interpretations.

"YOU ARE PETER . . . ." WHAT SURE DEDUCTION CAN WE MAKE FROM THIS WORD?

1. Jesus was speaking of the church. She is not a human invention or institution. She corresponds to the will of Christ.[2]

2. He spoke of her at the moment when for the first time a disciple recognized and confessed that He was the Christ. So we should not be surprised later on to learn that the confession of the Messiahship of Christ is closely linked to membership in the church.

3. Jesus said, "My church." This church belongs to Christ alone. Why? Because He obtained it for Himself with His own blood (Ac 20:28; 1 Pe 1:18-19). So He has over her all the rights of the owner: that of giving her *His name*, church of Christ (Ro 16:16; Ac 20:28). Should we permit another man's name to be coupled with her—even a great Reformer's—or should she bear the name of a particular doctrine? Christ has the right to direct this church, to give her the constitution and framework which seem to Him the most suitable. He did it through the authoritative voice of the

apostles. On what grounds should we substitute human rules, constitutions and traditions with no biblical basis for the rules of the apostles? Because of obedience to an authority which He did not institute in His church? (See Jn 8:31; 10:3-5.) "My church" clearly contrasts the Christian church with the theocratic ecclesia of the old covenant and at the same time with the Greek *ekklesia.*

4. Jesus said, *"I will build."* So Jesus Christ is both the Architect and Builder of this church.[3] It is He who drew the plans for her and no man is authorized to follow his own personal plans in place of Christ's. It is also He who assembles the stones after having drawn them from the quarry of the world, who cuts them, adapting each one to its place, cementing them together. Only the buildings which conform to His plan and are made with materials fashioned by His hands should have the right to be called the "Church of Jesus Christ."

5. "My church." "These words should necessarily awaken in the minds of Christians the thought that unity belongs to the very nature of the church of Christ," says Marc Boegner.[4]

6. This church will be the target of the adversary, but he will never conquer her. Why? Because she is built not on the sand but on the rock: "on this rock."

"And on This Rock"

Who is "this rock"? Opinions differ. There are three conflicting theses:
1. The rock refers to Peter.
2. It refers to Jesus Christ.
3. It is Peter's confession.

THE ROCK IS THE APOSTLE PETER

The opinion of all Catholic interpreters and also of a good many Protestant theologians is that the apostle Peter is the rock. The whole argument of the papacy is built on the interpretation of this verse. "Jesus Christ founded a monarchical church by conferring on Saint Peter the primacy of jurisdiction over the entire Church . . . the foundation is to endure as long as the building itself . . . one is to deduce from it that the primacy, principle and foundation of the structure are to endure as long as *it* does and that Peter is to transmit his authority to successors. . . . Peter's successors to the primacy are the bishops of Rome."[5]

To establish the Catholic argument, it is necessary to prove
1. that the rock is Peter
2. that by that word Christ assured him of a spiritual primacy in His church[6]

3. that this primacy was transmissible[7]
4. that Peter came to Rome[8]
5. that he was the bishop there[9]
6. that he transmitted this primacy to his successors, the bishops of Rome[10]
7. that these bishops transmitted without a break this primacy from Peter to the present pope

"Just one break in the argument and everything collapses, that is our risk. We are gambling our whole spiritual fortune on just one blunder."[11] A very dangerous game if one discovers that the Bible and history contradict not only one but each one of the last six points. Supposing then that the exegesis declares the Catholics to be right on the first point, that still does not prove the Roman thesis to be true concerning the infallibility of the pope.[12]

Is Peter the rock? This is the explanation that appears to be the most natural, otherwise one would not well understand the progression of the sentence, nor the play on words evident in Aramaic (*Kepha*) as well as in Greek (*Petros:* proper noun, *petra:* common noun), in Latin and in French. However, a more thorough study of the text in the original brings to light a difficulty which has caused many interpreters to hesitate to accept this "natural" explanation.

In Greek, the first stone (*Petros*) is in the masculine and indicates a pebble, a movable stone; the second (*petra*) is in the feminine and has a different meaning: rock, high rock; so, literally, the passage should be translated: "You are a pebble and on this high rock I will build My church."[13] "This distinction in the wording should warn us not to impute this high service to Peter alone."[14]

In face of this difficulty, other meanings have been sought for the word *rock.* From the first centuries, interpreters have proposed two views:

THE ROCK IS JESUS CHRIST

This opinion has in its favor a certain number of Bible verses designating Christ as the foundation stone of the building: Jesus Himself said that He is the principal stone. "Did you never read in the Scriptures, 'The stone which the builders rejected has become the chief corner stone . . .'" (Mt 21:42; see Is 8:14)? (According to many exegetes, the cornerstone would be the foundation stone.) This word is recalled twice by the apostle Peter himself: before the Sanhedrin (Ac 4:11) and in his epistle (1 Pe 2:4-7) in which he couples it with another quotation from the Old Testament (Is 28:16), proving that the foundation stone is Jesus Christ Himself: "See, I place in Zion a chosen, precious cornerstone, and he who believes in Him will never be put to shame." "Come to him, to that living stone, rejected by men but in God's sight chosen and precious."

That is also the thought of the apostle Paul: "For none is able to lay another foundation than the one already laid, which is Jesus Christ" (1 Co 3:11). "You are constructed on the foundation of the apostles and prophets, of which the cornerstone is Christ Jesus" (Eph 2:20).[15]

The foundation stone, which gives stability to the whole building, could not be a fallible man like Peter (Jn 18:15-27; Gal 2:11-14); Jesus Christ alone can guarantee this solidity.

However, one must acknowledge that the explanation which here likens the rock to Jesus Christ scarcely seems any more natural. Why not have said: "You are Peter, a loose pebble; I will build my Church on myself, the immovable Rock"?

It is true that according to the works of Strack-Billerbeck[16] the Aramaic text which is the basis of the Greek text, that is, the text in the language which Jesus spoke, would be translated as follows: "I also I say to you, yes to you, Peter, that on this rock I will build my church." So it would be Jesus as the Messiah who would be the foundation of the church. However, this interpretation has not won unanimous approval either.

A third solution has been proposed!

THE ROCK IS PETER'S CONFESSION

It is on this confession, "You are the Christ, the Son of the living God" that Jesus wants to build His church. All who confess that they believe Jesus to be the Christ will be members of the church.[17]

That is what all who were received into the early church did at the moment of their baptism. For example: "The eunuch said, 'See, here is water. What is to prevent my being baptized?' [Philip assured him, 'If you heartily believe, it is permitted.' And he replied, 'I believe that Jesus Christ is the Son of God']" (Ac 8:36-37). "Whoever confesses that Jesus is the Son of God, God remains in him and he in God" (I Jn 4:15; cf. Ro 10:9-10; 1 Co 12:3).

The central theme of apostolic preaching was: "He is the Son of God" (Ac 9:20). The study of the oldest Christian confessions of faith shows that this confession, "Jesus is the Christ," was the basis of the church constitution, since that is what the new convert was asked to confess at the time of his baptism.[18]

The church Fathers had a preference for this explanation. When the Roman Catholic Church affirms that the church Fathers are unanimous in saying that "this rock" of Matthew 16 is the apostle Peter, she is forcing the facts a little, since out of sixty-one of the principal Fathers, only seventeen defended this opinion and, on the other hand, forty-four—of whom were Saint Justin, Saint Augustine, Athanasius, Saint Jerome, Cyril of Jerusalem, Origen, Pope Gregory the Great, etc.—affirm that the foundation stone of the church was the confession that Peter had just made, that Jesus was the Christ, the Son of the living God.[19]

Luther also says that "the confession of the Messiahship is indeed the only foundation stone on which the messianic community will be built." However, one must admit that neither is this explanation entirely satisfactory. But why might not each of these three proposed solutions contain a part of the truth?

Upon Whom Is the Church Built?

Let us consider conditions for the construction of houses in Palestine. Before building *anything*, they dug down to the underlying rock (Mt 7:24-27; Lk 6:47-48). This rock can be none other than Christ. On this rock they were placing the first stone, the corner or foundation stone. Why should it not be the apostle Peter? How long had he been Peter? For scarcely a moment, since Jesus had just pronounced him so. How did he become Peter? By his confession: "You are the Christ, the Son of the living God." By recognizing Jesus to be the Christ, the Messiah, a transformation has taken place in him.[20]

It is evident that we cannot identify this transformation with that of the believers after Pentecost. After the outpouring of the Spirit, those who confess Christ as the Son of God, who died for their sins and was raised for their justification according to prophecy, become "sharers of the divine nature" (2 Pe 1:4), of the same nature as the Rock, Christ.[21]

By this transformation, Simon, son of John, now became Peter and was made fit to enter into the construction of God's building, the church. It is the image which he himself developed in his epistle: "Come to Him, a living Stone . . . and be built up as living stones [therefore, partakers of His nature] into a spiritual house" (1 Pe 2:4-5).

What is Peter's place in this building? He is the first to confess Jesus to be the Christ; he is the first stone; this stone is the first one to be placed on the rock.

Thus the house is built at the same time on the Rock, Christ, and on Peter, the first stone in the building, and on the declaration which he has just made, since by that means he became Peter. Peter is the first stone placed on the Rock; he is not the only one; the church is built "on the foundation of the apostles and prophets" (Eph 2:20; cf. Rev 21:14). They also confessed that Jesus is the Christ; they also received—as, moreover, did all the disciples of Jesus (Jn 20:19-23)—this "power of the keys" which the Roman Church would like to reserve for Peter: "Whatever you will bind on earth shall be bound in heaven, and whatever you allow on earth will be allowed in heaven" (Mt 18:18). "If you forgive the sins of any, they are forgiven them; if you retain those of anyone, they are retained" (Jn 20:23). According to Jean Cadier, "There is the same progression for 'the keys' as for the Rock—Jesus is the Rock; the apostle is the first stone; Christians are stones. In the same way, Jesus has the keys (Rev 3:7); the apostle is the first to receive the keys; Christians also have the promise of the keys."[22] "Peter is the first part of the construction upon which the other stones will rest," says Schlatter.[23] "It is not at all a question of a primacy, but rather of a priority," comments J. Blocher. "In Matthew 16:16 ff.," according to O. Cullmann, "the rock, the foundation, will have to be understood in the chronological sense exactly as in Ephesians 2:20 and Romans 15:20."[24]

Also, Peter was the first to exercise the power of loosing souls until then held captive by sin and the devil. This he did on the day of Pentecost, at the time of the founding of the church, and again in the house of Cornelius when he preached the gospel to the Gentiles for the first time.

Notes

1. Concerning the authenticity of Mt 16:17-19, see the article by A. Legault in *L'Eglise dans la Bible*, pp. 35-52. For the history of the critical examination and exegesis of Mt 16:18, see Olof Linton, *Das Problem der UrKirche in der neueren Forschung*, pp. 157-83. For the exegesis of Mt 16:18 see G. Gloege, *Reich Gottes und Kirche im N.T.*, pp. 263 ff.; O. Cullmann, *Peter: Disciple—Apostle—Martyr*, pp. 113 ff.; Strack-Billerbeck, *Kommentar zum Matthäus-Ev.*, pp. 731 ff.; and the other commentaries on Matthew: Barnes, *Critical and Exegetical Commentary*, pp. 176 ff.; G. Kittel, *Neutest. Wörterbuch*, 3:522-30.
2. A number of critics deny the authenticity of these verses simply because "there could be a question of a future foundation of the Church only if this Church was already in existence" (J. Haller, *Das Papsttum*, p. 5).
3. "Furthermore, Christ did not say to Peter, 'You shall build my Church,' but rather 'I will build my Church,' thus indicating that no vicarial mediation is expedient between the believers and Himself for fear of compromising His personal deeds and nullifying the work of the Holy Spirit" (F. J. Leenhardt, *Catholicisme romain et Protestantisme*, p. 42).
   For the Christians of the first centuries, the Holy Spirit was the only true vicar of Jesus Christ (Jn 14:16-17, 26; 16:7, 13-15). Tertullian also wrote, "The Holy Spirit is the administrator of God and the Vicar of Christ."
4. Marc Boegner, *Le Problème de l'Eglise*, p. 172.
5. Canon Boulenger, *Apologétique*, pp. 335-39 passim.
6. "In the most ancient documents of the N.T. nowhere is there a question of the alleged preeminent position of Peter. Neither Eph. 2:20 nor Rev. 21:14 quotes Peter. In the midst of the twelve, he seems just one of them" (Gloege, p. 269). This silence is embarrassing to Catholic theologians: "Saint Paul did not say everything . . . concerning the doctrine of the Church. Thus, [there is] not a word of Peter the Primate and of his infallibility. Galatians 2:11-14 presents a problem: 'I withstood Peter to the face.' Likewise, not one word, or practically no word, was spoken concerning the authority of the bishops . . . that proves that the doctrine of the Church is not complete in Paul's writings. He is only a

link in the great chain of tradition, an instrument of divine revelation" (Abbé Hubert Paradis, article in *L'Eglise dans la Bible*, p. 95).

Moreover, such a spiritual primacy would run counter to the teaching of Christ (see Mt 23:8-12; Lk 22:24-27). Peter does not think he is invested with special privileges (see Ac 10:26; 1 Pe 1:1; 5:1). See note 2 of chap. 9.

7. Even Karl Adam, a Catholic theologian of authority, is obliged to recognize that "following the texts closely, one is of the opinion that the words reported in Matthew do not apply to Peter's successors" (*Le Vrai Visage du catholicisme*, p. 133). See Leenhardt, *Etudes sur l'Eglise dans le N.T.*

Another disturbing fact is that the three other evangelists omit these promises made to Peter. If, by these words, Jesus had really wanted to confer such an important spiritual primacy in His church, how can one explain that Mark (Peter's secretary) and Luke carefully relate the apostle's confession, but silently pass over the promise Jesus made to him? Nevertheless, Mark reports the reprimand the Lord gave to His disciple! Did Peter relate a fact perhaps which refutes in advance all claims to his infallibility by failing to mention the promise of it?

The real reason for the silence is doubtless the fact that, for the primitive church, the confession of the apostle was much more important than the promise. Peter's prerogatives were limited to: (1) being the first stone in the building, (2) opening the door of the kingdom to the Jews, (3) opening it to the Gentiles. The omission of the promise by three out of four evangelists is "proof that those temporary prerogatives were of little importance in the tradition of the apostles" (L. Bonnet, *N. T. expliqué*, 1:131). Also see R. Stier, *Discours du Seigneur*, 2:204 ff.

8. From the biblical point of view, Peter's coming to Rome was almost an impossibility. In any case, the version of Eusebius, according to which Peter is supposed to have founded the church of Rome and to have exercised the charge of bishop for twenty-five years (from A.D. 42 to 67), conflicts with a series of explicit statements in the Word of God. During the years A.D. 36-50, the book of the Acts shows him constantly at Jerusalem, at Caesarea, at Antioch. In 57 when Paul wrote his epistle to the Romans, Peter was not in Rome (an entire chapter is devoted to salutations; 27 names are given, but no mention is made of Peter) and certainly he had not been there before (see Ro 1:11, 15; 15:20). When Paul arrived in Rome in the year 60, there was still no trace of Peter. Paul called together the Jews (Ac 28:17-23), but the latter seemed never to have heard of him nor to have a very clear idea of the Christian "sect." If Peter, the apostle of the circumcision (Gal 2:7), had been in Rome, he would not have failed to contact them.

During his captivity in Rome, Paul wrote the epistles to the Colossians, the Philippians, and to Philemon. Peter's name was not mentioned among those whom Paul greeted in his salutations. In 2 Timothy 4:21 he mentioned, among others, Linus, whom tradition names as successor to Peter in the Roman Episcopate, but still no mention of Peter. "In my first defense no one supported me; instead, they all deserted me" (4:16). Can we charge Peter with this desertion? See A. Antomarchi, *Rome face à l'Evangile*, pp. 65-92.

In postapostolic literature, mention of Peter becomes more and more precise the farther we come from the first century. The discretion of Clement (1 Co 5), of Papias (cited by Eusebius 2:15), or of Irenaeus (*Adv. Haer.* 3:1, 3) contrasts strangely with the abundance of detail which we find in the writings of Jerome (who died in A.D. 420; see *De Viris Illustr.* 3:1, 5) or of Eusebius.

"Prior to the second half of the second century, no document confirms explicitly Peter's visit to Rome and his martyrdom there" (Cullmann, p. 113).

The explanation of this fact is found, without doubt, in the prestige enjoyed by the apocryphal writings in the second century (*Homilies of Clementine* and *Acts of Peter*) among the Christians. These accounts, relating the adventures of Peter pursuing Simon the sorcerer even to Rome, were taken seriously by writers like Justin, Irenaeus, Tertullian and Hippolytus (see quotations proving it in Moreton's *Rome et l'Eglise primitive*, pp. 93, 97-136). If "all *that* is henceforth classified in the realm of the legend," it also follows that "all that has been taught about saint Peter, the first pope of Rome, and his successors is based on grounds insufficient to warrant being accepted as history" (Mgr. Duchesne, *The Early History of the Church*, vol. 2).

9. Also, he could not have been bishop of Rome for the simple reason that the monarchical Episcopate was instituted there only toward the middle of the second century. We can deduce with certainty from the first epistle of Clement to the Corinthians that the primitive condition of the plurality of the episcopates was maintained there. "For Clement, the terms 'episcopate' and 'presbytery' have the same meaning and are interchangeable" (G. Bardy, *Théologie de l'Eglise de Saint Clément de Rome à Saint Irénée*, p. 40).
"The same synonym is again found in the Pastor of Hermas" (Ibid.). "They always appear together without either of them seeming to be superior to the other" (Ibid., p. 123). "Towards the middle of the 2nd century, the monarchical episcopate also comes before us as an undisputed fact . . . in the Western Christian communities of Rome" (Mgr. Duchesne, 1:67). "The monarchical episcopate developed at Rome later than elsewhere" (Moreton, p. 167). See Haller, p. 9.

10. In any case, facts prove that during the first three centuries "it is scarcely possible to define . . . in what measure Christianity is aware of possessing a supreme authority, charged with settling all controversies, assuring the unity of discipline, maintaining the integrity of the traditional doctrine" (Bardy, p. 122). "It [this authority] scarcely finds the occasion to manifest itself in deeds" (Ibid., p. 123). "During the first centuries all bishops were apostolically and canonically equal; all were successors of the apostles with the same rights. The Church Fathers were unanimous on this point" (Canon I. de Doellinger, *Les Origines de la Papauté*, p. 14). Cyprian defended this equality of all the bishops with special vigor before the claims of Pope Stephen. In his letter (A.D. 72) "to my brother Stephen, bishop of Rome," he writes, "We do not claim to restrain or compel anyone, each bishop being free to act as he deems advisable in the governing of his church, and having to give account only to God." At the seventh Council of Carthage, he rises up in rebellion against "those who try to set themselves up to be bishop of the bishops and claim that their colleagues should obey them by virtue of a tyrannical privilege." It is true that certain excerpts are often quoted from *De Unitate Eccl.* in favor of the Roman thesis, but it has been recognized even by Catholic scholars (e.g., Mgr. Battifol) that this text is filled with interpolations of a later date. See Moreton, pp. 173-75.
It is therefore preferable for these first centuries to confine oneself to the conclusions set forth by the Catholic scholars themselves: "One finds nothing in this early period which can serve as a foundation for the papal claims" (Cardinal Newman). "No document exists, dating from the first three centuries, which implies that a community has the right to excommunicate another local or independent church" (Dr. Zenov, quoted by Moreton, p. 167). "There was no guiding power, an effective expression of Christian unity. The Papacy, such as the West later knew it, was still to be born [in the fifth century]. . . . Such is not the law; such is not theory; but such is the fact" (Mgr. Duchesne, 2:522). "The Papacy has its origin in the Middle Ages" (Canon Doellinger).
As for infallibility, "evidently it would be an unnatural anachronism to attribute to the pre-Nicene Fathers belief in infallibility" (Mgr. Battifol, *Dict. cath.*, p. 672). "All historians are obliged to recognize the downfall of pope Liberius when he repudiated communion with Athanasius and signed the condemnation of that great bishop in order to be returned to the good graces of the emperor, a zealous disciples of Arius. The fall of the pope is attested by St. Athanasius, St. Jerome, and St. Hilary" (Mgr. Duchesne, vol. 2).
It was not before the year 607 that a pope proclaimed the authority of the bishop of Rome, and it was in 1049, at the Council of Reims, that he was declared to be "Apostolic Primate of the universal Church." The dogma of the infallibility is not proclaimed for another eight centuries.

11. Canon Christiani, *Catholiques, Protestants, Frères quand-même*.

12. It is known that the dogma of papal infallibility, not promulgated before 1870 at the first Vatican Council, encountered keen opposition from Catholic bishops. It was by a series of maneuvers and of "unforeseen expedients" that Pope Pius IX succeeded in having the doctrine, which was so close to his heart, voted in.

One third of the Fathers in the council were opposed to the new dogma. The fractional part of those who opposed the infallibility included in their ranks certain men of the highest authority in the Roman Church: Mgr. Dupanloup, bishop of Orleans; Mgr. Darboy, archbishop of Paris; Cardinal Mathieu, archbishop of Besançon; Mgr. Ginouilhac, primate of the Gauls; and more than a third of the French bishops. Most of the German bishops and the whole group of the Austro-Hungarians (including Cardinal von Schwartzenberg, archbishop of Prague, and Cardinal Rauscher, archbishop of Vienna) publicly declared themselves opposed to the dogma of the infallibility.

Canon I. von Doellinger, "the most illustrious nineteenth century German theologian of the Catholic Church and a brilliant man in the science of theology, for fifty years the true head not only of theological science but also of Catholicism on the other side of the Rhine" (A. Giraud-Teulon) prepared an impressive number of historical documents proving that the papacy did not exist before the ninth century and that the dogma of papal infallibility is of even more recent origin. In his book, *La Papauté et son Origine au Moyen-Age,* pp. 1-2, he wrote: "For thirteen years an incomprehensible silence reigned in the Church and in all of its literature concerning such a fundamental dogma. None of the ancient confessions of faith, no catechism, none of the writings of the Church Fathers destined for the religious instruction of the people, not one contains any word concerning the pope. Even less is there any allusion to the obligation to seek from him alone certainty in matters of faith and doctrine. During the first thousand or more years of the Church, the validity of any point of doctrine was never determined by a papal judgment."

"To justify the doctrine of papal infallibility by means of Church history, nothing short of the falsification of that history from beginning to end is needed" (Ibid., p. 265). "Similar to geological stratification resulting from successive deposits, layers of falsifications and alterations have formed their deposits, one on top of another, in the Church" (Ibid., p. 45). Canon Doellinger is not satisfied with affirming it, but in his work of close to five hundred pages, he enumerates the countless falsifications which have crept in to justify the privileges and powers of the pope. As proof of the fallibility of the pope, he cites the case of Pope Honorius I, who was formally condemned by the third Council of Constance for having supported the Monothelite heresy (this example was brought up at the council by Mgr. Hefele) and that of Pope Adrian I, condemned by the great assembly of the Church of Frankfurt (794) and by the bishops of Paris (824). At the council, Mgr. Strossmayer, bishop of Bosnia, solemnly declared: "I have read the whole New Testament, and I declare before God, raising my hand toward this great Crucifix, that I have found no trace there of the papacy as it now exists. . . . Reading the Holy Scripture with all the attention of which the Lord made me capable, I have found there not even one verse in which Jesus Christ gave to Saint Peter authority over the apostles, his fellow-workers. In none of Paul's epistles to the churches does he mention the sovereignty of Peter. If this pre-eminence had existed, that is if the Church had had a visible head infallible in the matter of doctrine, the great apostle to the Gentiles would certainly have mentioned it. What am I saying? He would have written a long epistle on this most important subject. For if, as is really the case, he set up the whole structure of Christian doctrine, would he have forgotten its foundation and cornerstone? Now we cannot and must not say that the apostolic Church was heretical, and we must recognize that the Church was never more beautiful, pure, and holy than she was when there was as yet no pope. . . . I claim that as long as the apostles lived, the Church never thought of the possibility of a pope. To claim the contrary, one should burn or totally ignore all Sacred Scripture" (Quoted by R. Stauffer, *Le Premier Concile du Vatican,* p. 35).

Pope Pius IX and those who held the dogma of infallibility remained inflexible. They stopped at nothing in order to reduce the opposition. "I know," writes Canon Doellinger the day after the council, "by a goodly number of irreproachable witnesses, by confessions that inadvertently escaped, that the Vatican Council was not free, that threats, intimidations and enticements were used on them. I learned this from bishops whose letters I still have in my possession or who confessed it to me by word of mouth. The very archbishop of Munich who ex-

communicated me came to my home the day after he returned from Rome and related details which left no doubt in my mind" (Doellinger, *Lettres et Déclarations au sujet des Décrets du Vatican*, p. 270, quoted by Stauffer, p. 48).
The final vote for the dogma by a quasi-unanimity was obtained only because of the untimely departure of the disregarded minority.
Finally, all of the bishops rallied to the new dogma. The archbishop of Munich, Mgr. Scherr, himself opposed to the claim of infallibility, dealt the blow of major excommunication to his friend, Professor Doellinger.

13. "In I Cor. 10:4, 'that rock was Christ,' we see that Abbé Crampon translates the word 'petra' with the word 'rock'; so also in Rom. 9:33 and I Pet. 2:7 'a stumbling stone and a rock of offence'; likewise, in Rev. 6:15 'said to the mountains and rocks . . .' 'Petra,' rock, is found only five times in the New Testament. Why does Abbé Crampon translate it with the exceptional word 'stone' in Matt. 16:18?" (Antomarchi, p. 24). Also, the Jesuit A. Durand admits in his commentary on this passage, "Rock is a more exact equivalent of petra" (*Verbum salutis*, p. 310).

14. *Lettre pastorale du Synode de l'Eglise Réformée des Pays-Bas.*

15. See also, Deu 32:18; 1 Sa 2:2; 2 Sa 22:2-3, 32; Ps 31:2-3; 62:2, 6-7; R. de Pury, *La Maison de Dieu*, p. 7; and Moreton, pp. 36-43.

16. Strack-Billerbeck, *Kommentar zum N. T. aus Talmud und Midrasch*, 1:731-32.

17. "When Jesus speaks of that which He wishes to build on Peter as His qâhâl, His quehilla (in Aramaic qohale), He thereby says that He wishes to build the true Israel with men who, by faith, confess Him to be the Messiah" (Wilhelm Vischer, *Die evangelische Gemeindeordnung*, p. 19).

18. Cullmann, *Earliest Christian Confessions.*

19. Justin: "The rock upon which our Lord promised to build His Church is Peter's confession of faith" (*Dialogue with Tryphon*).
Augustine: "What does 'On this rock I will build my Church' mean? On this rock of your confession . . . on this faith, on what you have said: Thou art the Christ, the Son of the living God."
Cyril: "I believe that one must understand 'rock' to mean the immutable faith of the apostles" (*Fourth Book on the Trinity*).
Hilary: "The rock is the blessed and unique rock of the faith confessed by Peter" (*Second Book on the Trinity*).
Chrysostom: "On this rock, that is to say on the faith of his confession, 'You are the Christ, the Son of the living God'" (*55th Homily on St. Matthew*).
"No one of the Fathers of this period who has explained exegetically the passages from the Gospels concerning the power transmitted to Peter (Matt. 16:18 and John 21:18) has made it apply to the bishops of Rome, as Peter's successors. How many Fathers have not given their attention to these passages, and yet not one of those whose commentaries we still possess (Origen, Chrysostom, Hilary, Augustine, Cyril, Theodoret and those whose explanations have been gathered together in the Catenes) has designated, even by one syllable, the primacy of Rome, as the consequence of the mission given to Peter and the promises he received. Not even one of them interprets the 'rock' or the foundation on which Christ wished to build His Church as a charge especially conferred on Peter, and after him transmissible by inheritance" (Doellinger, *La Papauté*, p. 12).
Again, at the end of the seventh century, a synod of Spanish bishops declared that the promise was made with relation to his faith.
"The holy Fathers never understood the famous passage, 'You are Peter, and on this rock I will build my church,' in the sense that the Church would be built on Peter, but on the rock (not on *Petrum* but on *petram*); that is to say on that apostle's confession of faith" (Mgr. Strossmayer, bishop of Bosnia, at Vatican Council, quoted by Stauffer, p. 36). For the patristic interpretation of Mt 16:18, see the very complete chapter which Moreton, pp. 57-76, devotes to it. See also H. Clavier, "Brèves remarques sur les commentaires patristique de Matt. 16:18" in *Studia Patristica I*, pt. 1, pp. 253-61.

20. Gore (*The Holy Spirit and the Church*, p. 48) quotes a passage from a Jewish author (see Taylor, *Sayings of the Jewish Fathers*): "When God saw Abraham who was going to arise, He said, 'Lo, I have discovered a *petra* to build and to found the world upon.' Therefore He calls Abraham a 'rock.'"

21. "When, enlightened by the heavenly Father, we make the profession of faith that Peter made, it is possible that we become like Peter; that is, that we are declared blessed as he was. Then we are made Peter (rock), and Christ says to us: You are a rock (Peter), since every disciple of Christ is a rock (Peter). If you think that the whole Church was founded on this Peter (rock), what about John and each of the other apostles?" (*Origène* in Migne 12:10-14).

22. Jean Cadier, *L'Apôtre Pierre est-il le Chef de l'Eglise?* p. 11.
   These promises made to Peter personally (the keys, all that you shall bind) confirm the interpretation which identifies Peter as the rock. The realization of these promises in Peter's life also indicates to us the significance and scope of the different prerogatives of which he was assured: the promise of the keys finds a double accomplishment in the entrance of Jews and Gentiles into the kingdom in response to Peter's message (Ac 2 and 10). The words "whatsoever you bind on earth" have been interpreted in various ways. In studying them with John 20:23, one can see the remission of sins (loosing souls by pardoning their sins; Peter had many occasions to exercise this power). If one considers the context of Mt 18, one will see there an allusion to church discipline: to bind is to banish (Josephus uses the verb with this meaning); to loose is to liberate or free from banishment. Nothing indicates, however, that one must limit the application of these words in Mt 16 to discipline. They have looked at this word also in light of the rabbinical use of the words "to tie" and "to untie or loose," which makes them synonyms for "forbid" and "permit" (e.g., to gather dead wood on the Sabbath day: the school of Schimmei "forbids," the school of Hillel "permits"). So these words would signify: that which the apostles permit in the church has divine authority (e.g., Ac 15:20). That would mean that Jesus gives them authority to determine the rules for church organization, rules which alone make up the law for Christians in all ages. The broader meaning of these words in the language of the rabbis is simply "to teach"; the teaching of the truth binds or looses souls, opens or closes. This promise would then confirm the preceding one. The teaching of the apostles has been considered by all Christian churches as the norm for all Christian teaching.
   Another interpretation associates the fulfilling of the promise of binding with the bond established between the Gentiles and the ecclesia of God by Peter's preaching. "Thus he created a new bond between Jews and Gentiles, a oneness in the Messiah, valid for earth and heaven. In like manner, he freed the Jews from the decree prohibiting them from having anything to do with non-Jews" (A. Waldstein).
   Whatever may be the accepted interpretation, it is in any case only a question of a temporary role accomplished by the apostle Peter during the course of his lifetime and not at all a transmissible prerogative. The accomplishment of the first promise should be of the same character.

23. Schlatter, *Der Evangelist Matthäus*, p. 507. This is also the conclusion in Cullmann's detailed study of the various exegeses of this passage. What Jesus says applies to Peter alone who lays on earth once and for all the foundation of the church yet to be built, the first stone which will support all the others. (See p. 191.)
   Certain men have even translated *epi* (*on* this rock) by "following" (this rock) which would resolve all the difficulties raised by this verse.

24. Cullmann, *Peter: Disciple—Apostle—Martyr*, pt 2: "Exegesis of Matt. 16:17-19."

Part V

BEGINNING OF THE CONSTRUCTION

9

The Birth of the Church

WHAT HAPPENED on the day of Pentecost? The Holy Spirit, promised by the Lord to His disciples (Mk 1:8; Jn 7:39; 14:16-17; 16:7-13; Ac 1:4-8), descended on them. They had indeed received a token: "And when He had said this, He breathed on them and said, 'Receive the Holy Spirit'" (Jn 20:22). But He had not come to dwell in them in a permanent manner: "I shall not leave you as orphans; I shall come to you" (Jn 14:18). "We shall visit him and make Our dwelling with him" (Jn 14:23).

All the promises of Jesus concerning this permanent home were still in the future because the Holy Spirit, which is the Spirit of the glorified Christ, could not descend upon the disciples before the Lord was glorified (Jn 7:39). Because if "anyone does not have the Spirit of Christ, he does not belong to Him" (Ro 8:9), and since it is by the Spirit that one receives the new birth (Jn 3:5), the disciples were not truly regenerated before Pentecost. That day was for them the day of their baptism by the Spirit (Ac 1:5; 11:15-16), of their new birth, of their integration in the body of Christ (1 Co 12:13; Gal 3:26-28). It was the first time that such a thing had ever happened; a new dispensation had begun. Pentecost marks the final outpouring of the Holy Spirit for the founding of the church and the regenerating of the believers. "The Holy Spirit is proof of the beginning of a new dispensation," says C. H. Dodd.[1]

That which followed this outpouring shows immediately the reality of the unexpected changes which took place: the disciples, until then fearful and timid (Mk 14:50-52; 14:66-72; Jn 20:19), were transformed into courageous witnesses. What Jesus did not achieve during the three years of His ministry—the establishing of a stable Messianic community (see Jn 6; Lk 19:37-38; 21:1-37; 22:1-71)—the Holy Spirit effected in a single day (Ac 2:41-42; 4:32-35). It is in this dispensation of the Holy Spirit that we are still living and will be until Christ returns. Therefore, only the events subsequent to Pentecost are to serve as norms for us; that is, they can serve as models for our individual as well as our collective spiritual lives. The experience of the disciples whose lives spanned a portion of two

121

dispensations could in no way serve in all points as the standard of what God expects of us; particularly the receiving of the Holy Spirit in two stages (Jn 20:23; Ac 2) is peculiar to their situation.

The events which follow during the course of the memorable day permit us

1. to verify the reality of the promises made to the apostle Peter
2. to establish a plan for the founding of a church
3. to isolate, by comparison with other accounts from the Acts, a certain number of exceptional and temporary elements by which the Lord wished to mark the inauguration of the church

THE ROLE OF THE APOSTLE PETER

The role of the apostle Peter on the day of Pentecost conformed in every respect to the promise the Lord gave him on the coast of Caesarea Philippi; his preaching is the amplified echo of the confession he made there.

Peter is the first stone of the building to be constructed, placed on the Rock, Christ. Today new stones are coming to be placed on this foundation, thanks to the testimony which Peter gave to the Messiahship of Jesus. So what is the message in brief? Acts 2:36: "Let the whole house of Israel know that God made Him both Lord and Christ—this Jesus whom you crucified."

He adds nothing to his previous confession: "You are the Christ, the Son of the living God," but he says it with assurance because of the resurrection and ascension of Christ and by the power of the Holy Spirit. During the early days of the church (Ac 2–12), Peter played a leading role in its life; he who had denied his Master in the most cowardly fashion, now transformed and revived by the Spirit, gives the most courageous testimony for his Lord (Ac 4:8-12, 19-20; 5:29). But nowhere does he assume the role of head of the church attributed to him by some.[2]

THE SCHEMA TYPE FOR THE FOUNDING OF A CHURCH

1. *Testimony of Christians and preaching of the Word* (Ac 2:4, 11, 14-36). All of the disciples were filled with the Holy Spirit and testified to the marvelous works of God. Peter addressed the crowd with a message based on the Word and work of God.

2. *Conviction of sin* in the hearts of those who heard (2:37).

3. *The way of salvation* as set forth by Peter (2:38-39).

   a. *Repentance:* changing one's opinion concerning Jesus. Until then they had seen Him as a seducer of the multitudes; now they must consider Him as the Christ, the Lord. This repentance implies *b. Faith:* This condition is not mentioned explicitly here as it is in other passages (Mk 1:15; Ac 20:21) but it is implied since the new attitude must result in

c. Baptism: It would be the public confession of this new conviction: Jesus is the Christ, my Christ (also according to Is 53), my Lord. By this confession, which resembles Peter's, one becomes "a living stone" fit to be used in the construction of the building. This confession is the condition to be met in order to receive.

d. Pardon from sin.

e. The gift of the Holy Spirit whose essential function is still to glorify the Son (Jn 16:14).

4. *Formation of the church in two steps* (Ac 2:41-42):

a. Subtraction (2:40): separation from this perverse generation

b. Addition (2:41): "Then those who welcomed his message were baptized, and there were added that day about three thousand souls."

The same method continued during the following days (2:47): "Daily the Lord added to the group those who were being saved." At the founding of each church in Acts, this same sequence is found: proclaiming the Word, repentance and faith, baptism, joining the Christian community.

EXCEPTIONAL AND TEMPORARY FACTORS IN PENTECOST

As at the time of an official inauguration, the Lord was careful to mark the founding of the church by a certain number of miraculous deeds which were to draw the attention of all men to the unique event unfolding before their eyes. These miracles were to give official recognition to this new community being formed and at the same time attest to its being of divine origin. Since "Jews request signs" (1 Co 1:22), God gives to them miracles in abundance to show that His good pleasure rests from this time forward on those who confess Jesus as their Lord.

These exceptional signs are:

a sound as of a rushing, mighty wind (Ac 2:2)
tongues like flames (2:3)
testimonies in foreign languages (2:4)
the conversion of 3,000 people mentioned only in Acts (2:41)

Just as the beginning of the old covenant was marked by a certain number of unique miracles and signs (the miracles of Moses, those in the desert, etc.) so this whole period of the Acts enjoys certain special favors from God by which He supplies the deficiency later met by the New Testament writings. Although God remains sovereign and free to repeat these miracles when and where He chooses (and He has done so many times throughout the centuries, particularly where the gospel was being introduced for the first time in a new land where conditions are analogous to those of the apostolic times), it does not seem that God's chosen means of approaching man is by miracles. The eternal God is a God who hides Himself (Is 45:15) and wants men to "feel for and find Him" (Ac 17:27). He does not violate their liberty by the use of miracles. Jesus never did that (Mt 4:6; 12:39; 16:1, 4; 13:58; 27:42; Lk 23:8) because He knew that miracles are unable to produce real faith (Mk 6:52; Mt 21:15; Jn 12:37). The greatest miracle, the one by which He prefers to draw men to Himself, is the transformation of a life into the likeness of Christ.

Notes

1. C. H. Dodd, *The Apostolic Preaching and Its Development*, p. 138.
2. The replacement for Judas was decided not by Peter but by the drawing of lots (Ac 1:21-26); the twelve asked the entire church to select those who were to assist them (Ac 6:5); Peter did not send apostles into Samaria, but he himself was sent with John by the others (Ac 8:14); he was obliged to defend his actions when criticized by others (Ac 11:1-4); he did not preside over the council; it was James who obtained the decision, and the letter bearing it begins: "The brothers, including the apostles and elders . . ." (Ac 15:23). Paul related that he did not consider it necessary to go up to Jerusalem to confer with the apostles (Gal 1:17). At Antioch Peter made it necessary for Paul to reprove him. He "opposed him to his face" because he was not upright in his walk and was at fault (Gal 2:11-14).
   In his epistles Paul says nothing of the function of "sovereign pontiff" or of a "vicar of Christ" whom God is supposed to have established in His church. "God has appointed . . . first apostles [plural; not *an* apostle] . . ." (1 Co 12:28; cf. Eph 4:11). The church is built on the foundation of "the apostles and prophets" (Eph 2:20; cf. Rev 21:14). In the New Testament as a whole, Paul occupies a much more important place than does Peter. When Paul quotes Peter in his epistles, it is never to call attention to a special privilege conferred upon him. When Peter's name is associated with others, it is never mentioned first (1 Co 3:22; Gal 2:9). Peter speaks of himself as "a fellow elder" (1 Pe 5:1-4) and gives to Jesus alone the title of "Chief Shepherd." Nisbet says, "It is as if someone today were to write a biography of Napoleon without once mentioning that he was an emperor" (*L'Evangile ne dit pas cela*, p. 44).

Part VI

THE MATERIALS

10

The Members of the Church

THE TWO GROUPS

THE QUESTION of whether a person must be converted to be a church member is certainly the most important and controversial of all that concern the church. It divides the Christian world into two unyieldingly opposed groups. On one hand, the churches "of the masses" or "the multitudinist churches" (all of the large churches) affirm:

> One can consider the visible or exterior church as composed of all the inhabitants of the Christian world, even the indifferent and unbelieving. . . . One comes into the world, thus into relationship with the lights and graces it sheds, here one is brought up in the knowledge of the truth; but after having been a member in fact one must become a member by choice; one must declare he is joining it on the conviction that it is evangelical. . . . This principle is recognized by all the great Christian communities. They baptize infants, but they do not admit anyone to the Lord's table until he is older, has received more or less serious instruction and testing at which time he is required to confirm his baptismal vows.[1]

On the other hand, the free churches believe that "the church is a society of believers and of believers only; entrance into the church is on the basis of accepting of one's own free will the grace of God in Christ."[2]

"We believe," says the confession of faith of one of these churches, "that conforming to the practice of the apostles, it is absolutely necessary for all those who make up a local church to have accepted the Gospel message, to have manifested the new birth by faithful Christian conduct, and to have testified to their faith by being symbolically buried."[3]

As Professor A. F. Odeberg says, "The Christian world is divided on the concept of the church. For some, it is the assembly of those who have come to the faith and have accepted the Gospel; for others, it is an institution which makes possible the spread of the Gospel and takes in as members those who are won by it."[4]

According to the first concept, true Christians constitute the church; according to the second, they are in the church. When everything is taken

127

into account, it is the contrast between the church as an institution and the
ekklesia of believers.[5]

THE LOCAL CHURCH: AN OPEN OR CLOSED SOCIETY?

The first question which will help to shed light on the problem is: Was
the primitive church an open or a closed society?

AN OPEN SOCIETY

An open society is a group which one joins with a minimum of conditions: the population of a city, the clientele of a store, and the audience
at a lecture are extreme types of open society. The conditions for belonging to these societies are limited to chance of birth or interests or to
material or intellectual attractions. Many state churches become just such
open societies in which one becomes a member by birth and remains by
conviction—or by inertia—the conditions for belonging being scarcely
more demanding than those imposed on the clientele of a store or the
audience at a lecture.[6]

At the extreme opposite is found the closed society: only he who has
asked to be admitted and has satisfied the requirements of the rules for
admission enters. In the secret religions of antiquity, for example (like
present-day Free Mason societies), those who had undergone the pre-
scribed tests and had subscribed to the promises required were admitted.

In the New Testament the church appears as both a closed society and
an open society. In fact,

1. *Its name* is derived from a closed society. The Greek *ekklesia* was
open only to citizens of the city. Only the circumcized were members of
the Jewish *qâhâl*. As E. A. Judge states,[7] the New Testament often em-
ploys terms which were used to characterize those who were excluded
from different civil societies, "exiles, sojourners," etc. (see Eph 2:19; Heb
11:13; 1 Pe 1:17; 2:11) in order to speak of the condition of Christians
before their conversion, before they belonged to the church.

2. The details given concerning *the organization* of the church make it
evident that it was a society with clearly defined limits. There is the question of the membership (Ac 12:2) of which the clearly defined number
can increase (Ac 2:47; 9:31; 16:5) or diminish, be it by defection (Heb
10:25; 1 Jn 2:19) or removal (1 Co 5:2; 3 John 10). There are plenary
assemblies (1 Co 14:23). The church can be gathered together (Ac 14:27),
so it is definitely known just who the members are.

3. A certain number of expressions which are scattered throughout the
epistles presuppose a collective, homogeneous framework, a well-defined
structure. Phrases like "brethren," (Ja 3:1), "among you," "in the midst

of you," "one of you," "anyone of you," "you who are in Christ" (1 Pe 5:14), "one another" (which is repeated a hundred times) presuppose a definite group in which people know each other, where they can distinguish those who are "among you" from "those who are without," where they can admonish one another, care for one another, encourage one another, etc. (see Col 3:16; 1 Co 12:25; Heb 10:25, etc.).

According to all of these passages, the early church appears to have been a closed type of society; however, certain verses show that their assemblies were also open to all: "Suppose at an assembly of the whole church they should all speak with tongues, and uninstructed or unbelieving persons came in, would they not say that you are demented?" (1 Co 14:23). So an unbeliever could enter unexpectedly into a church assembly.

Without doubt that is the situation in James 2:2-4: "For should there enter into your gathering a man wearing a gold ring and splendid clothes, and there enter also a poor man shabbily clad. . . ." It is not specifically stated whether these visitors are Christian brothers. Moreover, as "in the Orient people enter the homes of others as if they were entering their own, without ceremony, (cf. Luke 7:36 ff.), with all the more reason they enter an assembly of a public nature," says J. Chaine. The church could not have been an entirely closed society. But these passages, especially the first, which is very clear, show plainly that they distinguished between "the church" and "the man of the people, the unbeliever."

How Did They Become Church Members?

In every closed society one must choose to enter after having met a certain number of conditions. What conditions had to be met by those who wished to become members of the church? Let us look at a few examples of people becoming members of the church as found in Acts:

"Repent and be baptized, each of you in the name of Jesus Christ" (Ac 2:38-47).

"Then those who welcomed his message were baptized, and there were added that day about three thousand souls" (2:41).

"The Lord added to the group those who were being saved" (2:47).

The Word of God was proclaimed by the Jerusalem Christians dispersed by persecution; Philip preached Christ in Samaria (8:4-8).

"But when they believed Philip as he told the good news of Jesus Christ, they were baptized, men as well as women" (8:12).

Peter proclaimed the Word of God in the house of Cornelius, a Roman centurion; the Holy Spirit was poured out on all who heard the Word (10:34-46).

They were baptized in the name of the Lord (10:37-48). Paul preached Jesus the Christ in the synagogue at Corinth (18:4-5).

"Crispus, the leader of the synagogue, believed in the Lord, with his entire family, and many of the Corinthians who listened believed and were baptized" (18:8).

Where it concerns individuals, exactly the same succession of events is found: preaching of the Word, faith, baptism, church membership:

Paul relates his conversion experience (Ac 9).

He is baptized; he seeks to join the church in Jerusalem (9:18, 26).

He joins the church in Antioch (Ac 11:26).

Lydia hears the Word, believes, and is baptized (Ac 16:13-15).

There is a church in her house (16:40).

There is the same order of events in the case of the Philippian jailer (Ac 16:30-34).

We conclude from these examples that the condition for church membership was "faith" and its corollary, "baptism."[8] Were these conditions obligatory?

MUST ONE BE BORN AGAIN TO BE A CHURCH MEMBER?

Certainly, for the accepting of the unregenerated as church members and their normal presence there would be incompatible with:

1. the teaching of Jesus Christ and the apostles concerning the church
2. the call to conversion and to the new birth which is the very heart of all neotestamentary preaching
3. the names given to members of the churches in the New Testament
4. the description of their spiritual condition as given in the epistles
5. the practice of baptism in the primitive church
6. the details given on the practice of the Last Supper
7. the New Testament teaching concerning church discipline

THE TEACHING OF JESUS AND THE APOSTLES CONCERNING THE CHURCH

The presence of the unconverted as regular church members is in contradiction to the teaching of Jesus Christ and His apostles concerning the church. The first time Jesus Christ spoke explicitly of the church was when a disciple confessed his faith in Him as the Messiah (Mt 16:18); the second time was to mark the contrast between this church and the "pagan and a tax gatherer" (Mt 18:17) to whom one must compare the brother who refuses to submit to the verdict of the church. In the types which Jesus and His disciples used to represent the church, we have seen that the part which refers to members implies a certain identity of nature among them. These same types stress the fact that a living and constant relationship must exist between Christ and His members. The detailed study of the three types (the house of the living God, the bride of Christ, and the body of Christ) reveals that, in their development in the epistles, there was no place in the church for foreign elements which are not personally related to Christ.

The image of the body, in particular, advances the idea that it is not normal for those who are not "in Christ" to be in the "body of Christ." When Paul wrote to the Corinthian church: "But you are Christ's body and individually members of it" (1 Co 12:27), or to the church at Rome: "So the many of us form one body in Christ, while each is related to all others as a member" (Ro 12:5), it is evident that he could not include in "individually" those whom he elsewhere calls "outsiders" (1 Co 5:12), "uninstructed or unbelieving persons" (1 Co 14:23), "strangers" (Eph 2:19), "a crooked and perverted generation" (Phil 2:15), the "unbelievers" (1 Co 6:6; 2 Co 6:14), "enemies" and "false brothers" (2 Th 3:15; 2 Co 11:26; Gal 2:4; Col 1:21), the "disobedient people" (Eph 2:2; 5:6; Col 3:6).

Everywhere in the New Testament the church seems like the *ekklesia*, the assembly of those who are called out from the world. Now, what is the world if not all those who have not believed on Jesus?[9] So if unbelievers have their legitimate place in the church, there is no longer a line of separation, no longer any reason to speak of the world, to call the unrighteous "those who are without," to leave the "crooked generation" (Ac 2:40), to "come out from their midst and be separate" (2 Co 6:17). If the church and the world are now one, "Jerusalem" and "Babylon" become synonymous, and one can then no longer understand the calls of the Word (Is 48:20; Jer 50:8; 51:45; Rev 18:4). Why come out of Babylon? Come out from what? Where is Babylon in our "Christian" civilization? Does it still exist or do these expressions describe a situation applicable only to the early days of Christianity?

Every honest man recognizes that our civilization and our contemporaries bear the marks of what the Scripture calls "the world" (Jn 1:10; 15:18-19; 17:14-25; 1 Co 1:20-21; 2:12; 3:19; Eph 2:2; Ja 4:4; 1 Jn 2:15-17; 3:13; 4:5; 5:19) which is antagonistic to what it calls the church or the Christians. So it would be more natural to ask: Where is the church? Does she still exist?[10] The condition in the large established churches of today reminds one of the words of Rufus Jones, who said that our churches resemble Robinson Crusoe's goat pen—those on the inside are as wild as those that live outside the enclosure.

How can the presence of the unconverted as regular members of a church be reconciled with the apostle Paul's vision: that church which

Christ cleansed by the washing of water with the Word, that He "may present the church to Himself gloriously, having no spot or wrinkle or any of such thing, but holy and blameless" (Eph 5:27)? Note that it concerns more than the mystical body of Christ, a theoretical spiritual entity, since it is to a definite church that the apostle Paul writes that he wishes to present her "as a pure virgin to Christ" (2 Co 11:2), telling her that Christ "has now reconciled in His human body through His death, to introduce you into His presence holy and blameless and irreproachable—if you remain grounded and settled in the faith" (Col 1:22-23).

It is evident that God alone can search the mind and the heart. He alone knows definitely those who are truly converted. Church discipline can apply only to the outward profession, that is, to speech and conduct. However, if a church renounces even outward criteria, can she claim to remain faithful to the biblical concept?

All one needs to do to be convinced that a multitudinist church does not correspond to the first church is to reread what Paul says of the church and what he orders her to do. This remark is applicable, moreover, to all the New Testament writers.

THE TEACHING OF JESUS AND HIS APOSTLES CONCERNING THE NEW BIRTH

To permit unbelievers to become church members is to minimize the teaching of Jesus and His apostles on the need for the new birth. We have seen the place and the importance of repentance, faith, and the new birth in the preaching of Jesus and His apostles; it is the beginning of and the key to all of their teaching: "Repent and believe in the good news" (Mk 1:15); "You need to be born from above" (Jn 3:7). The apostles likewise testified "to both Jews and Greeks that they should repent before God and have faith in our Lord Jesus" (Ac 20:21).

The new birth is the principal event in the life of each man, the beginning of his Christian life; and all apostolic preaching is aimed, on the one hand, at producing it in those who have not yet experienced it and, on the other hand, in exhorting believers. It is the dividing line between "that which is born of the flesh" and "what is born of the Spirit" (Jn 3:6), between "the children of the kingdom" and "the children of the evil one" (Mt 13:38; Jn 8:42-44), between "unbelievers, the unjust, the perverse and corrupt generation" and "believers, saints, and brothers." Therefore, to admit as regular church members those men, women, and children who have not personally experienced repentance and the new birth, who have never professed faith in Jesus as their Saviour and Lord, is to ignore and obliterate this boundary drawn by Jesus and the apostles; it is to merge "people who are outside" with "those who are within," "strangers" with "members of the household of God." If a person can belong to the church whether he is converted or not, it would mean that conversion is less important than belonging to a church. In recent years we have been witnessing a very rapid rise in the identification of salvation with church membership. It is known what a fortune the Roman Catholic Church has made because of Tertullian's words: "Apart from the church, no salvation." Even in many non-Roman Catholic circles, this has become an article of faith which has supplanted the call to personal faith and new birth as a requisite for salvation. In fact, most of the multitudinist churches give little time to the teaching of the new birth.[11]

IDENTIFYING NAMES OF CHURCH MEMBERS

The presence of the unconverted in the church is incompatible with the names given to church members in the New Testament. The Acts and the epistles designate church members by certain names which could not apply to the unconverted:

1. *All who believed* or *the multitude of those who believed* (Ac 2:44).
2. *The disciples* (Ac 6:2; 9:1, 26; 11:26; 14:21-22; 18:27; 19:9). "The Church groups all who, having heard and believed the Gospel, have become disciples of Christ."[12] What does this word mean, which we find 31 times in Acts and 269 times in the New Testament? "The disciple adopts the doctrine of the master. According to the Gospels he does even more: the disciple stays close to the person of Jesus. Soul and body, the disciples are bound to the person of the Lord. In the Acts the term disciple is the equivalent of 'brother' or 'believer.' This use is symptomatic, for it again proves that the word disciple implies faith without reservation in the One who is the Lord."[13]

"The true meaning of discipleship thus is response to Christ's lordship," says H. S. Bender.[14] "The disciple follows the Master by obeying Him, identifying himself with His cause, serving His purposes and renouncing all other loyalties."[15]

3. *The saints* (Ac 9:13, 32, 41; 2 Co 1:1; 13:13; Eph 4:12; Col 1:12).

This word is found sixty-two times in the New Testament (especially in the epistles) to designate believers. According to Regin Prenter, "The saints are those who are in Christ. . . . They are the believers. For it is by faith that we are partakers of Christ's holiness."[16]

Bonnard says, "The idea of holiness is common to all religions . . . at the base one always finds the ideas of *separation* (set apart) and of spiritual *power*: that which is holy is what has been separated, consecrated to the gods."[17]

So the saints are those who are separated to God. This term in itself implies a separation from what is secular, not consecrated to God, so it can refer to Christians only. All Christians are referred to as saints (Ro 15:26; 1 Co 14:33; Heb 13:24; Rev 22:21). The word is always in the plural (Phil 4:21 refers to a plural number) in the New Testament, except in Matthew 27:52.[18] "God sets Christians apart to be His very own, but they also set themselves apart for Him."[19]

In addition to the word *brother* used in the New Testament to designate a Christian, the other names most often used are *believer, disciple* and *saint*, each of which appears several hundred times. "The first three terms emphasize man's response to Christ rather than the passive aspect of his new condition."[20]

4. *The brethren* (Ac 9:30; 10:23; 15:33, KJV). This term is used more than a hundred times to designate church members. It is derived from the idea of the new family, the spiritual family, which is apart from his own family "according to the flesh." All who have become children of God because they have believed the Word (Jn 1:12) are now Christ's brethren (Mt 28:10; Ro 8:29; Heb 2:11, 12, 17) and consequently brothers among themselves in Jesus Christ.

The use of this word to designate church members (especially in 1 Co 5:11; 8:11; 2 Th 3:6; 1 Ti 6:2) in contrast to what the apostle calls "false brethren" (2 Co 11:26, KJV), "the enemy" (2 Th 3:15) or "all men" (Gal 6:10, KJV) proves once more that those he calls "brethren" were all members of God's family.

"The term 'brethren' is the most frequent designation of Christians in the New Testament, being used some 250 times in this way in Acts and in the epistles, 130 times by Paul alone, 50 times in Acts, 35 times in I Corinthians," says H. S. Bender. "Peter calls the church 'the brotherhood' (1 Pet. 2:27)."[21]

5. *God's beloved* or *beloved* (Ro 1:7; 2 Pe 3:1, 8; 2 Th 2:13); and *God's chosen ones, holy and beloved* (Col 3:12). It would be difficult to use these expressions in referring to men who are still "objects of God's indignation" (Eph 2:3), "disobedient people" (Eph 2:2; 5:6), those "who once were estranged and of a hostile attitude" (Col 1:21).

6. *"Christianoi"* (Christians, Ac 11:26; 26:28; 1 Pe 4:16). This can refer only to those who belong to Christ and reflect Him in their lives.[22]

7. *Our people* (Titus 3:14; 1 Jn 2:19). This is a term characteristic of the closed society in which one can easily distinguish members from nonmembers. "The members of the church are disciples," says Bender, "confessors of the faith, believers, witnesses, ambassadors, pilgrims, stewards, the faithful: all terms which denote response and activity on the part of the members."[23]

THE SPIRITUAL CONDITION OF CHURCH MEMBERS AS SEEN IN THE EPISTLES

The presence of unconverted members would be incompatible with the details found in the epistles concerning the spiritual condition of true members. Almost all of the epistles are addressed to churches. The details given by the apostles on the past experience and present spiritual condition of the church members help us to identify these people.

Salutations. The salutations in these epistles in which the apostle in a few words characterizes the addressees are in themselves significant:

"To all God's loved ones in Rome, called to be saints" (or "called saints") (Ro 1:7).

"To the church of God at Corinth, those made holy in Christ Jesus and called to be saints, together with all who in every place invoke the name of our Lord Jesus Christ, their Lord as well as ours" (1 Co 1:2).

"To the saints and faithful" (Eph 1:1; Phil 1:1; Col 1:2).

"To the . . . chosen and destined by God the Father . . ." (1 Pe 1:1-2, RSV).

"To those who . . . have been allotted a faith as precious as ours . . ." (2 Pe 1:1).

"To those who are called, loved by God the Father and kept by Jesus Christ . . ." (Jude 1).

If there had been unbelievers in those churches, could they have thought, with good reason, that the apostles included them among those to whom their letters were addressed, or considered them church members? It would not have been difficult to hold that opinion, but the contents of the epistles would have set them straight very quickly.

Just what do the epistles teach us about the members of apostolic churches?

"Formerly—Now."

They are men and women who have passed through a decisive crisis which has divided their lives into very distinct periods: *formerly—now.*

Formerly:	*Now:*
You offered the members of your body in the service of impurity in one act of lawlessness after another.	Offer your members in the service of righteousness for holy living (Ro 6:19).
You were slaves of sin. . . . What good did you derive from things of which you are now ashamed? Death is their consequence.	But now, freed from sin and made slaves of God, the good you derive leads to holiness and the consequence is eternal life (Ro 6:20-22).

When we lived our earthly way, our sinful passions . . . were active in our bodily organs to bear fruit for death.

We are released from the Law . . . we serve . . . in the new relationship of the Spirit (Ro 7:5-6).

You were once disobedient to God.

You . . . now have received mercy (Ro 11:30).

People who are immoral, or worship idols, or are adulterers, or homosexual perverts, or who rob, or are greedy, or are drunkards, or who slander others, or are lawbreakers—none of these will receive God's Kingdom.

But you were washed and you were made holy and you were made righteous by the power of the Lord Jesus Christ and by the Spirit of our God (1 Co 6:9-11, TEV).

In your days of paganism you were drawn away after dumb idols.

Brothers (1 Co 12:2).

You were enslaved to gods that essentially are not gods.

But now, when you know God, or better yet, are known by God (Gal 4:8-9).

You too were dead in your trespasses and sins. . . . Among them we all once walked, as we indulged our fleshly desires and carried out the inclinations of our lower nature and mind, and our thoughts, and by nature we were objects of God's indignation, as were all the rest of mankind.

But God is rich in mercy, so that on account of His great love with which He loved us, He made us who were dead in trespasses, alive with Christ—by grace you have been saved. And in Christ Jesus He caused us to rise, and seated us with Him in the heavenly spheres (Eph 2:1-6).

Once you were physically Gentiles and were called uncircumcision by the so-called circumcision that is made with human hands in the flesh; . . . in those days you were separated from Christ, aliens without the right of Israel's citizenship, and strangers to the covenants of promise, living in the world without hope and without God.

But now in Christ Jesus you, who were once far away, have been brought near by the blood of Christ (Eph 2:11-13).

Strangers and immigrants.

You are fellow citizens with the saints and members of God's household (Eph 2:19).

Once you were darkness.

Now in the Lord you are light (Eph 5:8-9).

You, too, who once were estranged and of a hostile attitude with your evil activities.

He has now reconciled in His human body through His death, to introduce you into His presence holy and blameless and irreproachable (Col 1:21-22).

You, who were dead in your trespasses and your lack of physical circumcision.

He made alive together with Him, as He forgave us all our trespasses (Col 2:13).

. . . disobedient people. At one time you were addicted to them, when your life was spent in such ways [immorality, impurity, passion, evil desire, and greediness].

But now you must also put all these things away—anger, bad temper, malice, slander, shameful language (Col 3:7-8).

For once we ourselves were thoughtless, disobedient, led astray, slaves to passions and pleasures of all sorts, wasting our time in malice and envy, detestable, and hating one another.

But when . . . God . . . in agreement with His mercy, . . . saved us through the washing of regeneration and a renewing by the Holy Spirit (Titus 3:3-5).

You who once were no people.

But are now the people of God.

Who once experienced no mercy.

But have now received mercy (1 Pe 2:9-10).

You were straying like sheep.

But now you have returned to the Shepherd and Guardian of your souls (1 Pe 2:25).

For to have been practicing the ways of the Gentiles heretofore is quite enough, indulging in unbridled lusts, in passions, in drinking, parties, in carousings, in dissipations and forbidden idolatries.

He who has suffered physically has gained relief from sin, so that he no longer lives by human passions but for the rest of his natural life he lives by what God wills. . . . Be self-controlled so that you can pray (1 Pe 4:1-3, 7).

"Those who are without—you." This experience has also separated them from those with whom they formerly associated. In the epistles the apostles draw a definite line between the church to whom they are writing and the unbelievers, the Gentiles:

"You must no longer behave like the *Gentiles,* whose lives are spent in the uselessness of their ways of thinking. Their understanding has become darkened. . . . estranged from the divine life of God . . . this is not the way you have come to know Christ" (Eph 4:17-20).

"Do not be sharing with them" (5:7).

Live "not in lustful passion like the Gentiles who have no knowledge of God" (1 Th 4:5).

". . . who pay no attention to good news concerning our Lord Jesus" (2 Th 1:8).

"Be not yoked unequally with unbelievers, for what common ground is there between righteousness and lawlessness, or what association is there between light and darkness? Or what harmony is there between Christ and Belial, or what partnership between a believer and an unbeliever? What agreement has God's temple with idols? For we are the temple of the living God . . . 'Come out from their midst and be separate,' says the Lord" (2 Co 6:14-17).

See also 1 Corinthians 5:1; 9:12. "If, therefore, the whole church assembles . . . and *outsiders* or *unbelievers* enter . . ." (14:23, RSV). "To *you,* then, *who believe,* He is precious, but to the *unbelieving* . . ." (1 Pe 2:7). "Conduct yourselves well among the Gentiles . . ." (2:12).

Frequently the apostle includes himself with those to whom he is writing in using the words *we* and *us.* Here he is contrasting this group with those who have not believed:

"For the message of the cross is folly to those on their way to destruction, but to us who are being saved, it is God's power (1 Co 1:18).

". . . those who, because they did not welcome the love of truth for their salvation, are going to destruction . . . so that all who have not believed the truth but have taken pleasure in wickedness may be judged. But we are always bound to offer thanks to God for you, brothers, beloved by the Lord, as you are, because from the beginning God chose you for salvation" (2 Th 2:10-13).

"See what a wealth of love the Father has lavished on us, that we should be called the children of God. And we are. For this reason the world does not know us, because it did not know Him. Beloved ones, we are God's children now" (1 Jn 3:1-2). "Do not be surprised, brothers, if the world hates you. We know that we have moved out of death into life . . ." (1 Jn 3:13-14).

Conversion: a past experience. The epistles often allude to this decisive crisis. The apostles remind their readers of this experience as an event in their past:

"But thanks be to God that, though you were slaves of sin, you have become with all your hearts obedient to the standard of teaching to which you were introduced, so that with deliverance from sin you were made slaves of righteousness" (Ro 6:17-18).

"In Christ Jesus I became your father by means of the good news" (1 Co 4:15).

"For by one Spirit we have all been baptized into one body" (1 Co 12:13).

"In Him you also, after listening to the message of the truth, the good news of your salvation, have as believers in Him been sealed with the promised Holy Spirit" (Eph 1:13).

". . . with thanksgivings to the Father, who has qualified you for your share in the inheritance of the saints in the light. He has rescued us from the domain of darkness, and has transferred us into the kingdom of His Beloved Son" (Col 1:12-13).

"And you, who were dead in your trespasses and your lack of physical circumcision, He made alive together with Him, as He forgave us all our trespasses" (Col 2:13).

"For they voluntarily tell . . . how you turned to God from idols, to serve the living and true God and to await His Son from heaven" (1 Th 1:9-10).

"Not because of righteous works that we have done but in agreement with His mercy, He saved us" (Titus 3:5). "Voluntarily He gave us birth by the word of truth" (Ja 1:18).

"Call to mind those previous former days when, after enjoying the light, you endured sufferings that involved great struggle. On the one hand you were publicly exposed to insults and affliction, and on the other you made common cause with those who were thus treated" (Heb 10:32-33).

"With your souls purified by obeying the truth . . . you have been born again . . . through the living and lasting message of God" (1 Pe 1:22-23). See also 1 Peter 1:3 and James 1:18.

Salvation: a present reality. When addressing church members, the apostles speak as to people who have already chosen, who already possess faith and salvation:

"You . . . have become slaves of God" (Ro 6:22, RSV).

"You . . . have received mercy" (Ro 11:30).

You have been called (1 Co 1:26).

"You are in Christ Jesus" (1 Co 1:30, NASB).

"You are God's temple and . . . the Spirit of God dwells in you" (1 Co 3:16).

"You were bought with a price" (1 Co 7:23).

"I would further remind you, brothers, of the good news which I preached to you which you welcomed, in which you stand, and by which you are saved, if you keep hold of my message to you" (1 Co 15:1-2).

"For through your faith in Christ Jesus you are all sons of God. As many of you as have been baptized into Christ have clothed yourselves with Christ" (Gal 3:26-27).

"Hearing about your faith in the Lord Jesus and your love for all the saints . . ." (Eph 1:15; cf. Col 1:4; 1 Th 1:3).

"By grace you have been saved" (Eph 2:5, 8).

"As you have always obeyed . . ." (Phil 2:12).

"As you accepted Christ Jesus as Lord, live in union with Him" (Col 2:6). "For you have died, and your life is hidden with Christ in God" (3:3). "You have stripped off the old nature with its practices and have put on the new self" (3:9-10).

"You also became followers of us and of the Lord when . . . you welcomed the message" (1 Th 1:6).

"Your faith in God has been made known everywhere" (1 Th 1:8).

"Our witnessing among you was believed" (2 Th 1:10).

"From the beginning God chose you for salvation by the Spirit's sanctifying work and by faith in the truth" (2 Th 2:13).

"We have come up Mount Zion, the city of the living God, the heavenly Jerusalem, to ten thousands of angels in festal gathering, and to the assembly of the first-born, whose names are enrolled in heaven, and to God . . . to the spirits of the righteous . . . to Jesus, the Mediator . . . to the sprinkled blood" (Heb 12:22-24).

"An inheritance . . . kept safely in heaven for you who by the power of God are protected through faith for a salvation ready to be revealed in the last time" (1 Pe 1:4-5).

"Whom having not seen, you love. In Him you have faith, though now you do not see Him, and you rejoice with inexpressible and heavenly joy, while you obtain the salvation of your souls as the goal of your faith" (1 Pe 1:8).

". . . well aware that you have been ransomed from your futile ways such as traditionally came down from your forefathers, not with perishable things such as silver or gold, but with the precious blood of Christ . . . who through Him are believers in God . . . your faith and hope rest in God" (1 Pe 1:18-21).

"But you are a chosen race, a royal priesthood, a holy nation, a people of His acquisition, so that you may proclaim the perfections of Him who called you out of darkness into His marvelous light" (1 Pe 2:9).

"I am writing you, dear children, because for His name's sake your sins have been forgiven you. I am writing you, fathers, because you know Him who is from the beginning. I am writing you, young men, because you have conquered the evil one" (1 Jn 2:12-13). "Besides, you have an anointing from the Holy One and you know all things. The reason I am writing is not because you do not know the truth, but *because you know it*" (1 Jn 2:20-21; see v. 27).

"You are from God, dear children, and have defeated them [the false prophets], because the One in you is greater than the one in the world" (1 Jn 4:4). "I am writing this to you who believe in the name of God's Son in order that you may know that you have eternal life" (1 Jn 5:13).

"He who believed that Jesus the Son of Man was the Lord," writes Dean Nils Johansson, "and who declared himself to be His follower (sich zu Ihm als solchem bekannt hatte) belonged to the primitive church, which was an assembly of those who definitely confessed Christ."[24] And A. de Gasparin adds, "The apostles never hesitate, when writing to a church, to consider all members as entitled to be called believers, redeemed children of God."[25]

The primitive church: A church of perfect men? Were there no unregenerate members in the primitive churches? To affirm that would be to misunderstand the relative character of all that is human. The primitive church was not that holy and infallible church to which Coleridge claimed to belong, but of which he said he was the only member.[26] Certainly there were "conversions" which were not real, people responding in a certain measure to God's call but never truly repenting and placing their confidence in Christ. Such people had not been regenerated by the Holy Spirit. They were deceiving themselves and others. Certainly they could make a profession of faith, be baptized, and be admitted to the church, but they were not really born again. Simon the magician deceived even the apostles (Ac 8:5-17). In his epistle, John the apostle speaks of those who "went out from us but they never belonged to us." So they were among them for some time without being truly born again. However, he adds, "for had they been ours, they would have remained *with us*" (1 Jn 2:19).[27]

Among the twelve was one who was "the son of perdition," but neither did he remain in the apostolic community. Nevertheless, in a church filled with the Spirit of the Lord, these false situations are of short duration: the spirit that inspired Simon was soon exposed (Ac 8:18-24). In a "sick" church it can take longer to clear up these troublesome cases. The one who is not genuinely converted is hidden in the mass of lukewarm and carnal Christians. Perhaps that was the case in Corinth, for two verses from the epistle addressed to that church by the apostle Paul suggest this possibility.

"Come to your right mind, and sin no more. For some have no knowledge of God. I say this to your shame" (1 Co 15:34, RSV). This translation causes one to believe that unsaved people had crept into the church at Corinth. If that was the case, let us be careful to notice the comments of the apostle on such a state of affairs: "*I say this to your shame.*" Instead of furnishing an argument for those who would like to believe it is a normal situation when unbelievers are members of the church, this verse shows the apostle reproving the Corinthians for such a situation. However, it is not certain that the above translation is the best since *agnosia* can also be translated *ignorance*. In fact, some are ignorant of God (F. Godet, and Goguel-Monnier translations). So it could be an incorrect knowledge of God which would not necessarily imply the absence of conversion. Let us not forget that the verse is found in the context of false teachings concerning the resurrection. In that case, the shame or disgrace would fall on the teaching ministry of the church of Corinth.

"Test yourselves, whether you are in the faith; examine yourselves. Or do you not recognize by yourselves that Jesus Christ is within you, unless you fail to pass the test!" (2 Co 13:5 or "provided you stand the test" (Williams), "unless you are counterfeits disapproved on trial and rejected" (Amplified). "The idea is that of an examination in which one fails," says Goguel-Monnier.

The verse seems a priori to show that the apostle counted on the possible presence of some unconverted members in the Corinthian church. In order to understand the true meaning, one must look at it in context. The Corinthians were contesting the validity of Paul's ministry: "You are looking for proof of Christ's speaking through me" (13:3). But if Christ was not speaking through him, neither was He indwelling them. If Christ was in them, it was proof that He spoke through Paul since it was by Paul that they came to the faith. "Since you are looking for proof of Christ's speaking through me. . . . Test yourselves, whether you are in the faith. . . . Or do you not recognize . . . that Christ Jesus is within you?" (13:3-5). The response is understood to be in the affirmative: "Yes, Christ is certainly in you" (F. Godet). "You will find the proof of my ministry in your own faith. Unless, perhaps, by chance (*ei me ti*) you are not real Christians, unless you fail in the examination and discover that you are unbelievers." This would be an unbearable thought for the Corinthians, who certainly did not consider themselves to be reprobates. One cannot fail to see a trace of irony in the apostle's reasoning: The logical result or consequence of the doubt of the Corinthians "backfired." In a way it demonstrated, by establishing the absurdity of anything to the contrary, what the apostle sought to establish in the letter as a whole. To prove that Christ did not speak through him, the Corinthians had to show that they themselves were not Christians—when they believed that their Christianity ranked higher than that of the apostle! That Paul was far from drawing such a conclusion from the reasoning which he suggested is sufficiently proved by reading a few verses farther (vv. 11-13).

So, one cannot deduce with certainty from this verse any more than from the preceding verses that there were unbelievers in the Corinthian church. Even if one could, in face of the number of verses which affirm the contrary, it would seem impossible to draw any other conclusion than that Corinth was the exception which confirms the rule and that this exception certainly did not receive Paul's commendation. Even if unregenerate men had crept into the church, it had no right to tolerate their remaining there: "Expel that wicked person from your own company" (1 Co 5:13). That is the principle of the apostles to which we refer later in speaking of church discipline.

No calls to conversion in the epistles. If there were unconverted men in the early churches, it is difficult to understand why the apostles in their letters never exhort them to be converted. In fact, we have seen that the necessity of the new birth was the main thrust in the preaching of the apostles. Now, analyzing the exhortations found in the epistles, we find none for repentance, conversion, or faith unto salvation. In the gospels and Acts there are about twenty imperatives, such as: "Repent," "Come to me," "Be converted"; some fifteen calls to faith: "Believe the gospel," "Believe in Him whom the Father sent." But, in the epistles, nothing! How can that be explained except by the fact that the churches were made up of men and women who had already repented and believed?

The only verse which seems to weaken the argument just given is 2 Corinthians 5:20 (RSV): "So we are ambassadors for Christ, God making his appeal through us. We beseech you on behalf of Christ, be reconciled to God." However, before coming to any conclusion, we must study the verse in its context and verify the translation. The apostle is here defending his ministry, as he does throughout the whole epistle. Here he defines it by its essential characteristic: evangelization or entreating men to be reconciled to God. "This call is not addressed to the church at Corinth, nor to Christians in general in so far as they need daily pardon," according to Calvin, but to all the unconverted. It is Paul's mission to entreat men, all men, by saying, "Be reconciled" (F. Godet).

Also, the original text does not say "we entreat *you*" but rather, "we beseech on behalf of Christ, be reconciled to God." In Laubach's *Inspired Letters of the New Testament* we read: "Speaking for Christ I say to every man: 'Turn from your sins and get right with God.'" Moreover, rereading 1 and 2 Corinthians and calling attention to the many testimonies of the apostle concerning the faith of his readers would suffice to rule out any attempt to compare the church of Corinth with a multitudinist church or a people to be evangelized.

Exhortations to increase in faith. If the church were not made up of believers, one would not understand the exhortations of the apostles to "stand firm," to "grow," and to benefit from their position as Christians. Indeed, only once in the gospels and Acts do we find an exhortation to stand firm in the faith (Jn 15, where Jesus is speaking to His disciples); the epistles command this firm stand about fifteen times and advise or encourage it about forty times.

"Stand firm, then, and do not be held fast again by a yoke of servitude" (Gal 5:1). "Let us hold firmly to our confession" (Heb 4:14). "It is our desire, however, for each of you to evidence the same earnestness all the way through, to enjoy the full assurance of your hope to the end, so you may not become sluggish . . ." (6:11-12). "Do not throw away your confidence; it carries a rich reward" (10:35). "And now, dear children, remain in Him so that when He appears we may not shrink in shame from Him at His coming" (1 Jn 2:28). "Hold on to what you have until I come" (Rev 2:25). "Hold fast to what you have, so that no one may rob you of your crown" (3:11).

You cannot remain in a place unless you are already there; you cannot continue on a road unless you have started out on it. The faith, which the members of the early churches possessed, was to *grow*. No encouragement to grow in the faith is found in the gospels or in Acts. On the other hand, the epistles contain some twenty commands and about forty references concerning growth and increasing in the faith.

"We should grow up in every way toward Him who is the Head—Christ" (Eph 4:15). "Be perfect" (2 Co 13:11, KJV). This exhortation is often associated with the call to steadfastness: "Be steadfast, immovable, at all times abounding in the Lord's service" (1 Co 15:58). "Be alert; stand firm in the faith; play the man; be strong" (1 Co 16:13).

"Brothers, we beg of you and exhort you in the name of the Lord Jesus to continue living in the way you learned from us, a way that is pleasing to God (and as you are behaving), and that you keep on, doing still better

. . . you yourselves are taught by God to love one another, and you are practicing it toward all the brothers. . . . But we appeal to you, brothers, to keep advancing in it" (1 Th 4:1, 9-11). "The God of all grace . . . will . . . Himself equip, stabilize, strengthen, and firmly establish you" (1 Pe 5:10). "But grow in the grace and knowledge of our Lord and Savior Jesus Christ" (2 Pe 3:18). This growth was a reality held in high esteem by the apostles: "We are always bound to give God thanks for you, brothers, as is befitting, because your faith is growing so splendidly and the love of each of you for one another is increasing, so that we ourselves mention you with pride among the churches of God for your *fortitude* and *faith* amid all the persecutions and distresses which you endure" (2 Th 1:3-4).

Sanctification is meaningless without conversion! All the moral exhortations of the Scripture are based on the new position of its readers. The schema of these exhortations is not: "Do this in order to be saved or to become holy" (that would be salvation by works) but: "Since you *are saved*, do this; since you *are holy*, become this."

In the epistles of Paul: "So I exhort you . . . to conduct yourselves worthy of the calling you have received" (Eph 4:1; cf. Phil 1:27). "Be kind toward one another, tenderhearted, forgiving one another, even as God has in Christ *forgiven* you" (Eph 4:32).

"But immorality and every kind of impurity or greed should not so much as be mentioned among you; such is the proper way for saints" (Eph 5:3). "For once you were darkness but now in the Lord you are light; live as children of light" (5:8). "So, as you accepted Christ Jesus as Lord, live in union with Him, rooted and built up in Him and confirmed in the faith" (Col 2:6). "If, then, you have been raised with Christ, seek the things which are above. . . . Apply your minds to things above, not to things on earth; for you have died. . . . Therefore put to death whatever in your nature belongs to the earth—immorality, impurity, passion. . . . Do not lie to one another, since you have stripped off the old nature with its practices and have put on the new self. . . . Therefore, as God's chosen, set apart and enjoying His love, clothe yourselves with tenderness of heart, kindliness, humility, gentleness, patient endurance" (Col 3:1-12).

In Peter's epistles: The apostle Peter speaks in the same manner. In his first letter he gives about fifty different exhortations expressed by about seventy verbs, but he justifies almost every exhortation by the work which God has accomplished. Frequently we find such expressions as: so, therefore, so that, as, but as, but now, and if, likewise, because. God asks us to live holy lives *because of what He has done for us* (1:3; 5:7), *in us* (1:22-23), (*having purified*—by obedience to the truth *for* a sincere love of the

brethren, love one another earnestly . . . you *have been born anew* . . .)—
because of what we have become (1:14, as obedient children; 2:2, like
newborn babes; 2:5, like living stones; see also 2:9, 11, 17, 24; 4:10),
because of what we profess or do (1:15, 17; 2:13, 15; 3:12; 4:11; 5:5),
because of our calling (2:21; 3:9), *because of what is awaiting us* (3:9;
4:7, 13, 17; 5:4, 6).

In John's epistles: John follows the same line of reasoning in his epistles:
he who believes in Christ is "born of God," is "in God," and "God is in
him." Now, whoever is born of God loves God and the brethren (1 Jn
2:5, 7; 3:11, 23) and keeps the commandments of God. Those to whom
his epistles are addressed are born of God (2:12-14, 20-21; 3:14; 5:13), so
they ought to walk as He walked (2:6), ought not to sin (2:1; 3:6, 9;
5:18), ought to keep His commandments (2:3; 3:22-24; 5:2), ought to do
right (2:29; 3:7), ought to love God (4:19; 5:2) and the brethren (3:11,
18, 23; 4:7, 21; 5:2).

"Whoever reads the epistles (except for hypocrites and the undeserv-
ing) should see in them that every member of an apostolic church is
treated like a redeemed person, a saint, solely because he is considered to
be a believer," says A. de Gasparin.[29]

Become what you are. Because the members of the churches to whom
the apostles wrote were born of God and were in Christ or in God, the
apostles could exhort them to keep the commandments, to practice justice,
and to love the brethren. This would have been impossible for them
before their spiritual rebirth, because sin rather than God dwelt in them
(Ro 7:17). They were slaves of the law of sin and death (Ro 7:23; 8:2);
the law was weakened by the flesh (Ro 8:3); the flesh was incapable of
submitting to God's law (Ro 8:7); and to accomplish what was right was
not possible (Ro 7:18). But now the law of the Spirit of life in Christ
Jesus has set them free from the law of sin and death (Ro 8:2) and Christ
in them enables them to obey the Father's commandments (Col 1:28; Gal
2:20). Thus all of these exhortations once more confirm the fact that the
apostolic churches were made up of regenerate believers.

The tragedy of the preaching in most multitudinist churches is that it
continues in the style of the epistles, even though it addresses an audience
which resembles those in the gospels and the Acts more than it does those
to whom the epistles were addressed. "They speak to the world as if it
were the Church," said Dr. W. A. Visser't Hooft.[30] By hearing themselves
exhorted as if they were Christians, the unconverted in the churches
finally believe they are; but this belief does not take the place of faith nor
of the Holy Spirit when it is a question of putting into practice the admonitions. Finding that impossible in their lives, they believe it to be

generally true, and consider the admonitions to be merely pulpit eloquence. Those who hold the form of religion but deny the power of it
(2 Ti 3:5) cannot fail to be distressed by the requirements of Christian
ethics, whereas the good news of salvation by faith, of pardon from sin
secured by the death of Christ on the cross would meet all of their needs.
This message is often missing from the pulpit because one begins with the
false supposition that by infant baptism, by Christian instruction, confirmation, and regularly partaking of the sacraments, everyone is already a
regenerated Christian and has received the Holy Spirit. So preaching
often finds itself in an untenable position with respect to the audience:
instead of a message which offers liberation and life, the "Christianized
unbelievers" of the multitudinist churches receive exhortations which
discourage them because they cannot realize them in their lives.[31]

On the other hand, in a number of evangelical works and movements,
regenerated Christians, who make up the majority of the listeners, are
deprived of the exhortation and teaching which the apostles gave to the
believers to help them grow, because the minister of the Word has chosen
to limit himself to evangelistic preaching. A misunderstanding of the composition of the church as God established it is responsible for this serious
mistake.

THE PRACTICE OF BAPTISM IN THE PRIMITIVE CHURCH

*The presence of unconverted members in a church is incompatible with
baptism as originally practiced.* The question of baptism is examined more
in detail in the next chapter, where, using New Testament texts, we show
that the early church baptized only believers who had openly confessed
their faith. From that time we can establish a certain correlation between
baptism and church membership. Were all church members baptized?
Was baptism only for believers who had confessed their faith?

If the New Testament answers these two questions in the affirmative, it
becomes evident that the status of church membership was granted only
to those believers who had confessed their faith in Christ. This evidence
is obtained by a classical syllogism: all church members are baptized—all
who are baptized are converted; therefore all church members are converted.

a. WERE ALL CHURCH MEMBERS BAPTIZED? It should scarcely be necessary to show that baptism was required for church membership, since in
all Christian groups this requirement has been retained. All churches,
official or free, as well as almost all sects which have sprung from Christianity, required baptism for membership. "Baptism is the sign, common
to all Christian churches, of membership of the Church," says Brunner.[32]

The Council of Trent defined the church as the society of those who have been baptized. In many communities, this sacrament confers membership ipso facto. ("Baptism is a sacrament which . . . makes us Christians, children of God and of the Church," says the Catholic catechism.) But what is more important to us is to know what they practiced in the early church. What does the Scripture say? We saw that when the church was founded, the apostle Peter associated baptism directly with the call to repentance: "Repent and be baptized, each of you in the name of Jesus Christ for the forgiveness of your sins. . . . Then those who welcomed his message were baptized, and there were added that day about three thousand souls" (Ac 2:38, 41). Generally speaking, the apostles baptized immediately after conversion and a profession of faith (see Ac 8:12-16, 26-39; 9:18; 10:44-48; 11:16-17; 16:14-15, 33-34; 18:8). Indeed, there may have been people baptized in the days of the apostles who should not have been, people who fell back into their former lives, returning to the world (2 Ti 2:18; 4:9-10; 1 Jn 2:19). But it is difficult to think that anyone having been converted with the other Christians knowing of it would not have been baptized. The epistles which are addressed to the churches begin with the assumption that all church members have been baptized.

So it is that the apostle Paul writes to the saints in the church of Rome: "Do you not know that *all of us* who have been baptized into Christ Jesus have been baptized into His death? . . . Even so consider yourselves to be dead to sin, but alive to God in Christ Jesus" (Ro 6:3, 11, NASB).

To the Corinthians he writes: "Were you baptized in Paul's name?" (1 Co 1:13). He reminds them that he baptized Crispus, Gaius, and the household of Stephanas. He affirms indirectly that they have all been baptized: "For by one Spirit we have all been baptized into one body" (1 Co 12:13). Although this verse refers to the baptism of the Holy Spirit, it would have been inconceivable to a first-century Christian that one could be baptized by the Spirit without first having experienced water baptism. "This verse presupposes that water baptism was required of all Christians."[33]

To the Galatians Paul writes, "For through your faith in Christ Jesus *you are all* sons of God. As many of you as *have been baptized into Christ* have clothed yourselves with Christ" (Gal 3:26-27).

To the Colossians: "In Him, too, you were circumcised—not with a physical circumcision—in stripping off your fleshly body in Christ's circumcision, when *you were buried with Him in baptism* and thereby *raised to life* with Him" (Col 2:11-12).

Postapostolic testimony confirms, moreover, the unanimous practice in the primitive church of admitting into church membership only those who had been baptized. Only those who had passed through the waters of baptism had the right to partake of the holy communion. Justin Martyr writes, "We call this meal 'the giving of thanks.' No one can partake of it unless he believes that what we teach is true and has received baptism for the pardon of sins and the new birth and unless he lives according to Christ's teachings."[34] In the *Didache* it is also specified, "Let no one partake of the Eucharist except those who have been baptized in the name of the Lord. For concerning that the Lord said: 'Do not give dogs what is holy' (Mt 7:6)." Since all members of the church partook of the holy communion, these texts again prove that they all were baptized.

b. WERE ONLY BELIEVERS PERMITTED TO BE BAPTIZED? This question is examined more in detail in a later chapter. Basically, this is the crux of the problem, not only of baptism but also, to a great extent, of the composition of the church. "Admission for baptism and, with even greater reason, participation in the Holy Communion presuppose faith," says Dean M. Simon.[35]

If only those who personally confess their faith in Christ are permitted to be baptized, the church will count as members only those who know they are believers and professing Christians. Indeed, the choice of "baptism of believers" or "infant baptism" already implies the choice of "churches of professing believers or multitudinist churches." History proves that the primitive church of professing Christians gave way to the multitudinist church when infant baptism became prevalent. It was in order to preserve the multitudinist church that the Reformers retained infant baptism.

Karl Barth writes,

> Am I wrong in thinking that the really operative extraneous ground for infant baptism, even with the Reformers, and ever and again quite plainly since, has been this: one did not want then in any case or at any price to deny the existence of the evangelical Church in the Constantinian *corpus christianum*—and today one does not want to renounce the present form of the national church? If she were to break with infant baptism, the Church would not easily any longer be a people's church in the sense of a state Church or a church of the masses. *Hinc, hinc illae lacrymae* (Then what tears!) Has not the anxiety, which here shows itself, often unconsciously taken the quite primitive form to which Luther openly confessed on occasion: "there would not be too many people baptized if, instead of *being brought* to baptism, they had to come of their own accord"? We make no mistake about the difficulty of personal decision—historical, practical and actual—which is here indeed obvious. But in spite of it we may ask: are these legitimate anxieties? Would it not always turn out even in this matter that to be successful in what one intends, in any case and at whatever price, one must examine it closely? Are we so sure of the inner worth of the Constantinian system and of the present-day form of the

National Church, is our conscience in these matters so clear that we ought to and must resolve to hold fast to them, at whatever cost,—even at the cost of inflicting wounds and weakness on the Church through an incorrect baptism? . . . Where does it stand written that Christians may not be in the minority? Might they not be of more use to their surroundings if they were allowed to be a *healthy* Church? What would be the advantage for the Church to remain a National Church in the present-day sense of the term: a church *of* the people, instead of a church *for* the people? Whatever may be the theological answer, we must agree that the matter of a better ordinance of baptism is urgently needed.[36]

Professor Jalaguier, an ardent defender of the multitudinist church, in justifying infant baptism by the multitudinist principle, states clearly, "If the Church by nature and intended purpose can be multitudinist, infant baptism is justifiable."[37] This point is discussed later.

c. BAPTISM OF CHILDREN AND THE FREE CHURCHES. Certainly there are free churches which have continued to practice infant baptism; but, in their theology, these churches do not confer on the rite the true value of baptism; they equate it with dedication of children. Baptism is replaced by another ceremony by which the newly converted asks for admission as an active, conscious member of the community. (In the Darbyist assemblies one "asks for his place at the Lord's Table"; in the Salvation Army the mourners' bench takes the place of baptism, to a certain extent.) There are generally historical reasons which explain the replacement of the biblical symbol by a human tradition. Whether it is advantageous and whether its continuance is justifiable are questions which we will let the assemblies themselves answer.

THE PRACTICE OF THE HOLY COMMUNION IN THE PRIMITIVE CHURCH

The presence of unconverted people in the church is irreconcilable with the holy communion as practiced in the primitive church. The question of holy communion also would merit special study, but we shall concern ourselves here with only that which has a bearing on the problem of the composition of the church.

We have already seen, according to postapostolic testimony, that only baptized Christians were admitted to the holy communion. It would be easy to show that each time holy communion is mentioned in the Scripture, all those participating were baptized (Ac 2:41-42, 46; 1 Co 10:15; 11:23).

On the other hand, church discipline even excluded believers from the holy communion if their conduct no longer corresponded with their Christian testimony. "Whoever, therefore, eats the bread, or drinks the cup of the Lord in an unworthy manner, is a violator of the Lord's body and blood. Let a person look carefully at himself" (1 Co 11:27-28). With even greater reason the unconverted were excluded from partaking of the Lord's table. For was it not the visible form of the unity in the body of Christ? "Is not the blessed cup, which we consecrate, a fellowship in the blood of Christ? Is not the bread we break a fellowship in the body of Christ? The many of us are one bread, one body, since we all participate in the one bread. You cannot drink the Lord's cup and the cup of demons. You cannot participate in the Lord's table and the table of demons. Or shall we provoke the Lord to jealousy? Are we mightier than He?" (1 Co 10:16-17, 21-22). At the table of the Lord only those participate who are members of the body of Christ, those who have been baptized by the Holy Spirit and have thus become integrated in the body. The apostle Paul could write to the Corinthians, "But let a person look carefully at himself and in that spirit eat of the bread and drink from the cup" (1 Co 11:28), because he could also say: "You are Christ's body and individually members of it" (1 Co 12:27). "All the numerous parts of the body compose one body, so it is with Christ. For by one Spirit we have all been baptized into one body, whether Jews or Greeks, whether slaves or free, and we have all been imbued with one Spirit" (1 Co 12:12-13).[38]

Thus, in the primitive church there existed a simple, logical, and coherent order between the different steps in the Christian life and the symbols which represented them. He who was moved by the Word of God and responded to the call of the Lord with repentance and faith experienced conversion and the new birth, was baptized, and admitted to the assembly of those who also had answered the call, the ecclesia; then he participated in the holy communion. All the difficulties which these different points have caused in the historical churches come from the abandonment of the order established by God.[39] Thus, these difficulties can be resolved only by returning to God's plan.

THE UNITY OF THE CHURCH AND CHURCH DISCIPLINE

The presence of unconverted persons as regular church members renders meaningless the recommendations concerning relationships with unbelievers as well as the orders relating to church discipline.

a. "BE SEPARATE FROM THEM." Indeed, the apostles frequently exhort Christians to separate themselves from unbelievers or "false" believers:

"Be not yoked unequally with unbelievers; for what common ground is there between righteousness and lawlessness, or what association is there between light and darkness? Or what harmony is there between Christ and Belial, or what partnership between a believer and an unbeliever? What agreement has God's temple with idols? For we are the temple of the living God, as God has said, 'I will dwell in them and walk among them, and I will be their God and they shall be My people.' For that reason, 'Come out from their midst and be separate,' says the Lord, 'and do not touch anything unclean. Then I will receive you and I will be a Father to you, and to Me you shall be sons and daughters. The Lord Omnipotent speaks' " (2 Co 6:14-18; cf. Rev 18:4).

"Do not be misled. Bad associations corrupt good morals" (1 Co 15:33). "Be sure of this, that none guilty of immorality or of impurity or of greed, which is idolatry, has an inheritance in the kingdom of Christ and of God. Let no one lead you astray with empty words for on account of such things the indignation of God comes on disobedient people. *Do not be sharing with them* ['Carefully avoid those who give themselves to such things'—translation of J. P. Benoît]" (Eph 5:5-7). "If a pretended brother is immoral or greedy or idolatrous or abusive or a drinker or a robber, you must not associate with him, nor even eat with one of that type. What business of mine is it to judge outsiders? Do you not have those within the church to judge? But outsiders God will judge. Expel that wicked person from your own company" (1 Co 5:11-13).

b. "MAINTAIN UNITY." Therefore, looking at it one way, Christians should have no fellowship with unbelievers (2 Co 6:14-15), those who are still in darkness (v. 14), who serve false gods (v. 16), who are considered by God as unclean (v. 17), who live in debauchery or are covetous (Eph 5:5). Their company must be avoided even if they put on the outward appearance of Christians (1 Co 5:11-13). Had these nonbelievers been church members, how could one reconcile these recommendations with those given by the apostles in almost all of their letters? They were told to maintain *unity* among all the members of the assembly. "But in the name of our Lord Jesus Christ, I beg of you, brothers, that all of you agree, that you eliminate factions among you, and that you be *united in mind* and *attitude*" (1 Co 1:10). This unity is clearly manifested at the time of the holy communion: "The many of us are one bread, *one body*, since we all participate in the one bread" (1 Co 10:17), "making every effort to preserve the unity of the Spirit in the bond of peace" (Eph 4:3).

"Make my joy complete by being *in agreement*, having *the same* love, being *united in spirit*, having the *same attitude*" (Phil 2:2). "But we must hold on to what we have attained" (Phil 3:16). (In Phillip's translation we read: "It is important that we go forward in the light of such truth as we have ourselves attained to.") "We must continue to live up to that degree of success that we have already reached" (Williams), "Only, at the point where we have now arrived, let us keep in step" (Louis Segond, Fr.). Would this be possible with those who are following "the ways of this world system, controlled by the ruler of the kingdom of the air, the spirit of the one now working in disobedient people" (Eph 2:2), with those whose lives are spent in the "uselessness of their ways of thinking" (Eph 4:17)? And there is even this request which is given five times, at the end of the chapters: "Greet one another with a holy kiss" (Ro 16:16; 1 Co 16:20; 2 Co 13:12; 1 Th 5:26; 1 Pe 5:14). How can it be reconciled with the exhortation to not even eat with a "false brother"?

c. "DRIVE OUT THE WICKED PERSON FROM AMONG YOU." But more than that, the Lord and His apostles told the believers to break off their close association not only with unbelievers but even with those who bore the name of brother but who lived in immorality and sin. "If your brother should do wrong against you, go and show him his fault privately; in case he listens, you have won your brother. In case he does not listen, take one or two along, so that from the testimony of two or three witnesses the whole dispute may be settled. If he refuses to listen to them, tell the church; and if he will not listen to the church, *treat him like a pagan and a tax gatherer*" (Mt 18:15-17).

This is the rule the apostles asked the churches to follow:

"Purge out the old yeast, so that you will be a fresh batch. Expel that wicked person from your own company" (1 Co 5:7, 13). "We charge you, brothers, in the name of our Lord Jesus Christ, to avoid every brother who, instead of observing the tradition [teaching] that you received from us, is living in idleness. If someone does not follow our instruction in this letter, note him well; do not associate with him, so that he may grow ashamed. Do not consider him an enemy, but warn him as a brother" (2 Th 3:6, 14-15). He remains a "brother" in Christ since he has been redeemed and regenerated by Him; but on the human level of relationship, he is put to one side in the church.

d. AVOID THOSE WHO ARE OPPOSED TO THE DOCTRINE. Church discipline was exercised not only on those who had sinned or who no longer lived according to the instructions of the apostles, but it also affected those who preached doctrines which differed from those of the apostles, thus creating divisions in the churches.

Paul had foreseen the ravages these heretics would make among the flocks that he had gathered. "For I know that after I have left, savage wolves will make their way to you, that have no mercy on the flock; and from your own number also persons will arise who will teach distorted things to draw away the disciples after them. Keep on the lookout, therefore" (Ac 20:29-31). And he gave precise instructions to the churches concerning these instigators of schisms: "I warn you, brothers, to keep an eye on those who cause divisions and temptations, quite out of harmony

with the doctrine you have been taught; and to keep away from them"
(Ro 16:17).

"But even if we or an angel from heaven should preach to you a gospel
that differs from what we have preached to you—a curse on him! As we
said before and repeat right now, if anyone evangelizes you with a gospel
that varies from what you have received, *let him be accursed*" (Gal 1:8-9).
The glossary of the revised French Segond Version of the New Testament
says that "this word corresponds in the New Testament to the cursing or
excommunication of those who are the enemies of God" (Ac 23:14; Ro
9:3; 1 Co 12:3; 16:22). Hans Bruns states that he who was declared
anathema (accursed) in Judaism "did not have the right to teach or to
participate in teaching."[40]

In the day when Paul wrote his pastoral epistles, heretics were beginning to multiply: ". . . retaining a form of piety, they are strangers to its
power. *Turn away from such people.* Just as Jannes and Jambres opposed
Moses, so do these men oppose the truth, corrupt thinkers as they are and
counterfeits so far as faith is concerned" (2 Ti 3:5, 8).

"*Have nothing to do with a factious person* after a first and second warning, aware that such a person is perverted and goes on sinning, and is self-
condemned" (Titus 3:10-11).

The same warning but even more severe appears in the second epistle
of John: "For many imposters have gone out into the world, who do not
confess Christ as having come incarnated. Whoever assumes leadership
and does not remain in the teaching of Christ, does not have God. He who
remains in the teaching has both the Father and the Son. If anyone comes
to you who does not bring this teaching, do not receive him in your home
nor extend him your greeting; for he who bids him welcome makes himself a sharer of those wicked works of his" (2 Jn 7, 9-11).

If, therefore, church members were required to break off their relationship even with regenerated believers who had not persevered in the Christian life and the apostles' doctrine, with how much more reason was there
never any consideration of admitting to church membership someone who
had not even begun to live this Christian life and accept this doctrine by
faith.

Neglect of church discipline in churches descended from the Reformation changed them into very different institutions from those the Reformers had in mind. "It is true that Luther never tried to form a pure
church, but he practiced church discipline," says Dr. M. Jacobs.[41] Calvin,
for his part, wrote, " 'As the saving doctrine of our Lord Jesus Christ is
the life of the Church, so discipline is, as it were, its sinews; for it is owing
to it that the members of the body adhere together, each in its own place.'

It serves to 'lend a helping hand to doctrine to stimulate the lazy and indifferent.' "[42]

CONCLUSIONS

Thus, from the study of the New Testament it is clearly seen that the churches established by the apostles were made up of men and women who had experienced the new birth, had testified thereto by baptism, continued daily in the teaching of the apostles, in the Christian walk, and in the breaking of bread. Such communities were what we today call churches of professing believers or *free churches*. Were they "churches of perfect men"? All one needs to do is to cast a glance at the churches of Corinth, Pergamos, Thyatira, Sardis, and Laodicea to see how far apart are "professing believers" and "perfect men." On the other hand, not one of the churches founded by the apostles themselves could have guaranteed that all of its members were actually regenerated. If the deceit of Simon the magician had not been exposed at once, he would have been a member of the church of Samaria since he had just been baptized.

Thus, even in the primitive church, membership in the local church did not signify ipso facto that a person had been regenerated; only membership in the universal church carries this guarantee because that membership is recorded by God Himself. We have also seen that the gathering of the primitive churches was not closed to nonbelievers (1 Co 14:23). For all of these reasons, the assembly, insofar as it was a local assembly, could never claim to correspond 100 percent to what God had recorded as a local branch of the universal church.

However, there is an essential difference between the apostolic churches and the present-day multitudinist churches. To become a church member in the first century, one had to make a personal profession of conversion and give a testimony of one's faith at the time of admission by baptism. Certainly one could labor under a delusion concerning one's new birth or seek to produce this illusion in others; it was clearly known that personal regeneration was the condition *sine qua non* of belonging to the church. No one was added to the church register without personally desiring it and without meeting the requirements, or at least without giving the impression that he met them. One should also add that the Word was faithfully preached with clarity and power. Where the Holy Spirit was at work, false impressions were rare and of short duration. One can indeed wonder whether the incestuous man of Corinth had ever really experienced the new birth, but we know in any case that the apostle asked the Corinthians to "cast out that man from the fellowship of the church."

Brunner asks,

Who then has the right to call himself a member of the Body of Christ? Only the one who is united to Christ by actual personal communion, by faith. It is not just anyone who has been baptized, who listens to the preaching of the Word, who has received religious instruction, pays his contributions, agrees to be named a member of a council, holds a church office just simply because he is interested. The criterion for Church membership is plain, positive, unquestionable. Only the one who can say: I know who is my Savior, and say it sincerely, with real humility and profound faith, he only is a member of the Body of Christ; and he knows it. Only that man is a member of the Church, even though we also include in the Church those who are destined by divine election to become members, but are not as yet. They are not the present Church but the potential Church. As of now, only those who are regenerated belong to the Church.[43]

The confession of faith of the Reformed Church of France (art. 27) clearly states: "According to the Word of God, we say that the true Church is the community of the faithful who with one accord wish to follow the Word and the pure religion it teaches." And a Reformed Church pastor, P. Lecomte, affirmed in his report on the church member, "It is true that the idea which best corresponds to biblical teaching is that of the Free Churches, the Church of professing Christians."[44]

Lutheran theologians like Günther Harder or Fritz Hübner openly declare, "The Church is indeed the assembly of believers."[45] "Only those who through repentance and biblical faith come to a personal appropriation of salvation and regeneration, only they are the members of the Body of Christ."[46] Then why is there no apparent effort made in the churches to conform reality to the theory?

The most outstanding representatives of contemporary theology define the church as the society of believers:

Emil Brunner: "The Church is in reality the community of believers, all of them living together by the faith that is in them and by the Holy Spirit who governs and directs them. . . . Wherever men live together in obedience to the Word of God, there is the Church."[47]

Karl Barth: "Since here and there through the Holy Spirit men meet with Jesus Christ and so also with one another, a Christian community visibly arises and exists here and there."[48]

"No one belongs to it by birth or origin; no one is a member because he is from a Christian family or a Christian nation or even by virtue of some arrangements which others may have made for him."[49]

L. Newbigin: "The message that we hear and believe and the community founded on Christ's death and resurrection and into which we must be baptized, these are closely bound together by the Holy Spirit and the work of Christ. When these ties are broken by giving a central place to the spoken word and to the sacraments, we essentially draw away from the character of the religion of the New Testament."[50]

Why is there such a distance between what theology affirms and what the churches practice, churches from which these theologians come? Must one believe Brunner when he says that the men who preside over the destinies of these churches have no idea of the results of theological research? If so, how is it useful and what is its practical function in the church? Can one, under these conditions, continue to affirm that the Word of God is the only foundation of the church? How can one rightfully stigmatize as a "sect" those who practice what the theologians of the large established churches declare conforms to the teaching of the Bible? What are the real reasons for their clinging to these ecclesiastical systems which have been denounced for a long time as being contrary to Scripture by authentic representatives of the multitudinist churches? Was Kierkegaard really right when he claimed that it was a question of influence, power, and money?[51]

Notes

1. Paul Jalaguier, *De l'Eglise*, pp. 321-22. (However, the Orthodox churches give the eucharist to baptized infants.) Therefore, when Jalaguier defines the church as "the assembly of those who profess to know Jesus Christ, who invoke His name" he must add "or upon whom His name is invoked" (Ibid., p. 23). In the same book, he says, "The invisible Church is composed of all who invoke, or upon whom is invoked, the name of Christ . . . whatever may be their convictions or personal dispositions" (p. 170).
   Here we find reechoed the Catholic theory as Cardinal Bellarmin defined it: "For someone to be called a member of the Church, we do not think there are any grounds for requiring of him some inner quality; a verbal expression of faith and communion in the sacraments are sufficient" (Bellarmin, *Symbolie*, p. 15).
2. Henry Cook, *What Baptists Stand For.*
3. *Confession de foi de l'Association des églises evangéliques baptistes.*
4. A. F. Odeberg, "Der neuzeitliche Individulismus und der Kirchengedanke im N. T." in *Ein Buch von der Kirche.*
5. See E. Brunner, *The Misunderstanding of the Church.*
6. "The Church [evangelical reformed of Neuchâtel] considers to be members all who do not declare themselves excluded from it" (Art. 4 of the constitution of the aforementioned church, quoted by Francus, *Il n'y a pas de Protestants*, p. 160).
   "In our canton (Vaud) all who do not declare themselves not to be a part of the national church are considered to be members of it" (Pastor André Bovon, president of the synodical council).
   "The national Church of Geneva is composed of all people of Geneva who accept the organizational forms of the Church as later established" (Art. 114 of the political constitution of 1847). "These organizational forms are purely administrative which have nothing, either remotely or closely related, to do with the Christian faith and life. All the amendments tending to indicate that the National Church of Geneva was a Christian Church were ruled out by the Great Constituent Council" (Henri Heyer, *L'Eglise de Genève*, p. 155, cited by J. de Senarclens, "De la Vraie Eglise, selon Calvin," p. 45).
   "The matter of belonging to the Church rests upon the residence in the district of the community" (Constitution of the Evangelical Lutheran Church of Bavaria [1920], Art. 7, paragraph 2). "The child must be incorporated in the Church, the body of Christ, from his birth" (Reformed evangelical synod of Pau, quoted

by Francus, p. 38). "Our church is a multitudinist Church. One becomes a member of it by birth, not by the new birth, and is considered a member as long as he has not asked to be dropped from the church" (Church of Zurich, *Dienst der Kirche in unserer Zeit*).

7. E. A. Judge, *The Social Pattern of Christian Groups in the First Century*, pp. 28 ff. See also Hildebrandt, *Das Gemeindeprinzip der christlichen Kirche*, pp. 82 ff.

8. "How does one become a part of the Church? Solely and uniquely by the faith of the heart and obedience to the Word of God. . . . It is the obedience of faith which determines if one is a part of the Church" (Brunner, *Unser Glaube*, p. 142).

9. For more details on Jesus' teaching on the difference between the world and Christians, particularly as seen in John 17, see A. Kuen, *Que tous soient un*, p. 17, and the appendix of H. S. Bender in *These Are My People*, pp. 112-13.

10. One should reread what Blaise Pascal said concerning the difference between the primitive church and the church as it is today in *Les Opuscules* (parts 3-17): "Then one joined the Church only after much effort and a long, eager waiting period; now, without effort and concern, without any difficulty, one finds himself a member. Then one was admitted only after a very careful examination; now one is received before he is able to be examined. Then one was accepted only after he had sworn to renounce his past life, the world, the flesh, and the devil; now one becomes a member before he is of an age where he is able to do any of these things. Finally, formerly one had to leave the world to be received into the Church; today one enters the Church when he enters the world. Then, because of this method of proceeding, the essential distinction between the world and the Church was known. They were considered contrary the one to the other, two irreconcilable enemies, one of which does not cease to persecute the other, and the one which is apparently more feeble than the other will one day triumph over the stronger one, so one had to leave one of these contrary parties to enter the other . . . one left, abjured the world into which he had been born. . . . Now one finds himself in both groups at about the same time, and the moment he is born into the world he is reborn into the Church so that suddenly reason no longer makes a distinction between these two worlds which are so contrary . . . one now sees them intermingled so they are no longer discernible . . . the Church of the saints finds itself soiled by being constantly exposed to the wicked in their midst."

11. In an article entitled "That which is essential has been forgotten," Pastor Cadonau writes, "It is striking to see how little importance is attached to conversion and regeneration in the Church. She has resolutely left this aspect of the message to the sects and orders . . . nevertheless, one must recognize that this same conversion and regeneration are required in the Bible and in a way which shows they are not of minor importance. The call to repentance and conversion runs throughout the entire Bible . . . it is always a question of a personal decision which no one can avoid . . . the Church should recognize that her goal is to bring men to this new birth" (*Studium und Zeugnis*, no. 2 [1957], pp. 25-28 or *Gott hilft* no. 68). Professor E. Kellerhals of the Missionary Bible School in Basel says the same thing in his brochure *Bekehrung und Wiedergeburt*, p. 6: "It is necessary that we Christians of national churches should be clear today concerning this unquestionable Biblical truth. Indeed, we have too long permitted ourselves to be tempted to reject not only the words but also that which they represent and to consider them insignificant because of what we considered to be the erroneous and one-sided use of these words in the Pietist circles, in the "communities," among the Methodists, and in the Salvation Army. Yes, we have continued to harden ourselves against the call to conversion. The abuse of these words in other circles was our easy excuse to push far from us the thought of conversion and the new birth and to remain tranquilly the old Adam that we were. But the Bible, to which we like to refer, speaks very earnestly with a seriousness which we cannot fail to recognize, of the fact that conversion and the new birth are necessary for *all* men."

12. M. Goguel, *Le Problème de l'Eglise*, p. 12.
13. M. Bernouilli in *Vocabulaire biblique*.
14. Bender, p. 79.

15. Ibid., p. 81. See also the article "Mathetes" in G. Kittel, *Theol. Wörterb. N. T.,* vol. 4.
16. Regin Prenter, "L'Eglise d'après la confession d'Augsbourg" in *La Sainte Eglise Universelle,* p. 112.
17. P. Bonnard, *Vocabulaire biblique.*
18. See Bender, pp. 83, 119.
19. Ibid., p. 85.
20. See ibid., p. 67.
21. Ibid., pp. 51-52.
22. Even in the postapostolic period this name was given to believers only after their baptism (see Hermas, *Similitude IX,* 16.3; 19.2; Polycarp 6.3; Ignatius, *Eph.* 7:1).
23. Bender, p. 17. For the members see the article "melos" in Kittel's *Theologisches Wörterbuch N. T.,* 4:559-72.
24. Dean Nils Johansson, "Wer gehört zur urchristlichen Kirche?" in *Ein Buch von der Kirche.*
25. A. de Gasparin, *Les Ecoles du Doute et l'Ecole de la Foi,* p. 385.
26. Quoted by A. Keller, *Church and State on the European Continent,* p. 44.
27. In the first stages of its growth, darnel resembles wheat (Mt 13:23-43); it is found *among* the wheat (v. 25). But how did it get there? "While men were sleeping." So the presence of "weed Christians" in the church is due to a lack of vigilance. One argument against the exercise of church discipline is taken from the master's reply to his servants (not to root up the weeds). If this argument were true, Scripture would be contradicting itself, for, as we shall see farther on, this discipline is commanded in the Scripture. On the other hand, in the parable, to gather up the weeds represents eternal damnation; the harvesters who pull up the weeds at the close of the age (v. 39) are the angels, and the field from which they are pulled is the world (v. 38) and not the church.
28. It is true that in verse 1 of the following chapter we find: "We entreat you not to accept the grace of God in vain"; but even that does not permit us to conclude that the members of the church of Corinth were not converted, for:
    1. One can also translate it "not to have accepted the grace of God in vain" (J. Hering, *Comm. 2 Cor.,* p. 55), or in Williams' translation, "I beg you too not to accept God's favor and throw it away."
    2. The apostle is trying to tell them not to stop where they are or they will become "unfaithful to the grace of God; so it would be possible to have received it in vain" (Allo, *2 Cor.,* p. 173).
29. Gasparin, p. 390.
30. W. A. Visser't Hooft as quoted by F. H. Littell, *The Free Church,* p. 72.
31. "The primitive Church had an organization which enabled them to address themselves separately to listeners (not yet Christians) and to the community of believers. The Holy Communion, for example, is intended for the community of believers, but not for those on the periphery" (Brunner, *La Situation de l'Eglise,* pp. 22-23).
    W. Ninck also criticizes current preaching in the multitudinist churches, saying that, on the one hand, belonging to an age completely in the past (the old covenant) it has nothing to give believers; on the other hand, as its message has lost its power through politics, philosophy, and psychology, it is unable to lead to Christ one who is seeking Him. As it thinks the Christian truths are known, its preaching is too difficult, too moralizing, and too boring for those on the outside. (Ninck, *Christliche Gemeinde heute,* p. 94).
32. Brunner, *Dogmatics,* 3:53.
33. Erich Dinkler, *Religion in Geschichte und Gegenwart,* vol. 4, col. 629.
34. Justin Martyr, 1st *Apology,* 1:65-67.
35. Dean M. Simon, *Les Premiers Chrétiens,* p. 94.
36. Karl Barth, *The Teaching of the Church Regarding Baptism,* pp. 52-53.
37. Jalaguier, *De l'Eglise,* p. 74.
38. "In the Church of believers in the first centuries, the community of believers was gathered about the Holy Communion" (G. Hilbert, *Ecclesiola in ecclesia,* p. 88).
    "The sacramental meal—there can be no doubt about this—is that portion, or that form, of divine worship from which unbelievers were excluded. . . . It is es-

160 *I Will Build My Church*

pecially that, therefore, which constitutes the Christian community as such:
fellowship in and through Christ . . . the Ecclesia is constituted as the fellowship
of Christ" (Brunner, *The Misunderstanding of the Church*, pp. 64-65).
"In the Holy Communion the community presents itself simply as the church of
volunteers, as a community of professing believers. That is what God asks for
and He recognizes them as such" (Dietrich Bonhoeffer, *Sanctorum communio*,
3:186).
Bonhoeffer also speaks of unworthy participation in the Church as on a parallel
with unworthy participation in the Holy Communion. (M. Jacobs, *Evangelische
Lehre der Kirche*, p. 326).

39. "The Protestant commemoration of the Holy Communion is as far from that of
the primitive Church as is the Catholic eucharist with its dogma of transubstan-
tiation" (Karl Heim, *Die Gemeinde des Auferstandenen*, p. 171).
40. Hans Bruns, *Kleine Entdeckungsreise im N.T.*
41. Jacobs, p. 327.
42. John Calvin, *Institutes*, bk. 4, chap. 12, para. 1.
43. Brunner, *Le Renouveau de l'Eglise*, p. 25.
44. P. Lecomte, article in *Verbum Caro* (1958), p. 187.
45. Günther Harder, article in *Evang. Theol.* (1960), p. 72.
46. F. Hübner, *Weltreich und Gottesreich in Prophetie und Erfüllung*, p. 104.
47. Brunner as quoted by Desbaumes, *L'Eglise–Communauté*.
48. Barth, *Esquisse d'une Dogmatique*, p. 138.
49. Barth, *L'Eglise*, p. 63.
50. L. Newbigin, *L'Eglise*, p. 129.
51. See Søren Kierkegaard, *L'Instant*. A very important debate on the character of
the church, multitudinist or of professing believers, took place at the time of the
constitution of the confessional church of Germany in Hitler's times. See arguments developed in N. Glage, *Volkskirche oder Freikirche?* (1935); Burghard,
"Volkskirche, Freikirche," *Das Evangelische Deutschland* (1936), pp. 11-13;
M. Doene, "Was heisst Volkskirche?" *Theologia Militans*, vol. 1, (1935); J. Richter, "Volkskirche oder Freikirche?" *Christliche Welt* 51 (1937), cols. 723-26;
Barth, "Volkskirche, Freikirche, Bekennende Kirche," *Evangelische Theol.* 3
(1936): 411-22; Richter, "Volkskirche oder Kirche der Auserwählten," *Die
christliche Welt* 51 (1937), cols. 460-67; H. Asmussen, "Grundsätzliche Er-
wägungen zur Volkskirche," *Junge Kirche* (1935), pp. 288 ff. and (1939), p.
134; G. Mertz, "Volkskirche, Bekenntniskirche oder Volkstumskirche," *Junge
Kirche* (1934), pp. 784-90; G. Gloege, "Volkskirche, Freikirche oder Bekennende
Kirche," *Reformation oder Restauration* (1935), p. 50; Baumann, p. 68.
See the history of these struggles in the article by Harder, "Die Bedeutung der
Kirchengliedschaft im Kirchenkampf," *Evang. Theol.* (1960), pp. 70 ff.

For Further Reading

Blanke, F. "Wer gehört zur Gemeinde Gottes." In *Der Kirchenfreund* (1947), p. 1.
Mess, F. "Wer gehört der Kirche an?" In *Archiv des öffentlichen Rechts.* Neue Folge
10, 1926.
Schmitz, O. "Die Grenze der Gemeinde nach dem N.T." *Evang. Theol.* 14(1954):
6 ff.
Slenczka, R. "Die Grenzen der Kirche" in *Zeitwende* (1959), pp. 685-91.
Valeske, Ulrich. *Votum Ecclesiae.* For the Protestant and Roman Catholic concepts
of church membership, see 1:66-97.

11

Baptism and the Constitution of the Church

BAPTISM HAS ALWAYS OCCUPIED an important place in the thinking of the church; the New Testament mentions it more than a hundred times, often in connection with the formation of the church. From the first centuries it was the center of the most heated controversies. Even today it remains a major theme of theological research and ecclesiastical debates. The ecumenical evolution will depend to a great extent on the answer that is given to this problem.

The ties between baptism and the structure of the church are evident. Francus certainly is not exaggerating when he writes, "On the whole, it is on the question of baptism where the separation takes place between those who hold to the materialistic view of religion and the faithful who worship in spirit and in truth. The attitude adopted concerning it divides people into these two categories: the formalists and the spiritually minded."[1]

Günther Harder also confirms it: "The practice of infant baptism makes a church virtually a church of the masses. . . . The basis of infant baptism is in any case the same as that of multitudinism; it begins with the principle that the whole world must be taken by force for Christ."[2]

G. Steinheil observes, "If infant baptism is legitimate, so is the National Church."[3]

Karl Barth affirms concisely: "Infant baptism is the symptom of a very serious sickness from which the Church is suffering and which is multitudinism."

Emil Brunner expresses his thoughts in much the same way: "Catholic Baptismal doctrine which, of course, finds nothing objectionable in Infant Baptism is not only easily compatible with the Catholic conception of the Church, but is actually demanded by it."[4]

Elsewhere he writes,

> This question of baptism of children is not a single question in the large complex of Church problems, but rather is decisive for the entire churchly practice, since baptism is the basis for Church membership. He who has been baptized in the Lutheran or Reformed congregation belongs

161

to the Lutheran or Reformed Church. The host of correctly baptized persons who within and without the Church have been completely alienated from it must therefore be reckoned as belonging to the Church. . . . Objectivism in the concepts of sacrament and Church led to an expansion altogether too rapid which immediately must become manifest in directly tragic measures.[5]

That is indeed what the Scotch theologian *Geddes MacGregor* says: "Lack of comprehension of baptism stems from an even more serious lack, that of failure to understand the nature of the church."[6]

We shall limit ourselves to giving just a few facts:

1. Christian baptism is right in line with the symbolical acts of the apostles and the Jewish ritual baths.

2. The dissident groups of Bas-Judaism (Essenians of Qumran, a community of the New Alliance of Damascus) attached a particular importance to the ablutions. The postulant of Qumran, for example, had to submit to various ritual baths after two years of probation and a confession of sins in order to be admitted into the community.

3. The existence of the baptism of Jewish proselytes cannot be found before the second half of the first century of our era. So one cannot prove its influence on Christian baptism.

4. John the Baptist baptized adults who came to him, repented, and confessed their sins.

5. Jesus was baptized by John at the age of thirty.

6. His disciples baptized those who were ready to follow Jesus.

7. "John also was baptizing at Aenon near Salim, for there was plenty of water there" (Jn 3:23). "At once after His baptism Jesus came up from the water" (Mt 3:16). All the baptisms spoken of in the gospel are by immersion.

8. The apostles practiced this form of baptism (see Ac 8:36-39; Ro 6:3-5; Col 2:12).

9. The word *baptizo* always signifies to immerse, to plunge, to submerge.

10. The patristic allusions to baptism prove that baptism was always practiced by immersion except in circumstances outside of one's control.

11. History teaches us that up to the fourteenth century—the seventeenth in England—baptism by immersion rather than by sprinkling was preferred.[7]

12. The many baptistries in the form of tanks (they were built that way until the twelfth century) show that for centuries adults were baptized by immersion.

13. Theologians are unanimous in affirming that the early practice was baptism by immersion.

14. Immersion was discontinued because it was no longer the practice to baptize adult believers. "When infant baptism became a general practice in the eighth century, little by little the impractical installations were abandoned and the shallow font was substituted for the tank," writes Dom Cabrol.[8]

Should we have infant baptism or baptism of believing adults? This question plays a role of prime importance in the establishment or constitution of the church and must therefore be examined in greater detail.

BAPTISM IN THE ACTS: THOSE WHO WERE BAPTIZED

The book of Acts relates how the disciples of Jesus Christ carried out the orders and directives of their Master. Before leaving them, the Lord had communicated to them His last wishes: "Go, therefore, and make disciples of all the nations, baptizing them in the name of the Father, and of the Son, and of the Holy Spirit, teaching them to observe everything that I have commanded you" (Mt 28:19-20).

The first Christians not only respected the commands of their Master, but they observed them in the order given by Jesus:

1. "Make disciples": that is the purpose of apostolic preaching, missionary voyages,' conversations with individuals, Jews and Greeks.

2. "Baptizing them": *them* refers to the new disciples. (Consult again what was said concerning the precise meaning of this word in the New Testament.)

3. "Teaching them [these disciples] to observe everything that I have commanded you."

BAPTISMS IN THE BOOK OF ACTS

On the day of Pentecost the apostles carried out the Master's commands for the first time (Ac 2).

"Make disciples"   "Repent . . . you will receive the gift of the Holy Spirit. . . . 'Be saved from this crooked generation'" (vv. 31-40).

"of all the nations"   "Parthians, Medes, Elamites and residents of Mesopotamia, Judea, and Cappadocia, Pontus and Asia, Phrygia and Pamphylia, Egypt and the parts of Libya belonging to Cyrene, and visitors from Rome, both Jews and proselytes, Cretans and Arabians" (v. 10).

"baptizing them"	"Be baptized every one of you in the name of Jesus Christ. . . . So those who received his word were baptized, and there were added that day about three thousand souls" (vv. 38, 41).
"teaching them to observe everything that I have commanded you."	"They devoted themselves to the apostles' teaching . . . and day by day, attending the temple together . . ." (vv. 42-46).

Baptism occupies a relatively important place in the book of Acts: some twenty passages speak of it. The apostles spoke of it in their preaching and new believers were baptized immediately after their conversion:

The Samaritans. "But *when they [the Samaritans] believed* Philip as he told the good news of the kingdom of God and of the name of Jesus Christ, *they were baptized, men as well as women.* Even Simon himself *believed* and, upon his baptism, kept close to Philip" (Ac 8:12-13). Certainly there were children in Samaria. However, they were not baptized since, in addition to the condition "when they believed," the text specifies that "both men and women" were baptized (*andres te kai gunaikes*).

The Ethiopian eunuch. "Proceeding on the road, they came to some water and the eunuch said, 'See, here is water. What is to prevent my being baptized?' (Ac 8:36). Philip assured him, 'If you heartily believe, it is permitted.' And he replied, 'I believe that Jesus Christ is the Son of God.' So he ordered the chariot to halt, and both Philip and the eunuch went down into the water and he baptized him" (Ac 8:37-38).[9]

The apostle Paul. Ananias said to him: "Now then, why hesitate? Rise; be baptized and, calling on His name, be cleansed of your sins." "He arose and was baptized" (Ac 22:16; 9:18).

Cornelius and his household. "Cornelius had invited his relatives and intimate friends. '. . . all who believe in Him receive forgiveness of sins through His name.' While Peter was still saying these things the Holy Spirit fell upon all who listened to the message. Then Peter answered, 'Would anyone refuse the water for their baptism, since they have received the Holy Spirit as we ourselves did?' So he directed them to be baptized in the name of Jesus Christ" (Ac 10:24, 43-44, 47-48).

There again, they certainly did not baptize infants, since the account tells us that those who were baptized heard the Word, spoke in tongues, and glorified God.[10]

Lydia and her household. "And a certain woman named Lydia, from the city of Thyatira, a seller of purple fabrics, a worshiper of God, was listening; and the Lord opened her heart to respond to the things spoken by Paul. And when she and her household had been baptized, she urged us, saying, 'If you have judged me to be faithful to the Lord, come into my house and stay'" (Ac 16:14-15, NASB). "And they went out of the prison and entered the house of Lydia, and when they saw the brethren, they encouraged them and departed" (v. 40, NASB).

Were there small children in Lydia's household? Nothing in Scripture permits that assertion. We do not even know if Lydia was married. The term household (*oïkos*) used here designates the servants and slaves as well as members of the family.[11] Moreover, verse 40 specifies those who were in the house: "when they had seen the brethren." One must sorely need to find little children in order to find them in Lydia's home!

The Philippian jailer and his family. "'Believe in the Lord Jesus, and you shall be saved, you and your household.' And they spoke the word of the Lord to him *together with all who were in his house*. And he took them that very hour of the night, and washed their wounds, and immediately *he was baptized, he and all his household*. And he brought them into his house and set food before them, and rejoiced greatly, having believed in God with his whole household" (Ac 16:3-34, NASB) or "He and all the members of his household were happy in their faith in God" (v. 34, Williams).

Were there infants in the family who were baptized with the jailer? If so, they were awakened in the middle of the night so Paul could preach to them the Word of the Lord (v. 32) and they rejoiced with the jailer because they had believed in God (v. 34).

The disciples at Corinth. "Crispus, the leader of the synagogue, *believed* in the Lord *with all his household*, and many of the Corinthians when they heard were *believing and being baptized*" (Ac 18:8, NASB).

If Crispus was baptized with his whole family, it was because his whole family believed in the Lord. Another family in Corinth was baptized by Paul: "I did baptize also the household of Stephanas" (1 Co 1:16, NASB) but at the close of the letter he gives more details: "You know the household of Stephanas, that they were the firstfruits of Achaia, and that they have devoted themselves for ministry to the saints" (1 Co 16:15, NASB). "Infants cannot be called first-fruits or first converts, nor can they devote themselves to the service of the saints."[12]

The twelve disciples at Ephesus. "Paul . . . met some disciples, whom he asked, 'Did you receive the Holy Spirit on your becoming believers? . . . Into what, then, were you baptized?' They said, 'Into John's baptism.' Paul added, 'John baptized with the baptism of repentance, telling the people that they should believe in the One who was to come after him, that is, in Jesus.' On hearing this, they were baptized in the name of the Lord Jesus. . . . Altogether there were about a dozen men" (Ac 19:2-7).

> These twelve men were baptized (immersed, submerged) twice, because they had not been correctly instructed. It is the same today, after inaccurate teaching, many people have been "sprinkled" with a few drops of water or even really baptized (that is, plunged into the water, immersed) while yet infants. Now that they are really converted, by the grace of God, these children of God face the problem of their baptism. The reply is quite simple. The example of these twelve men at Ephesus is quite clear and was not given to us without reason. These men did not hesitate a moment to be rebaptized.[13]

In the case of infant baptism, one cannot truly speak of two baptisms since the first ceremony did not correspond in the least to the baptism of the Bible. The world of trade would never permit a label or a designating name which is closely inspected and controlled to be thus wrongfully used. He who is dedicated as an infant and sprinkled with a few drops of water cannot say that he is baptized in the biblical sense. When he experiences a personal faith, nothing should hinder or excuse him from obeying the command of the Lord and His apostles.

CONCLUSIONS, DRAWN FROM ACTS, CONCERNING BAPTISM

Thus, all the people who were baptized and identified in the book of Acts were adult believers. No specific case is given of infant baptism. Those who favor pedobaptism are compelled to suppose that the households baptized included children too young to have a personal faith. We have seen details given concerning these households which greatly weaken this position. Would it not be better to admit, as do many theologians from churches that practice infant baptism, that "all traces of infant baptism that have allegedly been discovered in the New Testament have actually been read into it (*müssen erst hineingetragen werden*)," as Prof. D. Fr. Schleiermacher puts it. "The practice of infant baptism begins at the end of the second century," says A. Harnack, "no proof has been found that it was practiced earlier."[14]

IS INFANT BAPTISM FOUND IN THE NEW TESTAMENT?

Listen to theologians who are members of churches that practice pedobaptism:

Herzogs Realenzyklopädie: "As a result obtained by scientific exegesis it can indeed be considered that there was no infant baptism in the New Testament."

Professor D. Feine of Breslau: "No record of infant baptism in apostolic and post-apostolic times can be found."[15]

Professor D. Drews: "We have no sure testimony concerning infant baptism during the time of the apostles. Every time that anyone has tried to find scriptural proof for the same he has wasted his time."

Karl Barth: "From the standpoint of a doctrine of baptism, infant-baptism can hardly be preserved without exegetical and practical artifices and sophisms—the proof to the contrary has yet to be supplied: One wants to preserve it only if one is resolved to do so on grounds which lie outside the Biblical passages on baptism and on the practice itself. The determination to defend it on extraneous grounds has certainly found expression from century to century."[16]

The conclusion reached by the Lutheran Professor Kurt Aland after intensive study of infant baptism is that there is no definite proof of its practice until after the third century. This, he believes, cannot be contested.[17]

Here are the conclusions of some Anglican theologians:

H. T. Andrews: "There is not the slightest real proof that baptism was ever administered to children during the apostolic era."[18]

P. T. Forsyth: "The origin of infant baptism is obscure . . . it is not found in the New Testament."[19]

J. R. Nelson: "That the New Testament says nothing explicitly about the baptism of little children is incontestable."[20]

A Catholic professor of theology, O. Heggelbacher, writes: "This controversy has shown that it is not possible to bring in absolute proof of infant baptism by basing one's argument on the Bible without the help of Tradition."[21]

And even Professor O. Cullmann, one of the few present-day theologians who try to defend infant baptism, is obliged to admit that "from sources which are available to us we conclude that it is in vain to question whether the primitive Church did or did not baptize newborn babies. The writings of the New Testament do not permit us to give any reply to this question, whether negative or positive, and it could be desired that everyone would yield to this evidence."[22]

We admire the sincerity of these acknowledgments but remain somewhat perplexed by the conclusion reached by the theologian from this state of affairs: "But the question of infant baptism should not rest on scriptural affirmation."[23] We used to think that for the churches of the Reformation the Bible remained "the supreme authority in matters of faith."[24] We will make progress in our study only if we accept as the fundamental principle what Markus Barth affirms from the beginning of his book on baptism, that the New Testament is the "norm by which all church doctrine should be measured."[25]

THE BAPTISM OF BELIEVERS IN THE NEW TESTAMENT

The New Testament contains no proof of baptism for infants or unbelievers; on the contrary, it often stresses that faith must precede baptism (Ac 8:12, 35-37; 10:34-48; 16:14-15, 29-33; 18:26; 19:4-5).

O. Cullmann concedes that the sequence "preaching . . . faith . . . baptism" is found in most of the cases related in the New Testament. It is quite true that the baptism of adults who have come out of Judaism or paganism, that is, the only ones which are clearly related in the texts, almost regularly give an opportunity to those to be baptized to confess their faith,[26] and in his studies on the earliest Christian confession he recognizes that "the developed confession of faith has its fixed place at several points in the baptismal ceremony."[27]

Heitmüller writes: "It is evident that faith is a condition which precedes baptism. Only those who believed were baptized."[28]

Rendtorff says: "It is an established historical fact that the basic presupposition of all that Paul said concerning baptism was faith."[29]

The Anglicans frankly admit that the original baptism was that of believers. As early as 1662 the *Prayer Book* contained this question and answer: "What are the conditions imposed on individuals who wish to be baptized? *Repentance*, by which they forsake sin, and faith, by which they firmly believe God's promises." So then the only way they justified the baptism of infants was by saying the requirements are met in the person of the *sponsors* (godparents).

"The New Testament references to Initiation assume that its recipients are adults," writes N. P. Williams, "and that the dispositions required of them are those of conscious and deliberate renunciation of sin and idols, and of personal faith in and allegiance to Christ."[30]

"Every expression in the New Testament concerning the rites of baptism assumes that the convert receives them with living faith and a renunciation of his old former life," says the report of the united Anglican committees on baptism, confirmation, and communion.[31] In the 1955 report the same committees concluded: "It is clear that the New Testament doctrine of baptism is established with reference to the baptism of adults. With two or three exceptions, the writers of the first three centuries are of the same opinion. In each case related to us in the New Testament, the Gospel had been heard and accepted, the condition of faith (and probably repentance) was conscientiously met by the one to be baptized before he received the sacrament."[32] The 1959 report confirmed: "In the New Testament the baptism of adults is the norm and it is only in the light of this fact that the doctrine and the practice of baptism can be understood."[33]

Even the present archbishop of Canterbury wrote: "The apostolic practice was the admission of adults into the Church and their anointing by the Holy Spirit in the rites closely connected to baptism and confirmation: *by faith.*"[34]

There are even Catholic theologians such as J. Bellamy, who declares, "We have wondered if Scripture also included infants among those baptized. It is certain that they are not expressly mentioned. . . . It is possible that Scripture chooses to mention only the baptism of adults on account of the natural dispositions which Scripture implies are found as a rule among those who are baptized."[35] This rule was maintained during the postapostolic period and it was only near the beginning of the fourth century that infant baptism began to replace the baptism of believers.

The Reformers rediscovered biblical baptism; but, for reasons which they considered to be only temporary, they did not introduce it in the churches of the Reformation. At present, after four centuries of Protestant tradition, it seems difficult to put into practice what they desired; however, Christians and theologians in greater and greater numbers declare themselves in favor of reestablishing the primitive baptism which was instituted by Jesus Christ and which was practiced by the first church.

We conclude this chapter by supporting what has just been said with several quotations from the church Fathers, from Christians of the Middle Ages, from Reformers, and from present-day theologians and Christians in favor of the baptism of believers.

TESTIMONIES IN FAVOR OF THE BAPTISM OF BELIEVERS

TESTIMONIES OF THE CHURCH FATHERS

In his reply to Emser in 1521, Luther wrote, "Christian controversy should be based on Scripture. The teaching of the Fathers should be used only to lead to the Scripture, for that was their source, and then let Holy Scripture alone be the support."

Clement of Rome. "When the apostles had received their commission . . . they departed filled with the joy of the Holy Spirit to announce the Good News that the Kingdom of God was near at hand. In villages and cities they preached and baptized those who were obedient to the will of God."[36]

Ebionite, Gospel of the Twelve. "When our Lord sent us to ignorant people to baptize them for the forgiveness of sins, He commanded us to instruct them first."[37]

Only in about the year 125 do we learn that they also baptized older children when they had been instructed and had become Christians.[38]

The Didaché. "Before baptism, both the one who is to be baptized and the one administering the sacrament should fast . . . ask the one who is baptized to fast one or two days . . ." (7:4). And The Didaché also required preliminary instruction for baptism: "Baptize in this manner after having taught all which precedes."

The Epistle of Barnabas (c. A.D. 100–105). "Blessed are those who have descended into the baptismal waters having placed their hope in the cross, for we go down into the waters covered with sins and stains, and we come up out of the waters bearing in our hearts the fruit of fear and having in our spirit the hope of Jesus by the Holy Spirit" (11:8, 11). The author of the epistle requires confession of repentance before the baptism (16:9). For Justin Martyr also, besides faith and the promise to live as a Christian, repentance is a requirement for baptism.[39]

Aristides (beginning of 2d century). "Servants, men as well as women, or children, if a Christian has any, are taught so they may become Christians, because they are loved by the master. And when they become Christians, he calls them his brothers without discrimination."[40] Baptism of infants, even though they may be from Christian families, is not permitted, according to Aristides.[41]

Hermas (c. A.D. 142). "Baptism is a seal, the seal of the sons of God; this sign is the water into which men descend, debtors of death only to come up out of the water as heirs of life." "It is by faith that the elect are saved, but baptism is necessary for salvation."

Justin Martyr (d A.D. 165). "All those who permit themselves to be convinced of the truth of our teachings and of our doctrine have faith and the promise that they will have the strength to live according to the teachings. Then we teach them to pray and to ask for the remission of sins during the fast. . . . Then they are led by us to the place where the water is . . . they are then washed in the water. . . . This ablution is called illumination because those who receive the doctrine have their spirits illumined . . . he who submits to immersion should feel within himself the strength to master himself."[42]

"We say to you that this baptism possesses the virtue of purifying men— on condition that they repent."[43] Therefore baptism follows repentance; it is preceded by teaching and accompanied by the promise of the new convert. "Our natural birth comes about without our will, our new birth with our willing participation."[44] Following that quotation are a

few short formal statements which were to be repeated "in the water."
He wrote, "Isaiah, even in his day, spoke of . . . this salutary bath for
those who are converted and purify themselves . . . it was the baptismal
bath which alone can purify those who repent."[45]

Tertullian. For Tertullian, baptism is an *obsignatio fidei*, the seal of
faith personally accepted (paean 6). That is why he says we must preach
first, then baptize.[46] He says expressly that the one being baptized confesses his faith by going down into the water and by answering the questions asked.[47] It is in his works that we find the first allusion to infant
baptism.[48] In order to condemn it, he cites it as a practice recently
introduced in the church:

> It is true that Our Lord said in speaking of children: "Let the children
> come to me, and do not hinder them." Let them "come" therefore as they
> grow older; let them come when they are able to learn, when they can
> be instructed whither they should "come" so they may understand to what
> they are engaging themselves. Why does the age of innocence hasten to
> the remission of sins? One acts with more wisdom in worldly things. One
> must accept a person for baptism when he has learned to seek salvation
> and when one can give him that for which he is asking. . . . Those who
> understand the seriousness of baptism will be more fearful of administer-
> ing it too early than too late. Sincere faith alone gives assurance of salva-
> tion.[49]

A *third-century* baptismal questionnaire has been preserved: "Dost thou
believe with thy whole heart in God almighty, the Father . . . and in
Jesus Christ, His Son . . . and in the Holy Ghost . . . ?"[50] Cyprian's Letter
70 of the Council of Carthage alludes to a question asked of the candidate
for baptism: "Do you believe in eternal life and in the remission of
sins . . . ?"

This confession had to be free and voluntary or it had no validity: "He
who was baptized during an illness could not be ordained as a priest;
for it was not a spontaneous resolve but from fear of death that he made
the profession."[51]

Christians of the first century required the candidate for baptism to be
fully conscious at the moment of baptism. "If, even in the famous
mysteries of Eleusis, admitting to initiation one who was not conscious
was forbidden," writes the Catholic Dr. O. Heggelbacher, "how much
more so should a request for baptism be free from everything which
could limit its voluntary character."

Gregory of Nazianzus says that one should ask to be baptized while
he is still in possession of his faculties. In the same way, Basil of Caesarea
warns a person not to wait until he has a fever which would prevent
him from being fully conscious at the time of his baptism.[53]

The frescos in the catacombs have sometimes been put forward to prove that children were baptized in the first centuries. But as F. Lovsky says, "Only baptism of adults was known to Christian art. . . . Any appeal to primitive Christian iconography to support pedobaptism is untenable."[54]

Origen (*c*. 240) and *Cyprian* (d. 258): Both considered baptism as absolutely essential for salvation, and supported infant baptism. But "in the third century, infant baptism was not generally and incontestably established."[55]

"It was not until the time of Constantine that infant baptism definitely triumphed," writes Secrétan, "when the Catholic Church became the State Church, the official Church of the Roman Empire."[56] In the middle of the fourth century, however, many children of Christian parents were not baptized before reaching adult age. Gregory of Nyssa whose father was a bishop (330) was baptized at the age of twenty-nine years; Basil of Caesarea (*c*. 330) was twenty-seven; Ambrose (b. 333) was forty; Rufinus of Aquilea (b. 340) was thirty-one; John Chrysostom (344) was twenty; Jerome (Hieronymous) (b. 347 in Dalmatia) was eighteen;[57] and there were others: Pauline of Nôle (b. 353 in Bordeaux), Augustine (b. 354), etc.

Basil the Great (d. 379) said: "One must first be a disciple of Christ and later be judged capable of receiving holy baptism."[58]

"The Edict of Justinian (527-65) made infant baptism a state law that had to be observed unless one wished to risk persecution."[59]

"From the fifth century to the eighth," says Lovsky, "children were baptized at the age of two or three years (except in cases when there was danger of an earlier death); from the eighth century to the tenth, children were one year of age. It was not until the eleventh century that infant baptism became a common practice."[60]

How can one explain the introduction of infant baptism in the church of the third century? Professor K. Aland gives two reasons: considerable growth in the numbers of the children of Christians at the beginning of the third century, and theological evolution. In the first century the Christians thought that newborn children were innocent, "holy" (1 Co 7:14), without sin. There are numerous quotations which would prove that the apostolic Fathers also believed this (e.g., Barnabas 6:11; Hermas, *Mandate* 2, chap. 1; *Similitude* 9, chap. 29; Aristides, *Apology* 15:11; Athenagoras [*c*. 180], *De resurrectione mort.* 14). The inscriptions on tombstones of children of Christians always bear the attributes: *innocens, innocentissime*. "They did not baptize infants because they considered them to be 'saints' or holy. The ancient Church held this position until the end of the second century. It was abandoned for reasons of theological order. As long as the Church took for granted that children of Christians were holy, it did not baptize them. From the very moment when this presupposition was considered erroneous, she began to require and introduce infant baptism."[61]

In the time of Augustine the starting point of reasoning was reversed. In his anti-Pelagian writings, he depends upon infant baptism to prove the dogma of original sin: "If children are not born sinners, why would one baptize them?"

Conclusions. Experts have arrived at these conclusions:

"In the entire New Testament we do not find the slightest allusion to the baptism of a newborn child . . . ," says Professor E. Menegoz, "even in the third century the Church was not at all uniform in its practice. . . . If the apostles had ordered infant baptism and had practiced it consistently and regularly, it would certainly have been continued by their successors and there would have been no differences of opinion in the Church."[62]

According to F. Lovsky, "The strict historical method is to emphasize that no written indications have been found to bear witness to the baptism of infants or little children during the first three or four Christian generations."[63]

Professor Kurt Aland, a learned exegete and historian of world reputation, a Lutheran by conviction and also a supporter of infant baptism, showed in his book that "no one can show proof of a case of infant baptism before the year 200. All passages from earlier sources tell only of the baptism of adults. This conclusion is incontestable."[64] He also said, "Definite testimonies in favor of the practice of infant baptism do not occur until after the third century."[65]

F. H. Kettler comments, "Until about the year 400 the baptism of adults was predominant; until the second half of the second century it was, so to speak, exclusive."[66]

TESTIMONIES OF CHRISTIANS FROM THE MIDDLE AGES

In the Middle Ages the baptism of adults was found only in a few groups such as the Paulicians or the Waldenses, who had remained faithful to the teachings of the New Testament. An Armenian book, *The Key of Truth*, written between the seventh and ninth centuries and describing the customs of the Paulicians, reads:

> Our Lord requires repentance and faith first; then comes baptism. We should therefore obey Him and not give in to the deceitful arguments of those who baptize the unconverted, unconscious, and impenitent. At the

time of the birth of a child, the elders of the Church should exhort the parents to bring him up in godliness and faith.

The Lord has taught us not to confer baptism on a person until he has reached the age of maturity. Consequently, following the words of the Lord, we should first lead him to the faith and to repentance before baptizing him.

No one should be baptized unless he has expressed a sincere desire to be. Baptism will take place in a river or at least out in the open air. The candidate for baptism shall kneel out in the water and fervently confess his faith before the assembled congregation. Prayer and Scripture reading will accompany this act.[67]

During this same period Charlemagne decreed his capitularies: "Every Saxon who is not baptized and refuses to be, wishing to remain a pagan shall be put to death. All children will have to be baptized within the year. Whoever shall neglect to present a child for baptism in the course of the year without the advice or excuse of a priest, shall pay to the treasury a fine of 120 gold sols if he is of noble birth; 60 sols if he is a simple man."[68]

In the doctrine of the Bohemian Brethren, baptism is of believers: "According to Lukas, justification and the new birth, brought about by God Himself, and faith, which is from the human side, must precede baptism. The purpose of baptism is twofold: to witness to justification by faith and assurance of salvation and to bring the new convert into the spiritual body of the Church."[69]

TESTIMONIES OF THE REFORMERS

The Reformers rediscovered the baptism of believers in the Bible and spoke out in favor of it.

Luther. In 1518 Luther wrote, "He who has faith, possesses; he who does not have faith, will profit nothing even from the sacrament."

In the *Babylonian Captivity of the Church* (1520) he said:

> God said: "He who believes and is baptized will be saved." . . . On this promise, if we receive it with faith, depends all our salvation. If we believe, our heart is strengthened by the divine promise. . . . Unless this faith is present or conferred in baptism, baptism profits us nothing,—nay, it becomes a hindrance to us, not only in the moment of its reception, but all the days of our life. . . . The efficacy of sacraments depends on faith and not on the visible rite. Thus, baptism justifies no one and helps no one; but the Word of God, which is in and with the water, and faith, which trusts this Word of God in the water, justifies and accomplishes that which baptism signifies.

In his *Large Catechism* he again says: "Baptism without faith is only a symbol devoid of any efficacy (*ein blosses wirkungsloses Zeichen*).

Those who are baptized without faith receive simple water, not the Spirit."

Baptism must continue to be linked with repentance and faith.[70] In 1525, in his sermon for the third Sunday after the Epiphany, he violently attacked those who baptize children even while convinced that the children do not personally believe:

Romans 10: Faith comes from what is heard, and what is heard comes by the preaching of Christ. Young children neither hear nor understand the Word of God; therefore neither can they have a personal faith. To this objection the Sophists of the schools of philosophy and the Pope's party made up this answer: young children are baptized without a personal faith, on the faith of the church which is confessed by the godparents. Even so the infant is transformed, cleansed, and renewed by the imparted personal faith through His grace, so he is transformed into a child newly born of water and of the Holy Spirit.

However, one is not enlightened by asking them on what they base their arguments and what Scripture supports them. They only show us their academic insignia and say: "It is we, the learned doctors, who say so; therefore it is true, and you need question no further." Almost all of their doctrines have no other authority than their own dreams and imaginations. And even if they do their utmost to answer you, they may present a quotation or two from St. Augustine or take some other far fetched argument from another Church Father. But that is not sufficient when it is a matter of the salvation of souls, since they are themselves, like all other Church Fathers, only poor human beings. Who will answer to me for their infallibility? Who wishes to place his full trust in their word and die with faith in nothing but their affirmations which have no basis in Scripture, the Word of God? Of what importance are saints to me? When it is a matter of losing or saving my soul for all eternity, I cannot rely on angels or saints, even less on one or two saints if they do not produce the authority of the Word of God.

Starting from this falsehood, they continued their reasoning and even went so far as to teach, what they maintain even today, that there is such virtue in sacraments that, even if you have no faith when receiving them, you obtain all the same grace and pardon for sins.

This they deduce from the preceding opinion, claiming that young children receive grace, without believing, only by the efficacy of baptism; that is purely the result of their imagination. . . .

Protect yourself from such poison and error, even if that was the explicit and unanimous opinion of all the Fathers and all Councils, for such an opinion cannot hold; it is not based upon the Scripture and rests only upon human dreams and vain subtleties. Moreover, it is in absolute contradiction to the essential Bible quotation in which Christ says: "He who believes and is baptized will be saved." In short, baptism without faith is of no value so should not be administered to anyone unless he believes: without a personal faith no one should be baptized. Saint Augustine also said this: it is not the sacrament which justifies but faith in the sacrament.

There are others . . . who deem it necessary that each man have a personal faith and receive baptism or the sacrament with a personal

faith, if not, neither baptism nor sacrament is of any value to him.
Up to that point they are perfectly right. But to continue to baptize little
children who have no personal faith, as they are doing, is to mock holy
baptism and sin against the commandment which enjoins us not to use
knowingly and wilfully the name of God in vain. Their pretext of baptizing children by virtue of the faith they will have, when in the future
they will have a personal faith, is valueless. For faith must be present before baptism or, in any case, at the time of baptism. If not, the child is
not liberated from the devil and sins. So if their opinion was correct,
everything practiced in the baptism of infants would be nothing but lies
and blasphemy. The person baptizing asks: "Does the child believe?"
and someone answers in the affirmative in his place. "Does he wish to be
baptized?" Again the answer is given in the affirmative for him. However,
no one is baptized in his place; the infant himself is baptized.

That is why he should believe also. If this is not so, the godparents lie
when they answer for him: "I believe."—Just the same way the one baptizing proclaims the child regenerated, his sins pardoned, and that he is
freed from the devil. . . . He behaves toward him as toward a new child
of the holy God.

All that would be nothing but untruth if there were no personal faith,
and it would be better to never again baptize an infant than to mock and
make fun of God's words and sacrament as if He were some idol or clown.
That is why if we cannot prove that infants can believe and have a personal faith, it is my personal counsel and judgment that one abstain from
it as early as possible and that infants never again be baptized so as not to
ridicule or blaspheme God's holy Majesty with such unfounded impos-
tures and antics.[71]

In his *Deutsche Messe und Gottesdienstordnung* (1526) he contem-
plated practicing baptism correctly in "private assemblies" (*Sonderge-
meinden*) that he intended to organize in "better days"; then

> those who wish to be serious Christians and profess the Gospel in word
> and deed would sign a list made out to this effect and, far from the mixed
> assembly, would gather in a house for prayer and Bible reading, to cele-
> brate baptism, to receive the Holy Communion and practice other Chris-
> tian works. . . . If there were these people who seriously wished to be
> Christians, the rest would follow naturally. But I neither can nor wish to
> establish such a church or assembly because I have not as yet the persons
> for the same.[72]

Elsewhere the Augsburg Confession says: "The sacraments demand our
faith, and one makes salutary use of them when he receives them with
faith." But later, in a struggle against the Illuminist group of the Anabaptists, Luther defends infant baptism by quoting church tradition. He
writes to Melanchthon: "Besides, what does the Church confess? Here
is a question of fact and not of right. There can be no discussion if the
Church must believe that faith is imparted during infant baptism, for
there is no text which constrains us to believe that. What should we do?

We have the profession. What does the Church profess?"[73] He had recognized that faith is, of necessity, to precede baptism; and here he is led into upholding infant baptism. So he can justify it only by assuming that faith is instilled in (that is, poured into the soul quite naturally) the newborn child[74] and this by attributing to the church the *opus operatum* (regeneration effected by the sacrament). Besides the Scripture, he here admits another source of revelation: the profession of the church, that is, tradition.[75]

So, for the sake of infant baptism, Luther overthrew, without realizing it, both justification by faith and the sovereign authority of the Scripture which he had set up as the very principles of the Reformation. He fell back into Roman sacramentalism by affirming that the water of baptism "frees us from sin, death, and all misfortune, helps us to have access to heaven and eternal life. Thus it has become a precious syrup, an *aromaticum* and a medicine . . . because God is in that water, it must of necessity be the true *aqua vitae*, which destroys death and hell and gives eternal life."[76]

So it is not astonishing to find in Lutheran dogmatics certain phrases which strangely remind one of the Catholic doctrine of the sacraments: "Very aptly our dogmaticians have called Baptism 'a means of justification.' . . . Baptism . . . works the forgiveness of sins . . . it sanctifies and purifies, . . . regenerates and saves. . . . In fact, Baptism confers all divine spiritual blessings. . . . 'By the Word such power is imparted to Baptism that it is a laver of regeneration.' (Luther) The effect of the Word and of the rite is the same."[77]

Calvin. On the question of baptism, Calvin follows somewhat the same steps as Luther. In chapters 14 and 15 of book 4 of his *Institutes* he presents a baptism which is truly faithful to the texts of the New Testament. He strongly insists upon the ideas of "the consciousness of the one to be baptized, of his understanding of the significance of the symbolical act, and of his understanding and faith without which the sacrament is inexistent."[78]

> What is the sacrament without faith, unless it is the destruction of the Church? . . . [Baptism] serves as our confession before men, inasmuch as it is a mark by which we openly declare that we wish to be ranked among the people of God, by which we testify that we concur with all Christians in the worship of one God, and in one religion; by which, in short, we publicly assert our faith. . . . To this Paul referred when he asked the Corinthians whether or not they had been baptized in the name of Christ (I Cor. 1:13); intimating that by the very circumstance of having been baptized in His name, they had devoted themselves to Him, had sworn and bound themselves in allegiance to Him before men,

so that they could no longer confess any other than Christ alone, unless
they would abjure the confession which they had made in baptism.[79]
    For it is God's will that all who have believed be baptized for the re-
mission of sins. . . . We are to receive it in connection with the promise,
"He that believeth and is baptized shall be saved" (Mark 16:16).[80]
    Let us realize then that we are baptized with this understanding: that
we are to give ourselves wholly to our God.[81]

"The Calvinist doctrine postulates the baptism of only believers," says
Dr. A. Lamorte.[82] However, in the same book (chap. 16) Calvin defends
infant baptism. Why?

    The reasons for the conflict between his doctrine of the sacrament and
    his method of baptism are summed up by him in five words: "the peace
    of the Church." . . . Not being able to abandon a doctrine which he held
    as being scriptural, at a crucial period in the religious history of the
    world, at the hour when minds were very restless, caught between the
    errors of secular Romanism and the anarchical subjectivism of the Ana-
    baptists which risked compromising the work of the Reformation, Calvin
    believed it his duty to find a practical solution by compromise. He
    thought that in this very period of the history of the Church, when the
    fate of the Reformation was being decided, peace should carry on, in the
    meantime, in the interest of the truth, even at the price of delaying the
    application of the whole truth. That is the tragedy of the Calvinistic
    paradox.[83]

Calvin also gets around the difficulty by appealing to the faith of the
godparents who present the child and who pledge themselves to instruct
him in the faith so as to make a disciple of him. Baptism is therefore
only in anticipation. He writes to John Knox: "We confess that it is
indispensable for them to have sponsors. For nothing is more preposter-
ous than that persons for whom we have no hope of their ever becoming
His disciples should be incorporated in Christ. Wherefore, if none of
the child's relations presents himself to pledge his faith that he will undertake the task of instructing the infant, the rite is a mockery, and baptism
is used for unworthy purposes."[84]
    "The statement may be hazarded," writes Karl Barth, "that the confu-
sion with which Luther and Calvin and their followers on both sides have
thrown themselves in this matter, is hopeless. . . . It still has to be said
that the actual information which one gets from them on the decisive
point is, in fact, as incredible as its exegetical grounds are unsatisfac-
tory."[85]
    Paul Lobstein says, "Their theological arguments are at times incon-
testably weak; they often resort to hypotheses which resemble expedients
rather than solutions or proofs."[86] And according to J. Baillie, "Calvin
and the Reformed theologians rather think out their doctrines of regenera-

tion in terms of men and women coming to Christ by conscious decision in maturity and then try to fit baptism into that scheme."[87]

In the Anglican Church there is maintained a curious mixture of authentic tradition and altered reform. For example, according to the *Prayer Book*, the godfather is called upon by the one who administers the baptism to make profession of repentance and faith and to promise for the child to be obedient to God's commandments. "Do you renounce the devil and his works? . . . I do. . . . Do you believe in God . . . in His Son? . . . I do . . . . Will you henceforth obey the one in whom you have believed? . . . I will." Before the Reformation these questions were asked of the child himself. These are the questions asked by Hippolytus at the time of baptism.[88]

But we are not bound by the word and writings of the Reformers. Alexandre Vinet writes, "The Reformation as a principle is permanent in the Church. . . . So that, even today, however important the event may have been in the sixteenth century, the Reformation is still something to be continued . . . the Reformers did not reform the Church once and for all, but they did affirm the principle and laid down the conditions for all future reforms."[89]

On this question of baptism, a movement to return to the practice of the primitive church is taking form in certain churches of the Reformation, opposed, it is true, by the ecumenical current which sees in infant baptism one of the few common denominators with the Orthodox and Roman Catholic churches. Nevertheless, the voices of some of the greatest theologians of our day who have declared themselves in favor of the baptism of believers have not failed to have profound repercussions in Protestant churches.

TESTIMONIES OF SOME GREAT THEOLOGIANS OF OUR TIMES

"In all branches of historic Christianity an uneasiness is manifest today concerning the significance of baptism,"[90] concluded the national ERF Synod of Lyon in 1946. This uneasiness is not a recent development. F. Lovsky says that "in French Protestantism, as soon as baptism was no longer either the introduction into a Christian society or the protest of the churches which make the Cross their central theme, doubts were noticed in the Reformed thought concerning pedobaptism."[91]

Anglican. The Anglicans give a clear account: "From the earliest days, repentance and the acceptance of the belief of the church was the condition *sine qua non* of baptism into the Body of Christ," says Dom Gregory Dix.[92] He also comments, "Christian Initiation in the New Testament is described and conceived of solely in terms of a *conscious* adherence and response to the Gospel of God, that is, solely in terms of an adult initiation."[93]

According to W. F. Flemington, "It is obvious that the most characteristic New Testament teaching concerning baptism, originally formulated with specific reference to the baptism of adults, must undergo some measure of restatement before it can be applied to a situation in which the typical subject of baptism is an infant."[94]

Methodist. A Methodist, Snaith, declares: "During the early days of the Christian Church, things were different, and the significance of the rite was clear. It was the baptism of. believers and a baptism by immersion."[95]

Reformed. In his report on the church member, the Reformed pastor P. Lecomte writes, "In the New Testament, baptism requires a personal step and is accompanied by an intervention of the Holy Spirit in the life of the one baptized."[96]

However, P. Marcel, one of the only defenders of infant baptism in our day, writes: "Conditions for being admitted for baptism cannot be different from those which are required for participation in the Holy Communion, for becoming and continuing to be a Church member. It is universally admitted in all Christian churches that the candidate for baptism must show signs of repentance and faith and must declare his purpose to obey Jesus Christ."[97]

In an article published in 1926, H. Windisch affirms that, when the church was begun, baptism was a confession and an act of personal decision on the part of the one baptized. "The baptism of infants in the Catholic Church represents an apostasy from primitive Christianity."[98]

"Without any doubt faith is a condition which precedes baptism," says Erich Dinkler, "this fact alone permits a confession of faith to be added to it (Rom. 19:9)."[99]

"Infant baptism has no Biblical foundation," says W. Ninck.[100]

Emil Brunner writes:

> The Pauline teaching does, however, suggest that the full sense of baptism can be realized only where it is understood as a dying with Christ and therefore where Christ's death, as having taken place for our salvation, is believed in.[101]
> It is impossible to harmonize Paul's teaching about faith and, in particular, his explicit teaching about baptism with the thought of infant baptism.[102]
> One thing is established beyond all doubt: that the baptismal doctrine in the New Testament is orientated not to Infant Baptism but to Adult Baptism, and never separates baptism from the faith that receives it.[103]
> It is not the act of baptism as such, but the baptism affirmed in a per-

sonal act of repentance and faith and coupled with a personal declaration of faith which truly incorporates the believer in the Church; that is Biblical and that is according to teachings of the Reformation.[104]

The present practice of infant baptism cannot be described other than scandalous.[105]

Catholic. Even Catholic theologians recognize the truth concerning the primitive practice of baptism. Pascal noted that

> in the nascent Church, they taught the catachumens, that is, those who were asking for baptism, before conferring it on them; and they were not accepted until after having been fully instructed in the mysteries of religion, after having repented of their past life, after having learned a great deal about the grandeur and excellence of the profession of faith and of Christian maxims, which they were desirous of constantly delving in, until after having shown many distinguishing marks of a heart conversion, until after a very strong desire to be baptized. These things being known by the whole Church, the sacrament of incorporation was conferred on them, by which they became members of the Church.[106]

According to François Amyot, professor at Saint-Sulpice,

> Baptism assumes that one has confessed his faith in Jesus Christ. . . . But faith in Christ is not only a mental adherence to the evangelical message; it requires a total conversion, a giving of one's whole self to Christ, who transforms the whole life. It normally leads to asking for public baptism, which is the sacrament for it and in the receiving of which it is perfected. Paul never separates them. . . . He always assumes that profession of faith is crowned by the receiving of baptism.[107]

Mgr. Cerfaux writes: "In the book of Acts, which faithfully guards the memory of these ideas in the early Church, baptism places the seal on those who have believed in the resurrection of Christ . . . faith and baptism appear to be connected . . . in Acts 8:36-38 faith is presented as the condition essential for receiving baptism."[108]

"Faith is the essential condition for baptism; moral conditions are usually found included: previous repentance is considered as a matter of course," comments Dr. O. Heggelbacher, professor of ecclesiastical law at the Catholic school of law at Freiburg.[109]

Dr. J. Marx acknowledges,

> The custom of baptizing infants became general in the third century. . . . Adults were baptized as soon as they confessed their faith in Christ, without special preparation. Later on catechism courses were instituted, which seem to us to have already been fully developed with Tertullian.[110] . . . Very often in the fourth century, even the children of Christian parents and converted pagans did not receive baptism before they reached a more advanced age. . . . In the fifth century infant baptism was practiced everywhere.[111]

Abbé Mollard suggested to the Vatican Council II that "the children be only enrolled on the registers of the Roman Catholic Church, baptism being given to them later on following a personal step of faith."[112]

Lutheran. The Lutheran theologians are among the only ones who defend the apostolic origin and intrinsic value of infant baptism. Beasley-Murray notes that if the last decade has witnessed a marked swing of popular opinion back to infant baptism it has been due especially to two scholars, Joachim Jeremias and Oscar Cullmann.[113] However, even in their works one finds unexpected statements. "The incorporation into the Church, which takes place at the time of baptism," says Cullmann, "should of necessity correspond with the faith of the new member."[114] And Jeremias writes in his book: "According to I Cor. 7:14 Paul seems to know nothing at all about any baptism of children of Christians."[115] Citing Acts 21:21, he concludes, "Toward the middle of the first century in Christendom, Hebrew Christians as well as Gentile Christians in all probability did not baptize the children of Christians."[116] According to him, infant baptism was not introduced until the years 60 to 70. His whole argument is based on the distinction between the *Uebertrittstaufe* (baptism on "crossing over to" Christianity) and baptism within Christendom.

Kurt Aland has shown that this distinction existed nowhere in the documents and that it was a pure figment of the imagination.[117] Basing his decision on a close analysis of all documents on baptism between the first and third centuries, the author establishes irrefutably that no case of infant baptism can be shown before the third century.

In spite of the extremely rigid position taken by the theologians of Tübingen (they asked that pastors who taught or practiced "rebaptism" or even those who did not condemn it as heresy should be excluded from the ministry and from the Protestant Church), they admitted in their report that "a compelling and direct proof cannot be brought from the Scripture in favor of the possibility of infant baptism."[118]

Certain Lutherans have risked some daring statements:

> Is our baptism, which we receive as newborn infants, also an appropriation of the grace of God, the pardon of all our sins, a baptism of regeneration? If one's answer to this question is negative then our baptism or the baptism practiced within Christendom is not the baptism commanded by the Lord Jesus. If it is not that, it is not baptism at all: there is no purification from sins, no death with Christ, no resurrection with Him—it is nothing . . . no, it is less than nothing. For then it keeps one from the real baptism which the Lord commanded, and consequently it is a hindrance to attaining grace and accomplishing redemption in us.[119]

Regin Prenter draws the following logical conclusion:

> If it is debatable whether or not infants can believe, there is only one solution: discontinue infant baptism. If we do not admit that infants have faith and in spite of that uphold pedobaptism, maintaining that insofar as the role of faith is concerned at the time of the administration of the sacrament we are talking about a different baptism from the one for adults,—then we are in disagreement with the New Testament which knows nothing of two baptisms. Insofar as it is a sacrament of the new birth, baptism is the living Word of the glorified Christ, and this Word can be received only by faith. *Baptism, therefore, makes the Church a community of believers.*[120]

Thus, there is only one baptism, the baptism received by faith. If the infant does not believe, he should not be baptized. Indeed, that is what Luther said.[121] One realizes that the Lutheran idea of infant baptism rests on a presupposition which cannot be proved. In any case, one can affirm that a faith which infants might have has nothing in common with what the New Testament calls faith.

Emil Brunner clearly shows the relationship between infant baptism and the multitudinist church:

> The popular Church inherited from Constantine has been maintained by infant baptism, that is, the baptism of infants which is required by the authorities and protected by punitive sanctions. Woe to the man who would get the notion not to have his newborn child baptized as soon as possible! There is no longer any obligation, but the custom has been continued even where faith and the inner ties with the Church of Christ have long ago disappeared.
>
> The discrepancy between these two Churches, the gigantic Church of those baptized and the tiny Church of those assenting to confession, is one of the chief causes of the present difficulties of the Church in all places. Seen in the long Church-historical perspective, the essence of the situation in which the present-day Church finds itself is above all the replacing of the people's Church of Constantine by the pre-Constantine Church of those making confession.[122]

Karl Barth is certainly the contemporary theologian who has attacked infant baptism the most vehemently. After having defended it in the first edition of the *Prolegomena to Christian Dogmatics* in 1927, he was convinced through the study of the New Testament that only the baptism of believers corresponds to the biblical idea. In *The Teaching of the Church Regarding Baptism* he writes:

> Baptism without the willingness and readiness of the baptized is true, effectual, and effective baptism, but it is not correct; it is not done in obedience, it is not administered according to proper order, and therefore it is necessarily clouded baptism. . . . It is, however, a wound in the

body of the Church and a weakness for the baptized . . . how long is she [the Church] prepared to be guilty of the occasioning of this wounding and weakening through a baptismal practice which is, from this standpoint, arbitrary and despotic?[123]

He bluntly reveals, as we have shown earlier, the reason for their attachment to infant baptism:

> The really operative extraneous ground for infant baptism, even with the Reformers, and ever and again quite plainly since, has been this: one did not want then in any case or at any price to deny the existence of the evangelical Church in the Constantinian *corpus christianum*—and today one does not want to renounce the present form of the national church [*Volkskirche*].
>
> Whatever may be the reason from the theological point of view, one must affirm that the question of a better ordering of our baptismal practice is urgent. This is what one must say concerning the ordinance of baptism and concerning the one to be baptized, the question calls for a restoration. Putting it simply, instead of the baptism of infants as it is practiced it requires a baptism where the one to be baptized is responsible. In order that things may be done correctly, the baptized person, instead of being a passive object, must again become the free partner of Jesus Christ, that is to say, a partner who decides for himself and who confesses his faith freely, who attests, for his part, that he desires to be baptized and is ready to be.[124]

What remains to be added to these words? Nothing but deeds—that is, obedience to the recognized will of one's Master. "The slave who knew what his master wanted and neither got ready nor did it, will be severely lashed" (Lk 12:47). "The person who knows what is right to do and fails to do it, to him it is sin" (Ja 4:17). Many Christians from various religious backgrounds—other than Baptist churches—have, in order to carry out God's plan, been baptized even though their church has not yet changed its practices. Eminent men in God's work such as Ami Bost, Henry Pyt, Guers, Daniel Lortsch, George Müller, B. W. Newton, S. P. Tregelles, C. H. Mackintosh, Hudson Taylor, A. B. Simpson, A. T. Pierson, G. Campbell Morgan, Katherine Booth-Clibborn, Herbert Booth, Philip Mauro, Pandita Ramabai, Prince Oscar Bernadotte, Count Korff, Badaeker, David Baron and many others at the head of many Christian works and enterprises have been baptized by immersion as believers.[125]

SIGNIFICANCE AND VALUE OF BAPTISM

The wealth of meaning in baptism revealed in the epistles confirms that it was destined for believers only. They teach that baptism is the symbol:

1. of union with Christ (Ro 6:3-8; Col 2:12-13; Gal 3:27; cf. 1 Co 10:1-2)

2. of death and burial (Ro 6:3-11; Gal 2:20; 6:14)

3. of our resurrection with Christ (Ro 6-8; Col 2:13; 3:1-4; Eph 2:5-7; 2 Co 5:17; 2 Ti 2:11)

4. of a purification bath (Ac 22:16; Eph 5:26; Jn 3:5; Titus 3:5; Heb 10:22; 1 Co 6:11)

5. of putting on Christ (Gal 3:27; Ro 13:14; Eph 4:21-24)

6. of the seal of our being accepted by God and our alliance with Him (Eph 1:13-14; 4:30; 2 Co 1:21-22)

7. of passing into a new nature (1 Pe 3:18-22; Col 1:13)

It is evident that infant baptism cannot express all of these spiritual realities. The apostle had in view the immersion of adults who had consciously accepted by faith the salvation offered in Christ. It is only by reducing its meaning considerably and making it a "bath of purification" and a "seal of our acceptance by God" that the theologians from the second to the fourth centuries succeeded in applying it to children who were not aware of anything.

Since then its meaning also has developed. According to the New Testament, baptism is for the believer:

1. an act of voluntary enlistment
2. the outer and visible expression of an inner experience
3. a testimony, a confession of the Lord
4. a proclaiming of the great truths of salvation
5. a test of faith (not of knowledge)
6. an aid toward sanctification
7. an act of homage and obedience

It is clear that infant baptism could not be viewed under any of these aspects. Of what value is it to the infant? None, unless it is imbued with some almost magic power. There again, as far back as the second century, theological thinking was changing. Instead of its being the testimony of the regeneration effected by the Holy Spirit, baptism becomes the agent of this transformation. It alone "obtains the remission of sins" (Barnabas 11:1), and "eternal life" (Irenaeus), and "introduces one into the kingdom yet to come (Barnabas). It becomes "indispensable for salvation" (Tertullian), and it "makes us children of God" (Pacien). Sacramentalism is born. Theologically, there are no more obstacles to infant baptism. Sacramental thought dominates the whole Catholic concept of baptism. "Sacraments are causes which produce grace by their own virtue *ex opere operato*," said the Council of Trent.[126]

The Reformation broke away only partially from this teaching. After having broken away from it in 1526, Luther returned to it in order to retain the favor of the masses of the people. For Calvin also, sacraments are "instruments which God uses to give to us His grace," "means by which God works effectually . . . they are as necessary for salvation as is the preaching of the Gospel" for "in this the spiritual graces of God are communicated to us."

The Lutheran and Reformed catechisms often reflect this sacramentalist concept: "Baptism effects the remission of sins, delivers from death and the devil, and grants eternal life. . . . It is the bath by which man is purified from original sin, and which, by the Holy Spirit, causes him to be born again as a child of God."[127]

And Durand-Pallot says, "Baptism delivers from the stain of original sin."[128]

Two tendencies stand out very clearly at present in Protestantism. Some (Taizé, Vatja, etc.) are happy to see in the residue of Catholicism found in Protestantism that the sacramental theology of the Reformers constitutes one ecumenical meeting point. On the other hand, others wish to continue the principle of the Reformation and to return to biblical sources.

Brunner affirms in his *Dogmatics:*

> The sacramental concept was unknown to the New Testament witnesses to Christ.. . . . At this point above all, even the Reformation failed to penetrate through mediaevalism to the sources of the New Testament faith. The fact that here the stream of the movement of the Reformation divided and lost its impetus has not been without significant consequence. . . . Above all, the retention by the Reformers of the Catholic practice of Infant-Baptism, which was based really, though never avowedly, on the desire to retain the National Church, made it clear that the new understanding of faith was incompatible with the Church as an institution and brought both concepts under the suspicion of ambiguity and muddled thinking. Men of today, at least, have no time for a Church which on the one hand indiscriminately baptizes every child and declares it to be a member of the Body of Christ, and on the other hand preaches justification by faith alone.[129]

"It becomes more and more clear," writes Pastor Wilhelm Busch, "that we cannot expect a new comprehension of what the Church is and what the community is, unless we are given a new biblical comprehension of that which we call the sacraments. All discussion of the Church should begin there."[130] And Pastor Venske says, "I discover more and more that all the trouble in our multitudinist churches comes from the fact that the Reformers did not return to the source in their teaching concerning the sacraments."[131]

Two tendencies, two ways; we know to what they lead. One leads to Rome, to religious materialism, to Christianized paganism; the other leads back to the faith and the church as Jesus Christ and the apostles instituted them. Baptism is at the crossroads of these two ways. It is up to us to choose which one we wish to follow.

Notes

1. Francus, *Il n'y a pas de Protestants*, chap. 4.
2. It was one of the points brought out in favor of retaining the multitudinist type of the "Confessing Church" of Germany in 1934. See Günther Harder, "Die Bedeutung der Kirchengliedschaft im Kirchenkampf," *Evangelische Theologie* (1960), p. 80.
3. G. Steinheil, quoted by F. Lovsky, *Foi et Vie* (1950).
4. Emil Brunner, *Dogmatics*, 3:54.
5. Brunner, *The Divine-Human Encounter*, pp. 183-84.
6. Geddes MacGregor, *Corpus Christi*, p. 138.
7. See on this subject the testimonies of Bossuet, Grotius, Calvin, Luther, Neander, Wesley, and Karl Barth in the *Dictionnaire de Théologie catholique;* and those of Abbé Crampon and Dom Cabrol.
8. *Dictionnaire d'Archéologie chrétienne*, vol. 1, col. 391.
9. These words, starting with "Philip assured him . . ." are missing in all of the ancient uncial manuscripts except one (E), in more than eighty minuscule manuscripts, in the best manuscripts of the Vulgate, in the Syriac Peschitta versions and those of Héracleá, in the Sahidic, Bohaïric and Ethiopian versions. Also the critical editions of the Greek New Testament of Tischendorf, Westcott-Hort, von Soden, Nestle, and Vogels agree to omit them, and many French translations mention them only as an added thought in the footnotes. So it seems that we are faced with an interpolation due to a copyist of the second century. As for the question with which we are concerned, that makes it all the more valuable since it brings to us the testimony of the church which still in the second century considered that a profession of faith had to precede baptism. See Barnes, *Notes on the Acts;* R. Jamieson, A. R. Fausset and D. Brown, *A Commentary, Critical and Explanatory on the Old and New Testaments;* P. Adrien Boudou, *Actes des Apôtres* (Verbum salutis), p. 181; Davidson, Stibbs, Kevan, *New Bible Commentary;* L. Bonnet, *Nouveau Testament expliqué;* F. F. Bruce, *The Growing Day*, pp. 113-14.
10. Luke specifies that "the house of Cornelius" means the relatives and close friends who are gathered together (10:24); it is to them that he speaks; the Holy Spirit falls on them (10:44); it is they who speak in tongues (10:46) and who are baptized (10:48).
    "We are here dealing . . . with a meeting of like-minded adults coming from different families" (K. Aland, *Did the Early Church Baptize Infants?* p. 91).
11. Fustel de Coulanges as quoted by J. P. Ramseyer, *Histoire des Baptistes*, p. 6. See also Jean-Daniel Benoît, *Calvin et le Baptême des Enfants*, p. 458. "Let us note that it is the only passage in the New Testament where the baptism of the 'house' is mentioned. Lydia is either an unmarried woman or a widow. *She* is the one whose vocation is described. *She* invites Paul to take lodgings in *her* house. Therefore no other conclusion seems possible. To assume that the entire family would renounce their former religion and be converted to Christianity while the husband was away on a business trip is unthinkable within the framework of ancient family tradition" (Aland, p. 89).
12. Louis Secrétan, *Baptême des Croyants ou Baptême des Enfants*, p. 32. See G. R. Beasley-Murray, *Baptism in the New Testament*, pp. 315-16.
13. J. R. Couleru, *Le Baptême selon la Parole*, p. 30.
14. A. Harnack, *Die Mission und Ausbreitung in den ersten drei Jahrhunderten*, 1:399.
15. D. Feine, *Realenzyklopädie für prot. Theologie und Kirche*, bk. 19, p. 403.

188   *I Will Build My Church*

16. Karl Barth, *The Teaching of the Church Regarding Baptism,* pp. 45, 49.
17. Aland, *Did the Early Church Baptize Infants?*
18. H. T. Andrews, *Lectures on the Church and the Sacraments,* p. 150.
19. P. T. Forsyth, *The Church and the Sacraments,* p. 198.
20. J. R. Nelson, *The Realm of Redemption,* p. 129.
21. O. Heggelbacher, *Die christliche Taufe als Rechtsakt nach dem Zeugnis der frühen Christenheit,* p. 70.
22. O. Cullmann, *Le Baptême des Enfants et la Doctrine biblique du Baptême,* p. 20.
23. Ibid., p. 22.
24. Cf. Luther at the Diet of Worms: "Unless I am convinced by Scripture or by evident reasons, I am bound by the texts which I have presented and my conscience is captive to the Word of God."
25. Markus Barth, *Die Taufe—ein Sakrament?* p. 11.
26. Cullmann, pp. 23-44.
27. Cullmann, *Earliest Christian Confessions,* p. 21.
28. F. Heitmüller, *Taufe und Abendmahl bei Paulus,* p. 14.
29. Rendtorff, *Die Taufe im Urchristentum im Lichte der neueren Forschung,* p. 32.
30. N. P. Williams, *Ideas of the Fall and Original Sin,* p. 550.
31. *Theology of Christian Initiation* (1948), p. 9.
32. *Baptism and Confirmation Today* (1955), p. 34.
33. *Report . . . Baptism and Confirmation* (1959), p. X, 2 ff.
34. A. M. Ramsey, *The Doctrine of Confirmation Theology,* 48 (1954): 201.
35. J. Bellamy, *Dictionnaire de Théologie catholique* de Vacant-Mangenot, Fasc. X, 176-77.
36. Clement of Rome, *Epistle to the Corinthians,* 42:4.
37. *Homilies and recognitions attributed to Clement,* Hom. 17, 7.
38. See *Aristides* 15:6.
39. Justin Martyr, *Apology I* 61:10.
40. Aristides, *Apology I* 15:6.
41. Aland, p. 33.
42. Justin Martyr, *Apology I* 1:61.
43. Justin Martyr, *Dialog with (the Jew) Tryphon* 14:1.
44. Justin Martyr, *Apology I* 61:10.
45. Justin Martyr, *Dialog with Tryphon* 13.
46. Tertullian, *De Baptismo* 14.
47. Tertullian, *De spectaculis* 4, *De corona mil.* 3.
48. Tertullian, *De Baptismate* 18:5 (written between 200 and 206).
49. Ibid.
50. Cullmann, *Earliest . . .,* p. 21. The custom of having godfathers and godmothers testifies against infant baptism. Why must the godparents, in place of the child, reply to the questions asked by the one baptizing? Because the form of words used (for example, the baptismal questionnaire of Hippolyte) addressed these questions to responsible adults and because the baptismal liturgy anticipated a reply from the one being baptized. "When they began to baptize infants so soon after their birth they continued to use the same formulary" but they had to "substitute a godfather, who replied for the infant being baptized" (Aland, p. 108).
51. The Council of Neocesarea, Canon XII (between 314 and 325). Lovsky, who quotes this text (p. 122) adds: "This text casts into disrepute the baptism of one confined to a hospital bed by critical illness; but by that it implies the habitual practice of delayed baptism, not only of adults but also of children."
52. Heggelbacher, pp. 55-56. See G. Foucart, *Les Mystères d'Eleusis,* p. 311.
53. Gregory of Nazianzus, *Oratorio* 40:11; Basil of Caesarea, *Homilia* 13, 5.
54. See demonstration in Lovsky, pp. 110-11.
55. Paul Lobstein, "Essai d'une Apologie du Baptême des Enfants," *Par le Christ à Dieu,* p. 221. One realizes in what a free and easy manner certain theologians of great renown handle the arguments when it is a question of proving a thesis at all costs. When we read, for example, from the pen of Joachim Jeremias that Origen is supposed to have learned "from his father and probably from his grandfather that they had been baptized as infants" (*Die Kindertaufe in den*

ersten vier Jahrhunderten, p. 77), Jeremias seems to have overlooked one small detail in his argument, that the name Origen signifies "son of Horus." How can one explain that the son in an old Christian family bears a name which is typically pagan? E. de Faye, an authority on Origen, thinks that Leonidas, Origen's father, was converted only after the birth of his son. Moreover, to make infant baptism legitimate, Origen relies not on the Scripture but on the "traditio ecclesiae." It is his most forceful argument—proof that he had no better one. The resistance to this custom of infant baptism (between 230 and 250) in Palestinian quarters proves that it was a recent innovation. See Aland, pp. 49-51.

56. Secrétan, p. 42.
57. See Lovsky, pp. 122-25.
58. Basil the Great, *De Baptismate,* bk. 2, chap. 1.
59. Secrétan, p. 42.
60. Lovsky, p. 126.
61. Aland, p. 84.
62. E. Menegoz, "Le Baptême des Enfants d'après les Principes de la Théologie paulinienne," *Revue chrét.* (1884), quoted by Secrétan.
63. Lovsky, p. 113.
64. Aland, p. 73.
65. Ibid., p. 22.
66. F. H. Kettler, *Religion in Geschichte und Gegenwart,* vol. 6, col. 638.
67. *The Key of Truth* as quoted by E. H. Broadbent, *The Pilgrim Church;* and H. Wheeler Robinson, *Baptist Principles,* pp. 58-61.
68. Charlemagne's ordinance promulgated in 785 (quoted by Halphen, *Etudes critiques sur l'Historie de Charlemagne*).
69. Rudolpf Rican, *Die Böhmischen Brüder,* p. 316.
70. See Luther, W. A. 6:529; W. Jetter, *Die Taufe beim jungen Luther.*
71. Luther, W. A. XVII-II—79 to 81.
72. Julius Boehmer, ed., *Martin Luthers Werke* (Deutsche Verlags Anstalt), p. 246; W. A. 19, 72-113.
73. Luther as quoted by Secrétan, p. 45.
74. In 1528 Luther was still saying, thus indicating his hesitancy: "The infant is baptized not because he has faith but because the Lord commanded it. Baptism without faith is unprofitable but not harmful" (A. Lemaître, *Foi et Vérité,* p. 470).
"Luther was determined to keep Infant Baptism at all costs. Both *sola fide* and Infant Baptism were to be retained. In the dilemma into which Luther thus fell nothing availed except the absurd assertion that in fact the infant had faith; an assertion that was made more extreme in post-Reformation theology by the pedantic claim that the infant in fact had real faith in the threefold sense of knowledge, assent and trust (*notitia, assensus* and *fiducia*)" (Brunner, *Dogmatics* 3:55).
"Luther postulated the presence of faith in an infant in order to bring his doctrine of infant baptism into line with justification by faith" (Beasley-Murray, p. 347).
75. Luther as quoted by Secrétan, p. 45.
76. Luther, W. A. 52:102, as quoted by K. Barth, p. 13.
77. J. T. Mueller, *Christian Dogmatics.*
For the development of Luther's concept of baptism see *Mennonitisches Lexikon,* 2:703.
Brunner says about the Lutheran doctrine that no faith is necessary for baptism, and that baptism is effective as an act of the saving institution, the church. . . :
"Their self-contradictory doctrine was obviously created only in order to give theological justification and legitimacy to infant baptism, which they were determined at all costs to retain, whatever their grounds for so doing may have been" (Brunner, *Dogmatics* 3:55).
78. A. Lamorte, *Réflexions à propos des doctrines de la prédestination et du Baptême chez Calvin,* p. 9 (ouvrage primé par le Comité du Jubilé Réformé).
79. Calvin, *Institutes,* bk. 4, chap. 15, no. 13.
80. Ibid., no. 1, p. 513.
81. Calvin, *Sermon sur Deut.* 6:20-25, *Opera* 26:490.

82. Lamorte, p. 16.
83. Ibid., p. 20.
    However, one must admit that Calvin sincerely believed that infant baptism could be biblically justified. In chapter 8 of the same book he says, "It would be a very weak support if, in order to defend infant baptism, we were forced to resort to the pure and simple authority of the Church" (*Institutes*, bk. 4, chap. 8, no. 16). From the beginning of chapter 16 he informs us that if one had proof of the human origin of infant baptism, that would be sufficient reason to reject it (16:1). "Infants are in the Church since they are counted among the people of God and belong to the kingdom of heaven," so they must also receive "the sign of their cleansing."
    It is by comparison with Jewish circumcision that infant baptism can be defended, according to Calvin. "The defense of infant baptism by the argument of circumcision implies, in Calvin, the whole interpretation of the Old Testament. According to him, children of believers are *already* members of the body of Christ (Inst. IV, 15, 22; 16, 9, 22) and some of them are already *regenerated* (IV, 16, 17)" (H. Blocher).
    "The chapter that Calvin devotes to this thought of the sacrament is probably one of the most ambiguous of the Institutes" (J. de Senarclens, *De la Vraie Eglise, selon Calvin*, p. 48).
84. Calvin, *Letter to John Knox*, quoted by Beasley-Murray, p. 348, who notes that judging by these words Calvin denies the efficacy of baptism to "make anyone a Christian."
85. K. Barth, pp. 48-49.
86. Lobstein as quoted by F. J. Leenhardt, p. 66.
87. J. Baillie, *Baptism and Conversion*, pp. 28-29.
88. Wittacker makes the following observation on this subject: "These passages presuppose the infant to be capable at present of faith and repentance and to have experienced them . . . as in the case when a mute adult is baptized" (E. C. Wittacker, article in *Theology* 59 (1956): 104).
89. Alexandre Vinet, *Hist. de la Littérature française au XIXᵉ Siècle*, 3:392.
90. Decision 28 du Synode national ERF de Lyon 1946.
91. Lovsky, p. 132.
92. Dom Gregory Dix, *The Shape of the Liturgy*, p. 485.
93. Dix, *The Theology of Confirmation in Relation to Baptism*, p. 37. See also the testimonies of church Fathers cited earlier in the chapter.
94. W. F. Flemington, *The New Testament Doctrine of Baptism*, p. 130.
95. Snaith, *The Methodist Recorder* (June 17, 1948).
96. P. Lecomte, "Rapport sur le Membre d'Eglise," *Verbum Caro* (1958), p. 185.
97. P. C. Marcel, distinguishing between the conditions addressed to the adults and those addressed to children.
98. H. Windisch, *Zum Problem der Kindertaufe im Urchristentum* (ZNW, 28: (1929): 118 ff.
99. Erich Dinkler, article in *Religion in Geschichte und Gegenwart*, vol. 6, col. 633.
100. W. Ninck, *Christliche Gemeinde heute*, p. 47.
101. Brunner, *The Misunderstanding of the Church*, p. 66.
102. Brunner, *Dogmatics*, 3:54.
103. Ibid., 3:270.
104. Brunner, *Le Renouveau de l'Eglise*, p. 17.
105. Brunner, *The Divine-Human Encounter*, pp. 182-83.
106. Pascal, *Opuscules*, 3ᵉ partie, p. 204.
107. François Amyot, *Vocabulaire de Théologie biblique*, p. 86, as quoted by Francus, p. 256.
108. Mgr. Cerfaux, *La Théologie de l'Eglise suivant Saint Paul*, p. 122.
109. Heggelbacher, p. 66.
110. J. Marx (Th.D., Ph.D.), *Lehrbuch der Kirchengeschichte*, p. 116, as quoted by L. Vogel, *Kindertaufe*, p. 12.
111. Ibid., p. 225.
112. Abbé Mollard, *Revue Esprit* (Dec. 1961), p. 728.
113. Beasley-Murray, p. 331.

114. Cullmann, *Le Baptême* . . . , p. 41. When Cullmann's arguments are quoted in favor of infant baptism, it would perhaps be useful to ask those who quote them if they have given any thought to the scathing words with which J. L. Leenhardt refuted them (in *Foi et Vie* [1949], pp. 76 ff.). It is particularly difficult to resist the logic of Cullmann's argumentation showing into what a maze the physiological concept of holiness leads us.
F. J. Leenhardt challenges a certain number of illogical statements in Cullmann's work on infant baptism: "distinction between the sacramental event and the effect following baptism. If faith is lacking after baptism, regeneration loses its effect but not its reality. Since baptism consists in the gift of the Holy Spirit, 'the gift retains all of its reality' in spite of the unbelief of the one who is baptized! Does that imply that the Holy Spirit remains? Well then, what is lost by unbelief? And if the Spirit does not remain, let someone tell us what does remain!" (F. J. Leenhardt, p. 79).
115. Jeremias, p. 54.
116. Ibid., p. 57.
117. Aland, pp. 50 ff.
118. "Gutachten des Evang. Theol. Fak. der Univers. Tübingen über: Fragen der Taufordnung" in "Für Arbeit und Besinnung," No. 21-1951, p. 419 *Z.T.K.*, (Aug. 1950).
119. H. Cremer, "Taufe, Wiedergeburt und Kindertaufe" in *Kraft des Heiligen Geistes*, 3d ed., pp. 30-32.
120. Regin Prenter, "L'Eglise d'après la Confession d'Augsbourg" in *La Sainte Eglise universelle*, p. 123. See the development of this thought in his doctrine, *Schöpfung und Erlösung*, pp. 447 ff.
121. Luther, W. A. XVII–II–80-81.
122. Brunner, *The Divine-Human Encounter*, pp. 186-87.
123. K. Barth, pp. 40-41. One wonders what meaning Barth gives to the words *true*, *effectual* and especially *effective*. Would he himself not remain subject to the sacramentalist concept that his son fought against so brilliantly? See his final position in his last book, *Dogmatics* 4: 4, devoted to this question of baptism.
124. K. Barth, *The Teaching* . . . , pp. 53-54.
125. List given by R. Dubarry in *Le Lien fraternel* (1930), p. 317.
126. Council of Trent, session 7, canons 6 and 8.
127. *Catéchisme luthérien* (Strasbourg, 1932), p. 83.
128. Durand-Pallot, *Baptême, Confirmation, Sainte-Cène*, p. 47.
129. Brunner, *Dogmatics*, 3:98.
130. Wilhelm Busch, preface to H. Venske's *Vollendete Reformation*, pp. 7-8.
131. Venske, p. 9

For Further Reading

WORKS WHICH DEFEND THE BAPTISM OF BELIEVERS

Beasley-Murray, G. R. *Baptism in the New Testament.*
Schneider, Johannes. *Taufe und Gemeinde im N.T.*
Sondheimer, F. *Die wahre Taufe.*
St. Winword, *The New Testament Teaching on Baptism.*
Warns, S. *Baptism, studies in the original Christian baptism, its history and conflicts in relation to a state or national church and its significance for the present time.*
White, F. H. *Christian Baptism.*

AUTHORS WHO SUPPORT INFANT BAPTISM

Aland, Kurt. *Did the Early Church Baptize Infants?* (*Die Sauglingstaufe im Neuen Testament und in der alten Kirche.* Eine Antwort an Joachim Jeremias.)
Heggelbacher, Othmar. *Die christliche Taufe als Rechtsakt nach dem Zeugnis der frühen Christenheit.* Catholic .
Jeremias, Joachim. *Die Kindertaufe in den ersten vier Jahrhunderten.* See a resumé of the theses of Jeremias and something of their reputation in Aland, pp. 8-17.

Part VII

THE FRAMEWORK OF THE BUILDING

12

The Free Church Through the Centuries

"Yes," you say, "we papists have remained in the primitive Church, the one of apostolic times; that is why we are the true Church; but you have withdrawn from us and have raised up a new Church against us."

Reply: "But what would happen if I were to show that we have remained in the true Church, yes, that we are the true Church, the early Church, but that you have withdrawn from us, that is to say from the Early Church, and have established a new Church in opposition to the early Church? Let us see!"

LUTHER (W. A. 51, 478, 13-479, 3)

SINCE THE PRIMITIVE CHURCH was a church of confessing Christians, how does it happen that all the large historical churches of the present are multitudinist churches? In particular, how can one explain that the Reformation, which tried to restore the church to its original form, gave rise to churches of the multitudinist type?

History alone can give a reply to these disturbing questions. By scarcely perceptible modifications over the centuries, the primitive church has been transformed into an institutional ecclesiastical system.

IN THE FIRST CENTURIES

During the first centuries the way in which members were added to the church remained relatively consistent with the biblical principle. The churches of which we catch a glimpse through the writings of the apostolic Fathers and the church Fathers remain *grosso modo* churches of professing believers. However, a close observer will notice a number of factors which change the image of the church rather imperceptibly as early as in the second century.

MORALISM

The teaching departs from the apostolic message little by little to return to the beaten paths of *morality* and salvation by works. Thus we find the idea of conversion and, consequently, the definition of a Christian falsified at the very foundation. The Christian is no longer the one who, despairing of himself, has by faith seized the lifeline of salvation which is offered to him through the death of Jesus for his justification; but he is the one who follows the precepts and ordinances of Christ, just as the Jew did his utmost to fulfill the law of Moses.

All the writings of the apostolic Fathers breathe a moralism which is disconcerting to the reader who is familiar with the epistles of the New Testament.[1] It is evident that if one connects the degree of Christian excellence with moral attainment, the borderline between Christian and non-Christian will be blurred; one enters right into the domain of the relative. One who is in sympathy, who leads an honest, moral life, is he not just as good a Christian as the average church member? What right would one have to refuse to baptize him if he recites the creed correctly?

INTELLECTUALISM

Running parallel with the moralization of Christian teachings is the *intellectualism* of the church. The struggle with newly arising heresies forces church leaders to make more and more detailed the creed to be recited at the time of baptism. On the other hand, many pagans are drawn to Christianity because they are seeking a "gnosis" (knowledge) superior both to that offered by popular religions which have fallen into disrepute, and to the contradicting philosophies. In order to meet the needs of "gnostics," learned Christian doctors elaborate intellectual systems which strive to combine revelation with philosophical thought. This is the birth of "theology," the teaching of which replaces that of the Word of God in catechetical schools.[2]

Having followed catechetical teaching for several months or even several years, the new believer—if he knows how to answer correctly all doctrinal questions put to him, and if he can recite an orthodox confession of faith—finds nothing standing in the way of his baptism.[3] Instead of a testimony of faith and confidence in Christ, baptism is more like the sanction for a pass at the close of a course of initiation into a mystic religion. Intellectual faith gradually replaces the faith which originally was the spontaneous impulse of the whole being by which a man entrusted his destiny to Jesus Christ.

From the second half of the second century there was a new shift in the definition of a Christian: to the moral conditions are added the intellectual. The good Christian is one who knows the orthodox doctrine and adheres to it intellectually. As this condition was easier to identify than a genuine spiritual experience, the entrance door to the church was again made broader.

It is probable that many church members of the second and third centuries experienced only a type of intellectual conversion. Thus, conversion to Christianity became a religious phenomenon rather than a spiritual experience. A superior religion always attracts adherents of inferior religions. It was noticed in Africa that when young fetishists attended a school with Muslims and Catholics, they left the school either as Catholics or Muslims.

Intelligent people have of necessity established the religious superiority of Christianity over Greek and Roman myths, its moral superiority over mystic cults. So they may have been attracted to Christianity by reason, without their hearts having been necessarily touched by the call of Jesus Christ.

SACRAMENTALISM

A third fact leads to the disintegration of the apostolic churches: *the concept* that baptism and the holy communion become more and more *sacramentalist*. From the beginning of the second century, baptism was seen to be, more than anything else, a bath of illumination "which purifies from all sin."[4] Church leaders taught that the rite itself brought about regeneration: the, church door was then open to all who were ready to submit to baptism. Consequently, why should they refuse to admit baptized infants?

Thanks to this doctrinal expedient, all churches remain theoretically churches of the regenerated since they admit as members only those who are baptized.[5] "Infant baptism appears to be a great discovery which permits one to avoid conversion."[6] In fact, the growing practice of baptizing children of Christians before they reach the age of personal, conscious conviction has enrolled in the church ranks many people who remain in the Christian faith and in the church more out of filial reverence than of personal godliness.

ECCLESIASTICISM

This *evolution* on the doctrinal level produces as consequence another one on the *ecclesiastical* level. Here we are witnessing a transformation which will finally produce the Roman Catholic system. "The origin of the Roman Catholic Church . . . lies in two factors which reciprocally influenced each other: the sacramental view of salvation and the assertion of formal legal authority."[7]

Baptism and the holy communion became the crystallizing points in a concept of salvation which is of pagan origin and which we find nowhere in the New Testament. If a rite became a depository of spiritual blessings, that would carry with it profound modifications even into the very structure of the church. Brunner says,

> In the Ekklesia it is known that the community is a brotherhood which together celebrates the Supper. No special accent falls on the administering, not a word is said of a differentiation between the one who administers and the one who receives. But if what is distributed is itself the means of salvation, it is inevitable that differentiation should enter in; the priest as the one who administers, the community as the recipient. The Ekklesia becomes the Church of the priests who, as mediators of the means of salvation, stand over against the laymen. . . . So the Church is, in the first instance, the institution whose means of salvation the priests administer. This differentiation would necessarily receive a quite particular emphasis after the Sacrament began to be considered as a sacrifice. Everywhere in the field of religion the principal function of the priest is the offering of sacrifice. . . . There is once more a holy place, the altar, and with it a barrier between those who administer holy things, the clergy, and the "profane" people.[8]

In a church of priests—where the pastor alone is the priest of God— the important person is obviously the pastor. The ordinary member of the congregation is reduced to an increasingly passive role: he is "the one who receives"; his position and his spiritual state are much less important than they are in a church where every Christian is actually a priest and a sacrificer. "The Catholic institution of the priest reinstated Christianity in the prison of Judaism," says A. Vinet.[9] A clerical church will inevitably become a multitudinist church.

If, in spite of these four factors working to the same end—that of lowering the spiritual level of the candidate for membership—the character of churches of professing believers was maintained in most of the communities until the fourth century, it was because of persecutions which the church passed through periodically. As long as belonging to the church brought with it rejection from the social life with threat of banishment, prison, or even death, the temptation to become or remain a church member without having a personal conviction was not great. All one needs to do is reread the writings of the adversaries of Christianity (Pliny the Younger, Tacitus, Suetonius, Celsus) to realize in the midst of what scorn the first Christians had to live and make their way.

THE GREAT TURNING POINT

When at the beginning of the fourth century Emperor Constantine left paganism to become a Christian and when Emperor Theodosius, in addition, lifted Christianity to the rank of the state church, they dealt "a mortal blow to the individual profession of the Christian faith. Belonging to the church became an obligation to the State by decree of Emperor Theodosius. Masses of superficially christianized pagans poured into the church."[10] Many bore the name *Christian* for financial gain, without experiencing the new birth and separation from the world. The multitudinist church made its appearance and developed rapidly. "The Church, in the thinking of the sovereigns, was to have as many members as the emperor had subjects," writes E. C. Babut. "Soon every one was to belong to the Church by bishopric, as he belonged to the empire by a city."[11]

The "Christian era" was beginning. A multitudinist, ecclesiastical system, highly organized and hierarchical, ruled the entire body of Christianized countries during the entire "dark millennium" of the Middle Ages. In official religious teaching, more and more dependent on Greek philosophy, biblical truths concerning conversion and the new birth disappeared. Inexpensive regeneration was obtained by the sacraments. The title of church member conferred by baptism on an infant was for the adult linked by submission to the clergy and to the commandments of the church. "By his anti-Donatist writings which culminated in the famous and notorious 'compel them to come in!', Augustine . . . contributed not a little to the development of the compulsory Church," Brunner comments.[12] In another place he says,

> It is understandable that at a later time when this original power and unity no longer existed in the same abundance, one should seek to find a substitute for what was lacking and to secure the presence of what was fast disappearing. This attempt to achieve security and replacement assumes three different forms: the living Word of God is secured— and at the same time replaced—by theology and dogma; the fellowship is secured—and replaced—by the institution; faith, which proves its reality by love, is secured—and replaced—by a creed and a moral code. It is so much easier to discuss from an intellectual and theological standpoint the ideas implied in the revealed Word of God and to analyze them conceptually than it is to allow oneself to be transformed at the center of one's life by the action of the Holy Ghost.[13]

W. Hobhouse writes,

> It is my conviction that the great change which began in the relationship between the Church and the world at the time of Constantine's conversion is not only the turning point in the history of the Church, but it also gives us the key to many of the practical difficulties of the present. At that time the line of demarcation between the Church and the world was fatally obscured. The world . . . got into the Church and we have never since been able to get it out. I am also convinced that the Church of tomorrow is destined more and more to return to a situation similar to that which reigned in the Church before Nicaea.
> That means that instead of seeking to include the world she would consider herself as a church of the minority and adopt an attitude of

conscious opposition to the world. As a compensation she will again find, to a certain degree, her former inner unity.[14]

IN THE MIDDLE AGES

Biblical teaching and churches of the apostolic type have not entirely disappeared; they are condemned to secrecy and, like an underground current of water, survive in movements and groups considered heretical by the predominant church. W. Ninck relates the following:

> The first opposition to the State Church and "the Church of the priests" came from a Spanish nobleman Priscillian who, laid hold on by Christ, furnished the impetus for a vast movement of laymen who crossed Spain and France and were joined by many clergymen and bishops. Those who had come to the faith gathered together in brotherhoods and many men went from place to place to strengthen the communities. But as the movement troubled the conscience of the leaders of the Church, Priscillian and six of his followers were executed at Treves in 385—the first judgment of heretics.[15]

Priscillians, Paulicians, Bogomiles, Culdees, Petrobusians, Patarenes, Waldenses, Berghards, Lollards, and many others were persecuted, tracked down, and executed by the thousands by an organization monopolizing the name *Church*, which they had usurped. Why this persecution? Because they had committed the crime of wishing to follow the teaching of the apostles as it is transmitted in the New Testament.

In the heart of the Roman Catholic Church, while the mass of "Christians" is sinking deeper and deeper in gross paganism, the cloisters are becoming a place of refuge for pious souls who are seeking a truly Christian life. The abbeys and convents are, in their way, churches of professing Christians; you can enter them only with a "solemn profession" of the vows by which one pledges himself to lead a Christian life conforming to the established standards.[16]

Certain movements, like the one started by Francis of Assisi, were real revivals in the heart of the Catholic Church; but instead of resulting in the formation of churches like those of the first centuries and after the seventeenth, they emerged in the form of a new monastic order. Furthermore, in the Middle Ages—and in the Roman Catholic Church even now—the word *conversion* was used to evoke the call to a monastic life and entrance into the convent.[17] Devotional books (e.g., *The Imitation of Christ*) were written exclusively for monks and nuns. "No devotional book was written in the Middle Ages for Christians living in the world as opposed to in monasteries,"[18] because only the monastic communities were considered to be the pure church.

In case of need, these orders took on a secular form also, seeking to include those who had remained "in the world." Thus a whole line of "tiers-ordres" (church members who though living in the world are affiliated with a religious order), brotherhoods, and masculine and feminine religious movements were formed. Many a time the people of the Catholic parishes called these organizations "sects."[19] Tauler, for example, has to defend the "Friends of God" against that accusation: "Today the prince of this world has sown weeds among the roses, and at times the roses are choked and torn by the brambles. Children, a difference must be established, a sort of separation, whether it be in the cloisters or outside of them. The fact that the 'Friends of God' do not resemble the friends of the world does not constitute them a sect."

A few spectacular reappearances of the underground stream—quickly suppressed—called the attention of upright souls to forgotten truths. "As early as the eleventh century stations of light appeared in Italy and spread into France."[20]

"Muffled revolts are springing up throughout the entire Christian world," wrote Raoul Stephan.[21] All of these movements emphasized again, not only the fundamental truths of salvation and sanctification, but also those which concern the church.

AT THE TIME OF THE REFORMATION

The truths of the sixteenth century, which having rapidly become a forceful river now reappeared, owed their survival to the sum total of favorable exterior circumstances. The great biblical truths of justification by faith and of the universal priesthood of all believers could again be proclaimed in broad daylight. Why did the churches of the Reformation remain in the groove of Roman Catholic Church doctrine? Why did the Reformers set up their communities as multitudinist churches instead of returning, as they did on many other points, to the apostolic model of churches of "professing believers"?

This is without doubt the great tragedy of the Reformation of the sixteenth century, the source of the "misunderstanding of the Church," as Brunner calls it, from which present-day Protestantism is suffering, the origin of numerous schisms during the past four centuries, regrettable confusion in the present, and reconciliations which risk seriously leading to new difficulties in the future.[22]

What is most heartrending is that the Reformers saw—or at least caught a glimpse of—the true nature of the church in the Word of God but, because of varying circumstances, were hindered from communicating their conviction on this point to the movement to which they gave the impetus.

LUTHER

Evidently the first place among the Reformers goes to Luther. He was the first to make a breach in the Roman Catholic system. He was also the one who most clearly saw the true nature of the church. All of the Reformers, more or less, were inspired by his work, as much by its positive aspects as by its omissions. That is why we examine the historical progression of his thought concerning the church in more detail. As has been emphasized many times, Luther was primarily interested in the salvation of the individual.[23]

Personal salvation and the church. The principal event in Luther's life, the one that determined his thinking, was his discovery in the Holy Scripture of justification by faith. "One day after having read Hab. 2:4, 'The righteous shall live by his faith,' it seemed to him that scales fell from his eyes. 'I felt as if I had been born again,' he said. This inner work is like the key to his whole life."[24] That occurred in 1507. *Sola fide et sola scriptura* (faith alone and Scripture alone) are two pillars of all the work of the Reformation. This experience of salvation by faith is, in the first place, an individual experience. Luther's thinking is controlled by the vision of personal salvation.

Nevertheless, the idea of the church was not absent from his thoughts; it runs through his teaching on justification by faith.[25] Of whom is the church composed? Those who like him have experienced justification by faith. As early as 1513 the first outlines of his vision of the church took form in his commentaries on the Psalms and on Genesis.[26] "One is a member of the Church, the mystical Body of Christ," Luther wrote, "when faith has been created in his soul by the Word of God."

In 1520 he wrote that "the Church is, according to the Scripture and the Apostles' Creed, solely the assembly of all believers in Christ [*Versammlung aller Christ-gläubigen*] and is composed of all who live in true faith, hope, and love so that the essence, life, and nature of Christendom is not to be an assembly of bodies, but the reunion of hearts in just one faith. This spiritual communion is quite sufficient to create Christendom."[27]

Luther and the church of believers. "It is surprising," writes Dean S. Strohl, "that Luther did not organize groups of believers and set up with their aid reformed churches in which all believers would have a responsibility and carry on some activity."[28] In a short treatise published in 1523 Luther develops a plan by which a group of souls who have been touched by the Word can be formed within the parishes (*grosse Haufen*—grand masses). This would be the embryo of a community (*Gemeinde*) in which the universal priesthood could be exercised. Luther wanted to form such churches, but circumstances hindered him from doing so. In fact, it was only after the pope and emperor opposed him and the gospel officially that the Reformer had to consider reorganizing the church. At Wartburg he elaborated upon his concept of the church.

On September 29, 1521, with Luther's consent, Melanchthon and his students for the first time took, in privacy, both the bread and the wine of holy communion. Luther hoped that the renewal of the entire church would be accomplished in this way, by the regrouping of true believers around the holy communion. The ill-timed intervention of Carlstadt, who by means of authority introduced the reformation in the great assembly, ruined everything. Luther wanted the need for communion to come from the inner life; first "put in fresh wine skins," that "the souls themselves" may come "driven by spiritual hunger to ask for the sacrament."[29] He wanted the assemblies for holy communion to be made up of those who came of free choice, on the basis of "faith alone."[30]

After his return to Wittenberg, Luther reestablished the ancient order of the mass in the great assembly, abolishing the chalice; but for the "worthy ones," the true believers, there was a private ceremony with the chalice.[31] "If we truly practiced this doctrine," Luther wrote in April, 1522, "there would not be as now a thousand or so who would partake of the sacrament, but scarcely a hundred. There would then be fewer of these horrible sins . . . we would be at last a Christian assembly instead of what we are now, scarcely any better than pagans bearing the name of Christians. We could separate from among us those who show by their works that they have never believed and have never had life, which is now impossible for us to do."[32]

How can we attain this "Christian assembly"? "I have no other advice to give than to preach the Gospel, turn away people from the sacrament and from all exterior observances until they feel they are Christians and show it, and until they themselves aspire to faith and love first, then to the outer sacrament and other similar things."[33]

But once more events combined to thwart his plan. Near Easter of 1523 the crowds were exerting pressure on the preachers to give them the sacrament, not because of "spiritual hunger" but in order to follow tradition. Luther, feeling that he could not stand against this pressure, sought a means to avoid unworthy participation in holy communion. In his sermon on Good Friday, 1523, and more explicitly in his *Formula missae* of December, 1523, he developed the idea of an examination before communion closely following the one given in the early church before baptism. The faithful who wished to partake of the communion were to submit to a double examination: (1) the pastor questioned them concerning their religious knowledge and their conduct, (2) at the time of communion, they went forward and gathered around the altar. Thus the entire assembly could judge them and, should the occasion arise, could oppose giving the holy communion to notorious sinners.

By participation at the table of the Lord, Luther said, they would publicly proclaim that they were Christians.[34] Therefore, one had to be on guard that those whose lives contradicted their profession of faith did not come in among the Christians without being observed.[35] "Communion at the Lord's Table," said Martin Kähler, "should separate in the church because it represents the unity of the Church."[36]

According to G. Hilbert, "By linking the receiving of the Holy Communion with the meeting of certain conditions and by separating the eucharistic community from the masses, Luther introduces, in reality, a separation within the Popular Church and prepares a 'selection' which will go farther."[37] In the same sermon of Good Friday, 1523, Luther also said, "One could gather separately those who believe correctly. . . . I have been wanting for a long time to do it, but it has not been possible; for there has not yet been sufficient preaching and writing."[38] Luther at that moment was still impressed by the life of the flourishing communal body of the Bohemian Brethren.

In December, 1525, Luther had an important interview with Schwenck-feld on the subject of *the constitution of a church of the neotestamentary type.* He admitted that until then the spiritual and moral condition of the people had scarcely been improved. According to Schwenckfeld's notes, Luther wished to "draw up a register with the names of Christians in order to observe their walk"[39] but "true Christians are not numerous as yet. I would certainly like to see two of them together; I do not know a single one." Several times between 1522 and 1527 he expressed the desire to form a true church of those "who seriously wished to be Christians." He developed this subject especially in his prologue to the *Deutsche Messe* in 1526.[40]

"There are three kinds of divine service," he said:

> 1. The Latin Mass [which he maintains for the young people who are learning that language];
> 2. German Mass and divine worship . . . they are held publicly in the churches before all the people among whom there are many who do not yet believe so are not Christians. . . . For here there is not yet any ordered and certain assembly in which one could govern the Christians according to the gospel, but there is a public incitement to faith and to Christianity.
> 3. But the third kind, which should have the true nature of evangelical order, would not have to take place so publicly among all kinds of folk, but those who earnestly wish to be Christians and confess the Gospel

with hand and mouth would have to register their names and assemble themselves somewhere in a house alone for prayer, for reading of the Scripture, for baptism, and to receive the Sacrament, and to practice other Christian works. In such a reunion one could know which ones did not conduct themselves like Christians, one could revive them, correct them, exclude or excommunicate them according to the rules laid down by Christ in Matt. 18.

Why did not Luther put this plan into action? A few lines farther on he explains it himself:

> If one had people and persons who earnestly desired to be Christians, the order and manner would soon be devised. But I cannot and do not yet wish to set up or to organize such a congregation [*Gemeinde*] or assembly. For I have not yet people and persons for this, and also I do not see many who ask for such a thing. But if the time comes when I must do it and am so compelled, so that I cannot with good conscience leave it undone, then shall I gladly do my part in it, and give the best help that I can for its realization. In the meantime, I wish to continue with the two kinds of worship first mentioned and start a public worship service for the young and so that the others may be called and encouraged to the faith until Christians who seriously desire to live according to the Word may spontaneously form a group.

According to Brunner,

> What he really intended, what appeared to him as the ideal form of the Christian fellowship, he has expressed in his *Deutsche Messe*—a writing which has been found distressing by the Lutheran Church and Theology and is more or less absolutely ignored. . . . Thus, in principle, he realized that the inheritance of the compulsory and popular Church of Constantine and Theodosius was something to be got rid of, and in 'the third manner' regarded the simplest brotherly fellowship as something worth striving for.[41]

That way he came very close to the *ekklesia* of the New Testament. Pastor H. Venske writes:

> That is Luther's tragic mistake, indescribably tragic, that he did not put it into effect. His Reformation was not a complete success. That is the point where he should have put a final end to that sacramental multitudinist system which had developed and was constantly manifested in the Roman Catholic Church. That was not done. Totally inconsistent compared with his understanding of the apostolic church, Luther again ended with a popular sacramentalist church. One cannot put the blame for this wrong formation of the church on anyone but Luther himself.[42]

After 1526. The thoughts quoted earlier continue to dominate Luther's concept of the "true Church" and reappear from time to time. In a letter to Nicholas Haussmann on March 29, 1527, he differentiates between the

assembly (*Sammlung*) of the Christians for public meeting and that of
the non-Christians in the public *theatralis concio* (theatrical assembly).
He expresses the hope that Christian assemblies will be organized after
the *visitatio* (visit in the churches of a team of two pastors and two laymen).[43] "The parishes are to be thus visited so that communities may be
organized."[44] In a letter to the clergymen of Hesse in June 26, 1533, the
same thought is expressed: only within the framework of this assembly
can church discipline be exercised.[45] "All must be taught according to
the Gospel but all cannot be governed by it. The censure of people has
its place only in the assembly of Christians."[46]

"Among the others neither law, nor ordinance, nor warning will be of
any value; all one can do is let them go; in any case, forced services do not
please God and are useless and wasted." Exterior discipline in the present
life is, as far as Luther is concerned, a matter for the Christian authorities,
but not for the church. On this point his concept differs totally from
that of Calvin, who would subject the popular church to church discipline
and would have the whole population of Geneva pledge themselves to the
confession of faith. In his large catechism of 1529 Luther defines the
true church thus:

> I believe that there exists a small holy group [*heiliges Häuflein*] and
> community on earth made up only of saints, under just one head, Christ,
> called out and assembled by the Holy Spirit in *one* faith, *one* sentiment,
> *one* thought, with diverse gifts, but united in love, without quarrels or
> divisions. I also am a part and a member of it; I am a participant and
> co-beneficiary of all its wealth. I have been brought into it by the Holy
> Spirit, united to it by having listened to the Word of God and by still
> listening to it. Before becoming a part of it, we all belonged to the devil
> and knew nothing of God and of Christ.[47]

Luther remains constantly faithful to that vision. In 1541 he writes:
"In the beginning they taught what Saint John said: (I John 2:19) 'They
went out from us, but they were not of us' and *In ecclesia sunt, sed non
de Ecclesia* (They are *in* the Church but not *of* the Church), item:
Numero, sed non merito (They are of the number but do not merit the
title.) From that one draws this distinction: not *all* of those who claim
to be Christians really are."[48]

In his work on the councils and the churches, Luther gives seven
distinguishing marks of the true church, which show that his first concept
has not changed.[49] "The Church is always there and only there where
the Holy Spirit gives to men faith in Christ, thus sanctifying them, writing
God's commandments on the tablets of their human hearts. He gives
the true knowledge of God; he sanctifies Christians. . . . Where you see

and hear the Word preached, believed, confessed, and put into practice, there, without any doubt, must certainly be a true, holy, Catholic Church, a holy, Christian people, even though they may be few in number."

Ecclesiastic, public and private discipline, public worship service with praise and thanksgiving, the ministry of the Word and the "virtues of the Cross," that is, the sufferings for Christ, are the other different signs of the true Church.[50]

What then was the substance of Luther's thought concerning the church? According to Brunner, "Of all the great teachers of Christianity, Martin Luther perceived most clearly the difference between the Ecclesia of the New Testament and the institutional church."[51] A. von Harnack comments: "Luther never could forget that the true church was the community of believers."[52] Only the free assembly of believers portrays "the authentic form of the Lutheran Church organization,—still better the organization of the communities," says Walter Köhler.[53]

So he never called the mixed groups of believers and unbelievers a "church." The great church of Wittenberg was to him not a church but the *civitas Viteberga*.[54] The church was only "the communion of believers."

For the *gathering of the believers* Luther uses the words "meeting" (*Versammlung*) or "private community" (*sonderliche Gemeyne*). One would have to say *eine christliche Gemeine oder Sammlung* (a Christian community or assembly).

> The best expression and the clearest of all would be *eine heilige Christenheit* (a holy Christendom). The word *communio* which is added to it should never really be translated as communion, but by community. . . . To say it as the Germans do one should say: the community of the saints, that is to say, the community where there are only saints, or more clearly yet, a holy community. . . . That is the meaning of this addition, "I believe that there is on the earth a holy community, a small group of saints whose only head is Christ."[55]

Luther had wanted to establish this "community of the saints" by gathering together those who were truly believers "in a house separately." According to Schwenckfeld, he planned to hold these assemblies in a convent or in his home.[56] Only those who would "enroll"[57] would be permitted to enter, those who "confess the gospel by word and deed" and are capable of "defending their faith, teaching others, and helping to spread the kingdom of Christ."[58]

In that assembly there would not be much singing[59] and there would be no liturgy, only the teaching of Christians,[60] prayer and Bible reading, baptism, and holy communion. Luther's plan was inspired not only by the apostolic model but also by the practice of the early church which distinguished between the *missa catechumenorum*, which was open to all, and the *missa fidelium*, to which only the baptized had access.[61] "There it is recommended to each member that he care for the others."[62]

One can "recognize those who do not conduct themselves as Christians" and exercise church discipline. One can also require of the Christians gifts for charity, given voluntarily and distributed to the poor according to the example given by Paul (2 Co 9).[63] But since the time has not yet come,[64] one must continue to preach the gospel "until the Christians who take the Word seriously find each other and ask for an assembly." Luther wanted them to evangelize on several consecutive days, as is now done in evangelistic campaigns.[65]

Therefore, for him the *popular church* was a mission field. The meetings were for those who "have yet to become Christians,"[66] "principally for the young people and to stimulate the common people"[67] to the faith. The "German Mass" intended for the popular church was to be "a public excitation to the faith and to Christianity"[68] in order to attract the crowds "who stand around and watch to see something new, exactly as if we were holding a worship service in the midst of Turks and pagans."[69]

Luther did not scorn exterior methods: "If it would help, I would be willing to ring all the bells, pump all the organs, and cause to resound everything which can give a sound."[70] He maintained the liturgy and ritual forms in this assembly to avoid confusing the people,[71] but he labored under no delusions concerning the composition of these "churches": "The crowd is and remains non-Christian, even though they are all baptized and call themselves Christians."[72] That is why, he continued, "one must not count among the number of Christians those who do not live godly Christian lives; one must not console them as if they were Christians, by speaking to them a great deal of the pardon for sins and of the grace of Christ."[73]

> There are among the people of God, secretly, a few false Christians who do not believe. They do not take away holiness from God's people because they are secretly unbelievers.
> The church or the people of God do not tolerate false, unbelieving Christians who are such openly; they punish them and try to lead them into the way of salvation also, or else, if they will not believe, they exclude them from the holy place and consider them as heathen as in Matt. 18:17.
> Where there are no keys [church discipline] neither are there any people of God.[74]

That is not the "ecclesiology of the *young* Luther," since the Reformer writes these words fifteen years after the beginning of his struggle against the Illuminists.[75]

"The church of professing Christians is the fixed goal of the popular church."[76] "The base remains the popular church, but the supreme goal is the constitution of a true community of confessing believers."[77] "Those who do not wish to be converted and sanctified," said Luther, "let them be excluded from this holy people."[78] In any case, "to recognize equal rights for believers and unbelievers is absolutely contrary to Luther's ideas," says Dr. G. Hilbert.[79]

The concept of a popular church in which believers and unbelievers live together without distinction was far from the Reformer's mind.[80] It was not the congregation politic or the community of neighbors, but rather the community of Christians truly filled with the Christian Spirit which he considered to be the Church . . . he asked for voluntary membership and an individual declaration of faith from the members of the community."[81]

Causes of the failure. In practice, however, Luther was not able to realize his vision of the church. Why? Brunner gives one of the reasons for it: "But in practice, at the time of the construction of his Christian community, Luther found it an absolute necessity to have both the co-operation of the State and the use of a legal administration. He allowed the territorial princes to organize the Church and to govern it by law."[82]

According to Karl Müller, "The aggressive and conquering power of Lutheranism at its inception was lost in all places at the very moment when the authorities took everything into their hands and produced the Lutheran confession."[83]

Professor H. Strohl thinks that it was the particular moral and spiritual condition in Saxony which hindered Luther from putting his plans into effect.[84] Another reason is that Luther retained *the concept of the Constantinian corpus christianum* in his thinking. He did not want to break away from the ecclesiastical institution; he wanted to reform it. In his Ninety-Five Theses Luther attacked only the papacy's misuse of its power, indulgences, etc. He continued to ask for a council to reform the church.[85] Bender claims that "his maintaining the second concept and its dominant role over the course of the years is proof of the influence of the Middle Ages on Luther's thought."[86]

"Although Luther saw the true nature of the Ekklesia as the church which one can perceive by faith alone," Brunner said, "he was too much influenced by Augustine and the Middle Ages to ignore the other aspect,— the institution governed by laws."[87]

K. Ecke believes that "*sacramentalism* is the real reason that Luther's Church did not become the nucleus of apostolic communities with an outreach of popular missions, as the Reformer had foreseen, but that instead it took the form of a Church with regeneration invested in baptism and the Holy Communion, thus lowering it to the level of a superficial, popular custom."[88]

The fatal turning point. Beginning in 1526, one notices a change in Luther's concept of the church. From that time on it returned, more or less, to the Catholic concept, abandoning faith in the power of the Word alone to bring about reforms, and placing reliance on the support of the civil authorities.

Luther began launching into insults and slander, directed not only toward the papists, but just as much toward all evangelical Christians who, out of obedience to the Word of God, could not go along with him in his concept of the territorial church, baptismal regeneration, and the holy communion offered to the masses. In his youth, Luther had written: "One must force no one to believe; one must permit each one to exercise his free will whether it be to follow or not to follow . . . conscience and faith should be subordinate to God alone."[89] But this change makes Heitmüller comment, "Luther is responsible for the martyrdom of thousands and tens of thousands of God's children."[90]

From 1530 on he approved the death penalty for all those who contradicted his doctrine. In his explanation of Psalm 82[91] he said that all Christians who were teaching and preaching the Word of God publicly, unless they were pastors, must be executed, "even if they are teaching correctly."[92] Melanchthon also asked for capital punishment for the leaders of the Anabaptists.[93] The two Reformers, in reply to the Elector of Saxony, wrote that he should condemn to death the Anabaptist leaders and their congregations.[94]

According to Dr. Karl Müller, "The doctrine of the sacraments assumes a more and more Catholic character; sacramental pomp is substituted for justification by faith; instead of the church in which the saints who have believed joyously assemble, a hierarchical, ecclesiastical system is formed."[95]

After the peasants' revolt—peasants who, at the beginning asked for nothing but justice while placing their reliance on the Word of God (see *The Twelve Articles of the Peasantry*, especially articles 1, 2, 3, 12, which are concerned only with the kingdom of God)—Luther abandoned his own people and took his place beside the princes. In *Wider die mörderischen und räuberischen Rotten der Bauern* he wrote: "Aim, flog, massacre however you can. Should you die while so doing, be sure that you could never find a more blessed death." History teaches that Luther's advice was never more faithfully followed.

"It was not worthy of Luther to take this step [to return to the Catholic system] the consequences of which caused greater harm to the evangelical truth than any one can tell," says Dr. M. Baumgarten.[96]

Luther's contemporaries well understood his sudden change. The Silesian Reformer Schwenckfeld wrote,

> In the beginning Luther's doctrine was clearly better, purer, and more sound than it is at present,—which his first books prove! In time the scholars strayed far from the truth. How I wish he had remained true to his first calling and had not permitted his own wisdom, apart from the Spirit and contrary to the will of the Lord. . . . He has become very much taken up with the outward or external forms, since the revolt of the peasants and since he fought against the truth on the question of the sacrament, and has linked external things with internal things, and without these he does not want to allow anyone to be saved. . . . Even if, by a gracious revelation from God, he discovered many mistakes in the papacy, it was not given to him to reform the sacraments; even today the papists praise him for this, even if they condemn him for everything else; and because they can now keep the essential cause of all error, Luther having confirmed it, papacy subsists.[97]

Toward the end of his life, Luther regretted having decided in favor of the territorial system of multitudinist churches. He wrote:

> Among a thousand parishioners one can scarcely find one true Christian.[98]
> We are scarcely anything more than pagans bearing the name of Christians.[99]
> If you find one peasant who is a Christian, you find a thousand who are not.[100]
> If one were to baptize adults and the old people now, I can wager that there would most certainly not be even a tenth who would be baptized.[101]
> I would prefer that the peasants, the middle class people, and the nobility who now misuse the Gospel, were still under the Papacy. They are only an obstacle, a shame, and a loss to the Gospel.[102]
> If I were to start over again to preach the Gospel, I would do it differently. I would leave the great masses under the government of the Pope; they are not improved by the Gospel,—on the contrary, they abuse liberty.[103]

Even if Luther had wanted only to reform the Catholic Church, he had, however, fixed as a definite goal the restoration of the church to its original state. "Only primitive Christianity is the true Church," he said.[104] It is still the objective which the Reformation must reach. The multitudinist church was for him nothing but a makeshift, a means of access to the true community of believers. What would he have said had he known that his temporary solution would be considered by his successors to be the only valid expressions of his thought, and that those who would quote his name as their authority would relentlessly pursue the Christians who were daring enough to put into effect the ideal that he had set forth in his *Deutsche Messe!*

Is it not time today, when conditions have changed so much, when the walls of the "corpus christianum" have crumbled one after another, to take the thought of the great Reformer seriously? "We know today that Luther wanted to accomplish something else"; Brunner says, "but he could not do it. This is a historical fact. What Luther wanted to accomplish but could not is what we today should do our utmost to bring to pass."[105]

MELANCHTHON

The young Melanchthon. Melanchthon also at first considered the church "properly and principally" as "the assembly of the saints." In the *Confessio Augustana,* he defines it as "the assembly of all believers, where the Gospel is preached in its purity and where the sacraments are correctly administered according to the Gospel." In the variant of 1540 he even says specifically that "the Church, in its proper meaning, is the assembly of the members of Christ, that is to say saints who truly believe and who are obedient to Christ, even if, in this life, many wicked people and hypocrites are mixed in among them." In the apology of this same confession (article 7) he says:

> When we confess "I believe in the holy Christian Church" we are saying that the Church is holy. Those without God and the wicked cannot be the holy Church. Then comes "the communion of the saints" which explains even more clearly and more precisely just what the Church signifies: that is to say the mass [*Haufen*] or the assembly of those who confess the same Gospel, who have the same knowledge of Christ, the same Spirit which renews, sanctifies, and rules their hearts.
> The wicked are in the Church only by name, not by their works; [they are] dead members of the churches.
> According to the Gospel, only those who have received spiritual blessings, who have received the Holy Spirit, are a part of the people of God. This Church is the kingdom of Christ as opposed to the kingdom of the devil. . . . The true Church is the kingdom of Christ, that is, the gathering of all the saints, because those without God are not directed by the Spirit of Christ.

Later on Melanchthon turns to a different concept:

> The visible church is a gathering of those who accept the Gospel of Christ and use the sacraments correctly; in this gathering God is at work and renews many unto life eternal; in this assembly there are many who are not regenerate but who, however, accept the true doctrine. . . . Others have an orthodox faith; they are not the enemies of the Church

nor are they heretics, but have only a few moral vices. . . . Those people are not excommunicated; however, they are called dead members; they are only a part of the exterior society of the Church. The marks of the true Church are the whole Gospel and the legitimate use of the sacraments.[106]

Melanchthon seems to want to take the opposite view of the Anabaptists and, in the prospect of a struggle against them, changes his opinion: "I have touched upon this briefly in order that godly people may be made firm against the Anabaptists and that they may remember that in the Church it is often the wicked who rule; as Christ said, the Church resembles a net in which there are good and bad fish."[107]

In the thinking of the humanist, little by little reason takes precedence over faith: "Belonging to the true Church is not based on saving faith but on accepting the correct doctrine," says M. Jacobs.[108] The church, then, becomes the saving institution. This line of reasoning is parallel to Luther's throughout all of Lutheran theology. We find it again, for example, in the writings of Martin Chemnitz (1522-86): "The Church is a body in which there are many rotten and dead members, but among whom unity reigns where doctrine is concerned."[109] Johann Gerhard (1582–1637) and David Hollatz (1646–1713) place the emphasis on the institution, the purity of doctrine, and on the sacraments which are considered to be valid even if administered by unworthy ministers.[110]

CASPAR SCHWENCKFELD

Melanchthon's evolution had repercussions on Luther's thinking. It has been claimed that Melanchthon was his "evil genius." But there was among Luther's disciples a man who could have been of inestimable help to him: the Duke of Silesia's counselor, Caspar Schwenckfeld von Ossig (1480–1561).

Professor K. Heim writes: "The vocation of that man was to reestablish a close relationship between Luther the Reformer, whose student he was, and the living Church of apostolic times. How many worries our Church would have been spared if, from the beginning, this man's voice had been heard with Luther's and if he had been able to exercise his influence on the Reformation."

Schwenckfeld and Luther. Schwenckfeld welcomed Luther as a "messenger from God" and in 1519 was won over to his ideas. He diligently read Luther's writings but also reserved enough time each day to read four chapters from the Bible. Although he was not a theologian, he began to preach, encouraged by Luther, with whom he corresponded constantly. He organized private gatherings for edification which were attended by members of the best families of Silesia. Many pastors were

keenly interested and drawn into a revival movement which soon spread
all across Silesia in all social classes, from duke to peasants. Rather than
seeking masses of people to join the group, Schwenckfeld sought those
with the "serious and inward Christianity" which bears fruit in one's
daily life. The faith that justifies must develop into a transformed life.
"The question of the moral fruits of the Reformation becomes the decisive
question for him."[111]

In December, 1525, Schwenckfeld went to Wittenberg to see Luther,
who received him cordially. The two Reformers discussed the sacraments,
church discipline, and the future of the church. Schwenckfeld was desirous "that they should all be able to join hands with a view to the building
of a Christian Church." It was largely owing to the influence of this
interview that Luther wrote his *Deutsche Messe* in the early part of 1526.

It was not before 1527, after having worked eight years "for the Word
of God and Luther's doctrine" that Schwenckfeld obtained the assurance
of his own salvation after a *personal experience of the new birth*. It was
the decisive turning point in his life and the basis of his concept of the
church. With him it was not in the least a question of a "mystical experience" as some have claimed. Schwenckfeld insisted upon faith alone
which lays hold on the promises of God without feeling having any part
in it. "Cling to His sacrifice for sin," he wrote. "Comfort yourself with
complete trust in His justice." Contrary to the mystics (Tauler, Münzer,
Carlstadt, S. Franck) whom he condemned, Schwenckfeld wished to know
no other source of inspiration than the Bible shedding light on the Bible.

In his assiduous study of the Bible, Schwenckfeld came upon a number
of points where Luther's doctrine seemed to deviate from the teaching
of the apostles. He called attention, in particular, to *five dangerous articles in Lutheran preaching:*

1. that faith alone saves, without any mention of a new life
2. that we have no free will
3. that we cannot keep the commandments of God
4. that our works are nothing
5. that Christ did everything for us

These positions, correct if seen in their biblical context, bear bitter
fruit if they are arbitrarily taken out of context. To that add Luther's
new sacramental view: baptism makes Christians; therefore, all who are
baptized may partake of the holy communion.

Schwenckfeld hesitated more and more to follow Luther in his new
antiscriptural ways. His doubts as to the legitimacy of infant baptism
and the holy communion to be given to the Christianized masses grew in

proportion to his delving into the study of the apostolic church. He believed that "the sacraments were instituted only for Christian believers."

"Instead of evangelizing, they baptize," J. Schmidt writes. "Baptism becomes the new birth and replaces the personal testimony of the Holy Spirit; sanctification of the life disappears; the Holy Communion is given to the masses; the universal priesthood of believers no longer exists except on paper; the unfortunate joining of Church and State bears dangerous consequences: suspicion, persecution of Christian brothers. . . ."[112] According to K. Ecke, "Lutheranism is directed toward a unilateral orthodoxy."

The rupture. Schwenckfeld warned Luther, orally and in writing, of the dangers of the new way that he was taking. Luther replied by writing *Wider die Schwarmgeister*, in which he cited Occam and the Catholic theologians of the Middle Ages as grounds for the defense of his concept of the church.[113] Belonging to the Christian church does not depend on one's personal faith, he maintained, but on adhering to a certain number of theological propositions.

From that time on Luther pursued Schwenckfeld with implacable hatred, launched into insults and slandered him. No longer did he call him anything but *Stenckfeld* (an ill-smelling field), "an insane fool, a demon-possessed, a heretic, an illuminist, who understands nothing, knows nothing, through whom the devil spews out books." He sent back Schwenckfeld's writings, in which he had exposed Luther's doctrine, without even reading them. Many times Schwenckfeld declared his readiness to debate with the Lutheran preachers, when, where, and as long as they would like on all points that would seem useful to them. The only replies to his offer were insults and cursing.

The publishing of Schwenckfeld's writings by Oecolampadius in 1527 and by Zwingli in 1528 seems to have stirred up Luther's animosity toward their author. Ferdinand I, influenced by his court theologian, Fabri, also declared himself against Schwenckfeld. Harassed by the Lutheran preachers, who "blow their master's trumpet," the Silesian Reformer was soon obliged to go into exile. For thirty years, until seventy-two years of age, he was forced to wander across Europe, tracked like a wild beast.

Schwenckfeld, however, remained respectful and deferential toward his former teacher. In 1524, after ten years of banishment, he wrote: "Let Dr. Martin Luther think what he will of me; being a man of honor I am indebted to him for love, honor, and every good." (Calvin was treated scarcely any better by Luther than was Schwenckfeld. But the Reformer from Geneva displayed the same Christian qualities as did

Schwenckfeld: "Even if Luther called me a devil, I will honor him by recognizing him as an experienced servant of God with brilliant qualities as well as great faults.") Schwenckfeld added, moreover: "Though I have benefited from his services, I am not obliged to accept what is false."

The work of Schwenckfeld. The *exiled Reformer* went from place to place, spreading the gospel. In 1529 he arrived in Strasbourg, was received by Capiton and Zell, and stayed there for five years. His ecclesiastical concepts drew him to Bucer, but a discussion with him led him to leave the city and to stay in Ulm and Augsburg for some time. Schwenckfeld saw "his vocation to be that of working with individuals." He would have liked to "proclaim to the entire world the gospel of Jesus Christ and the riches of His grace."

Orally and in writing he counseled thousands of people in eastern and southern Germany. His correspondence and his writings for special occasions, published in 1961 by the Schwenckfelder Library of Pennsburg, Pennsylvania, filled nineteen volumes. The essential themes of his message are: repentance, conversion, a living faith in the crucified and glorified Christ, sanctification by the Spirit, redemption in Jesus Christ, and communion with the resurrected Lord.

Living communities were formed in many places: Strasbourg, Augsburg, Ulm, and even in Prussia. These were especially "churches in the homes," "reading communities," where the Word of God was read and the people prayed. "Let the Christians meet, comfort, and strengthen one another," he wrote. "It is a good thing to have someone with whom you can speak, as often as possible, of the kingdom of the Lord and talk of your understanding of Him. You can comfort one another, pray together, question each other on the Scripture and thus make the way easier for both."[114]

By means of these contacts in the homes, nuclei of a church life conforming to that of New Testament times sprang up in many places. There they prayed, sang, read, and commented on the Bible passages; then they talked over their problems and experiences. Each one had the right to add "his grain of truth" and to verify by the Word of God what had been said.

The elders traveled from one community to another to strengthen the believers. To avoid divisions in the Reformed churches, Schwenckfeld refrained from introducing biblical baptism and the holy communion in these assemblies. He believed that true baptism is the baptism of the Holy Spirit, "the baptism of a new birth and a changed heart," and named the Holy Spirit, the Word of God, and the blood of the Lamb as the three active factors in this new birth. He maintained that faith that lays hold of the work of Christ is indispensable from the human side. However, water baptism was not in the least scorned as it was among the spiritualists. He who has been baptized by the Holy Spirit may be baptized with water, which serves as a symbol of the baptism of the Holy Spirit.

Schwenckfeld's thought. Schwenckfeld vigorously opposed the doctrine of baptismal regeneration: "We are taught that we should not doubt our salvation since we are baptized, as if nothing else were necessary. 'For as soon as we are baptized,' wrote Luther, 'we have Christ dwelling in us and with us . . . so that all who are baptized can glory in being just and holy.' One can see only too clearly by our conduct and life that this is not true! May God have pity on us."[115]

Infant baptism, in his sight, was a return to the circumcision of the Old Testament. According to him, only those who have experienced liberation from the power of Satan should participate in the holy communion.

Schwenckfeld saw the weaknesses and limitations of the Lutheran Reformation with a keenness of insight which astonishes us. "At the beginning," he wrote, "Luther raised his voice against papism; nevertheless the sacramental idea which forms the very foundation of papism he sanctioned, thus confirming the idolatry of the papists. What is more, he included justification in the sacrament instead of leaving it entirely dependent upon Christ."[116]

"The preachers withhold from their listeners half of all that Jesus wishes to be and to give to those He has redeemed," he claimed. "They should preach Christ in His entirety and not only the satisfaction He has obtained for us: One must speak of regeneration and sanctification through Him, not only present the Christ who redeemed us on the Cross, but who is also at present glorified, who reigns, and who sanctifies us."[117] "That which is totally lacking is a reformation of life. This results from speaking of the experience of Christ in a manner contrary to apostolic teaching."[118]

Schwenckfeld was grieved over those churches where "neither those who teach nor those who listen are regenerated believers and saints, but all live in sin and abominations."[119] "The preachers," he stated, "are remarkably tolerant of the unbelievers in the multitudinist Church; but they are manifestly intolerant of any movement of apostolic life, of any effort to form a true ecclesia within the religious institution. The preachers cannot tolerate in their churches true Christians who do not say exactly the same things as they do or who are not in perfect agreement with them on all points."[120]

"Their goal is not the true conversion of individuals nor the forming of living communities of the redeemed; they seek only the result of impressive numbers."[121] "Provided a person believes what they say, praises them, and takes the Holy Communion with them, he is considered to be a good Christian even if he lives as he pleases."[122]

Schwenckfeld vigorously opposed the use of force in religious matters. "How can we permit ourselves to force other people? Who ordered us to do so? Where is it written? What apostle ever did that? Paul never proposed converting the whole city or making such a commonplace thing of the mystery of the faith. . . . In the New Testament the Holy Spirit starts to build from the inside and works toward the exterior; He does not work from the outside toward the inside as in the Old Testament."[123]

The progress of the work. The friends and disciples of Schwenckfeld increased more and more, not only in Silesia, but in all of southern Germany. In 1540 a whole section of Wurtemberg embraced his ideas. The lord of Justingen offered him refuge in his castle and entrusted to him the education of his children. A flourishing and radiant community sprang up there in the center of southern Germany. In 1544 people of all ranks were found among his devoted followers in Schwaben, in the Algäu, in the Graubünden. Among his friends were scholars and pastors, many of whom interceded in his behalf and defended him in their writings. In 1559 the elector of Brandenburg wrote to him that he highly esteemed his books and would very much like to talk with him.

He was also in contact with the Anabaptists: "They are a people who fear God and can be distinguished from the great masses by their irreproachable conduct and their extreme seriousness in religious matters. They have the natural aptitude for sacrifice." He pointed out that "all those who sincerely wish to live with Jesus Christ and to walk in obedience to Him are accused of being Anabaptists."

However, Schwenckfeld seems to have known only the Illuminist and revolutionary branch of Anabaptism. The names he mentions (Thomas Münzer, Hans Hut, L. Hetzer, B. Hübner, A. Bader, H. Schneider, Melchior Hoffmann, Socinus, Servetus, S. Franck, etc.) enable us to understand the severe judgment he brought against them elsewhere: "They lack the true knowledge of salvation; they have no experience of salvation; they have no personal relationship with Jesus Christ . . . few gifts of the Holy Spirit . . . a spirit of judgment . . . little esteem for the Word of God; they consider water baptism to be the new birth . . . there is no sound doctrine among them."[124] These judgments, perfectly justifiable in the case of the Spiritualists and revolutionary Anabaptists, do not relate to the evangelical branch of the Anabaptist movement, as we shall see.

Schwenckfeld died peacefully in Ulm in 1561. His many disciples continued to assemble after the manner of the apostles. Lutheran pastors endeavored to force them to return to the Lutheran Church. They were imprisoned; their children were taken from them. The Catholics tried by trickery and force to bring them back to the Roman Catholic Church. Later on, Count Zinzendorf intervened in their behalf, but without succeeding in persuading the emperor to set them free. He extended to them a welcome to his estate, but the Roman Catholic Church succeeded in having them exiled. A large number of them found a welcome in Pennsylvania, where they were able at last to serve God according to the dictates of their consciences.

Main points of his message. J. Schmitt gives a ten-point summary of Schwenckfeld's main teachings:[125]

1. Regeneration by the Holy Spirit.
2. Justification is just as important as sanctification; faith, as experience; the Word, as the Spirit.
3. The doctrine of baptismal regeneration is antibiblical.
4. The holy communion is reserved for the community of believers.
5. Scripture is the infallible source of knowledge.
6. Evangelization and the healing of the soul are duties incumbent on the Christian church.
7. All believing Christians have the privilege and the responsibility of gathering together to meditate on the Word of God and to pray together. The Holy Spirit bestows gifts on these assemblies.
8. The unity of the Spirit must be cultivated among all the children of God.
9. One should avoid and flee from preachers who, according to the Word, are not preachers of the Word.
10. The church has no right to join forces with the state.

If Luther and the other Reformers had followed Schwenckfeld in these ten points, the churches of the Reformation would have been spared much unprofitable strife, and the biblical ideal of the church would have been realized at least four centuries earlier.

It has been said, as an excuse for the relativity of the great work of the Reformation, that it was impossible for one or two men to perceive and to clear away all the rubbish accumulated in the church during the course of fifteen centuries. An impartial examination of history reveals that such an argument is not entirely accurate. The Reformers were alone only because they chose to be. Had they been able to recognize the areas of biblical truth in the work of Christians like Schwenckfeld, John of Lasco,

Hubmaier and many others, and work together with them, what an irresistible moving of the Spirit would have been seen in the sixteenth century! At least it would have prevented the Catholic theologians from advancing that ready and artificial argument: since the Reformation did not reestablish the church as Jesus and the apostles had instituted it, the Roman Catholic Church found it their duty to oppose it as being false (see H. Küng).

Opinions concerning Schwenckfeld. "Schwenckfeld was a gift of the Grace of God at the time of the Reformation, a complement of the Reformers, by the will of God, so that certain Biblical truths which were being practiced might shine with a new brilliance," says J. Schmitt.[126]

According to K. Ecke, "Among the Reformers it is he who undertook to make accessible to the Church the treasures of the experience of primitive Christianity. By doing this he filled in what was lacking in the practice and theory of the Reformation message, a lack which we keenly feel even today."[127]

"Schwenckfeld had seen that the Church needed to be reformed according to the model of the primitive Church. Luther refused to do it," says H. Venske. "From Luther's refusal of a neo-testamentary reformation sprang a new Babylonian captivity for the Protestant Church which is evident even today."[128]

Even if Schwenckfeld remains, in G. Maron's words, "a figure of great mystery,"[129] and as Erich Sauer says, even if "one cannot entirely agree with him on certain points [it was said that he was slightly tainted with gnosticism] we are, however, astonished again and again at the great spiritual insight in his christology, at his moderation, at his spiritual judgment, and at the nobility of his attitude toward friends and enemies alike."

"Schwenckfeld was neither a heretic nor an Illuminist, but a true Biblical Christian in the midst of innumerable nominal Christians. He sought to awaken and develop an apostolic life, and he succeeded. He shows us the beginnings of the formation of a Biblical Christian Church," says Dr. T. Haarbeck. "That is the principle to which we and the Church must return," according to F. von Bodelschwing.

"May the Holy Spirit, the architect of Christ's Church, now grant that He Himself use the apostolic message which He entrusted four hundred years ago to Caspar Schwenckfeld, a chosen instrument, to lead God's people, and especially the messengers of the Gospel, to a new reflection and introduce them to the whole truth, according to the promise of the Lord," writes O. S. von Bibra.[130]

MARTIN BUCER

Oecolampadius, the Reformer of Basel, was the first one to make a great effort to bring about the admission of a distinction between the church and the state which called itself Christian. With a prophetic glance he grasped the situation of the church. "Now it is true," he said, "that the authorities are Christian, but others could come who would lead the Church into a great tribulation; then what would become of her if she had no autonomous organization?"[131]

He won over to his side Martin Bucer, the Reformer from Strasbourg, who carefully worked out in detail an ecclesiology very much like that of the New Testament: "The members of the church must be drawn out of the world [*von der Welt versammelt*] and united in Christ so as to form one body, an active community in which no member is idle."

His early concept of the church, like that of Luther and his compatriot, Capiton, was the church of the redeemed. If the excesses of certain Anabaptists forced him to abandon the establishing of such a church and if it led him to accept the multitudinist church, it was

> only on the condition of being allowed to transform it, to purify it, and to bring some warmth into it by means of a strict discipline within it to be exercised by the clergy and by willing lay associates. However, he was not permitted to put this discipline into practice. So, leaving the church of the masses as it was, he endeavored to form within it "Gemeinschaften," groups of the faithful willing to submit to the discipline desired . . . who would serve as an example to the Church and raise its spiritual level.
>
> He was quite aware of Martin Luther and his Haufen, the godly groups with which the Reformer had thought to begin to restore the Church, even wondering whether the true Church was not formed in just this way. But they persuaded Bucer (that is, the Magistrate did) not to circulate what he had written on that subject.[132]

The history of the "Christian Community" of Strasbourg is one of the most instructive. In 1545 the pastors of Strasbourg proposed to the city council that they reestablish church discipline with excommunication and banishment. They wanted a "second Reformation" in order to put into effect the "communion of the saints." Bucer carefully worked out a detailed plan according to which the pastors were to go from house to house, instructing their godly parishioners concerning the nature of a true Christian community. After some time they were to gather those who had been thus prepared and explain to them the meaning and purpose of the "Christian community" which was to be built up. If they agreed, the "volunteers" would elect two or three of the "best men" as elders. Their duty would be to supervise the pastors, the community, and the church.

The other people were to be allowed a certain extension of time to enroll with a view to the "entrance examination," a "public interrogation concerning their faith." With a handshake they would pledge themselves to submit to the discipline of the brethren of the community. Their names would be written on a special register.[133] Only those who were a part of the community would be granted full rights to participate in the holy communion.

This project encountered keen opposition from the city council. Nevertheless, several pastors began to put it in practice in their parishes and no longer served holy communion to any who were not members of the community.[134] Bucer, in his explanations to the city council, affirmed that those who had been baptized as infants were to receive instruction before being admitted into the community and were to confess their faith before all the members of the assembly and personally reaffirm the confession made for them by their godparents at the time of their baptism as infants. From the year 1523 Bucer had seen "how meaningless it is to believe that the salvation of infants is linked with the baptismal ceremony and that one must stop considering water baptism as a magical means destined to obtain salvation."[135] This is where the origin of Protestant confirmation is found which Bucer introduced in Hesse after having been prevented from doing so in Strasbourg.

Bucer stressed the mutual edification and exhortation within the communities. Discipline was practiced according to Matthew 18:16. Only those who were members of the community had a right to be called Christians. When the council prohibited these gatherings, the members of the various communities met in a church in secret for mutual edification.[136] "They wanted to form a real *ecclesiola in ecclesia* able to withstand the persecutions which they vaguely foresaw. Since the publishing of Bucer's work on Christian communities had been prohibited, Bucer was forced more and more to withdraw from the leadership of the group. Twelve elders and some laymen took in hand the leading of the brotherhood."[137]

However, after Bucer's departure, in "unexpected devious ways" ("it is clerical art," said Vinet), the pastors succeeded in "decentralizing" this community by holding out to its members the bright prospects of a beneficial multiplication of these groups.[138] In reality, they were no longer authorized even to gather together in the various parishes where they were scattered. Thus this fine beginning came to nothing.

"To my knowledge," writes W. Ninck, "that is the only attempt of the Protestant Church, even up to the present, to bring about a 'second reformation,' that is to say, a restoration of the primitive church as a free community. It was wrecked on several reefs: the close union between

Church and State, the pastors' lack of assurance, and the renascent power of Catholicism."[139]

So neither did Bucer succeed in working out the ideal church of which he had caught a glimpse, because he was not able—or willing—to break with the Constantinian *corpus christianum.* At crucial moments the civil authorities of Strasbourg intervened and it was they whom Bucer asked to organize the new society. His ideas, however, made headway.

We find them again in *François Lambert d'Avignon*[140] and *John of Lasky* (or Lasco). In October, 1526, a synod was held in Homburg (Hessen) to consider the organization and constitution of the Protestant churches. Under the influence of *François Lambert,* a detailed church constitution was carefully worked out which was inspired by Luther's *Deutsche Messe.* The parish was divided into two concentric circles, the smaller constituting the church.

Landgrave Philippe of Hessen was a supporter of this constitution, but Luther and Melanchthon strictly advised him against it. Why? Instead of maintaining his ecclesiastical ideal, Luther had yielded to the influence of his collaborators, Niklaus Haussmann, Justus Jonas, and Melanchthon, who wished to impose everywhere the system of the popular churches founded on the territorial principle. The political prospect of possible peace with the empire induced Luther to repudiate his ideal and to decide in favor of the territorial churches.[141] As for *John of Lasco,* he built up a real church of professing Christians among the refugees in London. The constitution of that church served as a model for a number of churches of the biblical type in the Anglo-Saxon countries.[142]

CALVIN

Calvin, who spent some time in the company of Bucer in Strasbourg, was strongly influenced by him in his concept of the church. Particularly his chapter on church discipline was the key to the Calvinist idea of the church.[143] After having visualized the church especially in its invisible aspect, Calvin was influenced by Bucer to turn his attention to the visible church.

"All of his ecclesiology [Calvin's]," writes J. de Senarclens, "had its beginning in a radical and dramatic doubt which he conceived concerning the validity of his own Church, the church in which he had grown up, which he doubtlessly loved and which occupied a central place in the society of his time. No, that church was not the true one! This was his initial discovery . . ."[144]

The true church is that of the apostles, the one of the early days of the church; it is that one which must be rediscovered and reestablished. "It is the Church first organized by the apostles which we must follow unless we wish to greatly err and to fail," Calvin said. This is what he wrote to Sadolet: "You well know, Sadolet, that not only do we correspond more closely to the church of antiquity than you do, but that we also ask for nothing more than that the Church sometime be restored and set up again just as it was in its primitive days."[145]

Luther's concept of the church was derived from his essential doctrine: justification by faith. Calvin's idea was closely connected with Luther's on predestination. "God's secret choice," he wrote, "is the foundation of the Church."[146] For him, the church is more than anything else the assembly of the elect (*universus numerus electorum*). One comes into the church by the new birth. "The passage and entrance into the Church is a second birth." The church is not an autonomous and initial entity which makes us children of God. We are not members of the church unconditionally from our birth. It is only after our regeneration that we come into the church. That is clearly expressed by Calvin:

> Christ becomes the bridegroom to the faithful on this condition, that they forget their people and their father's house and that, fashioned and regenerated by incorruptible seed into new creatures, they begin to be children of God as much as of the Church. So it is not the Church which is the beginning, it is Christ; the Church does not make new creatures, Christ does; and only when we are new creatures do we come into the Church. The man of faith who is regenerated by Christ becomes a member of the Body of Christ, the Church. . . . Jesus Christ, by enlightening us by faith, grafts us into His body to make us participants of all that is His.[147]

When Calvin began to establish his churches, he profited from the thirty years of the Reformation already passed. These thirty years had shown that having the Word preached in all of its purity, as Luther thought, is not sufficient, but that the Word must also be "rightly understood" if a church is to result from it. Calvin called this church *aliqua Ecclesia*. It is the human church which does not go beyond the local boundaries; it is the "two or three who are gathered" in the name of Christ (Mt 18:20). It is especially on these words of Jesus that Calvin took his stand at that time.[148]

"We acknowledge as members of the Church all who by confession of faith, an exemplary life, and participation in the sacraments unite with us in acknowledging the same God and Christ," Calvin said.[149] "In this Church there is a very large mixture of hypocrites, who have nothing of Christ but the name and outward appearance";[150] this is not a normal state which should be encouraged or perpetuated. "When churches are well regulated, they will not bear the wicked in their bosom."[151] If the believer is to have certainty of faith,[152] "he should also know that he is a member of the Church."[153] He maintained that those who have the responsibility of the churches must, if necessary, help the believer who is troubled by his conscience by urging him to confess his faith, or by excommunicating him from the church if his life contradicts his confession.

The organization of the church in Geneva. "Let all the inhabitants of your city be required to make a confession and to give a reason for their faith in order to know which are in accord with the Gospel," Calvin stated. "All townsmen and inhabitants of Geneva must swear to preserve and maintain" the confession of faith.[154]

Likewise, Calvin wished to achieve in the members of the church of Geneva a Christian conduct and zeal conformable to what may rightfully be expected from every faithful member of the church: "Let every person in every home come to the place of worship every Sunday . . . under penalty of three sous. Let those who do not do their duty by attending, and their families, be warned by the 'guards.' If, after the warning, they continue to fail in their duty, let them be fined a penny for each time." For failure to participate in the holy communion: the same procedure was used;[155] the guards required all church members who were not excommunicated to participate in the sacrament.

Before being admitted into church membership, each one had to be "sufficiently instructed," then he had to "solemnly recite all" that he had learned and make "a profession of his Christianity in the presence of the whole Church."[156] Only then could he be admitted into the church and be received at the communion table. "Let no one be received at the Holy Communion unless he has first made a confession of his faith, that is, until he has declared before the minister that he wishes to live according to the reformation as seen in the Gospel and that he knows his credo [his Creed], the Lord's prayer, and the ten commandments."[157]

Of course, when one has met all of these conditions "one must make up his mind to take the charitable view that all who are called are called to salvation . . . and Christian good-nature requires that one think that all who have entered upon the straight road of salvation are still in the race."[158]

The exercise of discipline. However, if certain members showed by their lives, even after admonition, that they were not truly converted, those in charge were not to hesitate in excluding them from the church. They were to be exhorted publicly on three consecutive Sundays after each member of the church had been "advised to pray for them and to try in every way possible to bring them to repent of their sins in order to avert their being cut off and excommunicated." But the Lord has provided the means to prevent the corrupt members from spreading their corruption throughout the whole Church body. For this purpose excommunication was ordered in order to wipe out and expel from among the people of God those who falsely claim to have faith in Christ and who by dishonest and wicked lives bring disgrace upon His name.[159]

Since the Church is the body of Christ it must not be contaminated by corrupt members lest a part of the shame revert upon the Head.[160]

If he is not converted but preseveres in his hardness of heart and in his obstinacy, on the fourth Sunday the pastor will announce publicly that said shameful and hardened person (naming him) is no longer recognized as a member of the Church and his name is being stricken from the roll.

In the excommunication form it is written that "Having for so long a time sustained, invited, exhorted, and beseeched him to be converted to God, and even having tried every possible means to bring him to repentance, since he perseveres in his impenitence . . . we have cut off said person from the communion of the Church, from the society of the faithful . . . until this sinner gives glory to God by his conversion. . . ."[161]

So one cannot say that Calvin did not have a vision of a church of converted people and that he wished to establish a church in which believers and unbelievers would have the same rights. What one can say is that the manner in which he intended to bring this church into existence certainly bears the marks of his times. He counted on laws and force to get each one to take his place. "If a multitudinist church requires all of its members to recite the confession of faith, it is either violating consciences or it is signing its own death warrant, and thus becoming a church of professing believers."[162]

On the other hand, being the good humanist that he was, he was constantly tempted to confuse, as did Melanchthon, faith with intellectual adherence to the reformed doctrine. Another fatal confusion was that of the spiritual state with the moral state. By repentance and faith, by the new birth, we are placed in a new position before God, we are children of God, members of the body of Christ. Are we suddenly transformed 100 percent morally? Do we become incapable of sinning or at least of committing serious moral mistakes? Unfortunately, experience and Scripture answer in the negative. That is what Calvin seemed to forget in his controversy with the Anabaptists. Speaking of moral mistakes committed by the Corinthians, he concludes:

"What does the Apostle do about it? Does he seek separation from them? Does he discard them from Christ's kingdom? He not only does none of these things, but he acknowledges them and heralds them as a church of Christ and a society of saints. If the church remains among the Corinthians [where these moral sins are found] . . . who will presume to deny the title of church to those to whom even a tenth part of these crimes cannot be imputed?"[163]

But neither let us forget that the apostle Paul, far from sanctioning the state of the church at Corinth, demanded that they remove the wicked one from among them, which Calvin, by a strange lack of logic, also asked the reformed churches to do a few lines farther on. But Calvin was no more successful than the other Reformers in freeing himself from the setting of medieval thought of Constantinian Christianity.[164] The ecclesiastical ordinances of 1541, in which the magistrate plays a great role, give a characteristic reflection of his thinking of this point.[165]

The condemnation of Michel Servetus by the secular branch, repudiated by Calvin's successors, shows how difficult it was for the men of the sixteenth century to get away from the ideas which had been governing the Christian world since the time of Augustine. As Dr. Visser't Hooft says, "The institutional Church, indissolubly linked to society and the state in one vast Corpus Christianum, has been too strong for the Reformers. They could not bring themselves to break completely with the sociological forms in which the Church had lived ever since the days of Constantine. And so the inherent law of the institution acted as a strong brake upon their work of renewal."[166]

ZWINGLI AND THE ANABAPTISTS

This limitation appears most particularly in the work of Zwingli, the Reformer of Zürich. For him also the true members of the church were the elect,[167] and the church was the local gathering of all who confessed Christ in that place.[168] He hesitated, however, to follow the Anabaptists in their demand for separation between church and state. Indeed, he preached for three years in Zürich before breaking with the Roman Catholic Church. He had become an influential political personality, highly esteemed by the city council. As a good disciple of Erasmus, he sought to act prudently.

It was he who asked the council to summon an assembly in January, 1523, which was to be called "the first discussion in Zürich." So he put into the hands of the civil authorities the leadership of the Reformation. "The council had made possible the Reformation in Zürich for which Zwingli was indebted to the state. If Zwingli had accepted or supported the free church movement, the entire Reformation would have been smothered by the state and Zürich would have returned to Catholicism."[169]

The tribute exacted for this official protection was as heavy for Zwingli as for the Reformation movement as a whole. In fact, Zwingli had to part company with certain ones among his intimate friends and collaborators and deliver them up to the fury of the "Christian" authorities. As Professor F. Blanke proved, Zürich is the cradle of the oldest Anabaptist community, and its founders were faithful disciples and collaborators of Zwingli.[170] G. Rousseau writes, "As early as 1521 Zwingli had formulated a reforming principle of capital importance, namely: All that in matter of doctrine and practice is not positively *ordered* by the Scripture, should be rejected (whereas for Luther, only the doctrines and practices condemned by Scripture were to be rejected). As early as 1519 he refused to believe that nonbaptized infants would be lost. Two years later he designated as superstition the doctrine according to which baptism purifies from original sin.

The question of baptism was soon on the agenda of the Zürich Reformation. According to Rousseau, "In 1523, Zwingli wrote a document composed of 67 articles, in view of a public debate, the eighteenth of which established that in the apostolic Church baptism was conferred on catachumens who had confessed Jesus Christ as their Savior and had given proof of a living faith. By that Zwingli opened the way to a group of cultured young men who worked with him and whose scholarship had not quenched their fearless zeal."[171]

These collaborators of Zwingli were Conrad Grebel from an old aristocratic family of Zürich, son of a member of the council, former student of the universities of Vienna and Paris;[172] Felix Mantz, son of a canon in the church of Zürich, an experienced Hebrew scholar also influenced by humanism;[173] Georg Blaurock, a former monk who came to be one of the finest evangelists;[174] and Simon Stumpf, a former priest. "Other men of the surrounding areas also joined this group occasionally. They were Ludwig Hätzer of St-Gall, a former student in Freibourg and a distinguished Hebrew scholar like Mantz; Wilhelm Roüblin, formerly parish priest of Wytikon;[175] and especially Balthasar Hübmaier, formerly a disciple of Dr. Eck, then professor of theology and chancellor at the University of Ingolstadt, preacher at the imperial cathedral of Regensburg."[176] These friends of Zwingli, who have been called the "radicals" or "the left wing of the Reformation,"[177] urged the Reformer to take up the cause of a definite reformation.

Since Zwingli could not make up his mind to do that, the "radicals" began to meet among themselves. In a letter dated September, 1524, Grebel explained the reasons for their separation from Zwingli.[178] In substance, what he said was

> Zwingli put the Bible in our hands[179] and recommended that we study it. We did so, and through the reading of the New Testament we discovered a Church different from the one Zwingli is teaching about. According to

the New Testament (Matt. 7:14) the Church is the community of the few who believe correctly and who walk in conformity with their faith.
    The real aspiration of the Anabaptists did not have baptism in view, but rather the Church. . . . The Baptism of believers was only the most visible result of this new form of Christian community. Because of this outer sign of recognition, Zwingli called Grebel and his friends "Anabaptists," the name which has ever since clung to the movement. They called themselves the "brothers" and "sisters" according to the early Christian custom.[180]

In the autumn of 1524 Grebel had a son. He refused to have him baptized because, according to the New Testament, faith should precede baptism. But since baptism was obligatory according to the civil law, conflict with the council became inevitable. They published an edict specifying that the baptism of newborn babes was obligatory and was being maintained as it was before the Reformation. After several interviews with his former friends, Zwingli sided with the council and published a work against the "catabaptists."

At this time numerous groups of believers were already gathering together in many places throughout the area for Bible study, prayer, and to celebrate holy communion. At Zürich, Zwingli and his colleagues were again celebrating mass, and continued to do so until Easter, 1525. Under the powerful preaching of Georg Blaurock a great number of people repented and were converted.

"On January 17, 1525, after a public debate on baptism organized at Zwingli's request, and where the verdict was favorable to him, the Council ordered that all infants not yet baptized should be 'brought to baptism' within a week under penalty of the banishment of the parents."[181] This was the signal for the creation of the first free church of professing believers. "It was a turning point of historic dimensions. For in that time, in all of the Christian world, State Christianity reigned. In that important village of Zollikon, a group of revived Christians dared to establish a Christian fraternity, that is to say a church, without the help of the authorities."[182] Grebel baptized Blaurock, who baptized about fifteen brethren. It was the cradle of the Baptist movement, which therefore has nothing in common with the "Spiritualists," heirs of the Catholic mystics of the early part of the Middle Ages, nor with the German revolutionaries like Thomas Müntzer.[183]

Professor F. Blanke concludes: "I know of no revival events from the period of the Reformation like those told us from Zollikon. Above all, I have nowhere encountered this almost stormy eruption of the spirit of repentance which grips an entire group of people."[184] He also says, "Only men who repented could be baptized. Conversion or personal repentance became at that time the essential and decisive condition for baptism. Without repentance, no baptism, that is to say no salvation."[185]

The reaction of Zwingli and of the council of Zürich was not in the least Christian. Zwingli published a virulent pamphlet against the "catabaptists." The council, with the approval of Zwingli, condemned the leaders of the movement to prison. Grebel died there; Blaurock, who was flogged as he went through the streets, was banished and took refuge in Tyrol where he was burned at the stake; Mantz was drowned. All who fell back into the "heresy" suffered the same fate.

Zwingli organized the Church of Zürich more and more according to the pattern of the old covenant.[186] Professor Farner, casting a retrospective glance over the evolution of the Reformer, concludes:

> My conviction becomes stronger and stronger that Zwingli, who compromised with the world of his day, was mistaken in his expectations. With Zwingli considering the Gospel to be an ideal which could not be realized, we are scarcely any more advanced. Shall we be forced to say to ourselves for another four hundred years: patience! one cannot expect everything all at one time. Let us give glory to the truth and frankly avow: History has judged Zwingli's teaching, and its verdict leaves no room for doubt; are we people of Zürich noticeably closer to the Kingdom of God than was the population of Zürich in 1523? Was Zwingli right in having faith in the possibility of educating an entire people by means of a policy both realistic and idealistic?[187]

Progress of Anabaptist churches. Meanwhile the Baptist movement was rapidly spreading, not only around Zürich, but also throughout all of Europe. "As a reaction against the severe measures enacted, a popular movement in favor of baptism came into being in all of the surrounding region during the two months which followed . . . assemblies of baptized believers were formed."[188] The exiled brethren carried their evangelical ideas into Italy and through the valleys of the Rhine and the Danube as far as the Netherlands and into Moravia. As early as 1530, Anabaptists were found in England and Scandinavia.

During a synod held in February of 1527 at Schleitheim, the Anabaptists determined the principles of church organization:

1. Baptism is to be granted only to those who have repented and who believe that their sins have been taken away by Christ.
2. Church discipline must be exercised according to Matt. 18.
3. Those who participate in the breaking of bread must previously have been united to the Body of Christ by baptism.
4. Believers must separate themselves from the world and from evil. They must not take up the sword.
5. Local churches elect their pastor who is in turn responsible to them.

6. Christians are not to have their place among the authorities of this world.
7. They must not take an oath.[189]

These articles—refuted by Zwingli and Calvin—spread rapidly, and the Anabaptists of all Europe were governed by them.[190] As Professor W. T. Whithley says, "The Anabaptists were the first Protestants who, in France especially, carried out the principle of an alliance of spiritually autonomous congregations, a principle which was adopted in 1559 by the first re-formed synod in Paris and the following year in Scotland."[191]

A historian of the sixteenth century wrote that Anabaptism spread with such rapidity that one had reason to fear that the majority of the common people would join the sect.[192] "People flock to them as if they were living saints," complained Bullinger, Zwingli's collaborator.[193] One could count by tens of thousands the Christians who had rallied to Anabaptism in spite of the persecutions of which they were the object.[194] In Moravia the churches founded by Hübmaier numbered as many as six thousand baptized members.

> In certain places these Anabaptist churches were very important. At Augsburg they had 1100 members, several of whom were municipal counsellors and aristocrats of the city. Also at Strasbourg, Cologne, and in the cities of the Netherlands, the Anabaptist churches had several hundred members. When the municipal magistrates and the princes were tolerant, there were no persecutions or executions, even if the fanatical preachers demanded them. Landgrave Philip of Hesse, for example, never sanctioned the death penalty for an Anabaptist. "I see," he wrote, "more holy living among those who are called Illuminists than among the Lutherans."[195]

Numerous Christians paid with their lives for adhering to the apostolic doctrine as they rediscovered it among the Anabaptists. "Between four and five thousand men and women perished by the flame, water, and sword as Anabaptist heretics. In that crusade of extermination Protestant and Catholic authorities joined hands in a friendly fashion."[196] "In Holland and in Friesland 30,000 Anabaptists were put to death between 1535 and 1546."[197] "We can affirm concerning Anabaptism that no other movement for spiritual liberty has had so many martyrs as it has had," writes Dr. Rufus Jones.[198]

Different Types of Anabaptists. All Anabaptists did not share the apocalyptical dreams of Illuminists like Melchior Hoffman, nor did they participate in insurrections like those of Thomas Müntzer and of John of Leyde of Münster. Rather, they expressly repudiated the views and acts of these revolutionaries.

The real "Anabaptist drama" is not only the long and painful martyrdom of peaceful Christians exterminated even by those who claimed their authority from the Reformation, but also after that there followed the scorn which they suffered because they were compared to the revolutionaries of Münster in Westphalia and the "Zwickau prophets," mystic "Spiritualists" with whom they had nothing in common. For three centuries church historians blindly followed the Catholic Kessenbroick's interpretation of the Anabaptists which gave them a supposed connection with the visionaries and communists of Münster.

Professor Blanke wrote that up to that time historians had sought to invent an image of the Anabaptist movement by relying on the enemies of the Anabaptists for their source of information. "It is as if we sought to describe Luther's activity by basing our opinions on the writings of Luther's adversaries."[199] "This scorn is all the more unpardonable since documents clearly show . . . that the state church investigators were capable of distinguishing in court between those who adhered to revolutionary Münster, those who belonged to the voluntary communist communities in Moravia, and those who were simple Bible-believing folk."[200]

Recent historical research has shown that there were in the sixteenth century, as well as in the centuries following, three types of major Christian protest against the established order:

1. the revolutionary type ("Maccabean Christianity") such as that of Thomas Müntzer;
2. the Spiritualizers (Schwärmer, etc.);
3. "integral" Christianity of the classical Free Church style.[201]

Later on, the revolutionary ideology broke away from its religious bounds (except among the Jehovah's Witnesses where religion of the "Maccabean type" still exists). Nazism and Bolshevism are spiritual heirs of the Münster movement on the secular level. The truly spiritual heirs of Anabaptism are the free churches, the Mennonites, the Baptists, and, to a lesser extent, the Congregationalists and Methodists; these include the majority of the Christians who claim to descend from the Reformation.[202]

OPINIONS CONCERNING THE REFORMATION

"Originally," writes Dr. W. A. Visser't Hooft, "the Reformation of the sixteenth century was a movement of repentance, of returning to the Lord of the Church in total abandonment to His mercy and grace. . . . The Word will work; the Word will bring about the form it desires. . . . The Church which results from the new proclamation of the Gospel is in principle an *open* Church, a Church on the march, anxious to fashion its life in obedience to the Word of God in every circumstance."[203]

"In the beginning," "in principle"—but the original movement was soon left behind and its principles were soon abandoned. "The Reformation was a cleansing of the Church but not a totally new beginning," Brunner says.[204] "The theology of the Reformers is not drawn only from the Bible with no other help," writes Secrétan.[205]

"Calvin's influence has been incomparably stronger than Luther's in the formation of the Protestant western world," comments Brunner. "But in spite of that, anyone who is determined to lend an unprejudiced ear to the witness of the New Testament Christian community must recognize that Calvin's claim to have revived the primitive Christian Ecclesia is unfounded."[206]

And H. S. Bender adds, "It is one of the incredible paradoxes of history that the Reformers, who so boldly and effectively recaptured the Gospel of Grace from its medieval distortion and restored the central message of justification by faith, should have retained the mass church of the mixed multitude, the territorial church of the Constantinian compromise, in which real faith was not a requirement for membership."[207]

According to Brunner,

> The Constantinian and Theodosian concept which considers the people of the State as identical with the people of the Church—a dominating concept during the Middle Ages, the Reformation, and the post-Reformation period until it was shaken by the Enlightenment and the French Revolution—was possible only because of the secularization of the Church. It [the church] had to renounce her basic requirements of the individual and be satisfied with an exterior adherence which the State made certain by means of constraint.[208]

"Why was the sixteenth century, which was so magnificent at the beginning, suddenly stricken with barrenness and powerlessness?" asks Gasparin. "Because it made only half an effort instead of the all-out one required to break free from the traditions of Catholic paganism and from a collective religion. . . . In that, as in many other things, Protestantism remained Catholic. There are no insignificant violations of principles; principles violated are always finally avenged."[209]

FROM THE SEVENTEENTH TO THE TWENTIETH CENTURY

Our main purpose has been to find the reason why the sixteenth-century Reformation, which sought to restore the church to its primitive state, succeeded only in forming the mass church of the mixed multitude; so we shall pass very rapidly over the history. A river, once having formed its bed, changes its course with great difficulty. All of the great institutional churches that were started during the Reformation retain the pattern adopted by the Reformers.

FREEDOM AND FORMALISM

In France, because of the persecution which the young churches of the Reformation had to endure, most of them were practically churches of professing believers. But the return of religious freedom dealt them a fatal blow: the principle of the mixed multitude was soon to bear its bitter fruit, so much so, that on the eve of the revocation of the Edict of Nantes, pastors who had remained true to the Christian faith deplored the lamentable spiritual state of a great number of parishes and of their leaders. Indeed, hundreds of thousands of Protestants renounced their faith under compulsion.[210]

In the seventeenth century the Protestant churches were actuated by a "spirit of institutional demands," according to Visser't Hooft.[211] He quotes Torrance in saying that the churches of the Reformation "tended to erect a rigid tradition by stabilizing the forms of the Reformation period, forgetting that the Holy Spirit moves on and that the Church can fulfill its mission here on earth only when it allows itself to be broken on the anvil of the Word and reformed again and again."[212]

Melanchthon's theory of the visible church led the Lutherans to limit the true church to the church of the Augsburg Confession ("Never has anyone proved that our confessions were erroneous even on a single point!" said Wilhelm Löhe) and to identify it with the body of Christ.[213]

"In Germany the seventeenth century was a period of spiritual death, of fruitless theological disputes, and of formalism," says S. Samouélian. According to Bonhoeffer, "The justification of the sinner in the world degenerated into a justification of sin and of the world. Costly grace was turned into cheap grace, without discipleship."[214] "Active, dynamic repentance became a restrained repentance," writes Visser't Hooft, "and a change for the worse was once again the result of the Reformation."[215]

REVIVALS

But, as Calvin had already said in his Commentary on Micah 4 and 6, "The history of the Church is the story of many resurrections." Each time that a breath of revival would pass, communities of professing believers would spring up, whether it was the "collegia pietatis" of Spener, the Moravian communities in Germany, the Methodist classes of Wesley in England, the churches born of the revival in Geneva in the nineteenth century, or the revival in France.[216] Each return to the source of the individual spiritual life was followed by a return to the source of the collective spiritual life, to the biblical model of church life. Most of the live churches owe their birth to a spiritual awakening.

Pietism in Germany was a resurgence of the principle of churches made up of professing believers. Pietistic theologians differentiated between "the true and pure Church of the Gospels and of the time of the apostles, the Church which is a virgin and betrothed to Christ" and "the false, fallen church which has become, according to the New Testament, a prostitute because from the time of Constantine she has embraced hypocrites and evil doers."[217]

JEAN DE LABADIE

In this context, Jean de Labadie, a Frenchman, merits special mention. His spiritual journey led him from Catholicism to the church of professing believers. After having studied theology with the Jesuits, he left that order, repulsed by the dead scholasticism and the life, far from edifying, which he found there.

At Amiens, where he was a canon in 1640, he tried to bring about the regrouping of true believers into small fraternities, which was his main goal in life. There they partook of holy communion, both the bread and the wine. Twice a week they assembled to study the Bible; almost every participant had his French New Testament. Labadie was ordered to Paris where Mazarin explained to him that what he was doing "disturbed the peace of the State." He was forbidden to preach and then sent to southern France where a number of believers followed him. Persecution pursued him there also and Labadie, after a careful study of the writings of the Reformers, embraced Protestantism. He was appointed pastor, then professor, and in 1655 he became rector of the University of Montauban.

Exiled by order of the court, he took refuge in Geneva, where he brought new life to the lethargic Calvinist Church and continued to gather about him those who desired wholeheartedly to follow Christ. Churches were again filled, inns were forced to close their doors, and even the business world felt the effects of this pietistic revival. Among the students who gathered about Labadie were P. J. Spener, T. Untereyk, and F. Spanheim, men who later were to serve in directing the German pietistic movement.

Meanwhile, Labadie's zeal antagonized his colleagues in Geneva, who arranged first to have him called to Holland and then to get him to accept the call. At Middlebourg also, Labadie instituted his pietistic assemblies which met twice a week. In 1668 he published a book defending the right of believers to have these reunions: "Discerning a truly Scriptural church, containing thirty remarkable signs by means of which she can be recognized." It was the first writing which proved from the Bible and theology that the assembly of believers is legitimate.

Labadie showed in it that "only those who are truly born again constitute a true church where, by the Holy Spirit, all are united into one body and where all the members of the assembly are led by the Spirit of Christ."

Group meditations on the Bible "presuppose a true church," Labadie wrote. "Every church of authentic believers should have them." He gave practical suggestions for conducting these gatherings: introduction and prayer, hymn singing, Scripture reading, and then free exercise of "prophecy" according to 1 Corinthians 14:24-26, or a united meditation of the Scripture text. Each one contributes to the common edification.

The Middlebourg assembly was imitated by a number of German pastors, among whom were Spener of Frankfurt, Untereyk of Mülheim, and Neander of Düsseldorf. The center of religious life moved from the church to the home, from the sacrament to the Scripture, from the priest to the believer.

However, in spite of the renewal which he brought to all of the churches, Labadie encountered the same opposition in Holland as he had elsewhere, opposition from the Protestant clergy because "he persisted in trying to gather the Christians in small flocks," according to J. A. Bost. The synod at Leiden suspended him; the synod at Dordrecht (Dort) removed him from his office and excommunicated him.

Labadie founded an independent church at Veere, then at Amsterdam. The crowds were enormous, but his former colleagues accused him of attracting to himself "the best Christians and the most pious souls." The unfortunate experience of one private community forced him to leave Amsterdam and take refuge at Herford, then at Altona where he died in 1674.

The influence of his writings and of his accomplishments was very great. The pietistic movement considers him one of its initiators. Certainly he is one of the most valiant defenders of the idea of the church of professing believers in the seventeenth century.[218]

P. J. Spener (1635–1705), founder of *pietism*, believed that the unregenerate do not belong to the invisible church.[219] It is the new birth which makes one a member of the church.[220] "The Church," wrote Christian Schoen, "is an assembly, a community, a gathering of those Christians who together confess the true faith and serve their God with a sincere heart according to the same understanding and confession."[221]

Brunner says that pietism contained a part of the truth: "What is true is its teaching that faith regenerates man, that the Church is the community of true, regenerated believers; and it is then again his affirmation that only a living faith is important if one is to become a part of the true Church."[222] He states further,

> The so-called sects or societies which arose as struggles in the wake of the Reformation all sprang from the desire to get nearer to the New Testament *Ecclesia* than the great Reformed churches had done, which they accused, and with some justification, of having been insufficiently cleansed of the Roman leaven. They reproached those churches above all with having failed the age-long sinister association of Church and State and so with having taken over from Rome the Constantinian-Theodosian inheritance. . . . At the same time it ought not to be disputed that many of the characteristics which marked the New Testament *Ecclesia* have left upon them [these "sects" or societies] a clearer and stronger impress than upon the Reformation churches. In particular, it is the element of fellowship, brotherhood, and correspondingly the close relationship between Christian faith and the practical realities of daily life. . . .[223]

"The philosophy of the eighteenth century and the appearance of modern humanism endeavored to point out the separation between the Christian community and the world," Brunner says. "Indeed, the Church found herself in a situation similar to the one that had existed before the time of Constantine. Unfortunately, the Church did not understand this change and retained her inner organization and manner of working as the Constantinian tradition meant it to be."[224]

Visser't Hooft comments, "In light of the experiences of the century before the Reformation, one sees more clearly that the Reformation is not a unique historical act, but rather a permanent mission of the Church."[225]

Certain theologians of the liberal school had a correct vision of what the church is according to the New Testament. Schleiermacher, one of the fathers of liberalism, says: "The Christian Church takes shape through the coming together of regenerate individuals to form a system of mutual interaction and cooperation."[226]

The works of the legal writer R. Sohm proved that the ecclesiastical law was incompatible with the principle of the primitive ecclesia.[227] E. Troeltsch showed that the ecclesia of the New Testament is much more closely related to what the official churches classify as the "sect type" than it is to what they have agreed to call the church. H. von Campenhausen pictures the primitive church in a similar manner.[228]

In the nineteenth century, Wichern in Germany and Grundtvig in Denmark recognized that the church was nothing but a mission field. So it was for the purpose of evangelizing the people in the churches that they established the inner mission, an organization independent of the church. This mission, however, deviated from its original purpose and in turn became a charitable "institution" specializing in social service and in philanthropic works.[229]

In France the question of the church of professing believers was not raised before 1848 by the founders of the free church. Count A. de Gasparin said, "It is impossible for me to understand the idea of a church unless the members make a solemn profession of the doctrine on which it is established."

Adolphe Monod defines the goal of revival thus:

> At the beginning revival did almost nothing but rekindle the dying faith in the hearts of individuals by preaching to them Jesus Christ. . . . But today when this goal can be considered attained . . . the revival instinct drives it to new conquests . . . it aspires to move forward to a new position, the practical application of the Christian faith to the life, no longer of certain isolated individuals only but of a society in which a full and well developed faith can reach out as well as concentrate. Briefly, *the time has come to replace the church in which there are believers with the church of believers.*[230]

And let us carefully note that, in speaking thus, Adolphe Monod was not thinking of the free churches but of the established church that he did not wish to leave because he hoped to see it transformed into a church of believers.

Individual profession of faith and separation from the world were the two constituent principles of the free churches of France. "The multitudinist point of view," writes Pastor A. Roy, "begins with the notion of the Mother Church, the institutional Church, and then comes to the idea of a local church. First the whole, then the parts." The founders of the Union of Free Churches believe that "since the Church is the society of those who freely claim they belong to Jesus Christ, who are born again, one must go from the local church to the general church, from the part to the whole."[231]

In Switzerland, Alexander Vinet established, by arguments which have not yet been disproved, that apart from the solidarity created by the profession of a common faith in Jesus Christ, there is for the church neither stability, nor dignity, nor power effective over the world. Vinet is the author of the theory of "Christian individualism." . . . "It is not by institutions, no matter how perfect they may be, but by sanctified individuals that the Gospel is propagated and that the kingdom of God is established here on earth."[232]

SEPARATION OF CHURCH AND STATE

In the early part of the twentieth century, the law of the separation of church and state brought partial satisfaction to the promoters of free churches. The ideas of Rostan and Vinet finally triumphed in most countries. With the exception of a few unusual enclaves in which the conditions of the Middle Ages still survive, the Constantinian system has been abolished. Where the believers themselves are obliged to defray the expenses of their worship services and of their ministers, the only financial guarantee the church has is the interest of the members. Due to circumstances, the Reformed churches tended to become churches of professing believers, in the broader sense of the word, and to encourage lay ministries.

Today it takes a minimum of religious need to cause a person to attend a Protestant church and to support it with voluntary gifts. The church has again become a community of those who become members of their own free will (*Freiwilligkeits-kirche*).[233] Actually one is witnessing today in many places what Professor E. G. Léonard calls a "general trend to the church of professing believers": "Reinforced by promises and signatures, groups are being established in traditionally semi-multitudinist churches which do not quite succeed in transforming the churches into communities of professing believers, but which do take from them their own peculiar character."[234]

One example of the typically multitudinist form of Protestantism is the Anglican Church. It and other multitudinist Protestant churches as well as the Catholic Church, which is multitudinist, show a tendency toward becoming more like churches of professing believers. "In Catholicism the high regard for baptism is beginning to disappear and the Church is becoming a community of professing believers."[235]

"It is not disrespectful, I hope," says Professor Léonard, "to state that one of the rules of practical theology is 'the grapes are too green.' The multitudinist churches which do not gather the masses conform quickly to the philosophy of the communities of professing Christians and finally proclaim their doctrine."[236]

However, is it not useless to expect spiritual results from economic and political circumstances alone? Should not the Christian church take the initiative in reforms which compel recognition? At best, exterior circumstances tend to cause unwilling church members, who are a dead weight, to withdraw. But one who has merely chosen to be a member does not comply ipso facto with all the conditions which the Lord has laid down for one who wishes to be a member of His body.

Often the churches are only too glad to have the participation and support of a few faithful ones in their life and activities, and thus they do not dare to lay down any condition other than "good will," hoping that living faith will come through this simple participation. The regular failure of all experiments which try to transform the multitudinist churches into churches of believers (Richard Rothe, Sulze, etc.) should be given more serious consideration by those who are tempted to renew the experiment.

However, since the Reformation, as well as in the Middle Ages, the restoration of the apostolic-type church has been sought after principally in movements independent of the large institutional churches.[237]

NONINSTITUTIONAL CHURCHES

The "radical reformation" of the Anabaptists gave rise to the Mennonite and Baptist churches.[238] The moderate, well-balanced, peaceful churches, which sprang up in many parts of the world, proved that the Illuminist and revolutionary tendencies of some Anabaptist groups of the sixteenth century were not faults inherent in the Baptist principle, but in subversive foreign elements, fortuitously introduced in certain places. The missionary zeal and social work of these communities also demonstrated that the principle of "the churches of the redeemed" did not necessarily create closed conventicles which, for better mutual edification, abandon the world to its perdition. On the contrary, the consciousness of being the depository of the only message of salvation for this world awoke within these churches a sense of responsibility and of missionary endeavor during a period when the field of vision of the large institutional churches went scarcely beyond the frontiers of their denominations.

The ideas of Count Zinzendorf, carried out among the Moravian Brethren, met with little sympathy in official circles. It was with distrust and hostility that the Moravians were received in the established churches. The same lack of understanding was faced by Wesley in the Anglican Church, and it finally obliged him to continue, outside of the established church, his work of reformation, which, however, later saved the Anglican Church.[239] The restoration movement in America from 1790 to 1890 (T. and A. Campbell, B. W. Stone) and Stundism in Russia were just so many attempts to rediscover the church in its primitive form.[240]

NEW MOVEMENTS

In the nineteenth century the Brethren movement again brought out the principle of the universal priesthood. By giving to their assemblies the form of communities of brethren, J. N. Darby, G. Müller, and the brothers who were their associates, certainly took an enormous step in the direction of the primitive communities.[241] The two branches which issued from this movement created assemblies of believers throughout the entire world—assemblies in which, as in the early church, several laymen together carry out the duties and ministries of elders, evangelists and pastor.

In the twentieth century the Pentecostal church sprang up and spread throughout the world with astonishing rapidity. Its leaders also wanted to pattern their church after the primitive ecclesia, with the fullness of the gifts of miracles which characterized it. Their evident weaknesses have been pointed out many times:[242] theology based on experience more than on the Bible, excessive emotionalism which often causes both individual and collective spiritual lives to be drawn into an unwholesome seeking for the sensational in trying to transcend the walk by faith, ecclesiastical exclusiveness which results in divisions in the churches touched by Pentecostalism as well as within the Pentecostal churches themselves. In spite of that, one finds in many believers belonging to these churches a real love for the Lord and an exemplary missionary zeal. A number of these assemblies, which resolutely repudiated the excesses of the initial period and which bear the authentic marks of the early ecclesia, have forced the large institutional churches themselves to listen attentively to their testimony.

In addition to these churches and assemblies, a number of *movements* whose original purpose was solely evangelization (like the Salvation Army) or some particular work (like the spreading of the printed Word by the Bible societies) finally resulted in assemblies which bear most of the marks of a true church, without counting the diverse projects for which members often group themselves spontaneously for mutual edification as well as for common action.[243] "The Christian Free communities, the independent evangelical societies and institutions have constituted for more than a century one of the most important elements in the life of the church," according to Karl Barth.[244]

Certain readers will feel that we have used too many quotations from historians and theologians from churches of the multitudinist camp, but in this "conjectural science" which is history, as Renan said, one cannot surround himself with too many guarantees to avoid being reproached for partiality. Shall we avoid it? What serious historian could claim that? (Did not Louis Madelin say that there was a royalist manner of relating how a dog had been run over!) At least it will be noticed that we are not the only ones who see the unfolding of history as it has been presented.

We are happy to pay homage to the honesty and courage of those men who had to set their faces against the ideas and opinions of their milieu, men like those of whom we have written. Their frank acknowledgments are all the more valuable to us at a time when, before "the crisis in the Church in Europe," many men are beginning to question whether the way taken in the time of Constantine and in the sixteenth century was the right one. All those who do not admit a priori the Hegelian theory that all that has been was to be, are within their rights when they wonder: would not the keeping or the restoration of the primitive order of the church have preserved Christianity from many disappointments and tragic mistakes?

In any case, all Christians who do not feel bound by a defeatist fatalism ask themselves this important question today when the church again finds itself "at the crossroads," to use the words of Visser't Hooft. Shall we continue on the road which the Word of God, as well as history and the greatest theologians of our day, denounces as an impasse or shall we resolutely pledge ourselves to follow in the way of faithfulness to the Word of God?

Notes

1. "It was long ago established that except for the letters of Ignatius, the ideas in the writings of the Fathers called apostolic . . . differ considerably from the ideas of the New Testament and in a large measure slip back into a moralism which ignores the idea of grace and of the redeeming death of Christ, both so central in apostolic theology" (O. Cullmann, *La Tradition*, p. 50). See also T. F. Torrance, *The Doctrine of Grace in the Apostolic Fathers.*
   "It is clear that . . . in Tertullian the 'nomostype' dominates and that the eschatological conception of renewal as radical and total *metanoia* is replaced by the relative concept of fulfilling new moral commandments. In this respect, the situation is therefore that two concepts of renewal, the biblical one and the moralistic one, operate in the church and in its theology at one and the same time" (W. A. Visser't Hooft, *The Renewal of the Church*, p. 56).
2. It was this task particularly which the school of Alexandria had set for itself, the school which trained the Greek thinkers: Clement, Origen (see the studies of E. de Faye, *Vie, Oeuvre et Pensée d'Origène* and *Esquisse de la Pensée d'Origène*). But all the church Fathers conformed more or less to this fashion.
3. "Reference must be made to a further fact which is important for the understanding of the Roman Catholic Church: the development of theology and dogma. . . . But now it is held that belief in the theological sense is necessary, and that faith comes into being through the teaching-Church putting forward certain theological propositions to be believed—*ad credendum*. This *credendum* was then defined in its principal tenets in the law of faith (*lex fidei*), and in dogma, and determined by Church law. Everyone *has* to believe this and this, otherwise he is a heretic and (since the time of Theodosius) punished by the State" (E. Brunner, *Dogmatics*, 3:69-70).
4. See A. Benoît, *Le Baptême au II⁰ Siècle.*
5. "All churches agree on one point: that baptism constitutes entrance into the church" (John Baillie, *Baptism and Conversion*).
6. Francus, *Il n'y a pas de Protestants*, p. 79.
7. Brunner, p. 60.
8. Ibid., p. 65. The use of the word *priest* by Brunner is without doubt an anachronism for the period considered. Seen from the point of view of the millennial evolution, his remarks contain a great deal of truth.

9. A. Vinet, *L'Education, la Famille et la Société*, p. 307.
10. S. Samouélian, *Aperçu historique des Eglise de Professants*.
11. E. C. Babut, *Priscillien et le Priscillianisme*, p. 57.
12. Brunner, 3:71.
13. Brunner, *The Misunderstanding of the Church*, p. 53. "Primitive Christianity, which is pure Christianity, condemned the world and foresaw its end; historical Christianity was a compromise with the world in order to rule it" (C. Renouvier, *Philosophie analytique de l'Histoire*, 2:460).
14. Walter Hobhouse, *The Church and the World in Idea and History*. For a more thorough study of the history of the primitive church, see *The Fathers of the Church*, 42 vols. For this period see these evangelical authors: Philip Schaff, *History of the Apostolic Church*, 3 vols.; *The Anti-Nicene Fathers;* F. F. Bruce, *The Dawn of Christianity, The Growing Day*, and *Light in the West*. Also see J. G. Davies, *Daily Life of Early Christians*.
15. W. Ninck, *Christliche Gemeinde heute*, p. 216. See E. H. Broadbent, *L'Eglise Ignorée*, pp. 38 ff.
   E. Schnepel says of Priscillianism: "Perhaps we have before us that which was the most beautiful in the Christian communities of the fourth century" (*Jesus im Römerreich*, pp. 88 ff.).
   E. C. Babut, who devoted much study to this movement, compares it with what English-speaking countries call a revival: "The active and enthusiastic pietism of the Priscillianists wins over a part of the Spanish nobility, all of the clergy, and an entire province in the country" (*Priscillien et le Priscillianisme*, Bibliothèque de l'école des Hautes-Etudes [Paris: H. Champion, 1909, p. 135]).
   G. Bardy in the *Dictionnaire de théologie catholique XIII* (1, col. 391-400) says the Catholics continue to accuse Priscillian and his friends of "latent Manicheism" or of "weakened Montanism" so as not to repudiate the anathema of the Council of Braga, forcefully uttered against the movement almost two centuries after the death of its protagonists. However, after G. Schepps' discovery of eleven authentic treatises of Priscillian, it becomes difficult not to recognize the fundamentally biblical character of his doctrine. Apart from asceticism and a preference for the apocryphal writings, nothing distinguishes the Priscillianist communities from the apostolic churches: they formed small fraternal groups, religious brotherhoods, which one entered by conversion and baptism, where Bible reading and practical holiness were insisted upon, and where the worship services, held in the homes, were very simple (readings, exhortations, prayers, psalms, and hymns). It was indeed "the persistent trend to resume the practices of apostolic times as taught in the Gospel, coupled with an unquenchable liking for small churches of saints" (Babut, p. 59).
   "In the New Testament there appears to be found the seed of this so-called heresy which, the first time it appeared, was called Montanism. Priscillian had a part in the resurgence of this regressive or, as they said, apostolic error" (Ibid., p. 134).
   We shall study in this chapter the various appearances of this "regressive error." For Priscillianism see also F. Paret, *Priscillianismus, ein Reformator des IV. Jahrh*; A. d'Alès, *Priscillien et l'Espagne chrétienne à la Fin du IVe Siecle* (1936).
16. To be exact, one would have to say that "the religious profession is that which is essential and the vows, the means of leading to perfection, in a stable condition, a perfection evidently understood according to the norms of the Catholic Church" (G. Millon).
17. Baillie, pp. 71-73.
18. Pourrat, *La Spiritualité chrétienne*.
19. See H. Grundmann, *Religiöse Bewegungen im Mittelalter*. Evidently everything was not absolutely true in these movements; the sole fact of being opposed to Rome is not yet a guarantee for truth.
20. Gustave Isely, *Chrétiens, Sectaires et Mécréants*, p. 33.
21. Raoul Stephan, *L'Epopée huguenote*. See also Broadbent, *Pilgrim Church;* and Günnar Westin, *Geschichte des Freikirchentums*.
22. See Brunner, *The Misunderstanding of the Church*, p. 169.
23. H. Strohl, *La Pensée de la Réforme*, pp. 15 ff.
24. A. Bost, *Dict. d'Hist. ecclés.*, p. 526.

244 *I Will Build My Church*

25. K. Holl, *Festschrift*, p. 424.
26. Will Maurer, "Kirche und Geschichte nach Luthers Dictata super Psalterium" in *Lutherforschung heute*, pp. 85-101. See especially p. 97, the role of faith in church membership. See also in the same volume Jaroslav Pelikan, "Die Kirche nach Luthers Genesis Vorlesung," pp. 102-10.
27. Luther, *Vom Papsttum zu Rom*, W. A. 6, 292, 35. See also in *The Dispute with Alveld:* "The Church is an assembly of all those who believe in Christ."
"The point of departure of Luther's thought is that only the one who believes personally in Jesus Christ is a Christian. That is why he puts the masses of the popular churches on the same level as the Turks and Gentiles" (G. Hilbert, *Ecclesiola in ecclesia*, p. 61).
"Just as his conception of faith is through and through personalistic, so is his understanding of the Church; the Church is the community of the faithful, those who through Christ are 'called to be saints'" (Brunner, *Dogmatics*, 3:74-75).
28. Strohl, p. 181.
29. Luther, W.A. 10b, 26, 27 ff. (W.A. is the usual abbreviation for Weimarer Ausgabe, the most recent complete edition of Luther's works. As far as possible, we give those references in this book. Sometimes the W.A. reference is preceded by another in the Erlangen edition (E.A.) or in Enders. In these cases the first reference will be more precise than the W.A.)
30. Ibid., 10b, 36, 29 ff. See Hilbert, p. 5.
31. Luther, Enders 3, 320, 28 ff.
32. Luther, W.A. 10b, 39, 10 ff.
33. Ibid., 10b, 39, 17 ff.
34. Ibid., 10b, 27, 19.
35. Ibid., 12, 216, 25 ff.
36. Martin Kähler, *Die Sakramente als Gnadenmittel*, p. 64.
37. Hilbert, p. 7.
38. Luther, W. A. 12, 476 ff.
39. T. Kolde, "Luthers Gedanken von der Ecclesiola in Ecclesia," *Zeitschrift für Kirchengeschichte* (1892), pp. 554-55.
40. Luther, W. A. 19, 44 ff.
41. Brunner, *Dogmatics*, 3:75.
42. H. Venske, *Vollendete Reformation*, p. 80.
Dr. H. Boehmer, the famous authority on Luther, says about this passage from the *Deutsche Messe:* "There the Reformer found a solution to this difficult problem—the discovery of an organization which corresponded to his religious ideal." (Quoted by V. F. Heitmüller, *Die Krisis der Gemeinschaftsbewegung*, p. 82.)
43. Luther, E. A. 53, 399 ff. (W.A. 19, 623 ff.).
44. Luther, Enders 6, 10, 5 ff. and 6, 32.
45. Ibid., 9, 317.
46. Luther, E. A. 53, 400 (W. A. 19, 623 ff.).
47. Luther, *The Large Catechism.* Commentary on the 3d article. (The Article of Faith of the Evangelical Lutheran Church.) 2d ed., p. 657. See also *Oeuvres de Luther*, 7:97.
48. Luther, *Wider Hans Worst* (1541) W. A. 51, 521, 24.
49. Luther, W. A. 50, 629-41.
50. Luther as quoted by Brunner, *Le Renouveau de l'Eglise*, pp. 26-27.
51. Brunner, *The Misunderstanding of the Church*, p. 15.
52. A. von Harnack, *Das Wesen des Christentums*, p. 184.
53. Walter Köhler, "Enstehung der reformatio ecclesiarum Hassiae 1526," *Deutsche Zeitschrift für Kirchenrecht* 16 (1906): 217.
54. Albrecht Ritschl, "Luthers Anschauungen von der Unsichtbarkeit u. Sichbarkeit des Kirche," *Th. St. p. K.* (1900), pp. 416 ff.
55. Luther, *The Large Catechism.* E. G. Léonard, who quotes this passage, adds: "Here we are again looking at the ecclesiology of the 'first Luther.' So the Reformer remained faithful to his vision of the Church, which was one of the bases, we must repeat, of the Reformation" (*Histoire générale du Protestantisme français*, 1:110).
56. Kolde, p. 554.

57. Luther, W. A. 19, 75, 6.
58. Ibid., 19, 73, 20 ff. "Luther is not afraid to use the word 'to separate' (*sondern*) in this context; a real communion of the faith cannot be cultivated with all the members of the popular Church" (W. A. 10b, 39, 12; Hilbert, p. 42).
59. Luther, W. A. 75, 13 ff.
60. Ibid., 76, 11.
61. See ibid., 80, 28 ff.
62. Ibid., 6, 413, 7.
63. Ibid., 19, 75, 11 ff.
64. Luther, E. A. 59:166.
65. Hilbert, p. 17.
66. Luther, W. A. 19, 73, 13 ff.
67. Ibid., 19, 112, 1.
68. Ibid., 19, 75, 1.
69. Ibid., 19, 74, 26.
70. Ibid., 73, 23 ff.
71. Ibid., 72, 23 ff.
72. Ibid., 11, 21, 35 ff.
73. Luther, *Von Konzilii und Kirchen*, W. A. 50, 625, 21.
74. Ibid., and E. A. 25, 363.
75. Brunner, *Le Renouveau de l'Eglise*, p. 26.
76. Hilbert, p. 43.
77. Holl, *Festschrift*, p. 445; and his *Erganzungsheft*, p. 59.
78. Quoted by Brunner, *Le Renouveau de l'Eglise*, p. 27.
79. Hilbert, p. 29.
80. Paul Drews, "Entsprach das Staatskirchentum dem Ideale Luthers?" *Zeitschrift für Theologie und Kirche* (1908).
81. K. B. Hundeshagen, *Beiträge zur Kirchenverfassungsgeschichte und Kirchen politik*, 1:85, 58.
82. Brunner, *The Misunderstanding of the Church*, p. 97.
   See also L. Fèbvre, *Un Destin: Martin Luther*, which shows how Luther's followers often ran ahead of him.
83. Karl Müller, *Kirchengeschichte*, vol. 2, no. 1, p. 476. Quoted by H. S. Bender, *Das Täuferische Leitbild* (p. 43), who says: "Can we not say that the decision of Luther and Zwingli to renounce their first vision constituted the tragic turn in the Reformation?"
   William Hadorn states: "One must recognize that not only Zwingli but also other Swiss and German Reformers such as Oecolampadius and Capito, had originally the same views as the Anabaptists" (*Die Reformation in der deutschen Schweiz*, p. 104).
   Köhler says "Luther's community of the autonomous church also capitulated to the authorities" (*Zwingli's Werke*, 4:29).
84. Strohl, pp. 184-87.
85. "That Luther and the other Reformers wanted only a reformation within the Church is universally recognized today" (S. Grundmann, "Kirchenverfassung" in *Religion in Geschichte und Gegenwart*, 3:1571).
86. Bender, p. 42.
87. Brunner, *Dogmatics*, 3:48.
88. K. Ecke, *Schwenckfeld, Luther, und der Gedanke einer apostolischen Reformation*, p. 42.
89. Luther as quoted by Heitmüller, pp. 188-89.
90. Ibid., p. 189.
91. Luther, E. A. 39, 250; W. A. 31, 1, 189 ff.
92. Luther, *Commentary on Matthew*.
93. Luther, *Corpus Reformatorum*, 2:549.
94. Ibid., 4:737-40.
95. Luther as quoted by Jakob Schmitt, *Die Gnade bricht durch*, p. 32.
96. M. Baumgarten, *Zwölf Kirchengeschichtliche Vorträge*.
97. Schwenckfeld as quoted by Ecke, pp. 63-64.
98. Luther, E. A. 2.65; W. A. 52, 764 ff.
99. Ibid., 28. 315; W. A. 10, 11, 11 ff.

100. Ibid., 23. 326; W. A. 51, 331 ff.
101. Ibid., 23. 165; W. A. 30, 11, 595 ff.
102. Ibid., 5. 254; W. A. 52.
103. Ibid., 5. 254; *Hauspostille*, W. A. 52.
104. Luther, *Vom Papsttum zu Rom*, W. A. 6, 297, 36.
105. Brunner, *Le Renouveau de l'Eglise*, p. 31.
     For the development of Luther's concept of the church, see Holl, "Die Entste-
     hung von Luthers Kirchenbegriff" in *Gesammelte Augsätze*, 1:288 ff.; and his
     Oeuvres complètes, pp. 326-89; and *Luther und das landesherrliche Kirchen-
     regiment*. Also see Heinrich Boehmer, *Der junge Luther*; and Julius Köstlin,
     Martin Luther, sein Leben und seine Schriften, and *Luthers Theologie in ihrer
     Geschichtlichen Entwicklung und in ihrem inneren Zusammenhang*; Gerhard
     Müller, "Ecclesiologie und Kirchenkritik beim jungen Luther," *Neue Zeitschrift
     für systematische Theologie und Religionsphilosophie* 1 (1965): 100-28.
     For Luther's texts on the church, see E. Hirsch, *Hilfsbuch zum Studium der
     Dogmatik* and Manfred Jacobs, *Die Evang. Lehre von der Kirche*.
     For how Catholics view the evolution of Lutheran thought concerning the
     church, see J. Lortz, *Die Reformation in Deutschland*, 4th ed., pp. 393 ff.
106. Melanchthon, *Loci praecipiu theologici* (1559) in Stupperich, ed., *Works of
     Melanchthon*, 2:476, 492.
107. Ibid., p. 491.
108. Jacobs, p. 432. "The Church is becoming a learned assembly (*coetus scholasti-
     cus*). On one hand there are the teachers, on the other, the listeners." See
     Melanchthon, ed. P. Leyser, (1690), p. 117.
109. Martin Chemnitz, *Loci theologici* 3:117.
110. For the evolution of Melanchthon's ecclesiastic doctrine, see the bibliographical
     references in Jacobs, p. 432.
     For Melanchthon's thoughts on institutionalism, see G. Wehrung, *Kirche nach
     evang. Verständnis*, pp. 81-87; and H. Busch, *Melanchthons Kirchenbegriff*.
111. G. Maron, article in *Religion in Geschichte und Gegenwart*, vol. 5, col. 1620.
112. Schmitt, p. 32.
113. Luther, *Wider die Schwarmgeister* (W. A. 23, 64 ff.).
114. Caspar Schwenckfeld as quoted by Ecke, p. 96.
115. Ibid., p. 71.
116. Ibid., p. 64.
117. Ibid., pp. 70-71.
118. Ibid., p. 64.
119. Ibid., p. 77.
120. Ibid., p. 75.
121. Ibid., p. 73.
122. Ibid., p. 74.
123. Ibid., p. 73.
124. Schwenckfeld as quoted by Schmitt, p. 42.
125. Ibid., pp. 45-46.
126. Ibid., p. 44.
127. Ecke, p. 99.
128. Venske, pp. 81-82.
129. Maron, vol. 5, col. 1620.
130. O. S. von Bibra. For the life and work of Schwenckfeld, see Ecke, *Schwenck-
     feld*. . . . Also see C. Bertelsmann, Kaspar Schwenckfeld, *Ungelöste Fragen der
     Reformationzeit*. The abridged edition of the preceding book to which the
     references of this text refer, reedited in 1965 under the title *Fortsetzung der
     Reformation*. See Schmitt, pp. 27-47; Maron, vol. 5, col. 1620-21; and Hirsch,
     Zum Verständnis Schwenckfelds.
131. Oecolampadius as quoted by Ninck, p. 274.
132. Léonard, 1:177.
133. According to Bellardi, *Die Geschichte der "christlichen Gemeinschaft in Strass-
     burg*," pp. 24-25.
134. Ibid., pp. 40, 64, 79-80.
135. J. Courvoisier, *La Notion d'Eglise chez Bucer*, pp. 54-55.
136. Bellardi, p. 64.

137. Ibid., pp. 79-80.
138. Ibid., p. 85.
139. Ninck, pp. 225-26.
140. See V. W. Maurer, "Franz Lambert von Avignon und das Verfassungs ideal der Reformatio ecclesiarum Hassiae," *Zeitschrift für Kirchengeschichte* 11:209 ff.; also see his bibliography.
141. Heitmüller, p. 83.
142. Bellardi, pp. 113 ff.; and Naunin, "Die Kirchenordnungen des Johannes Lasci," *Deutsche Zeitschrift für Kirchenrecht* 19 (1909): 24 ff., 196 ff., 348 ff.
143. "The principle of church discipline is fundamental in Calvin's ecclesiology" (Geddes MacGregor, *Corpus Christi*, p. 62).
144. J. de Senarclens, *La Vraie Eglise, selon Calvin*, pp. 9-10.
145. Calvin, *Epître à Sadolet*, p. 53.
146. Calvin as quoted by MacGregor, p. 45.
147. Calvin as quoted by A. Albert, *Les Fondements de l'Eglise d'après Calvin*, p. 18.
148. Léonard, 1:227.
149. Calvin, *Institutes*, vol. 2, bk. 4, chap. 1, para. 8, p. 230.
150. Ibid., vol. 2, bk. 4, chap. 1, para. 7, p. 230.
151. Ibid., vol. 2, bk. 4, chap. 1, para. 15, p. 236.
152. Ibid., bk. 3, chap. 2, sec. 24: "Yet we do not thus accept that most pestilent philosophy which certain half-papists are furtively beginning to fashion today . . ." that one can have no certainty of his faith.
153. Calvin as quoted by Léonard, 1:276.
154. Calvin as quoted by Léonard, "Le Protestantisme entre l'Eglise de Multitude et l'Eglise de Professants," *Revue réformée* 1(1953):8.
155. Léonard, ibid., p. 10.
156. Calvin as quoted by ibid., p. 9.
157. Ibid.
158. Calvin as quoted by Albert, p. 19.
159. Calvin, *Institutes*, chap. 4 of 1541 ed., 2:136.
160. Ibid., p. 137.
161. Calvin, *Disc. ecclés.*, chap. 5, art. 9; V. Bruston, *La Discipline ecclésiastique réformée dans la Pensée de Calvin*.
162. Hilbert, *Volkskirche und Bekenntniskirche*, p. 11.
163. Calvin, *Institutes*, vol. 2, bk. 4, chap. 1, para. 14, p. 235.
164. "The historical association of the Renaissance with the Reformation has often obscured the fact that the Reformers—Calvin in particular—were brought up entirely in medieval thought. Although they returned to the origin, according to the new school of thought, they continued to think in medieval concepts, in terms of scholasticism and canon law in which they had been educated" (MacGregor, p. 23).
165. Calvin, *Homme d'Eglise*, pp. 27-57.
166. Visser't Hooft, p. 80.
167. See the *Fidei ratio* of 1530 (art. 6).
168. See also W. Hildebrandt, *Das Gemeindeprinzip der christ. Kirche* (Zurich: Zwingli, 1951), p. 85.
"Zwingli wished to carry out the ideal of the Old Testament to 're-establish the sovereignty of God on the earth. . . .' It is true that he had also passed through a period when the primitive Church was everything to him, when he rejected infant baptism, and approved bookseller Castelberg's private gatherings for Bible study. In those days his powerful preaching gave rise to real communities. . . ." But under the influence of humanism and the ideal of the universal culture of humanity, he could not bring himself to turn away from the masses. "He adopted a temporary solution: the majority of the people were not ready for the Gospel . . . so one had to be content to raise them to the level of the religion and morality of the Old Covenant" (Ninck, pp. 221-22).
169. F. Blanke, "Täufertum und Reformation" in G. F. Hershberger, *The Recovery of the Anabaptist Vision*, p. 64.
170. See Blanke (professor of church history on the theological faculty of Zürich), *Brüder in Christo*.
171. G. Rousseau, *Le drame anabaptiste*, p. 12.

172. See Harold S. Bender, *Conrad Grebel, 1498-1526, the Founder of Swiss Brethren.*
173. See Felix Mantz's biography by E. Krajewski, *Leben und Sterben der Zürcher Täuferfuhrers Felix Mantz.*
174. See J. A. Moore, *Der starke Jörg.*
175. See *Mennonitisches Lexikon*, vol. 3, under Röubli.
176. Rousseau, p. 12.
177. Roland Bainton, *Here I Stand* (New York: Abingdon-Cokesbury, 1950).
178. See L. von Muralt and W. Schmid, eds., *Quellen zur Geschichte der Täufer in der Schweiz*, vol. 1, no. 14 (1952), pp. 14-16.
179. About twelve editions of Luther's translation have come from the printing presses of Basel since 1522.
    "The translation of the Bible in the vernacular, the printing press, humanism, and the Reformation directed the attention of the laymen more and more to the Biblical idea and consequently to the baptism of believers" (*Religion in Geschichte und Gegenwart*, vol. 1, col. 862).
180. Blanke, "Täufertum . . . ," p. 58.
181. Rousseau, p. 14. "Let us note that it was a matter of the baptism still administered—until Easter of 1525—according to the Catholic rite with exorcism, the sign of the Cross, anointing with oil, with saliva, etc." (Blanke, *Brothers in Christ*, p. 6).
182. Blanke, "Täufertum . . . ," p. 56.
183. Ibid., p. 51. See also Blanke's *Brothers in Christ*, p. 45; and Westin, p. 55.
184. Blanke, *Brothers in Christ*, p. 35.
185. Ibid., p. 36.
186. For the development of Zwingli's thought beginning with the defense of the neo-testamentary type of church to the veterotestamentary, see O. Farner, *Zwinglis Bedeutung für die Gegenwart.* Köhler, (*Jubiläumsband 1519-1919*) also says, "His theology becomes theocentric, but not Christocentric." See also Ninck, pp. 90 ff., 270-71.
187. Farner.
188. Rousseau, p. 15.
189. *Das Schleitheimer Täuferbekenntnis 1527.*
190. For a continuation of the history of the Anabaptists in the sixteenth century, see Westin, pp. 68-132; G. Neff, *Geschichte der Täufgesinnten Gemeinden;* George-Hunten Williams, *The Radical Reformation.* A very well-documented history of the movement of the radical Reformation in the sixteenth century.
191. Rousseau, p. 20.
192. F. Roth, *Augsburgs Reformations Geschichte*, 2:230.
193. Bullinger as quoted by Blanke, "Täufertum . . . ," p. 34.
194. In the time of the Reformation the partisans of the Anabaptists were especially humanists, peasants, and the lower middle class, but not members of the political ruling classes. See *Religion in Geschichte und Gegenwart*, vol. 1, col. 862.
195. Schmitt, pp. 19-20.
196. Blanke, "Täufertum . . . ," p. 62.
197. Rousseau, p. 25.
198. Rufus Jones, *Studies in Mystical Religion*, p. 392, quoted by Rousseau.
199. Blanke, "Täufertum . . . ," p. 57.
200. F. H. Littell, *The Free Church*, p. 20.
201. Ibid., p. 26; also see the article by E. H. Correll, "Harold S. Bender und die täuferische Forschung" in *Das Täufertum*, pp. 17-30; and Bender, *La Vision Anabaptiste*, p. 2 and the bibliographical information. The one to trace the dividing line between the Anabaptists and the Spiritualists of the sixteenth century was the historian Alfred Hegler, *Geist und Schrift bei S. Franck.* See E. Troeltsch, *Die Soziallehren der christl. Kirchen und Gruppen*, 1:796 ff., who made this distinction popular.
    The Spiritualists, moreover, did not place any value on water baptism; to them, only the inner baptism of the soul was important. Sebastian Franck (1499-1543), one of the most typical representatives of the Spiritualist line, was excluded by the Anabaptists. These Spiritualists, heirs of the mystics of the Middle Ages (Joachim de Flore, etc.), are situated in the line of illuminism which proceeds from the Montanists to present-day liberals and to all those

who place the "Spirit" above the Word of God. The Anabaptists fought vigorously against that tendency. Menno Simons contended with the Spiritualists as much as Luther did. He said he would hear nothing of visions, revelations, dreams, etc.; his sole support was the Word of God. See Cornelius Krahn, *Der Gemeindebegriff des Menno Simons im Rahmen seines Lebens und seiner Theologie*, pp. 6-7.

202. As early as 1848 Max Göbel recognized that "the real characteristic of this movement and its essential distinctive criterion is its insistence on true personal conversion and the true birth of each Christian by the Holy Spirit. . . . It wished to assemble all true believers. . . . This movement wanted what was basically the main objective of the Reformation" (Max Göbel, *Geschichte des christlichen Lebens in der rheinisch wesph. Kirche*, 1:134, as quoted by Ritschl, "Täufertum," *Geschichte des Pietismus*, p. 39.

So Anabaptism put into practice the original plan of the Reformers which had been abandoned under the pressure placed on them by events and by those in authority. To get an idea of the present-day theologians' opinion of Anabaptism, see, for example, Brunner (*Dogmatics*): "The sources reveal to us a sober faith, based entirely on New Testament doctrine which is taken as its only authority, a faith which agrees perfectly with the doctrine of the Reformers" (3:79). "The only thing for which Zwingli could have reproached them was that they came too early in history" (3:55). "The Reformers claimed for themselves the right to be considered a reformation of the Roman Catholic Church; so why did they refuse this right to the Anabaptists?" (3:78). "Research has shown that they were tainted with neither perfectionism nor Illuminist pacifism nor with subjectivism" (3:79).

"When they [the Reformers] called the attempts of the Anabaptists 'sectarianism,' they took over a concept of the Roman Catholic Church which inevitably characterized every Christian form of fellowship outside the Roman Catholic Church a sect" (3:78).

"This was a 'high' doctrine of the Church, and can be considered 'sectarian' only if one accepts the territorial definition of the Church, or exaggerates the importance of the spiritualizers in the Free Church tradition" (Littell, p. 39).

"The best way to understand Anabaptism is to consider it the attempt to transplant the religious ideas of primitive Christianity directly into contemporary reality" (G. Anrich, *Martin Bucer*, p. 34).

"The Anabaptists with the monks, the Waldenses, and the Hussites share Jesus' reactions against the worldliness of His Church" (Prof. Wernle as quoted by Schmitt, p. 20).

203. Visser't Hooft, *Le Renouveau de l'Eglise*, p. 51.
204. Brunner, *The Misunderstanding . . .* , p. 101.
205. C. Secrétan, *Philosophie de la Liberté*.
206. Brunner, *The Misunderstanding . . .* , p. 103.
207. Bender, *These Are My People*, p. 70.
208. Brunner, *La Situation de l'Eglise . . .* , p. 4.
209. A. de Gasparin, *Paganisme et Christianisme*, 1:4; 2:74; quoted by Francus, p. 278. For the period of the Reformation in general, see Léonard, *Histoire générale . . .* , and its bibliography; Iain Murray, *The Reformation of the Church*; Schmitt, p. 455; Hershberger, whose book, *The Recovery of the Anabaptist Vision* is a Mennonite work containing a series of studies by Bender, Fritz Blanke, J. H. Yoder, Littell et al. See Fritz Blanke, *Brüder in Christo*, p. 88; the history of the oldest Baptist community, Zollikon, 1525; and J. H. Yoder, *Täufertum und Reformation in der Schweiz*, p. 184.
210. See on this subject Samouélian, pp. 8-13, who quotes among others the testimonies of Jean Claude, Claude Brousson, David Ancillon, and César Missy, stressing the cause for this condition: a dreadful laxity of godliness and morals.
211. Visser't Hooft, p. 53.
212. S. F. Torrance, *Scottish Journal of Theology* (1951), p. 290, quoted by Visser't Hooft, p. 79.
213. Jacobs, p. 323.
214. D. Bonhoeffer, *The Cost of Discipleship*, p. 44.
215. Visser't Hooft, *Le Renouveau de l'Eglise*, p. 54.

216. "The revival in Geneva established the church of professing believers. On May 18, 1817, Pyt, Porchat, Guers . . . decided to found in Geneva an 'independent church' composed, as far as possible, of true believers" (Samouélian, p. 18).
217. Gottfried Arnold, *Unparteiische Kirchen—und Ketzerhistorie von Anfang des N.T. bis auf das Jahr 1688*, preface, para. 30.
218. For more details see Broadbent, *Pilgrim Church*, chap. 12; Schmitt, pp. 51-60; Göbel, *Geschichte des . . .*; H. Heppe, *Geschichte des Pietismus in der reform. Kirche*; and Ritschl, *Geschichte. . . .*
219. Jacobs, p. 387.
220. Ibid., p. 436.
221. Christian Schoen, *Christianus Irenicus*, p. 3.
222. Brunner, *Renouveau de l'Eglise*, p. 17.
223. Brunner, *The Misunderstanding of the Church*, pp. 104-5.
224. Brunner, *La Situation de l'Eglise*, p. 9.
225. Visser't Hooft, p. 82.
226. F. Schleiermacher, *The Christian Faith*, p. 532.
227. R. Sohm, *Kirchenrecht*, vol. 1, 1892; vol. 2, 1922. H. Blocher says, "For Sohm and Brunner, there is antinomy between life and the communion of the brethren and the law, which are the practical structures. We do not find this antinomy in the Bible. Matt. 18, I Cor. 5, II Thess. 3 . . . , and the pastoral epistles show us that the liberty of the Spirit does not exclude judicial formation and the limits fixed by the law." The church, like her Lord, is an incarnate reality. Without these fixed limits of judicial appearance it is no longer anything but a phantom with neither consistence nor form. A church without structure, without organization, without members, does not resemble the apostolic churches any more than does a church governed by an invariable canonical law which no longer leaves any freedom to the Spirit.
228. Troeltsch, *Kirchliches Amt und geistliche Vollmacht in den drei ersten Jahrh*, 1953.
229. Brunner, *Dogmatics*, 3:95, 106.
230. A. Monod, "La Vocation de l'Eglise" in *Sermons choisis*, p. 71.
231. A. Roy, *Union des Eglises Evangéliques libres de France*, p. 11.
232. F. Lichtenberger, article in *Encyclopédie des Sciences religieuses*, 4:292.
233. M. Antonin, *Union des Eglises évang. libres de France*, p. 40.
234. Léonard, *Revue réformée*, p. 18.
235. Ibid., p. 23; See also Léonard, *Le Protestant français*, p. 149.
236. Ibid.
237. It is impossible for us within the limitations of this book to go into detail on the history of the different movements of restoration which have succeeded one another since the sixteenth century. For a comprehensive view, consult Broadbent, *Pilgrim Church*, and Westin, *Geschichte des Freikirchentums*.
238. See Neff, *Geschichte der täufgesinnten Gemeinden*. Also see Gwilym O. Griffith, *Pocket History of the Baptist Movement*.
239. G. C. Cell, *The Rediscovery of John Wesley*; I. Haddal, *John Wesley*; and Mathieu Lelièvre, *Wesley, sa Vie et son Oeuvre*.
240. See Broadbent, pp. 309-52.
241. See G. Ischbeck, *J. N. Darby*, Broadbent, pp. 353-93, and the bibliography at the end of this volume, under the heading "Assembly of the Brethren."
242. See Alexander, *Pentecôtisme ou Christianisme*; J. Besson, *Histoire du Pentecôtisme en Allemagne*; H. Dallmeyer, *Die Zungenbewegung; Sonderbare Heilige in Kassel; Erfahrungen in der Pfingstbewegung*; W. Geppert, *Die Pfingstbewegung*; W. H. Guiton, *Le Mouvement de Pentecôte*; Erich von Eicher, "Ein Beitrage zur Geschichte der Pfingstbewegung in Deutschland" in *Heiliger Geist, Menschengeist, Schwarmgeist*; and *Flugfeuer fremden Geistes*.
243. See, for example, *A Brief History of the International Fellowship of Evangelical Students*.
244. Barth, *Les Communautés chrétiennes dans la Tourmente*, p. 64.

Part VIII

"LET EACH MAN TAKE CARE
HOW HE BUILDS . . ."

13

Multitudinist Church or Free Church

In the preceding pages, the present-day situation of the churches placed us continually before the alternative: the multitudinist church or the church of professing believers. In this chapter we gather together the principal arguments for the latter. First we summarize what our study has brought to light so far. Then we draw some conclusions from various aspects of the life of the church.

NATURE OF THE CHURCH ACCORDING TO THE BIBLE

The churches established by the apostles remain the valid models for churches of all times and places. Everybody now agrees that they were churches of professing believers.

THE NAME OF THE CHURCH

The name "ekklesia." The etymological meaning of the word *ekklesia* is "called out of" and is applicable only to a church of believers. In the multitudinist church all the inhabitants of the country are members of the church. Just who is called out? What has he been called out of?

The historical background. The Greek political *ekklesia*, from which the Christian church took its name, was the assembly of only the citizens of the city who separated themselves from the whole body of the population. The church of the masses becomes identified with the population rather than with the *ekklesia*.

The Jewish "ekklesia." Israel was a people "called out from among" the peoples of the earth to be "a holy people belonging to the Eternal God."

THE LOCAL CHURCH AND THE UNIVERSAL CHURCH IN THE BIBLE

The first mention of the church is linked to a profession of faith (Mt 16:18). The true church is composed of those who, like the apostle, confess that Jesus is the Christ, the Son of the living God.

The second mention of the church contrasts it with the world. When Jesus speaks of the church for the second time (Mt 18:17), He contrasts

253

the "brethren" with the "pagan and a tax gatherer." The rule of discipline which He gives to His disciples is applicable to the whole period of the church. Wherever a church exists, the opposition between these two groups remains constant.

The composition of the local church is the same as that of the universal church. The universal church is composed of believers only. The local church, being the universal church on a small scale, should also be composed of only believers—at least, it should be structured as much like it as possible.

In the Bible the church is a community of believers, not an institution. In the book of Acts, each church was the result of the proclamation of the divine message and the conversion to Jesus Christ of a number of pagans resulting from the same. The Lord added to the church only "those who were being saved" (Ac 2:47). The local church is in existence from the moment there are some converted people—and only as long as they are there. The church of the masses is conceived of as an institution not dependent upon believers and of which Christians are a part.

THE CHURCH AND SALVATION

The people of the new covenant are enlisted one by one. As opposed to the people of the old covenant, those of the new are individually called; they have answered the invitation of Jesus Christ. In the church of the masses the method of enlistment is "biological," as is that of the Jewish people, while the church of professing believers is based on the personal adherence of each of its members.

The church must take into consideration the individual character of God's call. The gospel which Jesus and the apostles preached contained a call from God to individuals ("he who," "if anyone," "whosoever," "if any man"). The church of the masses places all "Christian people" under the benefit of the grace of God; it declares to be saved all who have had the privilege of being born in Christendom and of having the benefit of the sacraments. One enters this church by birth as did God's people of the old covenant.[1]

In the New Testament salvation is dependent upon certain conditions. The message of Jesus Christ and His apostles can be summed up in the call to repentance and faith, conditions for true conversion and the new birth. Jesus affirmed the absolute necessity of this new birth for entrance into the kingdom of God. Many multitudinist churches teach that the infant experiences the new birth during his baptism, and their preaching rarely stresses the fact that salvation is dependent on personal repentance and faith. The church of professing believers requires a personal repentance and faith for admission into membership.

The two possible responses to God's call fix the bounds of the church. The New Testament states that after the preaching of Jesus and the apostles, the hearers made a choice: some believed, others did not believe. "Daily the Lord added to the group [the church] those who were being saved" (Ac 2:47). But the multitudinist church accepts into its membership and retains all at the same time "those who believe, those who do not yet believe, and those who no longer believe." The church of professing believers recognizes the validity of a line of separation drawn by the Bible right down through the middle of humanity.

The New Testament uses a hundred expressions or types to differentiate between the two groups that are formed among human beings in response to God's call. Moreover, it points out fifty or more characteristics and privileges of the regenerated, in addition to about thirty which describe those who are not. The church of the masses removes the line which separates the two groups and fosters the illusion among all of its members that by baptism they enter the group of those who are saved.[2]

The call of Jesus Christ and His apostles requires a personal decision. The church of believers accepts only voluntary members. One cannot be a Christian against one's own will. But the church of the masses confers membership on those who do not know they are being received and are still incapable of making a decision. The confirmation ceremony, in which the adolescent is called on to reaffirm the vow he is supposed to have made by proxy at the time of his baptism, does not meet the condition of the act of the free will. Free choice, the basis of adding members in the primitive churches, has a very insignificant place in the multitudinist churches.[3]

Conversion was an experience of the past. The New Testament epistles teach us that the members of the apostolic churches had all passed through a definite crisis which separated their lives into two periods: before-after or then-now. The apostles frequently remind the Christians, members of the churches to which the epistles are addressed, that they *have* passed from death to life, from the camp of the enemies of God to God's camp. The apostles address themselves to people who have already chosen, so they never exhort them to be converted, but rather to continue in the way which they have chosen. The churches of professing believers also require that those who wish to be members testify that they have passed through that decisive crisis, having repented of their sins and accepted by faith the salvation offered in Jesus Christ.

The multitudinist church (which one of its greatest present-day theologians calls "the false church, the church of delusion," because of this "fatal fact that so many people join this Church and are considered members of it without having any right to be"[4]), requires no personal experience of salvation before admission. They are often reluctant to admit the legitimacy and divine origin of these experiences.[5]

Designating names given to church members in the Bible. The New Testament calls church members "saints, disciples, the elect, ours *or* of us, the brothers or brethren, the multitude of those who believed." All these names indicate a certain separation, and they contrast those who are thus designated with the rest of mankind. As the multitudinists see it, all who are baptized, that is, practically all the inhabitants of Christendom, are considered to be "saints, disciples, chosen ones, and believers," which does not correspond to the truth.[6]

THE TYPES OF THE CHURCH

Types of the church in the Bible reveal a personal and living relationship between Christ and the members of the church. This relationship can exist only with Christians who are born of the Spirit into a new life, not with just any member enrolled on the church register at birth, as is the case in most multitudinist churches.

They bring out clearly the identity of nature of all members. This identity of nature exists only among those who, by the new birth, have been made "partakers of the divine nature." In contrast, the church of the masses gathers into the same organization regenerated Christians and the unconverted alike.

The church, being the body of Christ, cannot include members who are not in Christ. These members, which the Bible very frankly calls "strangers, enemies of God and of Christ, them that are without" cannot be considered as church members.

THE SYMBOLIC ACTS OF THE CHURCH

The baptism of believers constitutes a church of confessing Christians. All the members of the primitive churches were baptized; only those who had believed and had confessed Jesus Christ as their Saviour and Lord were baptized. Therefore, the early churches were composed of only believers. The churches of the masses adhere to infant baptism, which admits as members all the newborn babes of Christendom. Most of the churches of professing believers have reintroduced the practice of the baptism of believers.

The testimonies in favor of biblical baptism argue in favor of the church of professing believers. The Reformers, many theologians, and

eminent members of multitudinist churches favor the baptism of believers
and affirm that it was the only method practiced in the early church. Thus
they approve the principle of membership practiced in the free churches
and repudiate the one used in the multitudinist churches to which they
belong. To support their thesis, the pedobaptists call on the Old Testament, tradition, and the peace of the church rather than on doctrine and
the apostolic tradition.

*The biblical significance of baptism can be reconciled only with the
churches of professing believers.* The significance of baptism as seen in
the epistles implies union with Christ of the one baptized: he is dead,
buried, and risen with Him; he is purified from his former sins; he puts
off the old man and puts on Christ; he passes into a new world with
Him. Infant baptism signifies nothing of this. The churches of believers
where baptism can retain its initial meaning remain in the apostolic
tradition.

*The multitudinist church can justify itself only by the theory of bap-
tismal regeneration.* In order to be composed of regenerate members,
according to the apostolic tradition, many multitudinist churches have
conferred on baptism the virtue of bestowing the new birth on the child
who receives it. The theory of baptismal regeneration is not a Bible
doctrine.

*The administering of baptism only to those who are fully aware of its
significance leads to the forming of churches of believers.* The practice
of baptism as one finds it in churches of believers gives to the ceremony
its original value, that of a conscious and valid promise, the outer and
visible expression of an inner experience, the manifestation of a decision,
a testimony, a sermon, an examination of one's faith, an act of obedience.

*The biblical observance of holy communion is possible only in the
church of professing believers.* In the primitive church only believers
who persevered in the doctrine of the apostles and in a life conforming to
the Word of God partook of the holy communion. It was like "partaking
of the Body of Christ," so it was unthinkable that nonbelievers, those
who were not "in Christ," should partake of the bread and the wine.
Since all church members are exhorted to partake of holy communion,
one can only conclude that the church was a church of believers. The
churches of the masses admit to holy communion all who have become
members by infant baptism and confirmation, whether they are converted
or not, whether their lives are consistent or not with the faith that has
been taught them. The assembly admitted to communion is thus not
limited to the *ekklesia*, but to the denomination or, in certain cases, to
an ecumenical intercommunion.

THE CHURCH IN HISTORY

The churches of the first three centuries were churches of professing believers. During the first centuries of Christianity, Christian communities were first of all churches of professing believers. The Roman Catholic Church, built on the multitudinist principle, persecuted these small groups of believers. Infant baptism and the union with the pagan state, in the third and fourth centuries, precipitated their transformation into churches of the masses. These latter are closely associated with the Constantinian era of Christianity, formally begun with the edict of Milan (313). That era is over and present-day Christians see more clearly than did their predecessors the necessity of a return to apostolic principles. "The future will know only two methods of forming churches: baptism and catholicism," said Cardinal Manning.

The faithful churches of the Middle Ages were churches of professing believers. The faithful communities of the Middle Ages were churches of believers. The Roman Catholic Church, built on multitudinist principles, persecuted these small groups of believers whose firmness, Christian character, and faithfulness to Christ, even when it meant martyrdom, verified their faith and recommended their principles.

The church of professing believers corresponds to the first vision of the Reformers. At first the Reformers did not want to restore the churches of the masses. Their early writings prove that they had discovered the principles of the church of believers in the Word of God. Unfortunately, under the political situation of the sixteenth century, the Reformers seemed destined to the same failure which former attempts at reformation had met, if they were to renounce the great masses and political power. The Reformers found themselves overtaken and carried along by the powerful movements for emancipation in their day. Moreover, the excesses of certain Illuminist Anabaptists turned them from their vision of churches of professing believers.

But we are no longer in the sixteenth century. Religious liberty, which most countries now enjoy, permits the formation of churches of believers independent of all outside aid. Mennonites and Baptists, whose predecessors were mistakenly thought to be Illuminists, have proved, by their Christian lives and by their exemplary church life, that the disorders of a few Anabaptists in the sixteenth century could not at all be attributed to their church principles. Many authorized voices have been raised to ask the present generation to complete the work of reformation in the church, a work begun in the sixteenth century.

Revivals have been the start of churches of professing believers. The renewals and revivals that the Spirit of God has set in motion in the

heart of Protestantism since the sixteenth century have led to the formation of churches of believers. If, after several generations, some of these
churches have become practically multitudinist churches, where the line
of separation between redeemed and unregenerate has slowly become
blurred, that is due to the abandoning of initial principles and to the lack
of vigilance on the part of those who have the responsibility of the
churches.

THE LIFE OF THE CHURCH

Principles and existing situations. By different avenues the Bible leads
us to the same conclusion: the communities founded by the apostles were
established on the principle of churches of believers. History now teaches
us that over the course of the centuries these communities have slowly
taken on the multitudinist form.

But, one might ask, was the early form of the church necessarily
superior to the latter? Does not the church of the masses, just as well as
the church of believers, permit one to carry out the various vocations of
the church?

One can examine this question from two different viewpoints. One
can say: God wanted the apostles to establish churches of professing
believers. He knew why. And, if we know our Bible and the human
heart well, we might even suggest many good reasons why the church
was led to prefer this structure [the free church] to the other one [the
multitudinist]. Or one might begin with the present-day situation of the
churches, compare the two types of communities, and compare the
advantages and disadvantages of each one.

Each method has its disadvantages. Beginning with the principles laid
down by God, we have one certainty: God's work is superior to the
human realization of it, but we can only surmise the reason for this work
when the biblical revelation does not indicate it.

The deductive method, starting with the examination of concrete facts,
arrives at general conclusions, usually true, but often contradicted by this
or that specific case. The rule is always clear and precise, but reality has
nuances and many forms. Thus it is possible that, for several of the
points examined in this chapter and the next, one could cite the example
of one of the multitudinist churches which contradicts the criticism made
of them and cite some church of professing believers which does not at
all conform to their ideal. However, the rule still holds true, for it is based
on verifications made of a great number of cases.

In order to limit the inherent disadvantages in each of these two
methods, we shall try to study them together by leaving it up to the

second one to verify the conclusions of the first. Beginning with the Bible, on the one hand, and with the present reality, on the other, we shall examine the principles governing the two ecclesiastical forms and the fruits which they have borne in various spheres of the life of the church: inner life, testimony to the world, places in the society of our day—always remembering the relative character of the conclusions to which they may lead.

Must one be reminded that the Holy Spirit "blows" where He wills and that a work reflects the value of its men more than it does its principles? "God, in His mercy, can bless even those who are not faithful in every respect—if it were not so who could be blessed?" says J. M. Nicole. Thus we find on one hand churches of the multitudinist structure which are alive, spiritual and zealous for the Lord; and, on the other hand, lukewarm churches of professing believers, unfaithful in many respects, sometimes torn by carnal strife. In order to be convinced of this, let us reread the epistles of the New Testament as well as the messages to the churches in the Apocalypse. "There are churches of professing believers where the Lord is at the door," said G. Millon. Having Abraham in one's genealogical tree was not sufficient to be a part of the Israel of God; it takes more than the constitution of a church of professing believers to be pleasing to the Lord. If that were not so, what would be the purpose of the epistles addressed to communities of this type? How many exhortations to love, to zeal, to the unity of the Spirit within the local community—even for churches of professing believers!

Are principles therefore useless? Far from it. Certainly men can temporarily weaken the effect of good as well as bad principles: under a false system spiritual men will produce spiritual fruit—in spite of the system—and carnal Christians, placed in the best of organizations, will succeed in turning them in the wrong direction, in the way of error. But principles and constitutions are generally more enduring than are men. Men are frail: they change, they are displaced, they die. Principles remain.

How many churches of the masses have known a flourishing time of revival: rousing preaching saturated with the vitality of the Word, conversions, circles for fervent prayer, a courageous testimony to those who are without. How lukewarm and flavorless the small neighboring community of professing Christians seemed beside what was happening in the "big church"!

Then times changed. With the growing opposition of the masses of those "who are as good Christians as——," the zeal of a great number of those who had been touched by the revival cooled off; perhaps the pastor himself, wishing to retain his place, had to moderate his position, or maybe the authorities intervened in some unforeseen, indirect manner; the pastor was perhaps transferred, or else, so as not to increase the discord, he was allowed to choose another field of activity, and then: all men are mortal. Time is stronger than men; it "does not spare what has been done without it," said Fayolles. "It does not allow the fruit of plants without roots to ripen, and it causes to ripen the fruits of those with principles solidly anchored in it." "Every healthy tree bears good fruit, but a rotten tree bears defective fruit" (Mt 7:17). Seen from the viewpoint of time, this word of Jesus is still true. After a more or less brief blaze, the system asserts itself, and one witnesses, in almost every case where there has been a revival in a multitudinist church, what the biologists call "a return to type": the characteristics of the species abide and gradually efface the temporary changes in the individual.

This law applies equally to the church of professing believers: after a longer or shorter time of lethargy, the Spirit of God can revive a church. Contrary to what happens in this case in a multitudinist church, it does not need to look long for a new procedure: the structure is there ready to receive the new life. "They put new wine into new skins, and both are preserved" (Mt 9:17).

This law has been verified in many cases in either sense or in both. Therefore, principles and the comparison of their fruits are important.

THE INNER LIFE OF THE CHURCH

The church and the worship service. The first call of the church is to praise God and to manifest His manifold wisdom before the angelic world (Eph 3:10). Only those who belong to God can praise Him, for in order to worship Him "in spirit and truth" they must first have received the Spirit and the truth. How can one who resists God fall down before Him and worship? The worship services of an assembly of believers may be devoid of the liturgical and artistic riches of certain great churches; those attending are often few in number; at least they are unanimous in glorifying the one who has saved them. They can truthfully sing hymns of adoration and consecration from their hymnals. Allowing the Spirit of God to guide and fashion them, they will also be witnesses of His infinite grace before principalities and powers in the heavenly places.

The church and the growth of Christians. The church of professing believers can perform the ministry which the Lord entrusted to it for the children of God. The local church is called to be both the family and the school of the believer. In the family the child receives nourishment and care which enable him to grow, and at school he is given the education and instruction which will make of him a useful and mature man.[7]

In the multitudinist church the minister of the Word finds himself faced with an almost unsolvable problem: if he considers his audience as a true church, that is, a community of believers,[8] his preaching greatly risks being irrelevant; it will pass over the heads of his audience and will discourage them.[9] On the other hand, if he takes into account the real state of his parish, he will need to limit himself to preaching the elementary truths of salvation in order to adjust his message to the real needs of his hearers. The real Christians, constantly fed only "milk," will have difficulty in growing.

In the church of believers, the attendance at gatherings for edification and enlightenment, generally more homogeneous (composed of a majority of Christians), more regular, often of smaller numbers, allows for the adaptation of the teaching and exhortation to the various needs of the believers and thus contributes to their harmonious growth.

The church and sanctification. The church is the milieu favorable to the growth of the Christian. There he should find new strength to enable him to remain faithful to the Lord. In the epistles all of the apostles earnestly warn the Christians to "not conform to the present world system" (Ro 12:2), to "no longer behave like the Gentiles" (Eph 4:17), in "your futile ways such as traditionally came down from your forefathers" (1 Pe 1:18), to "neither love the world nor the things in the world" (1 Jn 2:15). Everyone knows how very difficult and costly this nonconformity can be when one is alone in opposing the trend. The epistles invite the church members to "give daily warning to one another," to "admonish one another," to "edify one another," to "conduct yourselves worthy of the calling you have received" (Ro 15:14; Col 3:16; 1 Th 5:11; Eph 4:1; Heb 3:13; 10:25). If the Christian in his family or in his professional circle is judged, scorned, or even slandered because of his life which is different from that of "the world" (1 Pe 4:4), he should at least find in the local church brothers and sisters who are also doing their best to walk in the "narrow way" and who help him by their example, their intercession, and their counsel.

The spiritual atmosphere of a multitudinist church scarcely facilitates that kind of mutual exhortation. So as not to upset "the feeble members of the flock" (that is, really the unconverted), the pastor will avoid insisting on the necessity of a changed life, different from that of the people of the "world."[10] The fear of being treated as a "pietist" or as a "hypocrite" "who thinks he is better than the others" will hinder most members from exhorting and warning the others. Deprived of the support which God provided for him, the newly converted man will have great difficulty in progressing in sanctification.

The Protestant churches have been accused at times of putting the emphasis too exclusively on the "little problems of sanctification" of their members and losing sight of the cosmic dimensions of salvation as well as of the great social problems. These reproaches apply, in fact, to the pietist concept of the redemption of the world.[11] However, the church of professing believers is not necessarily associated with pietism. The apostles, founders of churches of this type, could certainly not be accused of pietism, but sanctification occupies a central place in their teaching. Is that not a sign that the terrestrial goal of redemption is the sanctified life and that to solve the serious problems of the world, God must first have new men? "The church of professing believers is not a pure church but a church which wishes to be purified, to be sanctified."[12]

The church and the communion of the brethren. The local church is the milieu chosen by God to open to us the community life. It is an ideal setting for the communion of the brethren. Man by nature has a tendency toward introversion, in the twentieth century just as much as in the nineteenth, for socializing at the present time touches only the very superficial aspects of the personality. Behind the mask, the person remains shut up in his solitude.[13] The first Christians "continued steadfastly in the apostles' doctrine and fellowship"; they "were of one heart and soul." A hundred times in the epistles we find the expression "one another" associated with the various aspects of the life of Christian brothers: "love one another—edify one another—teach one another—pray for one another—encourage one another—greet one another—have care for one another."

Where, if not in the church, will the Christian find surroundings which permit him to experience the privileges of such a relationship and also to be instructed in the duties which the community life implies? Only surroundings where all members are actuated by the same Spirit and the same life will be able to offer to the believer these opportunities of exchanging and sharing, of reciprocally loving and upholding. This is, without any doubt, one of the greatest privileges of the Christian here below, the earnest of the perfect communion which he will some day enjoy in the presence of God.[14]

Certainly, the happiness of being together could cause one to forget "those who are without." The churches of believers have not always avoided this trap. But a church animated by the Holy Spirit will constantly keep before it the vision of the world lost without God and a consciousness of its essential vocation: evangelization. The love of the brothers is for it a school where love for all is taught.

The universal priesthood. The universal priesthood can be effective only in a milieu of professing believers. The apostles laid down the principle for it: "You are . . . a royal priesthood" (1 Pe 2:9; cf. v. 5). "To Him who loves us . . . and has made us . . . priests to God, even His Father" (Rev 1:5-6). The medieval churches abolished it for the benefit of a clericalism which became more and more exclusive. The Reformers rediscovered and reaffirmed it: "All Christians belong to the ecclesiastical state," Luther said. "Through baptism absolutely all of us are consecrated to be priests."[15]

However, in the multitudinist context of the churches which sprang from the Reformation, this principle finds no practical application. "The Protestant Churches have remained essentially 'Churches of pastors,'" Brunner writes. And for a very good reason! He who is not one of God's people, can he be their priest? "The priestly character of believers is founded on personal faith and the new birth," says Dr. Manfred Jacobs.[16] What priestly functions can one entrust to one who is not regenerated? And since one must not distinguish between the converted and the unconverted, it is best to entrust these functions only to those who have been "regularly ordained."[17] By retaining the Catholic multitudinist principle, the Protestant churches have retained the very principle of clericalism, as E. de Pressensé has already pointed out: "A church of the masses is fatally doomed to become a sacerdotal and clerical Church; it annuls the universal priesthood, the most beautiful privilege of the New Covenant, or if it admits it theoretically, it annuls it in practice. From the day when the Church becomes nothing but a school, the priest turns up again to run it, and that is the end of a liberty so dearly acquired for us by the Son of God."[18]

The universal priesthood is in no way against specialized ministries or genuine preparation. Who would contest the fact that sound Bible study, the study of linguistics and history, etc., are valuable in exercising the different ministries of the Word? Let us not forget, however, that all through the history of the church, God has used many men and women who have had no formal theological training, and have not been ordained or set apart for the ministry.

Jesus Himself was scorned by the scribes because He had received no formal education. Among the twelve apostles not one had been trained as a rabbi. Almost all of the apostolic Fathers and the church Fathers would today be classed as "laymen." Several of those who exercised a dominant influence (Ambrose of Milan, Priscillien, etc.) were raised, without any preparation, from the position of laymen to that of bishop.

The few encouraging movements in the Middle Ages were begun by laymen (e.g., Pierre Valdo, Francis of Assisi).

The protagonists of the French Reformation had not had theological training: Calvin, a jurist who was never ordained, gave to the Reformation its doctrinal structure. William Farel, this layman "who is neither priest or monk," as the bishop of Gap wrote, founded a great number of churches and accomplished the work of an apostle of the Reformation. It was he also who in 1524 wrote the first French Reformed doctrine. Théodore de Bèze, another Reformer, was chosen to be Calvin's successor. He was a great scholar and translator of the New Testament, commentator, and dogmatist, but had studied only law and the humanities. Zinzendorf, the Reformer of the Moravian Brethren, was also a jurist. George Fox was a shepherd.

William Booth, founder of the Salvation Army, was a businessman, as was George Williams, founder of the Young Men's Christian Association. Evangelization, from Félix Neff to the pioneers of modern evangelism (J. Vetter, E. Schrenk, F. Binde, E. Keller, R. Saillens, etc.) owes a great deal to laymen.

Missions received their decisive impetus from a poor cobbler, William Carey. Some of its most illustrious representatives (Hudson Taylor, A. Judson, W. Bramwell, C. Studd, etc.) never had any theological education.

Among the famous preachers, Spurgeon did not attend Bible school; Dr. Martin Lloyd-Jones was a physician. However, that does not mean that they held studies in contempt: Spurgeon founded a Bible school (as did also other laymen: Dr. P. de Benoît, Rees Howells, Mr. and Mrs. Wasserzug, E. Sauer, Norton, etc.).

In the Orient, Christianity owes its most genuine revivals and its most effective movements to laymen such as T. Kagawa, Sadhu Sundar Singh, Bakht Singh, Watchman Nee and K. Utchimura.

And how could one forget that the most widely read Christian book next to the Bible was written by the tinsmith John Bunyan, that one of the greatest Christian writers in the French language was the mathematician and physicist Blaise Pascal, that among the best German translators of the Bible was a former headmaster, H. Menge—without mentioning numerous laymen who play most important parts in the Christian world of today. This function of the laymen will certainly be even more important in the world of tomorrow.[19]

The leadership of the church. The free church can apply biblical principles in the leadership of its community. In the New Testament, the offices of elder and deacon were filled by the church and were carried

on under constant supervision. The church often elected by the raised
hand (Ac 14:23, *cheirotoneo*) those who were called to direct and serve.[20]
As the proportion of unconverted members increased, the church realized
the dangers of this procedure. Would not the presbytery (the church
elders as a group) become an exact reflection of the heterogeneous composition of the assembly? Would not the leadership of the church be
removed from the true Christians when they came to be in the minority?
So it was necessary to abandon apostolic principles and resort to the
appointment of those who held positions of authority by someone in
higher authority.[21]

The churches of the Reformation reintroduced the principle of the
election of the elders and sometimes of the pastors, but multitudinism
scarcely renders the task of those who are called to take the responsibilities of the church an easy one. How many spiritual pastors have used up
their best energies in a struggle against a council of elders, most of whom
were unregenerate! And what shall we say of the inner suffering of the
Christian elders who are obliged to endlessly oppose the worldly and
carnal ideas of their colleagues and of a large fraction of the church?

In the free churches which follow the biblical model the elders and
deacons are church members whose spirituality, talents, and devotion
attract the attention of their brothers and sisters in Christ. After a period
of observation they are delegated these responsibilities (2 Ti 3:10). Since
the church is made up of regenerated Christians, the discerning of essential qualities for Christian service is relatively easy and the choice can
be made without the rivalry and jealousy which accompany all worldly
elections. Those elected know they are responsible before God and the
local church for the service entrusted to them. They know that as long
as they remain faithful to the Lord, they can count on the confidence
and support of the spiritual members of the church.

Is this ideal program easy to put into practice? Anyone who dares to
claim that is indeed naïve. That is failing to take into consideration the
malicious nature of the adversary who opposes all that comes from God.

Unfortunately, experience teaches us that it is the plurality in the leadership of the church which often causes the difficulties. "When there are
two stars in the heavens, the heavens become too small." The principle
is certainly not the cause of it; since it is biblical, it conforms to God's
plans. On the other hand, the carnal character and the lack of maturity
of the Christians charged with the responsibilities of the church are the
factors entering into many of the failures of the divine program (see
1 Co 3:3-4).

But experience also teaches us that where men have allowed their personal opinions and their wills to be nailed to the cross with Christ, they have discovered a fullness of joy, a security and riches which the "monarchical system" would never have been able to give them.

Ministries in the church. The exercise of biblical ministries is possible only in a church faithful to the principles of the Bible. The New Testament enumerates about twenty different ministries which the Holy Spirit grants to various members of the church: teaching, exhortation, evangelization, distribution of relief, chairmanship, gifts of miracles, distinguishing between spirits, etc. (see Ro 12:6-8; 1 Co 12; Eph 4:1-16; 1 Pe 4:10-11).

This is not a restrictive list, just the contrary; as in the human body each member and each organ has its function, so "to each is granted the evidence of the Spirit for the common welfare" (1 Co 12:7). "Each" person evidently designates only the true member of the body of Christ, for it is difficult to imagine that the Holy Spirit can grant spiritual gifts to those who have never been receptive to His influence and whom He has never regenerated.

In a multitudinist church, how does the Holy Spirit go about granting a gift to each of those who are born again without making visible the line of separation which is presumably not seen between the true Christians and the unconverted? How can a church devoid of spiritual discernment distinguish between the gifts of divine origin and natural gifts, when the brilliancy of the latter easily eclipses the humility of the former? The church which gives the Holy Spirit the liberty of putting His program into operation and which recognizes the gifts that He bestows, by entrusting her ministries and functions only to those who have received the gifts, ceases to be a multitudinist church. How can one deny that the application of these directives requires a great deal of wisdom and authority? Too often one confuses inspiration and improvisation, the ministry of the Word and natural eloquence.[21]

The church and doctrine. A church composed of mature believers will resist antibiblical heresies better than a church of the masses. He whom God has regenerated by His Spirit is also led by that same Spirit in discerning the truth (see 1 Co 2:16; 2 Ti 2:7; 2 Jn 1:2). Jesus said of the sheep belonging to the good Shepherd that they "follow him; for they know his voice. They will not follow a stranger but will run away from him, because they do not recognize the voice of strangers" (Jn 10:4-5). God does not want His children to remain "babes, swung back and forth and carried here and there with every wind of teaching that springs from human craftiness and ingenuity for devising error" (Eph 4:14). He has promised to guide those who follow Christ, in the light and "into all truth" (Jn 16:13).

The church of believers then will not accept just any teaching. Though one finds among the free churches a rather wide range of doctrinal variety in areas where the Bible does not give the full particulars, nevertheless, they generally oppose, more than do the multitudinist churches, the theological systems which undermine the authority of the Word of God, deny the divinity of Christ, or minimize the value of His redemptive work.

In churches of believers of the congregationalist type, those who serve and have been given charge of the teaching are named by the assembly and remain under its control. A church composed of true believers never entrusts the ministry of teaching to one who, although skilled in theology, denies all that is supernatural and rules out practically all the articles of the Apostles' Creed.

History proves that the churches of professing believers which have remained faithful to their principles, have offered the greatest resistance to negative theology, while the large established churches, filled with the unconverted who are without spiritual discernment, find wave after wave of it sweeping over them.

The communities of believers are still but islets of defense for biblical doctrine. It is not astonishing that they attract Christians who love the Word of God and wish to devote themselves to the apostles' teaching. The weakness of the free churches in matters of doctrine is often owing to the work of an amateur, to superficiality, to oversimplified generalizations, especially where the ministry of the Word is entrusted to laymen. Distrust of "theology" frequently engenders scorn of all thorough Bible study and of all genuine exegesis. Improvised "doctors" settle the most delicate doctrinal and exegetical problems with an assurance which ignorance alone can give. The evangelical churches are urgently in need of doctors of divinity "given by God" who are not afraid to add knowledge to their spiritual qualifications (2 Pe 1:5) so as to be able to successfully refute the fallacious arguments of "what is falsely called knowledge" (1 Ti 6:20).

The church and unity. In the local church, the Christian unity of which Jesus Christ and the apostles spoke can be realized only in a church of professing believers. Indeed, the New Testament invites us to be one with the other members of the church, and not to have fellowship with the unbelievers and false Christians. In the multitudinist church these two commandments are incompatible; Christians cannot obey both of them simultaneously.

In the church of professing believers the Christian learns to know the true unity in Christ, which shields him from counterfeits of Christian unity. Christianity of the world today has a "nostalgia for unity." The ecumenical movement and Ecumenical Council are in response to these aspirations, but the unity which they propose is not the one which Jesus and His apostles taught.[22] True Christian unity can be experienced only among the children of God. It can find concrete expression in the local church of believers by daily victory over all divisive agencies which assail it. The Christian who has succeeded in "maintaining the unity of the Spirit" with the brothers and sisters with whom he rubs shoulders every week will experience without difficulty the same unity with Christian brothers from other places whom he may meet occasionally. The experience of this true spiritual unity in Christ completely quenches his thirst for unity and keeps him from the compromise of imitation unity. Actually, true churches of professing believers are few in the Ecumenical Council of Churches, and those that do remain there usually have the hope—praiseworthy but no doubt utopian—of influencing the large established churches by their presence and testimony.

However, let us recognize, in light of the ecumenical progress, that the reconciliation of the free churches is still timid and sporadic. In agreement on the essentials, these churches often compromise their unity in testimony and collaboration by an exaggerated attachment to details of secondary importance.

Discipline in the church. In the primitive church those whose lives no longer corresponded to their profession of faith and who did not continue in the apostles' doctrine could be excommunicated. Thus there would never have been the question of considering as members those who were still strangers to the Christian life and who did not believe in the apostolic teaching. In the churches of the masses, church discipline is practically nonexistent. At best it is applied to glaring sins.[23] But churches of believers also must see to it that the progressing laxity in discipline does not transform them gradually into churches of the masses.

The church and finances. The church of professing believers can apply the biblical financial program. Even as financial problems are important in the secular world, so are they in the Christian world. The primitive church was a poor church, but each one put aside something on the first day of every week, the amount depending on "how much the Lord has helped you earn" (1 Co 16:2, Living NT), the believers gave cheerfully (2 Co 9:7), as they were able in order to meet the material needs of the community and provide for the needs of the saints. "They gave themselves first to the Lord" (2 Co 8:5) which made it easy for them to give a part of what they possessed, for they considered themselves to be nothing but stewards (Ac 4:32).

The problem is very different for the person who has never given himself to God. Sole proprietor and beneficiary of his possessions, he seeks happiness in the increase of his material wealth and in the pleasure which money can procure. It is with regret that he parts with even a part of his wealth; he will only give what he must to retain his rights in the religious organization of which he is a part.

Thus multitudinist organizations are always short of money, so they are always obliged to beg and to multiply the expedients which appeal more to the attractions of pleasure and to vanity than they do to generosity. These means are inevitable in a church where a great number of the members still bear in their hearts the love for this world and live according to the lust of the eyes, the lust of the flesh, and the pride of life, because they have never been gripped by the love of God. This word of Jesus is applicable to them: "Where your treasure is there will your heart be also," and the inverse is also true: "Where your heart is, there will your treasure be also."

If people are to give, one must appeal to the natural heart. But there is no biblical precedent for this, unless one refers to the sales in the temple, the profits of which were to replenish the holy treasury—not very probable considering Jesus' manifest condemnation of the same (see Mk 11:15-18; Jn 2:13-17). These means degrade the church in the eyes of the world, whose methods the Christian community is using even while claiming to be different from it.

On whom can the church of believers count for its financial needs? On the Holy Spirit, who has access to the hearts of all of its members. He alone can overcome man's natural greed and cause generosity to flourish to the point of complete self-sacrifice. Under His influence the numerical weakness of the free churches is compensated for by the liberality of all.[24]

THE TESTIMONY TO THE WORLD

Free churches and missions. Wherever the gospel takes root, in heathen lands or in Catholic regions, churches of professing believers are born. On mission fields, evangelical churches of professing believers are the most numerous, and most of the missionaries are not connected with the International Council of Missions which has merged with the Ecumenical Council of Churches.[25] Even the missions of multitudinist churches establish communities of the free-church type of professing believers in heathen lands, sometimes baptizing by immersion, whereas the church that sent them practices infant baptism by "sprinkling." The newly converted are quite naturally inspired by the biblical model, and they form churches which resemble the apostolic churches.[26] "Where the gospel of Paul is faithfully preached, communities of the Pauline type are formed," writes G. Nagel in *Der grosse Kampf.* Where, without any human agency, men have been converted by the reading of the Word alone, one finds, as a natural consequence, communities of professing believers organized on biblical principles.[27]

As to those converted who have come out from Catholicism, after having discovered in the Bible the true principles of the church, they often experience great difficulty in adapting themselves to a Protestant ecclesiastical system which differs too much from the biblical image. Also, experience proves that they generally integrate more rapidly in a church of professing believers which can justify all of its practices by the Word of God.

The adaptation of the church to circumstances. The assembly of believers is the most flexible form of the church, the one which adapts itself to all conditions, all forms of government, all situations. When the multitudinist church is deprived of great numbers, she feels awkward and frustrated. She grows like a plant transplanted in soil not suited to it. On the contrary, the genuine Christian assembly begins with two or three gathered in the name of Christ. Tertullian said: "Where two or three persons, even laymen, are gathered in the name of Christ, there is the church."

The community of professing believers need have no minority complex. On the contrary, she knows that the Lord and the truth are always found on the side of the "little flock" and that her safety lies in the spirit of humility. When the church grows, she tries to retain, whenever possible, the conditions found in the smaller group where communion and fraternal exchanges retain a force and effectiveness which the large assemblies never can. She will multiply prayer cells and Bible study groups in neighborhoods so much more easily since she can count on the gifts and working of the Holy Spirit in all her members.

There is absolutely no need for vast edifices in order to begin the work: the apostolic phrase "the church in . . . house" (Ro 16:5; 1 Co 16:19; Col 4:15) is still perfectly suitable for all churches at their inception. The place for the reunion grows as the community grows, and increasing material needs are met by the growing membership. Moreover, when the assembly reaches the size that requires a vast edifice perhaps she should ask the Lord whether He would rather have her divide than grow even larger.

The New Testament form of the church is also the one which is the most adaptable to the various geographic, ethnic, and political conditions in which the gospel is called to establish itself among men "out of every tribe and tongue and people and nation" (Rev 5:9). How many difficulties in missionary work have been caused only by the desire to closely apply the European ecclesiastical organizations in a setting which was not intended for them. "The work needs an institutional form which can be planted rapidly, can take root immediately, and can develop from the very first attempt in every soil and climate. The simplicity of the apostolic assembly meets these conditions," says H. G. Lang.[28] It is also the type of church which best withstands persecutions.

The church and evangelization. Evangelization is not easy in multitudinist churches. Its purpose is to bring the unconverted to conversion and the new birth; but are not all who attend the church Christians and regenerated since their baptism? Do they not benefit from all the "means of grace" of the church? Are they not exhorted each Sunday as though they were Christians? Would not the responding to the call for conversion be repudiating the teaching received in the church since earliest childhood? So one can well understand that many multitudinist churches never evangelize and are perhaps frankly hostile to evangelism. In any case, the churches which seriously accept the dogma of baptismal regeneration cannot envisage evangelization in any way other than as one aspect of their own teaching ministry among Christians entrusted to them who are already born again.

But does reality correspond to dogma? Does one not risk creating and maintaining in the minds of good parishioners the fatal illusion that all is in order? And that without their ever having taken a personal stand for or against Christ, without their ever having repented and personally accepted by faith the expiatory death of Christ, they will share in all the blessings promised to believers, and they are heirs to the kingdom of God.[29]

In the church of professing believers, on the contrary, in order to become a member one must make a profession of faith, generally at the time of his baptism. As long as one has not done this, he knows that something is not in order, that another step remains to be taken. By the evangelization which explains to all the nonconverted what God gives and requires, they know that this step concerns them especially.

Experience proves that in the countries where the majority of the churches are of the free-church type, evangelistic efforts are more numerous, less difficult, and more fruitful.

THE CHURCH IN THE WORLD TODAY

A church of the minority. A church of professing believers is a church of the minority. Many reproach her for that as if it were a defect, but actually it is her glory and protection. Even under the old covenant the truth was generally to be found on the side of the small number. As we pass from the old covenant to the new we witness a progressive decrease in numbers,[30] ending finally in the only remnant, Christ, depository of all the divine promises. About Him is grouped the "little flock" of disciples exposed to the pressure from the great number.

Pentecost created a church with a great number of people, but what are three thousand souls, if not a minority, in the large city which received for the feast more than a hundred thousand Jews and proselytes? All through Acts, the church is the few who believe and who find room in a house or a schoolroom. During three centuries the church remained a minority group, and that was her salvation.

The day when imperial favor drew to her the great numbers, that day she lost her purity, her power, and her essential character of "being called out of"—all at the same time. "If the salt has lost its taste, with what shall it be salted?" The spirit of the majority opens the door to the temptations of material security, the abuse of power, of repression, in truth, of the oppression of minority groups. When one feels he is with the crowd, he loses courage, the habit of the middle-class prejudices takes hold, and his testimony loses its validity.

The history of religions attests to the fact that all minority religious groups are dynamic, conquering groups whose moral and spiritual level transcends that of the majority group which it faces. So there is all the more reason that the Christian churches, which have the truth on their side, benefit from the advantages of being a minority group. The Christian who is a member of a church of professing believers will feel that he is constantly obliged to contend, to testify, to defend the challenged banner. He knows he is the focus of many eyes; the honor of the church and the salvation of several depend on his conduct. What better stimulant could one desire for his Christian walk? (1 Pe 2:12). The church as a whole must struggle, must evangelize in order to survive, must overcome the prejudices, the scorn, and the ostracism of the crowd. What is better able to bind them to their divine Head?

The church and the state. The free churches are churches separate from the state. Certain multitudinist churches also are separate, it is true, but the separation is usually accomplished against their will. As their parishes include practically the entire population, they feel justified in benefiting from state subsidies just as do other public services. Unfortunately, the attraction of an official function and the possibility of having recourse to the support of "the secular arm" hold a charm for many "church officials" even in the twentieth century. The temptation of power or, at least, of political action remains a dangerous snare for the churches of the majority. On the other hand, their vast buildings, their great social works, and their ecclesiastical coordinating and directing systems swallow up large sums of money—difficult to obtain from the spontaneous liberality of people for whom religion is of minor concern. Public funds offer a happy solution to this difficulty; so even where the multitudinist church had acquired its freedom from the state, following external circumstances, the religious authorities profited from the first political change to ask for the reestablishment of the regime of union of church and state.

But on the whole, the separation of church and state has caused the multitudinist churches to develop in the pattern of free churches. Since church membership involves financial obligations (other than symbolical), an automatic adjustment is made between a person's membership and his interest in the church. Only the more or less superstitious fear of divine displeasure, a fear coupled with that of seeing oneself refused the impressive church ceremonies at the most important hours of existence (birth of a child, marriage, burial) hinder many Christianized pagans from definitely cutting all ties with the religious organization. Certain countries that have known how to care for these anxieties have seen nominal Christians leave the church in a body.

In regimes where the church is not forging ahead and where the clerical garb is no longer highly esteemed, the situation clears up by itself. If we believe the Revelation, this state of affairs is destined to spread and to become more difficult; thus we can expect to see the dividing line between the church and the world become more and more distinct in the future. It is regrettable that financial considerations and political pressures have driven us to reforms in the church which Bible meditation and examination of conscience should have inspired.

"Wherever you find a State religion, you find a church which has denied its fundamental principle and which has slipped back from the New Covenant to the Old Covenant," says E. de Pressensé.[31] And Brunner comments, "When from the perspective of the Free Churches we see the Constantinian and Theodosian inheritance of the Churches of the Reformation in Europe, we recognize what a real curse it has been. . . . From the standpoint of the New Testament the Free Church is undoubtedly a more successful attempt to restore the primitive Christian Ekklesia than are the European institutional Churches."[32]

The church of the future. The free church is the church of the future.

The multitudinist church came into being with the Constantinian system of Christianity. All careful observers agree that this system has seen its day. "The multitudinist Church cannot prove itself to be a clerical Church unless it is a State Church at the same time."[33] Now the union of church and state no longer exists except in a few isolated instances.

In Europe we are witnessing the prolonged death struggle of Christianity, interrupted by a few sudden movements of life which certain men take to be a promise of renewal. But time marches on, and the Catholic Church itself, the last feudal estate of medieval Christianity, admits the "religious alienation of the masses" and the "paganizing of the Occident."

Toward what church are we going? Clear-sighted people like Professor R. Mehl reply without hesitation: toward "a minority church," toward "a humble church."[34] We are witnessing, as Professor E. G. Léonard said, "a general trend toward the church of professing believers." We return to this point later.

This tendency is especially important from the point of view of the world, as Kenneth S. Latourette states:

> It is from the radical wing that the majority of the missionaries have come who are proclaiming Protestant Christianity in other countries. That signifies that in the decades to come world Protestantism will be closer to pre-Reformation Christianity (that is, primitive Christianity and that of the faithful Christians of the Middle Ages) than the Christianity of Western Europe and the British Isles has ever before been. This tendency will probably gather strength if the "young churches" in the non-Western territory continue to grow.[35]

Here we are not facing secondary matters; it is about these last three points that the struggle between the church and the totalitarian regime has assumed a definite form. The church's attitude toward them will be the determining factor in the coming conflict between the church and the world.

All nations, Eastern or Western, exert a more and more complete hold on the mass of people, the money, and the power in all of its forms. If the church insists on exercising similar controls, conflict is inevitable. On the other hand, if this affects only a minority, if the church is satisfied with the modest means which her members place at her disposal for her material needs for evangelization and for the help of the needy, if she demonstrates by this fact that she intends to exercise no political influence and that her sole ambition is to change men into more conscientious workmen, more worthy fathers and mothers, better citizens, then in many cases, the church will be able to continue to lead a "tranquil and quiet life in all godliness and dignity" (1 Ti 2:2, NASB).

Will Build My Church

Many churches behind the iron curtain and the bamboo curtain have experienced this during these past years. That does not mean they were spared affliction, but at least they suffered as Christians. "None of you should suffer as . . . a meddler in others' affairs; but if you suffer as a Christian . . . praise God" (1 Pe 4:15-16).

The place of conflict has moved to the real center of gravity of the secular struggle between the adversary of God and the "people of the saints of the Most High." This conflict will not abate; quite to the contrary, the testing cycles through which the church passes in the end times, as seen in the Apocalypse, intensify as the end approaches. The fire through which some churches have already had to pass shows that only churches founded on the Word, churches which can count on the faithfulness and perseverance of each one of their members, will finally pass victoriously through the tribulation. On that day, all Christian "varnish" will crack, pretence will fall off, and the imitation Christianity of the pseudo-Christians will burn as tow in the fire. But the church built by the Lord on the rock will subsist and "the gates of hades shall not prevail against it."

Notes

1. "The National Church has reverted to the level attained in the Old Testament" (Caspar Schwenckfeld as quoted by E. H. Broadbent, *The Pilgrim Church*, p. 203).
2. The Christianity of the New Testament is based on the thought that one is a Christian in a relationship of opposition, that to be a Christian means to believe, to love God while setting one's face against the world" (Søren Kierkegaard, *L'Instant*, p. 64).
3. "He who does not want to confess Christ does not belong in the Church. The Church can hardly separate with certainty genuine from spurious faith—God alone can do that; therefore, the true Church is invisible—but it can and should determine who wishes to confess Christ and who not" (Emil Brunner, *The Divine-Human Encounter*, p. 184).
4. Brunner, *Le Renouveau de l'Eglise*.
5. "In the multitudinist church there is no foundation on which to build. One would have to begin by begetting the spiritual man before he could be cared for and educated" (G. Hilbert, *Ecclesiola in ecclesia*, p. 65).
6. "If the popular Church, by nature, is to be a church recruited 'biologically,' the majority of its members will never be true believers" (Ibid., p. 49).
7. ". . . the Church into whose bosom God is pleased to collect His children, not only that by her aid and ministry they may be nourished as babes and children, but that they may also be guided by her maternal care until they grow up to manhood and finally attain to the perfection of faith. What God has thus joined, let no man put asunder; to those to whom He is a Father, the Church must also be a mother" (Calvin, *Institutes*, bk. 4, chap. 1, par. 1).
8. "All the obligations divinely imposed on the local churches presuppose that those who fulfil them are true believers; for these Christian duties can be properly accomplished only by persons who have been genuinely converted; this applies also to mutual edification and exhortation. . . . If hypocrites wish to become members of the local churches, they must first 'repent and be converted' (Acts 3:19)" (J. T. Mueller, *La Doctrine chrétienne*, pp. 614-15).

9. "One concludes from many experiences in ministering to the healing of the soul, even among churchmen, that there are very few who know anything about what one might call the Christian experience: power of prayer, struggle for sanctification, discovery of the power of Christ and of the Holy Spirit, God's presence" (Brunner, *Situation de l'Eglise*, p. 7).

10. "When we read certain theological articles of our day, we have the impression that the principal concern of the Church is to emphasize the impossibility of overcoming sin, of combatting heresy. It remains to be seen if change is effectively brought about and if this change is visible. I do not wonder if this attitude is 'Reformed' or not, but it is not Biblical" (Brunner, *Eglises et Groupes*, p. 25).

11. See F. Rienecker, *Biblische Kritik am Pietismus*, pp. 22-27.

12. W. Ninck, *Christliche Gemeinde heute*, p. 190.

13. See P. Tournier, *De la Solitude à la Communauté*.

14. "Where there is the communion of the believers, where there is a close bond between the faithful and Christ and among the faithful themselves, that is not the Church; she is only where the elect meet together because they know they are the called and the elect. Consequently we see immediately that this Church is quite different from what we commonly call the Church. The believers know each other; there is an actual exchange of faith among them; they rejoice in the faith they possess; they help each other, as Luther says in the Smalkalde articles: 'by mutual support and by brotherly consolation.' The communion of the saints, an actual, living communion through the Holy Spirit, always presupposes faith, by which they all know one another" (Brunner, *Le Renouveau de l'Eglise*, p. 22).
"The Reformers in their commentaries on the Psalms and in their writings for moral enlightenment have many times stressed the importance of this exchange of experiences. But the Church, in most cases, has made very little use of it. They lack the ability for such exchange: the true communion of believers. And having things in common came to be regarded as something peculiar to the pietists or sects, while it was really the essential principle of primitive communities by which the life, which the apostles called the 'fruit of the Spirit,' was able to develop" (Ibid., p. 48).
"Paul clearly announced his conviction, based on the Gospels, that the true Church is bound together by the Holy Spirit and faith and that it is a spiritual communion of the brethren" (A. von Harnack, *What Is Christianity?*).
"In the light of our definition of fellowship it is clear that the basic experience of fellowship, as well as its growth in meaning and intensity, is dependent upon the awareness of a common experience of the grace of God in Christ, a common response of faith and obedience, a common expression of Christian love" (H. S. Bender, *These Are My People*, p. 50).

15. M. Luther, *An den christlichen Adel*. W. A. 6, 407, 13 ff. Luther affirmed this principle many times: "The pastorate is not a priesthood, but only one of the functions of the Church whose members are all priests and kings."
"The laymen, priests, dukes, bishops, and, as they say, the ecclesiastic and secular clergy, differ basically only by function, but not by rank (Stand). For they are all of the spiritual state, true priests, bishops, and popes" (Ibid.).
"Whoever wishes to be a Christian must be assured that we are all alike priests, that is to say, we have the same power in the Word of God and in each sacrament."
"Nobody can deny that every Christian possesses the Word of God, is instructed by God, and is anointed by God as a priest. . . . If this is so, if they have the Word of God, they then have the obligation to proclaim it. So it is certain that a Christian has not only the right and the power to teach the Word of God, but also the obligation; if he does not, he will lose his soul and fall from God's grace" (quoted by Brunner, *Le Renouveau de l'Eglise*, p. 43).

16. Manfred Jacobs, *Die evangelische Lehre von der Kirche*, p. 430.

17. "To many pastors the universal priesthood is doubtful. We are in the midst of a pastors' church, of a theologians' church" (Ninck, pp. 112, 114).

18. E. de Pressensé, *Discours religieux*, p. 35.

19. V. M. Gibbs; see T. R. Morton, *God's Frozen People*; J. Mott, *Liberating the Lay Forces of Christianity*; and the bibliography in *Religion in Geschichte und Gegenwart*, 4:206.
   We know that for some time these problems have preoccupied the Catholics ("the laymen are the Church"); Pius XII on this question of the laymen states, "It concerns nothing less than the foundation, the essence and the form of the Church" (Père Y. Congar, *Jalons pour une Théologie du Laïcat*, 1953).
   One must beware of illusions on this point; the Catholic sacrament of the order will always draw an impassable line between clergy and laymen in the Roman Catholic Church. The universal priesthood, as the New Testament presents it to us, could not, therefore, be applied to it. In the measure that Protestant thought follows in the wake of Catholic clericalism the churches of the Reformation will remain, they also, impregnable to the teaching of genuine, universal priesthood.

20. "There *cheirotonein* has nothing whatever to do with the laying on of hands; it is the technical term for 'to choose,' 'to appoint to an office,' and the underlying idea is not the laying on of hands but the raising of the hand—the customary manner of denoting assent to the election of some particular candidate" (Brunner, *The Misunderstanding of the Church*, p. 80). This term is found only twice in the New Testament, here and in 2 Co 8:18-19: "We are sending the brother . . . as an appointee of the churches, he travels with us in this ministry of grace."
   "Probably all that this passage means is that the apostles presided over the assembly from which the elders were chosen" (Barnes, *Notes on the New Testament*). On this point see also the notes of Calvin, Doddridge, Schleusner, etc.
   Other exegetes are less positive and think that this term could also signify: to name, to choose, to designate. The Catholics and the Anglicans translate it "instituted" or "ordained." The various concepts of the church and of the ministry become definite on this expression.

21. C. H. Mackintosh, one of the pioneers of the Assemblies of the Brethren of the past century, confessed toward the end of his life: "Unfortunately, we often see people get up in our meetings who should be kept in their seats by good common sense—not to mention spirituality. We have often thought that a certain category of ignorant people, who gladly hear themselves speak, consider the meeting to be a place where they can push themselves forward without going to school and studying" (quoted by G. Ischbeck, *J. N. Darby*, p. 104).

22. See A. Kuen, *Que Tous soient Un*, chap. 3, pp. 47-79, for proof of this assertion.

23. As C. Stoll remarks, "Church discipline is good fruit on a healthy tree . . . you cannot re-erect a church, which has fallen in ruins, by again introducing discipline or by handling it with increased severity, but by correctly performing the first duties of the church . . . we can see correct evangelical discipline only where a correct evangelical church exists" (*Kirchenzucht*, pp. 40-41).
   "The system of the churches of professing believers assures the exercise of church discipline which is almost impracticable in the State churches" (Philip Schaff, *Church and State in the United States*, p. 81).

24. American statistics show that in certain denominations of the free churches the average annual contribution per member exceeded $350 in 1967!

25. From the statistics published by the International Council of Missions, we gather that the expansion of Christianity is carried on mainly by the churches of professing believers, both in finances and in the number of missionaries sent out. (See *Interpretative Statistical Survey of the World Missions of Christian Churches*).
   In the United States, for example, the *National Council of Christian Churches* (NCC) connected with the Ecumenical Council represents 61.7 percent of the Protestant population, but only 34.7 percent of the missionaries are from the NCC.
   "The premise . . . that the Christian mission is the responsibility of every church member, has been an axiom of the Free Churches since the time of Anabaptists Georg Blaurock (1525) and Paul Glock (1550), and in organized form since

William Carey (1792) in London and Samuel F. Mills (1810) in Boston" (F. H. Littell, *The Free Church*, p. 4).

According to an article by Dr. Eugèn Smith which appeared in the *Ecumenical Review* of January, 1963 (pp. 182-91) the churches connected with the NCC have some 40 million members in the United States; the churches not connected with it, about 24 million. In 1960 the former had 10,324 missionaries and the latter had 16,066. The number of missionaries from the churches of the NCC had increased 4.5 percent between 1952 and 1960, whereas those not affiliated with the Ecumenical Council had increased 149.5 percent. The increase in giving for the same period was 50.5 percent and 167.3 percent, respectively. According to recent statistics, 62 percent of the Protestant missionaries in the world are from churches not in the Ecumenical Council.

26. The development of the Christian and Missionary Alliance is significant in this regard. This missionary society, born of the collaboration of Anglican, Presbyterian, Methodist and Baptist Christians, found itself facing a serious problem on the mission field: What form of church should they give to the assemblies born of their evangelistic efforts? The missionaries from the different groups agreed to take the apostolic churches as their models. By a kind of repercussion, hundreds of C&MA churches of the same type were formed in the United States to sustain the missionary effort of that alliance.

27. Dr. Alberto Diaz tells of the founding of the Baptist church in Cuba: "The believers wished to adopt a church organization but were not satisfied with those of the churches around them or those they knew. Consequently, they began to study prayerfully the New Testament to see if they would find a model church there. Following this study, they adopted a very simple organization: election of a pastor and deacons, and establishment of certain ordinances found in the New Testament. They did not know they had formed a Baptist church and were very much surprised later on to discover in America and in England many Christians called Baptists with whom they were in full accord. The Cuban brethren had organized a Baptist church two years before they knew that they were Baptists" (Henry Cook, *What Baptists Stand For*, p. 30).

28. H. G. Lang, *The Churches of God*, p. 33.

29. "The Gospel is preached in such a way that the unconverted man feels constantly at ease, though he is not in the least considering conversion" (F. Hübner, *Weltreich und Gottesreich*, p. 111).

30. O. Cullmann, *La Royauté de Christ et l'Eglise*.

31. Pressensé, *Discours religieux*, p. 32.

32. Brunner, *Dogmatics*, 3:82.

33. Hilbert, p. 51.

34. R. Mehl, "L'Eglise de l'Avenir," *Revue de L'Evangélisation*, no. 98 (1961), p. 483.

35. Kenneth S. Latourette, "A historian looks ahead: The future of Christianity in the light of its past" in *Church History* (1946), p. 14.

Part IX

RETURN TO GOD'S PLAN

"Workers Together with God"

14

Situation of the Churches in Europe Today

We have consulted the Bible and history to rediscover the divine plan for the church and to find the causes of its transformation into an ecclesiastical institution. Now we must use this information. What practical conclusions can we draw from the image of the church as God instituted it?

Everything that bears the name of church is at present passing through one of the most serious crises in history, at least in Europe. How is this crisis manifested? What is its cause? How can it be remedied? These three questions are inevitably asked of the Christian who takes seriously God's testimony in his generation. We shall evidently have to be satisfied here with a broad outline. The churches are sick; no one contests that. Recognizing objectively the symptoms of the disease in a sick person is not a sign of ill will toward him, but it is the condition necessary for rendering effective assistance.

THE POSITIVE ASPECT

If, in the following pages, we allow especially the critics of the church to speak, it is not because we fail to recognize the services rendered by the ecclesiastical institutions; we are not pointing out only their negative aspects.[1] We are certainly not forgetting that it is the church which has *transmitted the Word of God* down through the centuries and which has *led countless numbers of men to the truth and to the life.* Its social works and its charitable institutions have reflected the love of Christ in this world. Even today, we see her servants, both men and women, rendering acts of devotion; they bring to a suffering and undone humanity the testimony of the dedicated life and the consolation of the gospel of peace through their various ministries through the service of the deaconry.

Christ lives in the church through the many genuine Christians who are entirely devoted to Him. These believers diffuse the fragrance of Christ among the saved and the lost, often under very difficult conditions. Many of them are convinced that they are where God would have them to be. "Who are you to censure another's servant?" (Ro 14:4). Their affection for the church does not blind them, however, to her weaknesses and deficiencies. They suffer because of them more than do others, for they know, or feel, that when God created the church, He desired something other than what they are seeing and experiencing. They are most often misunderstood by their milieu and are exposed to vexations and difficulties caused by carnal men with whom they are associated.

It is for them, in the first place, that these chapters are intended. They will see that their suffering and their desire for change are shared by many believers and leaders of the church.

The Crisis of the European Churches

True love does not blindly and passively accept the faults of the beloved. Unconditional devotion to the church risks degenerating into participation in her faults and even betrayal of Christ and His body![2] To close one's eyes to the ecclesiastical crisis of today is not a proof of one's love for the church. He who truly loves her will make an effort to find the causes of and remedies for her present difficulties.

All observers agree that the churches in Europe are now experiencing the most serious crisis they have known since their inception.[3] How does this crisis manifest itself?

DE-CHRISTIANIZATION OF EUROPE

For the average European of the second half of the twentieth century, the problem of God no longer exists; God is dead. His heaven is on the verge of becoming a suburb of the earth; and men, the people of its satellites and its rockets. Since our earthly life is the only existing reality, our concern is to make it as comfortable as possible. Man's every thought becomes "existential"; all his efforts are concentrated on ameliorating the conditions of this present life.

One can understand that in this situation the Christian churches give the appearance of somewhat erratic blocks: witnesses and vestiges of a past era standing in the midst of a landscape which has developed; there they remain, partly due to the respect men have always had for historical monuments, partly due to inertia. But one must admit that even if these erratic blocks are the joy of the geologists, they are not greatly appreciated by the farmers; and, when a new proprietor decides to develop all of his land, they are moved back to the edge of the field. There they can, if need be, serve as a wall or as a boundary mark; they will still be a curiosity appreciated by the tourists!

In most of our Western countries the church has moved from the center of the scene to the marginal zone where only a few rare "faithful members" meet. "The great shadow of dechristianization and of practical materialism" hovers over "occidental Christianity."[4]

Entire countries have roughly thrown off the mask, instituting civil ceremonies to replace the religious church services. Even in Western countries, where the Christian ceremonies have retained the favor of the general public, the number of those who, out of honesty or indifference, free themselves from all church influence and from all religious ceremonies increases daily.

Statistics prove that there exists today "a situation which is new in the history of humanity. There are today millions of men and women in our multitudinist churches who confess no religious faith, who participate in no church rites and have no relationship whatsoever with any religious institution."[5]

Over against the Christian ideologies which have governed Western civilization until now, atheistic ideologies just as totalitarian and "religious" as Christianity, are presently rising up with an overwhelming force.[6]

DEPOPULATION OF THE CHURCHES

We first notice this de-Christianization in the practically empty churches.

France. "The eldest daughter of the Church," France, numbers today, according to what the Catholics themselves say, "40 million pagans; scarcely 3 or 4 million are still practicing Catholics."[7]

The percentage of those baptized remains rather large: 94 percent; however, in certain sections of the city, like the suburbs of Paris, it drops to under 50 percent. The proportion of practicing Catholics is not over 14 percent for the country as a whole—and nobody labors under any delusions concerning the amount of genuine faith which this term "practicing Catholic" implies. A significant detail is that the average monthly offering of the practicing Catholics of the diocese of Marseille in 1963 totaled 83 percent of a franc (20 cents), less than one-thousandth of the workingman's average pay.

Germany. The situation is scarcely any brighter in the countries of the old Protestant tradition. In 1906 there began a vast movement of defection of members of the German Lutheran Church, which suddenly opened the eyes of the ecclesiastical authorities. Whereas until the beginning of the twentieth century all German citizens were automatically compelled to be members of the church, a new thing began taking place: men were asking to leave the church. The state certainly tried to stop the move-

ment by requiring a certificate drawn up by the pastor, specifying that
the resigning member had explained to him his reasons for withdrawal.
It was in vain; whereas up to 1906 the number of annual defections in all
of the German Empire scarcely exceeded 6,000, it shot up after that date.
In the year 1906 there were 17,400; between 1907 and 1914 there were
from 14,300 to 29,300 a year. During the war of 1914 to 1918 the number
dropped to from 4,000 to 9,000 a year, only to reach 240,000 the day after
the armistice, and 315,000 in 1920. From that time on several hundreds
of thousands of "Christians" officially leave the ranks of the church each
year.[8]

England. Even during the last war—when the religious conscience of
many of the indifferent was rudely awakened—statistics of the Institute
of Public Opinion show that only 10 percent of the people participated
in the life of the churches.[9]

Switzerland. "The ecclesiastical reports point out that from 5% to 10%
of the population attend the Protestant churches; some speak of 1% to
2% of the adults. These percentages include the attendance on special
holidays. Of this number only a tenth partake of the Holy Communion,
as many as a third in the most favorable cases. Even then one would
have to discount those who participate for purely superficial reasons.
Therefore the number of those who really value the Church is very small;
often in one parish you can count them on your fingers."[10] Taking
Switzerland as a whole, 2.8 percent of the Protestants attend church services. All of these figures include special days (Christmas, Good Friday,
Easter, confirmation, etc.).

In a country as traditionally Christian as is the German-speaking part
of Switzerland, the average Sunday church attendance in the rural parishes is from twenty to thirty people; the number of men, as a rule, does
not exceed ten. Klaas Sluys also affirms that in the Flemish regions
scarcely 10 percent of the Catholic population are really practicing
Catholics.[11]

What shall we say of the Protestant regions of France? For example,
in the southwest, the Christian faith was still so vigorous at the end of
the last century that the parishioners built, with their own money, new
churches to accommodate the believers who thronged to the Sunday
worship services. In one of these localities where a second church was
built about 1880, the parishioners let it fall in ruins at about 1925; at
present, this small market town is one of six parishes served by the same
pastor—or rather, of five, for in one of them the church and the parsonage
were sold at an auction! The number of believers attending the services
rarely exceeds ten. A Protestant, passing through the town, went to one

of the most well known of these churches. He told me of his surprise on seeing the pastor preaching and observing all of the liturgy for only one person—his wife! Unfortunately, this case is not unique. The same religious indifference is found in many parishes in the Cévennes, where formerly faith impelled so many Huguenots to go to their martyrdom.

Conditions are no better in most of the other countries of the old Protestant tradition. I attended a morning service in one of the most beautiful Anglican cathedrals; the officiating priest was solemnly conducting the service for the beadle and two elderly women.

"Lord, have mercy," says R. Mehl. "Let us not take lightly the information that sociologists and statisticians are constantly placing before us: our sanctuaries are empty."[12]

"After having ascertained that, in our Church, the number of those who believe in Christ is a very 'small flock,' we must honestly ask ourselves what right we have to call it the 'popular Christian church' (*Volkskirche*)," comments W. Ninck.[13]

Ecclesiastical statistics complacently show an impressive number of "members" and a large attendance at the great solemn ceremonies (inaugurations, confirmations, Protestant assemblies, etc.). They seldom speak of the number of believers who regularly attend the Sunday services; yet, that is where the life of the church is manifested.

THE CHURCH, A CEREMONIAL INSTITUTION

For many "Christians" the church is now nothing but the frame which increases the value of a beautiful painting. Everyone likes to add a note of solemnity to the greatest moments of his life. Birth, the passing from adolescence to adulthood, marriage, and burial are, among all people, events where the individual and society meet. Everywhere and always such occasions are set in a religious framework. Let us not forget that "man is a religious animal"!

The modern pagans who people our Christianized countries do not readily renounce the splendor which a religious ceremony adds to the outstanding events of their family life, even if they personally feel free from all religious faith. One cannot, however, make of these events simple gastronomical occasions! How can one celebrate a birth without a baptism, a marriage without the nuptial benediction? How can one imagine a burial without any religious ceremony?

Do we not see even notorious atheists who call on the clergy to enhance the great events in their lives with that sacred glow of which the church has the secret and the monopoly? To meet this need, the majority of the large established churches have been transformed into ceremonial institutions. Under this title they are tolerated and even appreciated. In the large cities especially, the clergy have become, more than anything else, masters of ceremonies, and they complain that they spend their best energies and strength baptizing, marrying, and burying parishioners whom they do not know. Thus, there is no time left for the spiritual ministry, properly so called. The sizes of these churches seem to have been calculated by a malevolent spirit interested in transforming the clergymen into simple officiating priests.[14]

Fatal illusions. If only the church would use these ceremonies to proclaim the true message of the Bible! Unfortunately, they usually are only an occasion to consolidate the deadly illusions which the nominal "Christians" cherish.

"One says to the infant presented for baptism: 'You are now born again of water and of the Spirit'; to the one being confirmed who has submitted to the ceremony: 'You are a member of the Church!'; the newly married couple who has never set foot in the church but who could not think of renouncing the nuptial benediction, are addressed as 'Dear brother and sister in Christ.' The liturgy which was composed for the burial of believers is used beside each casket; they speak of the resurrection unto eternal life: 'We shall see you again, brother, in the eternal light.' "[15]

Who is responsible for the illusions in which all the inhabitants of Christianized countries live? Why does one complain of their lack of interest in the gospel and in the church when one assures them, by means of these few rites, that God is satisfied and everything is for the best in this best of all worlds!

The other side of the picture. This habit of religious ceremonies is so deeply rooted that it seems to have constituted the most tenacious bulwark against the abolishment of Christianity. In East Germany those who wished to supplant the church had to yield before the evidence that the people would not easily renounce their ceremonial festivals.

Would Christianity be saved because of these ceremonies? No, they merely formed empty bastions to be transformed into a base of operations against it. That is what happened in the Democratic Republic of Germany. In 1955 the government created a *Jugendweihe* (consecration of the young), copied point by point from the ceremony of the Lutheran confirmation. After the young person gives the social and political pledge, he is solemnly admitted into the community of workers; the gift of an antireligious book is given in place of the Bible given to the catechumen; the irreplaceable gastronomic family feast was to serve as a substitute for the former religious ceremony. In 1955, in spite of official propaganda and tempting gifts, only 15 percent of the young people participated in the *Jugendweihe*. In 1957 there were 32 percent; in 1958, 47 percent. The reports of 1964 indicate that in more than 90 percent of the cases the *Jugendweihe* replaced the confirmation.

Should not this example cause those to reflect who presume somewhat too readily on the faithfulness of the masses to Christianity?

INTERNAL SECULARIZATION OF THE CHURCHES

The numerical reduction of churches actually existing is alarming to be sure. However, this would not be catastrophic if the remaining nucleus were a fervent, living church and if those who remain devoted to her after this "sifting" were all genuine Christians. After all, the situation is scarcely different from that of the preceding centuries; only now that the masks have fallen, conditions are clearer and more honest.

But what is the situation within the churches? Brunner answers, "Since the eighteenth century (*Aufklärung*) our Church has become, at least in Protestant countries, unsure of her faith and of her own message; she has accepted into her doctrine and practices many pagan or worldly elements which are radically incompatible with the Christian faith; and so many manifestations of the true life of the Church have, to a lesser or greater degree, disappeared that this inner secularization presents a danger much more serious than that which comes from without."[16]

Some testimonies. Even the most faithful church members are not sparing in their criticism of the church. In the past century, R. Sohm complained in these words: "Even if she remains an assembly of the Eucharist and of the Word, the Church is nothing more than the world, the Christian world, but she is no longer the Christian Church."[17]

Those responsible for the churches, who prepared the report for the Ecumenical Conference in Evanston, said the same thing: "Our churches are sick. This illness is expressed by the fact that they are at home in the world and have adapted themselves to its ways."[18]

The spirit of the world has replaced the Holy Spirit. Roland de Pury affirms this: "In its complacency institutional Christianity manifests an unawareness of its need for the Holy Spirit; in other words, having lost sight of the 'scandal' of its foundation, it sees no need for true faith. This is the fraud which Kierkegaard denounces tirelessly. De Pury continues,

> From the two thousand years that she has been built on the Rock, the Church has obtained enough intelligence, experience, and knowledge of the world to be able to get along without the Founder, the Holy Spirit. She is strong enough to stand alone and to subsist by herself without the Spirit. She is voluble enough to speak even when God is silent and to

endure even when the heavens remain aloof. The Church has become so socially prestigious that she can exist even if God is no longer a living reality to her.[19]

But what results from such substitution? Karl Barth says,

> Instead of the Church, which is no longer a Church, appears not a vacuum but the phenomenon of the pseudo-Church or the semblance of a Church; it is an ecclesiastic substitute of the living congregation endowed with all the characteristics but devoid of all the substance. The result is one of two things: by reason of its inoffensive character, either the congregation knows a joyous complacency in its relationship with society and with the State, or its evident powerlessness in the world attests publicly the judgment which has struck it.[20]
>
> Having nothing but the outward appearance of a Church now, she would do well to ask herself if it is not by some linking of herself with the devil that she still exists or if she has not become the object of a well-deserved judgment from God.[21]

MULTITUDINISM

The intentional intermixing of believers and unbelievers in the church bears in its bitter fruits. "In fact," wrote Professor G. Hilbert, "the members of the popular churches, the great majority of them, are not yet 'Christians' and most of them are even less Christian than in Luther's day,"[22] and we remember what Luther said about them!

Emil Brunner states: "Today men are baptized in vain; for the most part, very few believe in Jesus Christ."[23] And F. J. Leenhardt adds: "One can practically establish the fact that infant baptism has not proved itself, for the multitudinist Church today is indeed multitudinist."[24] Multitudinism is no longer a blessing in the eyes of the present-day theologians; it is a wound, a sickness of the church. "Infant baptism," writes Barth, "is the symptom of a more serious illness from which the Church is suffering and which is multitudinism."[25]

Indeed, multitudinism is equivalent to being exempt from the necessity of making a decision for or against Christ; it is the "religion without decision" of which H. O. Wölber speaks. Such a religion no longer has a place and function in our world of today where all values, whatever they may be—philosophical, political or economic—maintain their position and progress only by a total involvement on the part of those who uphold them. The theologian Hans Hoekendijk said, "The multitudinist Church is not at all prepared to face such a situation of total involvement; in general, it has become an association where 'religion without decision' originates, is cultivated, and is propagated. It has become 'institutionalized indecision.'"

BECOMING MUNDANE

Thus, the majority of the large institutional churches are no longer either large or alive. In order to hold the few members who still participate in their activities, they feel obliged to make more and yet more concessions.

"The Church requires very little of its members"; says Brunner, "and they, moreover, scarcely permit her to make unreasonable demands of them. As much in the realm of the confession of faith as in that of Christian and church discipline, the people of the Church refuse to submit to definite standards."[26]

Church movie clubs, theater parties, and "pious" surprise parties vie with the world in attracting the youth,[27] but in this uneven race the church starts out seriously handicapped by the moral prejudices which its origin and its nature impose on it, unable to appeal forthrightly to instincts and covetous desires which constitute one of the surest attractions in the world.[28]

Moreover, even if she were a winner in this strange race, her victory would bear, nonetheless, the mark of final defeat. Those whom she will have succeeded in retaining by these deceptive means will leave her sooner or later in order to follow more openly the attractions of the pleasures to which the church has introduced them. As for the young who are in love with the truth, they will have renounced her some time earlier, disappointed because they had waited in vain for the brave word which would have saved them. "The Church would like to have many of us, but she offers us no help in solving our problems, and she asks nothing of us."[29]

SOCIAL CHRISTIANITY

The contemporary church lays great stress on her "presence in the world," her social works, her civic and political role. She boasts about these things as if they were her most recent acquisitions, and she thinks of them as characteristics which distinguish her from the "sects" which confine themselves to the religious role.

Jesus wanted His followers to be the "salt of the earth," but what example do we have from the primitive church which justifies the social role of the church and the present involvement of Christians in the world? Is it not disturbing to see the birth of this "social Christianity" coincide with the coming of liberalism, and are we not compelled to acknowledge that the "social gospel" has in many places replaced the simple gospel? It is claimed that Walter Rauschenbusch, one of the initiators of social Christianity, lost his faith in Christ when, during a trip in the Holy Land, he saw for himself the deplorable condition of the Palestinian roads for which Jesus had done nothing. Our Lord had better things to do than to busy Himself with comfort, but it seems that very often the church of today has nothing better to do.

That is the opinion of Father Paul Verghese, a member of the Orthodox Syrian Church and assistant secretary of the Ecumenical Council of Churches. He gives it in a report submitted to the Nyborg Conference of European Churches: "The temptation of the Protestant Churches of the West is to replace evangelization with service." A very small percent of the Western missionaries are, according to him, "engaged in a work of evangelization on the mission fields, with the objective of the establishing of the Church. On the other hand, pacifist agencies, work camps, operations crossroads, groups of voluntary service and other similar organizations spring up each year from all sides in the Occident." What are the reasons for this new direction in the churches? Father Verghese gives three of them:

> 1. A certain feeling that we have already *talked* too much in the past two hundred years and that we ought to *do* something for the nations and with them.
> 2. The materialistic milieu in which we live gives us an exaggerated idea of the physical needs of the world. . . . Today the speech for the defence which enables a person to collect the greatest indemnities is the one which consists in speaking of material poverty, of the homeless, of the condition of the orphans and the refugees . . . a purely emotional appeal. To speak of the spiritual needs is rather embarrassing for modern Christians of the West, perhaps because that makes them conscious of their own spiritual poverty. . . .
> 3. But the third reason is that the western Protestant Churches have become so spiritually impoverished that they unconsciously feel their lack of inner resources. How then can they tackle the spiritual needs of their own people, not to mention the needs of distant lands? It takes several years for some graduates in theology to perceive that theology alone has no value except to draw crowds and that it is without effect in the lives of people. And many others are honest enough to state that the only contribution which they can take to foreign people is their physical strength and their technical competence.[30]

THE WEAKENING OF THE MESSAGE

"Our Church has become very uncertain of its faith and of its message," said Brunner. And Karl Barth states: "To my knowledge and as far as I can judge, what is preached as the Gospel in the average sermons of our Church, in spite of all the calls to return to the Bible and to Lutheran terminology, is nothing but mysticism blended with ethics or ethics mixed with mysticism. It is not at all the Word of the Cross as the Reformers understood it."[31]

"If the salt has lost its taste, how can its saltness be restored?" After the sermons on hygiene and agriculture came social conferences or political controversies. They have tried everything, but the church is still without a message, without the power which attracts, without a hold on the people.

According to Walter Nigg, "The task of Luther's true heirs is to take fresh thought for the prophetical duty of criticism, as Herman Kutter has pointed out: I believe that if Luther and Zwingli were to rise from their graves today, they would drive us from our places and say, 'We know you not, in spite of all your fine Centenary Essays and Reformation celebrations. You are not Protestants; you make no protest of your own; you only keep on celebrating ours.' "[32]

CLERICALISM AND INSTITUTIONALISM

Feeling the situation slipping from her control, the church often reacts with clerical and institutional firmness. "It seems that the day of the Church as a great autonomous power is drawing to a close. The Church realizes this and, for the most part, seeks to defend and strengthen her former position. This attempt to save herself may end in her destruction instead."[33] Pastor Gerhard Bergmann, a doctor of philosophy who became an evangelist, ascertained this in many parishes that he visited: "The danger of clericalism is increasing at an alarming rate in the heart of Protestant Christendom."[34]

"On the whole," comments Brunner, "the Church has remained clerical, a Church of pastors."[35] He also says, "The whole misfortune of German Protestantism is rooted in the fact that from the very beginning the Reformation churches were served by pastors without the help of laymen. The same Church which discovered the priesthood of all believers has, up to the present day, never understood how to develop a real sense of responsibility in the Christian laity, with spontaneous cooperators in the local churches."[36]

THE SCATTERING OF THE CHRISTIANS

The consequence of this is that "many seek Christian fellowship outside of the Church, in the community life, a substitute for the communion of the saints which should be found in the Church."[37]

"The real tragedy of our time," according to W. A. Visser't Hooft, "is that we have an incoherent body of isolated Christians on the one hand, and on the other, we have powerful impulses, originators of new forms of communities. The Christians of today do not form a real community and the communities which the modern world gives rise to are not Christian."[38]

This scattering of true Christians in imitation-Christian communities is a phenomenon characteristic of our times. "Instead of trying to create a real community with living cells," states Brunner, "the Church has entirely neglected that function, so important, however, in primitive Christianity. . . . Thus the Church which, according to the New Testament, is to be a community, more than anything else, has become a very sparse scattering of individuals. She has blinded her eyes to this evil by retreating behind the doctrine of the invisible Church."[39]

Is it astonishing that in the face of such a situation the most clearsighted individuals should utter a cry of alarm?

"One can no longer assume the present method of Church procedure without uneasiness . . . to be satisfied with it is no longer possible," says Karl Barth.[40] He states earlier, "The time has come to call things by their real names. Whoever truly loves the Church today should calmly, ceaselessly, and with a loud voice, utter again and again: no farther, neither to the left nor to the right!"[41]

And H. Venske affirms,

> Sardis and Laodicea are types of these churches which have become sacramental institutions of salvation. . . . "You have the name of being alive, and you are dead. . . . For you say: I am rich, I have prospered, and I need nothing; not knowing that you are wretched, pitiable, blind and naked" (Rev. 3:1, 17). That which is artificial is to be destroyed. First of all there is a church which is not a church. She has almost nothing in common with the New Testament churches except her name. . . . Then there are Christians who are not Christians. . . . What an impressive number of important papers—baptismal certificates! They must be the cause of frenzied rejoicing in the infernal abyss! Everywhere there are Christian illusions from the cradle to the grave: baptisms which are not baptisms, confirmations which confirm nothing, church membership for those who are not members of the invisible Church, nuptial benedictions which simulate Christian marriages, religious burials which have difficulty in hiding the whole lie of one's "Christian" life.[42]

Evangelist Billy Graham, one of the men who best knows the present-day situation in the various churches, says in his recent book, *World Aflame:*

> Because the church, in turning to naturalistic religion, increasingly proclaims a humanistic gospel, thousands of laymen and clergymen alike are asking penetrating questions about the purpose and mission of the church. Thousands of loyal church members . . . are beginning to meet in prayer groups and Bible study classes. Multitudes of Christians within

the church are moving toward the point where they may reject the institution that we call the church. They are beginning to turn to more simplified forms of worship. They are hungry for a personal and vital experience with Jesus Christ. They want a heart-warming, personal faith.

Unless the church quickly recovers its authoritative Biblical message, we may witness the spectacle of millions of Christians going outside the institutional church to find spiritual food.[43]

Two questions are now asked of the one who examines the situation objectively: What are the causes of the present crisis? What remedies can we consider?

Notes

1. To avoid the confusion which might arise from the many quotations from ecclesiastical authors, we shall use the expression "the church" in these chapters in the sense which the theologians of the "established churches" give it. In their thinking, this expression often designates the ecclesiastical system from which they come or, following the expanded view of the ecumenical movement, the group consisting of the Lutheran, Reformed and Anglican churches as opposed to the scattered sects and communities which "revolve" about them.
2. "Many Christians are in danger of letting the Church take the place of Jesus Christ," says Erich Schick.
3. "It is unmistakable that today, in Europe especially, there prevails a far-reaching mistrust of everything that has to do with the Church even among such as are quite open to the Gospel of Jesus Christ. We must not forget that the idea of the Church is heavily compromised by nineteen hundred years of church history, and that the churches have accumulated obstacles between Jesus Christ and the individual man which are often impossible to surmount" (Emil Brunner, *The Misunderstanding of the Church*, p. 113).
4. M. Boegner, report of the Plenary Assembly of French Protestantism at Montbéliard, p. 15.
5. John Baillie, *What Is Christian Civilization?* p. 25. By "our churches" Baillie refers to the "large established Churches" like the Anglican Church.
6. "This 'baptized heathenism' is not new . . . for it was precisely the source of much of the protest of sixteenth-century radicals . . . against the whole idea of mass establishments. But it is new, at least, that there exist militant ideological alternatives to the faith, securely lodged in the centers of western civilization" (F. H. Littell, *The Free Church*, p. 3).
7. *Revue réformée* (1953), pp. 18-23.
8. See "Kirchenaustrittbewegung" in *Religion in Geschichte und Gegenwart*, 3:342 ff.
9. Tom Allen says in his book *The Face of My Parish* that his parish contained about 10,000 souls in 1946. Of these, the communicant membership stood at just over 400, which would represent about 4 percent of his parishioners. He claims that this proportion is quite typical of the problem of Britain today. According to *Towards the Conversion of England*, which he quotes, about 15 percent of the people regularly attend a place of worship.
10. W. Ninck, *Die Christliche Gemeinde heute*, pp. 28, 30. According to the study of the district of Zürich in 1963-1964 (*Dienst der Kirche in unserer Zeit*, [Zürich: Zwingli, 1966]), 6 percent of the members of the church are ready to work together in the church. Indifference has crept in among all classes of the population. Only 1 to 3 percent of the men attend the worship service (including holy days).
11. Klaas Sluys, *Das Wunder von Boechout*, p. 25.
12. R. Mehl, "L'Eglise de l'Avenir," *Revue de l'Evangélisation*, no. 98 (1961), p. 472.
13. Ninck, p. 32.

14. "They no longer turn to her except to give the luster of a doubtful and obscure consecration to human ceremonies and to have impressive funeral ceremonies" (Mehl, p. 475).
15. H. Venske, *Vollendete Reformation,* pp. 99-100.
16. Brunner, *Le Renouveau de l'Eglise,* p. 32.
17. R. Sohm, *Kirchenrecht,* 2:135.
18. Report for the WCC Evanston conference, *What is Christian Hope in the Christian Century?* no. 15 (1952), p. 428.
19. Roland de Pury, *La Maison de Dieu,* p. 19.
20. Karl Barth, *L'Église,* p. 112.
21. Ibid., p. 121.
22. G. Hilbert, *Volksmission und innere Mission,* pp. 3 ff.
23. Brunner, *Église et Groupes,* p. 43.
24. F. J. Leenhardt, *Foi et Vie* (Jan. 1949), p. 72.
25. Quoted by Francus, *Il n'y a pas de Protestants,* p. 83. "We no longer want groups in the Church" was the slogan. "All are baptized. Consequently, we must no longer form special circles. We must address all. But since everybody does not come, the peace of cemeteries is settling down over the parishes. We no longer hear anything but the steps of the pastor and of those who are being confirmed" (W. Busch, "Selbstmord der Kirche," *Licht und Leben-Ruf zur Entscheidung,* 1:66).
26. Brunner, *La Situation de l'Eglise,* p. 5.
27. In an article entitled "The Suicide of the Church," Pastor Busch shows by what means the church has driven out the life that was in it. Here is one of them: "New ways had to be found. Instead of Bible studies, evening dances were introduced. They began timidly with folk dances. Then they began shamelessly to compete with dancing classes." Then he quotes an article by a theologian who biblically justifies the dance as a means of contacting those who are without!
28. "That which is striking in the attitude of the Churches is their glib tongues. Panting for breath, they run with the times so that no one may escape them. 'We also, we also'! It is no longer as it was a few centuries ago. Now it is: Socialism? We also! Youth movements? We also. Sports? We also. These churches create nothing; they merely revise what others have created, what has developed among others into elements which can be useful to them" (Tucholsky, quoted by H. J. Schultz, "Christentum incognito?" in *Kritik an der Kirche,* p. 152).
29. Brunner, *La Situation de l'Eglise.*
30. Paul Verghese, "Vocation des Eglises à un service renouvelé" in *Report of Nyborg III.*
31. Barth, p. 33.
32. Walter Nigg as quoted by the Catholic Hans Küng (*The Council, Reform and Reunion,* p. 98), who adds, somewhat maliciously, "We would not have dared to say it, Catholics that we are."
33. Schultz, p. 125. "Sie kann sich zu Tode retten," or literally, "She can save herself to death."
34. Gerhard Bergmann, *Die Aufgabe des Volkes Gottesheute,* p. 70.
35. Brunner, *La Situation de l'Eglise,* p. 13.
36. Brunner as quoted by Littell, p. xiii.
37. M. Antonin, *Union des Eglises libres,* p. 43.
38. W. A. Visser't Hooft, *None Other Gods,* p. 70.
39. Brunner, *La Situation de l'Eglise,* pp. 10-11.
40. Barth, p. 125.
41. Ibid., p. 36.
42. Venske, p. 89.
43. Billy Graham, *World Aflame,* p. 86.

15

The Causes of the Present Crisis

THE ALLEGED CAUSES

THE SCAPEGOATS

MANY REASONS have been put forward to justify the present condition of the church: the progress in sciences and techniques which have multiplied the means of diversion, such as radio, movies, television, travel and reading; the infatuation with sports and other outdoor activities which keep people away from church on Sundays; a progressively materialistic viewpoint of all interests, such as material progress, comfort, the developing of the life of the body, which seem to monopolize all man's efforts and on which all his hopes for happiness are based; the appearance and propagation of *new* atheistic and anti-Christian *ideologies*, such as faith in Renan's "future of science," the philosophies such as Comte's which proclaim that the era of positivism always follows the religious and metaphysical ages, and the politico-philosophic systems of Hegel, Engels and Marx which are linked with historical materialism. These ideologies have known such a rapid growth that they are progressively replacing the Christian ideology.

CAUSES OR CONSEQUENCES?

All these factors undeniably play their part in the general alienation of Europeans from the "church." But, before being a cause, were they themselves not consequences? Why have the masses turned their backs on Christianity? Why is there this craving for amusement? Why have "Christians" sought their happiness in comfort, in developing the body, and in satisfying all of their penchants and their covetous desires? Why have they made scientific, economic and political progress the goal of their lives? Why have the new ideologies been so favorably received? Why have the upsetting and contradictory theories of a Renan, an Auguste Comte, or an Engels found followers at a time when the Word of truth was losing them?[1] Why was the call of Karl Marx heard at a time when the call of Jesus Christ was scarcely sounded forth anymore?

Why? Was it not that Christianity, which occupied the land and had the advantages of it, had become meaningless and distorted to the point that it no longer had any valid answer for man's problems, no desirable goal to which he could aspire? Was it not that the "church" which was to bring the world to Christ often created a gulf between them instead?

"The Church has again and again stood revealed as one of the major obstacles to the creation and preservation of the true *Ekklesia*. . . ," says Brunner. " 'Crush the infamous one' is also the cry of humanity oppressed by the Church and therefore the warning sign—never to be ignored—given by Christ Himself to a Christianity which is betraying Him in the interest of the Church."[2]

ARE THE PHILOSOPHERS MAINLY ACCOUNTABLE?

We have fallen into the habit of blaming the situation on the philosophers of the "Century of lights"; but honestly, are Voltaire, Montesquieu, and Diderot's arguments against the Christian faith so compelling? What Christian established in Christ would let his faith be shaken by reading their theories? Just as their attacks against the corrupt practices of the "church" scarcely succeeded in convincing their contemporaries, so their arguments against the Christian faith have been revealed as astonishingly weak, and their prophecies concerning the end of Christianity have discredited them in the eyes of their descendants.

When two religions or two philosophies confront each other, the victory always goes to the one which seems to contain the maxim of truth. When Christianity undertook the conquest of the old world, it not only had to overcome the old mythological religions of Greece and Rome, it found itself face to face with syncretic religions which have retained even up to this day their attractiveness for many Christianized people. It also had to firmly resist philosophies which had passed through a series of transformations, such as Platonism, Stoicism, and all their derivatives. Why did intellectuals, orators, and even philosophers turn to Christianity if not because they discerned in the Christian message a wisdom and life superior to those which their systems offered them? Was not the apostle Paul right in affirming that in Christ "all the treasures of wisdom and knowledge lie hidden"?

From the very moment that Christians lost confidence in the power of God's revelation alone to overthrow these philosophical fortresses and to "capture every thought until it acknowledges the authority of Christ" (2 Co 10:5, Phillips) and when they created "theological" systems by mixing fundamental Christian ideas with gnostic ideas, they laid the foundation for the de-Christianization of the masses even before they were Christianized.

In fact, the Christianity which is inculcated in the proselytes of the third century and in the masses, who beginning with the fourth century invade the ranks of the "church," owes as much to Neoplatonism and to Gnosticism as it does to the revelation of Jesus Christ and to the writings of the apostles. In the Middle Ages the thought took the form of Christian Aristotelianism while the life as it was practiced was nothing more than baptized paganism.

The Reformation threatened only slightly the union of Christ's revelation and philosophy. The simultaneous appearance of the Renaissance and the Reformation was more than a fortuitous coming together of two contradictory tendencies. Humanism, a rediscovery of pagan antiquity, placed man at the center of the world. More than once it influenced the Reformation, which tried to restore to the revelation and to God their central place which had been lost. Melanchthon, the humanist, stood by Luther; Calvin, like the other principal promoters of the Reformation, was influenced by humanism. Although in principle they proclaimed the exclusive authority of the biblical revelation, it is not difficult to show the unconscious influence of the medieval and contemporary philosophies on their thinking.

As soon as new philosophical systems began to appear, the Christian thinkers considered themselves obliged to adapt God's revelation to those systems. It is not surprising that their theologies followed the transitory vogue of those human systems, discrediting the Christian faith itself in the eyes of the world. Under those circumstances Christian teaching was in no position to struggle effectively against the attacks of the philosophers, and a message based on such fluctuating premises did not succeed in holding the church members in the churches.

THE REAL CAUSES

THE RESPONSIBILITY OF THEOLOGY

The foundation of the church. Luther wrote: "Wherever you see there is no Gospel (as we see in the churches of the Papists and of the Thomists) neither is there a Church and you must not doubt it, even if they baptize and partake of the Holy Communion."[3] And he stated that "false teachers of doctrine in the Church, false men who baptize, and false prayer books cannot be in the Church nor remain there should they enter."[4]

Calvin said, "If the doctrine of the Apostles and of the Prophets . . . is the foundation of the Church and one removes this doctrine, how can the building stand? So the Church must fall when the doctrine which alone supports it is overthrown." J. de Senarclens says Calvin thinks "a bad theology leads of necessity to a false Church, while the confession of the authentic Gospel, by the very faithfulness of God, must of necessity develop a genuine community."[5]

The foundation attacked. The prophetic word of Calvin was to be fulfilled only too soon in the churches of the Reformation because Luther's warning was not taken seriously. Theologians, desirous of suiting the gospel to the tastes of the day, attacked the authenticity of the Bible, the divinity of Jesus Christ, and the truth of the miracles. Some of them considered the thirteen epistles of Paul to be false; Jesus was no more than a rabbi among other rabbis, whose somewhat too enthusiastic disciples had, after His death, made Him a miracle worker and one who had risen from the dead.

That men could profess such doctrines was not catastrophic—there have always been unbelievers and enemies of Christianity[6]—but that a church which called itself Christian could welcome them to her bosom and entrust to them the training of future leaders of the churches, that is what should never have happened. Generations of pastors have been marked by the teaching of leading men who denied the doctrines of the Scripture, thus, in time, contaminating entire countries.

The repercussions. By means of an investigation made in a number of parishes in Germany, Dr. Gerhard Bergmann discovered that "before the invasion of theological rationalism there was a very intensive church life." Sunday worship services drew such crowds that everywhere balconies had to be built in the churches. During the week two supplementary services were held. From the Reformation until 1750, holy communion was commemorated each Sunday, or at least once in two weeks. What happened after the arrival of the liberal pastors? The weekly worship services disappeared, the attendance at prayer meetings decreased, the church was becoming empty even on Sundays, holy communion was celebrated only once a month, then once a year "in memory of the founder of the religion," the number of participants dwindled to almost nothing. In a small city in Friesland where there were between three and four thousand participants in the holy communion before the liberal crisis, there remained an average of approximately twenty. Records even show us who these participants were: they were the children of the confirmation class of that year and their mothers.[7]

In the French-speaking countries the situation is not any brighter. In a lecture devoted to the Protestant Church in the nineteenth century, Pastor A. Gaillard said: "French protestantism came out of the eighteenth century more weakened than it did after two centuries of persecution. Deism replaced the Gospel even in Christian pulpits which extolled 'fraternal gatherings of all cults.' Even the sermons of the famous Paul Rabaut were only ethical discourses. Faithful preaching, unknown in the official churches [state churches], could be found in the small pietist groups. The Moravians and the Methodists found themselves reproached by Paul Rabaut for preaching the death and resurrection of Jesus Christ."

In Geneva "the ministerial association" declared war on those who proclaimed the eternal divinity of Jesus Christ and free salvation by faith in Him. "Then began the separations and the schisms."[8] In innumerable Protestant parishes in France, Switzerland and Belgium the same thing was occurring that Dr. Bergmann had seen in Germany. Shortly after the arrival of a liberal pastor, the parish churches were practically empty and one could witness all the phases of the change: a flourishing parish with a pastor faithful to the Bible next to a liberal, dead parish—the downfall of the first with the arrival of a modernist pastor, and the renewal of life in the decimated community as soon as the Word of God resounded again in all of its purity.

What remained of the biblical message? "A God without wrath brought men without sin into a kingdom without judgment through the ministrations of a Christ without a cross."[9] One should not be surprised if this message no longer attracted anyone and if those who hungered and thirsted for spiritual nurture were abandoning the official churches and going to nonconformist communities.

"It is most presumptuous to expect church people to be faithful to their church," says Bergmann, "when its official representatives have ceased to be faithful to Jesus Christ and to follow him as the Head of the Church."[10] By welcoming the negative theologies, the church was closing its door to the Holy Spirit. "Wherever the Word of God is rejected—even by the slightest compromise with liberal theology—the Holy Spirit cannot work;" affirms A. Lüscher, "because the Holy Spirit will guide into all the truth (John 16:13) and not into [higher] criticism."[11]

It is a theologian, W. Stählin, who makes this confession: "No one is in such great danger of becoming incapable of perceiving the divine mystery as are the theologians. The time is not far off when we shall find out what fatal folly it was to think one could remove the Word of God entrusted to the Church from within the praying church and treat it professionally just like any other object of human research."[12]

Theological vogues. Father Congar harshly remarked that the Protestants are amazingly unstable and always ready to embark on the last ships to come out of the university "ship-building yards." The religious history of Germany in the nineteenth and twentieth centuries often corroborates this inconstancy. "Protestantism has multiplied the number of popes instead of abolishing them," comments F. J. Leenhardt.[13]

"You will retort," writes Werner Ninck, "that the teaching has been purified by dialectic theology. But why does not the church begin to flourish again? Perhaps because, in spite of this purification, the Holy Spirit, who alone can create faith, is missing as is the Word."[14] Brunner states: "The powerful movements for renewal of theology (Barthianism) have up to the present changed nothing decisively, not even in the preaching."[15]

Barth's teaching, by denying the absolute character of the truth and that the Scripture is in itself absolute truth, has remained in the tradition of Hegel and of relativist pragmatism. As opposed to "the one *or* the other" they substituted the dialectic which tries to reconcile "the one *and* the other," as Van Dusen puts it. Thus "one does not find among the neo-modernists—who address the world as if it were the Church and the Church as if she were the world—a radical distinction between the lost individual and the saved individual."[16] They claim that the Bible is not the Word of God; however, they act as if it were. "Let us imagine that you destroy a bridge," said F. Schaeffer, "then that you dash forward into the void as if the bridge were still there." Each one decides what is the Word of God. From this aspect, Barthianism, which fought against liberal subjectivism, itself remained subjectivist and prepared the ground for existentialist theologians who are lost in pure subjectivity. In the name of their inner sentiment of truth, R. Bultmann and his school decide what is true or false in the Bible, discarding practically all that is supernatural, that is, practically all the essential apostolic doctrines.[17]

After the publication of Bishop Robinson's books, one begins to realize just where these pernicious teachings lead. Concerning these books, J. P. Gabus writes, "It is to be feared that our Protestant churches, in this second half of the twentieth century, have to face distressing conflicts against these new forms of a completely secularized Gospel, which will not fail to raise up enthusiastic followers. It is henceforth clear that Bultmann's school will have served, alas, only to give rise to a neo-liberalism."[18]

OTHER SOURCES OF CRISIS TODAY

Let us take one more step. Why was theology so important in the churches of the Reformation? How could it exercise such a sweeping influence?

Intellectualism of faith. To the first of these questions one can answer, as does Bishop Newbigin, that the ministry of the Word and doctrinal agreement certainly occupy too great a place in the Protestant churches.

"The Word," said Luther, "is the *only* permanent and unerring mark of the Church." The logical consequence of this position is to give an increasingly important place to doctrinal rectitude.

"The true character of this mutual union of believers in Christ is falsified disastrously when one understands it to be doctrinal agreement,"[19] comments Bishop Leslie Newbigin, who speaks of the "superintellectualizing of the content of the word *faith*." It is the "misunderstanding of faith" which Brunner also denies and of which we spoke earlier.[20]

If by faith one means "intellectual acquiescence to the correct doctrine," to define this doctrine becomes the most important work of the church and it is the theologian who holds the keys of the kingdom.

Minor churches. How have theologians who deny the biblical truths been able to gain such an extensive influence in the churches? Why have unbelievers been allowed to occupy administrative positions in the church and to serve on faculties of theological schools? How does it happen that the believing members of the churches have not vigorously reacted against these pernicious influences of their (learned) doctors?

In seeking the answer to these questions, we are led to an older and more underlying cause of the present crisis, which is nothing else than the retaining of the church as it was under Constantine and Theodosius I, a compulsory state. This situation has for a long time disguised the actual condition by integrating officially all the new citizens of the Christianized world and the church.

The Constantinian system. Brunner writes of this system:

> The national Reformed Church, born of the national Constantinian Church, did not realize that its status and its task were changing at the time when state compulsion in confessional matters was disappearing. For more than a thousand years Europe had known this compulsory religion. The State exacted baptism and Church membership as a minimum of church observances, thereby identifying the people of the State with the people of the Church. . . . By a strange invention of the imagination, all baptized members of the State were Christians.[21]

"Up to the middle of the nineteenth century," says Liermann, "it was unthinkable that a man would not belong to a church."[22] Since the large institutional churches were made up of people, the majority of whom were unconverted and lacking in spiritual discernment, it was not difficult for a gifted preacher to get them to accept almost any doctrine. Since pastors were all-powerful in their parishes, and since they were appointed by the government or with its approval, the churches were at the mercy of all the new teachings which the professors in schools of theology—also controlled by the state—poured into their students.

Believers, reduced to the role of listeners only, had no means of actively intervening in the life of their church. Their number, in any case, was never large: "From the time of Theodosius there has been no more mission in Europe," comments Brunner, "since all are Christians."[23] "Evangelization has disappeared from the Church," says Ninck.[24] Having nothing to say in their church and, because of state subsidies, being exempted from having to make sacrifices in order to support her, the laymen became less and less interested in her, leaving the whole responsibility of her destiny in the hands of "specialists."

The late (deceased) Christendom. However, two world wars, the progress of sciences, and the mingling of civilizations have strongly shaken the Constantinian system of "Christendom." Man today has shaken off all the constraints which used to weigh heavily on him—especially religious restraint which had exerted pressure on him from the time of his birth.

It is a unanimously recognized fact that "we no longer live under the regime of Christendom."[25] We speak of the "end of the concept of Christendom," of "the collapse of Christianity,"[26] of "post-Christendom." In the coming years "the disintegrating process of Medieval Christianity will be completed in Europe."[27] "We seem to be coming to the end of this period ushered in by Constantine," says Roland de Pury, "and the challenge to Christian faith by all sorts of new faiths is a loud call to the Holy Spirit."[28] Karl Barth speaks of "the ruin, manifestly near, of the last bastions of the idea of the *corpus christianum.*"[29]

We are here and there witnessing a few spectacular revivifications of this idea. The Catholic Church, in particular, cannot resign herself to being divorced from the world which has served her so well. Present-day Christendom is trying to "resume the dialogue with its former partner." Encyclicals like John XXIII's *Pacem in terris* and Paul VI's *Ecclesiam Suam* are illustrations of the attempts being made today for reconciliation and for a union of Christendom and the world."[30] The different ecumenical efforts are along the same line and are "movements of Christendom," according to G. Millon, which interest the church of Jesus Christ only at a distance.

The future will reveal whether these efforts are the last convulsive movements of Christendom in the throes of death or the first signs of life of these great politico-religious systems which the Apocalypse foretells for the end times. Along with Christendom, the foundation of the multitudinist church disappears. "The time of the Protestant multitudinist Church is passed. It was an impossible ideal whose day is past," says Erich Steinbach.[31] "The so called 'popular Church' [*Volkskirche*, multitudinist church] has no promise in the Bible, no achievement in history, no significance in the present."[32] "One can in all honesty consider the masses of the popular churches only as a mission field."[33]

THE TESTIMONY OF THE AMERICAN CHURCHES

One fact corroborates this explanation of the crisis of the churches in Europe. That is the situation of the churches in America. From their very foundation the American churches objected to the Constantinian principle in force in European countries and were organized on the principle of liberty and voluntary service. Now, the "fundamentalist" churches of the New World are unaware of the crisis through which churches of the old Continent are passing. For instead of depopulation of the churches, one sees a very regular attendance at places of worship and continuous growth in the number of church members.

THE LANGUAGE OF STATISTICS

For America as a whole, statistics inform us that 36 percent of the Protestants go to church each week and 62 percent attend their place of worship at least once a month. Since the independence of the United States, the statistical membership in the churches has grown constantly. At the close of the state church regime, coinciding with the end of the colonial period, 5 percent of the population regularly attended a worship service. In 1800 the proportion had risen to 6.9 percent, in 1850 to 15.5 percent, in 1900 to 35.7 percent; and the census of 1926 showed that more than 50 percent declared they belonged to a church. From 1926 to 1934 the number of church members increased 32.8 percent, whereas the increase in population was only 13.9 percent.[34]

The growth of certain churches which are based entirely on the personal confession of faith is even more spectacular. In 1850 there were 700,000 Baptists in the United States, in 1900 there were 4.8 million, and in 1950 there were 18.5 million, which represents a growth of 260 percent. It is all the more significant since the figures do not include, as do statistics of multitudinist churches, the children and those who though baptized are unconcerned and who have neglected to withdraw their membership. These are not totals based on the enormous city parishes which number several thousand parishioners; the average church has fewer than 200 members.[35]

SOME CONCLUSIONS

Brunner points out that the great difference between the situation in Europe and in America is that there is a highly significant fact of a positive character; namely, that in the same epoch in which the Churches of Europe have been overtaken by the crisis, the Churches of the United States show an entirely contrary picture. There, instead of the European exodus from the Church, a strong increase of Church membership is to be noted. While the European Churches have lost more and more ground, a really astonishing increase of Church interest and sympathy on the part of the populace is noticeable. . . . The Churches in America have been protected from becoming "Churches" in the manner and degree of the Churches of Europe. The tradition of Constantine and Theodosius was radically swept away, so that voluntary Church membership alone remains. . . . The crisis of the Church is a specifically European phenomenon.[36]*

That shows us, he adds, that the origin of the crisis is not to be found either in scientific progress, since nowhere does one find such naïve faith in science as in America; or in the progress of rationalism, since it is in America that the rationalistic spirit has been the most radical. "The European church would do well to seek the cause of its crisis within itself and not in some exterior factor."[37]

Barth states that the Congregationalist churches resisted the current of rationalism in the eighteenth century better than did the Presbyterian and Episcopal churches. "It is the Congregationalist churches who shaped America, a country which does not lack order and which has produced young churches of which the dynamic force often amazes us today."[38] This fact also demonstrates to us how unwarranted is the argument of those who peremptorily claim that the principle of the free churches leads inevitably to a crumbling and disintegration of the church, and that only the state or institutional church is capable of maintaining continuity.

As early as the nineteenth century, E. de Pressensé exclaimed:

> Have we not the right to say to the system against which we are struggling: You have had Europe to yourself for centuries; what have you done with it? And if you had been the only ones serving, where would she be today? So also, where you have taught under the best circumstances in the land which was the cradle of the Reformation, this land of Germany where you have ruled too long, you must admit that a real paganism is supplanting more and more the fictitious Christianity. By the fruits one recognizes the tree. The fruit that the tree which you have planted is bearing, right under our eyes, is bitter and poisoned.[39]

Friedrich Loofs wrote in 1901, "Who knows if, some day, when the national Churches of the Old World collapse, the congregationalist form will not be planted in our country also?" Barth quoted this opinion in his

---

*Publisher's note: Since the French edition of this book was published, a crisis in the American church has become evident, perhaps for many of the same reasons as the author gives for the European crisis. Certainly some American denominations have become multitudinist in character.

report on the church, given at the Amsterdam Conference, and added as he concluded: "These words 'who knows?' could well be prophetic."

Notes

1. It is known that—height of irony—Auguste Comte finally created a new religion: the positivist religion (with churches, rites and ceremonies), of which he proclaimed himself the sovereign priest. Today there are still followers of this religion in South America.
2. Emil Brunner, *The Misunderstanding of the Church*, p. 117.
3. Martin Luther, *Ad. librum . . . Ambrosis Catharini*, W. A. 7, 721, 4.
4. Luther, *Wider Hans Worst* (1541), W. A. 51, 521, 19 ff.
5. J. de Senarclens, *De la Vraie Eglise, selon Calvin*, p. 18. He adds: "Transposed into our present situation, this reasoning would be translated as follows: Roman theology can engender only Roman ecclesiology; likewise, modern Protestant theology can lead only to a multitudinist and national Church."
6. Bonhoeffer said, "From the time of Adam's expulsion from paradise every man is born with this question, which Satan has put in Adam's heart. This is the first question of all flesh: 'Ought God to have said'?" (Dietrich Bonhoeffer, *Temptation*, p. 16).
7. Gerhard Bergmann, *Die Aufgabe des Volkes Gottes heute*, pp. 14 ff.
8. S. Samouélian, *Aperçu historique des Eglises de Professants*, p. 17.
9. H. Richard Niebuhr, *The Kingdom of God in America*, p. 193.
10. Bergmann, p. 25.
11. A. Lüscher, *Laodizäa die Christuslose Endkirche* (1939).
12. W. Stählin as quoted by Werner Ninck, *Die Christliche Gemeinde heute*, pp. 129-30.
13. F. J. Leenhardt, *Verbum Caro*, pp. 30-31.
14. Ninck, p. 90.
15. Brunner, *Dogmatics*, 3:99-100.
16. Francis A. Schaeffer, *Néo-modernisme ou christianisme*, p. 27.
17. V. G. Bergmann, *Alarm um die Bibel*; F. Rienecker, *Stellungsnahme zu Bultmanns Entmythologisierung*; F. Schindelin, *Es begann in der Ewigkeit*. Bultmann's theology is "a product of modern existentialism, but one will try in vain to lead the men of our time to give themselves to Christ or to create a living church with that" (Professor Karl Heim, at the end of his life, in *Ich gedenke der vorigen Tage*, p. 318). "Bultmannian and post-Bultmannian theology threaten the very substance of the Church of Jesus Christ in all confessions. . . . Rationalism has already led the Church to the edge of the abyss once. It will be no different with neo-rationalism if we do not take a resolute stand against it" (G. Bergmann, pp. 121-22).
18. J. P. Gabus with reference to *Honest to God* and *God Is No More* (*centre prot. etudes et doc.*, no. 83-84). Concerning Bishop Robinson's book, the English philosopher Alasdair McIntyre says, "Dr. Robinson is an atheist. That is the first thing in his book that impresses us. But he is not alone. The success of his book allows one to suppose that a combination between a religious vocabulary and sound atheism has a fair amount of attraction. This approval reveals to us one aspect of the present theological situation and one may well wonder: Is all present day Protestant theology perhaps atheistic?" (Quoted from *Diskussion zu Robinsons Gott ist anders*). See also M. B. Schlink, *Und keiner wollte es glauben*, pp. 50-70.
19. Leslie Newbigin, *L'Eglise*, pp. 67-68.
20. See Brunner, pp. 70-71, and the chapter "La foi" in *Il faut que vous naissiez de nouveau*. By denouncing here the intellectualizing of faith, we do not mean to blow the trumpet of liberalism (or neoliberalism), or that of sacramentalism, both of which have as a common *leitmotiv* the denunciation of the knowledge-faith (*foi-notitia*) cause of all the damage. It is certain that, from the biblical point of view, faith has an intellectual content and some Bible passages use the word *faith* in an intellectual sense (e.g., Ja 2:19), but that is only one aspect

of faith, and not the most important one; however, it is the one which has been
retained exclusively in many cases.
21. Brunner, *La Situation de l'Eglise*. For example, in Zürich until 1789 no one
    could become a citizen unless he was a baptized Protestant. When one was
    admitted for the first time to holy communion, he was also enrolled on the list
    of army recruits. See Ninck, p. 149.
22. H. Liermann, *Religion in Geschichte und Gegenwart*, 3:343.
23. Brunner, *Dogmatics*, 3.
24. Ninck, p. 59.
25. R. Mehl, *Verbum Caro* (1958), p. 179.
26. Newbigin, *L'Universalisme de la Foi chrétienne*, pp. 13-17. See the chapter
    devoted to this subject. Also see his *L'Eglise*, pp. 11 ff.
27. Mehl, "L'Eglise de l'Avenir," *Revue de l'Evangélisation*, no. 98, p. 469.
28. Roland de Pury, *La Maison de Dieu*, p. 19.
29. Karl Barth, *L'Eglise*, p. 117. *Corpus christianum* is an expression which we owe
    to K. Rieker and which designates Christendom as the "Christian body," basing
    it only on the fact that it is composed of those who are baptized.
30. G. Millon, *Combats pour l'Eglise*, p. 26.
31. Erich Steinbach as quoted by Ninck, p. 27.
32. Past. Lic. Hildebrandt (Berlin, Apr. 22, 1934).
33. Martin Kähler, *Zur Bibelfrage* (1907), p. 99.
34. According to Kenneth S. Latourette, *A History of the Expansion of Christianity*,
    4:117, and *Information Bulletin of the Federal Council of Churches* (Dec.,
    1945), quoted by F. H. Littell, *The Free Church*, pp. 116-17.
35. From "Baptisten" in *Religion in Geschichte und Gegenwart*. Even in France the
    Baptist churches tripled their total strength between 1945 and 1964. See J. P.
    Benoît, *Dénominations et Sectes*, p. 43.
36. Brunner, *Dogmatics*, 3:96.
37. Ibid.
38. Barth, p. 105.
39. E. de Pressensé, *Discours Religieux*, séries 1, pp. 36-37.
40. Barth, p. 105.

16

Remedies for the Present Situation

To whoever wishes to regenerate a decadent society, one prescribes,
and rightly so, that he take it back to its origin.

POPE LEO XIII

PROPOSED REMEDIES

THE CRISIS OF THE CHURCH is not a recent one; it has been latent since the
sixteenth century. So various solutions have been sought since the time
of the Reformation.

"REVIVE" THE CHURCH

The *collegia pietatis* (*ecclesiolae* in ecclesia)—cottage Bible study and
prayer meetings, the "Protestantenvereine" of Richard Rothe, the experience of Sulze in restoring life to the church through *religious activities*,[1]
friendly gatherings, and the "evangelical fraternities" were just so many
attempts, and just so many failures, to transform the church.

Various efforts have been made—popular evangelism, home missions,
social action—to reestablish the tie between the church and her people,
who were dissatisfied with her. However, one was soon forced to recognize that the gulf which separated the church from the mass of Christianized pagans was much deeper than he dared to admit and that any
new rapprochement between the churches and the masses could be
achieved only at the price of the church's yielding, renouncing her peculiar calling, and lining up her concepts with those of the world.

Even today many sincere Christians are still seeking to revive the
church by similar means: discussion circles, rooms where people work
together, charity bazaars, young people's clubs and groups; by these as
well as many other means they seek to gradually integrate the indifferent
with the church life. *Parish workers* go from home to home of enrolled
Protestants, doing their utmost to revive their interest in church activities.
Large *Protestant assemblies* and *church conferences* seek to demonstrate
to the parishioners, who often have complexes when facing massed Catholicism, the "vitality of Protestantism," and to give them again the con-

309

sciousness of their strength. Preparations for these gatherings include the forming of groups of specialists from all branches of the economy and culture to discuss their different points of view and to compare them with those of the Bible. These are certainly interesting experiences, but all of these temporary alleviations do not get to the root of the trouble.

Other people think that the revival of the church is connected with a *liturgical renewal* (e.g., Pomeyrol, Taizé, Grandchamp, and Berneuchen). According to still others, all the evils of Christendom are the result of its divisions, so they seek the remedy for them in a great nondiscriminatory union of all churches which claim Christ as their authority. The Ecumenical Council of Churches and the Ecumenical Council of the Roman Catholic Church are trying, each in its own way, to find the solution to the problem of Christian unity. Certain churches and some Protestant movements are conscious of the importance of the call to reunite the various historical branches of Christianity, even if it must be by a return of the "separated brethren" to the bosom of the holy Roman Catholic Church. The general public's infatuation with attempts at reconciliation encourages their promoters and risks precipitating the movement.

THE RESULTS

It is helpful to listen to what the scholars of the Protestant Church think of these attempts. After having studied the different systems proposed for renewal, Professor G. Hilbert concludes:

> I hold it extremely important that we forget these illusions and that we state clearly and firmly: It is impossible to transform all of the multitudinist churches into a living community. In vain we seek to give to our multitudinist churches, whose members become that by birth alone, the appearance—in the interior as well as on the exterior—of churches of professing believers! We must frankly and clearly state that our parish churches, in spite of everything we can do, are not true churches and can never become real churches.[2]

THE CAUSES OF THE FAILURE

Why do we fail? It is "because this false ideal leads churches to require of their members a life for which they are not ready and which, by nature, they can never live," not being born again. Hilbert terms this attempt *Schwärmerei* (Illuminism), which is the major reproach addressed generally to the "sects" by the established churches. According to him, it leads only to failure, to disappointments, to a waste of one's forces, and to total paralysis. "It is an impractical scheme, a Utopia, to expect people to live a Christian life before they are Christians; it is an illusion to think that by means of activity they will become Christians."[3] And as long as parish workers and those responsible for youth movements and various circles and sectors of church activity are not really born again, they will not be able to lead into a true Christian life those to whom they give their time.

If, as the result of the faithful preaching and the patient activity of a converted pastor, an *ecclesiola* of true Christians should be formed in a multitudinist church, this group will have to expect the greatest of difficulties from the majority of the members in the church. Many pastors have experienced this.[4]

In *Erweckung heute* Dr. Otto Riecker draws his conclusions from a revival which sprang up in a multitudinist parish church:

> In the Church assembly each member has the same rights. The church is constituted of all who have been baptized, who are in a more or less direct relationship with the church, and who contribute financially as well. What happens when, from the midst of those who have been "born into" the Church, a group of people step forward who have experienced the new birth? If one clings tenaciously to baptismal regeneration, such an event is not considered valid and will be rejected under the pretext that it is hyper-spiritual, Illuminist (*schwärmerisch*), and causes divisions in the Church. When such ideas are expressed by ecclesiastical officers in the exercise of their preaching ministry, the group of the "awakened" generally find itself forced back to the fringe of the Church or even excluded. This was the fate of A. H. Francke at Leipzig and of John Wesley in England. The static uniformity of the Church must not be broken; her "peace" is not to be jeopardized. . . . When the pastor defends the Biblical doctrine of the new birth, when he speaks of its gifts, of its grace, of its imperative, and of its spiritual dignity, even that creates a stir. But if a group of Christians is formed among whom this fact is not only preached, but lived, the excitement increases. The preaching is still accepted; it is considered in the category of the expression of opinions, which no one is required to follow—after that another pastor will come. But when a group of disciples is formed they prove that all these teachings are capable of giving life; they demonstrate by their very existence and even more by their behavior, the lie of the common, habitual, religious position; their presence reveals that something better than the habitual position exists, and this provokes tensions. Preaching conversion will never obtain such a revolutionary effect as will a group of young people who no longer frequent the taverns, no longer attend balls and society festivities, who hold in contempt the theater and the cinema, lead a pure life, and are beginning to work for Christ. The "world," which has just been rudely shaken from its tranquil state, declares that these "fanatics" are mad, and thereby establishes itself as the new norm, unlawfully even as an ecclesiastical norm. Christians accustomed to compromises loudly protest legalism when license ceases and definite steps toward sanctification are taken, for example, by avoiding places where the spirit of the world holds sovereign sway. Those most seriously affected are church members who are

well grounded but who do not have Life. They see the new life in the revived members and find themselves facing a dilemma: are they willing to recognize this new life and seek it or must they decline it under almost any pretext. . . . A manifest change in attitudes follows revival. What distresses the "old man" the most is that he cannot remain neutral. He must decide. By not saying yes, he says no. . . .[5]

There is nothing that the nominal Christian in the church finds more difficult to tolerate than the regrouping of believers.[6]

G. Millon says,

> In Roman, Orthodox, or Protestant Christendom, true reformation is practically impossible, for if it were carried out according to the will of the Lord, Christendom would cease to exist and would give place to the Church of Jesus Christ. In theory, one can admit the possibility of this radical change, at least for a certain privileged local assembly; but the facts seem to contradict this possibility. History relates nothing of a whole local body freeing itself as a group at one time. Doubtlessly its transformation can be only religious—not spiritual—since a small part, and sometimes even the majority of the group are unconverted men. The only solution to the problem is for the children of God to come out from Christendom.[7]

IS UNITY THE SOLUTION?

We have spoken elsewhere of the results that evangelical Christians expect from the present ecumenical efforts.[8] Let us hear what Emil Brunner, a doctor from one of the large institutional churches, thinks of the possibility of again finding the ecclesia by means of these unifications:

> By insisting on the necessity of a union of the judicial Church-bodies, one overestimates the institution and encourages clericalism, erroneous identification of the Church with the Ecclesia. Most often, where the merger of several Churches has taken place, the most clerical group has taken over and the least clerical has been repressed. This fact alone would lead one to the logical conclusion that this movement must result in the triumph of the Church which is the most "Church," that is to say, the Roman Catholic Church.
>
> Ecclesiastical men are trying to unify in one system the historical ecclesiastical Churches which have been fashioned over the centuries; how much more important it would be that the faithful and especially the persons who have the leadership of the Churches be ready to cooperate in the spirit of the communion of the brethren. . . .
>
> In certain ecumenical circles we have often heard the phrase "rediscovery of the Church" as implying one of the greatest events of our time. I suppose that it is here a question not of the rediscovery of the New Testament Ecclesia but of something quite different, namely, a revival of that false ecclesiasticism whose final goal—still unperceived at present— can be none other than the Roman Church. No true Ecclesia can be made out of twenty ecclesiastical institutions. Christian fellowship can

spring only from spiritual knowledge of Christ, which implies the desire for brotherhood in Christ.[9]

This is what Calvin said about it more than four centuries ago:

> Saint Hilary, in the book of the Councils, makes use of the following exordium: let it be known that unity is a name that looks good, and it is favored as a title, but there is no true peace in the Church other than that which is Christ. This is a statement worthy of being repeated each time someone negotiates to bring peace and concord to Christendom and principally when it concerns coming to an agreement on doctrine. Especially since God-fearing men of sane judgment avoid contentions and abhor dissensions, the proposal of appeasement is always agreeable to them. And who is the man (unless he is most uncivilized) who will not willingly listen when men are deliberating the re-establishing of peace in the Christian Church? . . . But since there are subtle and cunning enemies of the truth who steal in under the cloak of "unity" in order to alter the true Christian doctrine, one must carefully and prudently discern just what peace they are offering. And just as Jesus Christ enjoins us everywhere to peace, so He also teaches us that only the truth of the Gospel suffices to maintain it. Because of this those who are trying to turn us away from the pure confession of the Gospel must not delude us under the name of harmony. . . . [Then Calvin protests against] those who construct a camouflaged peace which leaves us half of the Gospel of Christ in such a way that there nevertheless is no part of His doctrine which they do not obscure or blur with some falsehood. And in order to make their maliciousness appear in a good light, they call it reformation.[10]

"The way to Church unity," says Karl Barth, "wherever it begins, can be only by its renewal. But renewal signifies repentance. Repentance denotes conversion: not that of others, but *our own*. The problem which the Roman Council poses to the World Council of Churches, is it not that of conversion, and therefore of the renewal of our Churches?"[11]

Need for a Second Reformation

RELATIVITY OF THE REFORMATION

No one still contests the fact that the church of the sixteenth century needed to be reformed, not even the Catholics, at least not the most courageous of them.[12] And no one denies the fact that this work of reformation could not have been achieved in a few years, not even the Reformers. Calvin wrote: "I certainly confess that when one cannot from the first day obtain an entire reformation, it is at least something to have obtained the principal points; however, one must not cease to follow after that which is lacking."[13]

In certain cases, however, they have tried to limit to a strict minimum the changes to be introduced into the church.[14] One recalls that after 1524 Luther came to a decisive and fatal turning point in his work of reformation, above all avoiding a break with the civil authorities of the empire. From that moment on he anathematized the promoters of the "radical Reformation." It has been pointed out that the Confession of Augsburg defined the church without any mention of the Bible.[15] Moreover, Luther claimed that the Scripture did not speak of the "exterior" church,[16] and that it permitted men to organize it according to their good pleasure,[17] "thus clearly renouncing all Scriptural support for his popular church."[18]

Zwingli, when placed before the alternative: Anabaptists or the council of the city of Zürich, chose to sacrifice the former in the hope of winning the masses. Calvin sacrificed several aspects of the apostolic church in order to maintain "the peace of the Church." In view of the choices which the principal promoters of the Reformation made, one can understand why the founders of the free churches called them the "middle-of-the-road men."[19] One also understands that the idea of the need for a "second reformation," or for a continuance of the work of the Reformers, found a very early foothold in the churches of the Reformation.

SEMPER REFORMANDA—ALWAYS BEING REFORMED

Ecclesia reformanda quia reformata: The reformed church should be reformed or, because the church has been reformed, it should be reformed. In this formal statement which probably dates from the time of Voetius (17th century) and which certain churches have taken as a motto (by giving it a greater emphasis: *semper reformanda*—always being reformed) probably lies the secret for the healing of the church. Many Christians and church men have affirmed it ever since the sixteenth century.

As early as 1690 John Robinson, addressing the Pilgrim Fathers about to set out for the New World, deplored the unconditional fidelity of the Lutherans and of the Reformed to the positions taken by their founders:

> I adjure you before God to follow me only in so far as you have seen me follow Jesus Christ. If God reveals something to you through another of His servants, be as prompt to obey it as if you had received it through my ministry. I am absolutely convinced that the Lord has other truths to impart to us through His Holy Word. Personally, I cannot sufficiently deplore the condition of these reformed churches which have acquired a certain degree of religion, but which do not wish to go beyond their reformation. The Lutherans can see only what Luther saw; they would die rather than accept a certain aspect of the truth revealed to Calvin. As for the Calvinists, they cling to the heritage left them by that great man of God, who, nevertheless, did not know everything. It is deplorable poverty, for even if these men in their time were lamps which burned and gave

light in the darkness, they had not yet entered into all the counsel of God. If they were living in our day, they would be ready to embrace a light which was more intense than the one which at first enlightened them. For it is indeed impossible for the Christian world so recently plunged into dense anti-Christian darkness to suddenly attain perfect knowledge.[20]

Voices from the nineteenth century. In the nineteenth century the men of the Awakening and the founders of the free churches spoke forcefully of the need for continuing the work of the Reformers. The supporters of the Revival of Geneva in the nineteenth century "were persuaded that the Reformers had never planned to give to the Church an exterior form which would be invariable and valid for all times, nor to impose on Christendom a faultless and unalterable organized system, but rather that they had sought to obtain for the Church liberty, above all, instead of Roman servitude."[21]

Alexandre Vinet proclaimed:

Even today, whatever may have been the importance of the event in the sixteenth century, the Reformation is still something to be accomplished, something for which Luther and Calvin only prepared a more even ground and a wider door. They did not, once and for all, reform the Church, but they affirmed the principle and laid down the conditions for all future reforms. . . . The Reformation was a sound and blessed work because it insisted on magnifying the eternal Gospel and nothing less in resolving all questions. To continue the work of the Reformation, do not consider it completed, but return without delay to the large, pure spring of all truth. . . . We must decide; Catholicism is pressing upon us; we must be openly Protestants. We have retained many shreds of Catholicism; now we must finally put on new clothes. . . .

The semi-Catholicism with which we stopped is now impoverished: only total Catholicism or total Protestantism endures; there is no life except in the Gospel.

What was lacking in the reformation work of the sixteenth century resulted from the fact that the doctrine of the Church was not studied thoroughly nor was the ecclesiastic question clearly resolved, whereas all the others were. What the Reformers, who could neither do everything nor see everything, left us as our task, is precisely that.[22]

Count Agénor de Gasparin declared:

When the Reformers of the sixteenth century did their utmost to recover the domain of Christian principle, they only partially succeeded; they discerned the dogma; the Church escaped their notice. . . . The Reformation must be completed.[23]

The principles which were violated in the sixteenth century are having their revenge in the nineteenth century. . . . We must complete the process of becoming Protestants in order to truly become Christians.[24]

Those who remained in the established church called for a reform no less than the others.

Adolphe Monod, in his sermon on the vocation of the church, criticizes those who "recreate a Luther more Lutheran now than he was in the sixteenth century and who wish to forever establish in the Church the thoughts and institutions of a fallible man who in advance devoutly protested such blind homage."[25] He says,

> There is a society on earth which has communion with Jesus Christ, which possesses Jesus Christ, which realizes Jesus Christ, which lives in Jesus Christ and in whom Jesus Christ lives. . . . This society is the Church. The Church, but what Church? The contemporary Church? I do not know, but it is the primitive Church. The Church as it is? I do not know that, but it is the Church as she ought to be, the Church which is the Church and which, if it does not exist, must be sought after by a reformation.[26]

Since then other voices have joined theirs to express the same desire. *Ernest Fontanes* warned, "The Reformation must not be limited to the sixteenth century, like a rebellion achieved once and for all, but it must be renewed and must continue without weakening, reminding us that there is no healthy, joyous life if the obsolete, worn out elements are not eliminated." And *J. Izoulet* noted, "The Reformation of the sixteenth century was entirely inadequate, only a partial reformation. It was a reform with respect to consequences but not in respect to principles."[27]

Present-day testimonies. At present these voices are becoming stronger and stronger, voices of men who are strategically placed to see the evolution of the church. *W. A. Visser't Hooft* is one of them: "The reformation of the Church, which transforms and renews it rather than conforms it to this world, should never be regarded as a definitive or isolated event, for the Lord calls His people back to Him again and again."[28]

E. Brunner has observed,

> It was especially in the Reformed Church, i. e. that branch of the Protestant Church which stems from Zwingli's and Calvin's Reformation, that this consciousness of the "semper reformanda" (which should constantly be in the process of reformation) remained active. True, the Reformed Churches of the European Continent are structures just as conservative, just as tenacious of old custom as the Lutheran churches. But this principle came to its full effectiveness above all in the Free Churches of the New World.[29]

J. Courvoisier comments,

> If the Reformation is a criterion of Protestantism, it invites us to a serious and careful examination of conscience. Whatever may be the

judgment that one brings against her, the distance that we record between what the Reformed Churches of the sixteenth century wished to be and what they have become in our days should cause us to reflect. . . . There is a way of saying 'We have the Reformers as our fathers' which strangely resembles 'We are descendants of Abraham.'[30]

H. S. Venske adds, "The Reformation of four hundred years ago stopped before it reached its goal; it must be completed."[31] And *W. Ninck* goes even further: "We are reaching the point where circumstances are ripe for a second reformation."[32]

At the *Third Ecumenical Assembly at New Delhi, 1961*, it was decreed,

> Our duty is to examine the structures of our Churches and to judge whether they help or hinder the work of evangelization. The scandal which deprives the Gospel of all significance in the eyes of the people of the unbelieving world and which turns away serious seekers from eventual conversion is no longer the real scandal of the faith: Jesus Christ crucified. It is indeed rather this false scandal of our own attitudes and ecclesiastical structures. That is what prohibits the Gospel from challenging the world. Thus the Assembly resumed an affirmation stated by the Study Commission of the Ecumenical Council some years before: The situation of the Church in the world today is so grave that many who have the cares of the future on their hearts are convinced that nothing but a revolution will be able to place it again in a position which would permit it to accomplish the will of God.[33]

Karl Barth has been very outspoken on the subject:

> The Reformation of our Church is always before her and never behind her.[34]
>
> The conserving of the Church and her salvation are realized only by the periodic return to the event which forms her basis, that is to say, by her periodic renewal of those who are gathered together in a congregation. A Church which is not in the process of a constant reformation which corresponds to her formation falls irrevocably into the abyss of non-existence or else into that of the pseudo-Church or one that has only the outward appearance of a Church.[35]
>
> We must seek a new form—perhaps also a forgotten ancient form—but in any case a better form, more discerning, more adequate, and better adapted to the conduct and deeds of the Church.[36]

Roman Catholic voices. One would think he was hearing an echo of the words of the famous Reformed theologians in those of Father Hans Küng who is preaching a reformation in the heart of his church: "Reformare: 'to give another form,' 'to restore an earlier better form,' 'to form anew something that has been deformed.' "[37]

Indeed, the need for a reformation seems to have been forced upon the Roman Catholic Church. Did not Pope Paul VI say in his opening address at the second session of Vatican Council II, "The Church looks at herself in Christ as in a mirror; and if this glance reveals some shadow, some deficiency on the 'face of the Church' or on her wedding garment, what should she do instinctively and courageously? Clearly, she should reform, which is her fundamental duty."[38]

Küng, in his preparatory work for the council, wrote: "If we put together everything that we have said, or might have said, about the Church as made of men and of sinful men, everything that has happened in the Church's worldly and sinful history—the human, the all-too-human . . . then only one thing remains to be done: metanoia, conversion of thought and deed . . . insofar as the Church is deformed, she has to be reformed: ecclesia reformanda!"[39]

The challenge of Rome. The work of internal reformation undertaken in the church of Rome is a challenge which the Catholics did not fail to throw out to the "reformed." Küng says, "There is no more dangerous description that a church could claim for itself than 'reformed.' To call oneself a 'Reformed Church' (whether Calvinist or Lutheran) could well represent a rejection of all further reformation; we *are* reformed."[40]

The Protestant theologians well understood this challenge and transmitted it to their churches. According to Roland de Pury, "At the moment when the Roman Catholic Church is attempting to institute reforms, what should one think of Protestantism in many respects more 'Roman' than Catholicism itself? Certainly Catholicism has integrated paganism into its system, but they control it, while Protestantism, after having rejected it with great display manifestly returned to it, almost without suspecting it, only to permit itself to be eaten away by this foreign influence."[41] And J. de Senarclens adds, "How does it happen that Protestantism is not seeking, with an energy at least equal to that of the Roman Fathers, a renewal, a bringing up to date, which seems as desirable in our midst as it does in theirs."[42]

In a study published in several languages after the first session of the council, Barth wrote:

> In light of the movement over there [Vatican Council II], do we think, speak, and act in anticipation of a movement which would be suitable for us, which would consist not only in preserving the famous "heritage of the Reformation," not only in maintaining our own conventions and traditions (as if among us all were in order), not only in all kinds of current informal discussions, uprisings, corrections, and innovations, but in the experience and productiveness of a fundamental crisis? In short, do we know—in the Churches which are so strong in the United States, for example, but also on this side of the Atlantic—what such a fundamental crisis could be and to what it could lead? We in western Europe, do we really live as *ecclesiae reformandae?* . . . Is there not also among us a

veritable hostility toward all really disquieting elements? . . . What should we say of the fact that Grundtvig exercises an incomparably greater influence in Denmark than does Kierkegaard?[43]

The purifying of the church. Voices are being raised clamoring for a purification of the church from all foreign doctrines, the return to the apostolic pattern, and the renunciation of the Constantinian system.

"To purify the Church—that would be the objective of the Reformation, as much in the twentieth century as it was in the sixteenth century," says de Senarclens. "To purify it from every influence foreign to the Gospel, whether it might come directly from without or from her own traditions. And to accomplish that, a systematic revision of all her doctrines and practices should be put into effect."[44]

According to Barth, "That which constituted the Church at its inception will always continue to do so; it confers on her continuous reformation. If she is not in the process of constant reformation, that indicates that she has succumbed to temptation and is no longer the Church."[45] "It is undeniable," he says, "that the communities of the New Testament present greater analogies with the Free churches than with our national Churches. One asks himself if the bond established between the Church and the State from the time of Constantine does not rest on a great error of the faith of the Church as well as on an error of judgment just as great, on the part of the State."[46]

And Rendtorff comments, "The return to Christianity can be accomplished by a complete break with the evolution of the Church up to this day."[47]

THE PRINCIPLE OF A REFORMATION

But what will be the principle of this "second reformation"? It could be nothing other than that of the Reformation of the sixteenth century: *sola scriptura*: the Scripture alone. But this principle will have to be applied to the church as simply as the Reformers of the sixteenth century applied it to individual faith. "The true principle of the Reformation is the pure and simple return to the authority of the Scripture," says Gasparin.[48]

Dr. Visser't Hooft writes: "There have been many who have sought the renewal of the Church by breaking away from the Bible or by adding to and improving upon the Bible. But we must maintain this simple truth that outside the Word of God there is in this world no true source of renewal. Why is this so? Because the Bible is the authentic record of the only radically new event that has ever taken place in the world. All other newness is either borrowed from that event or it is only newness in appearance."[49]

P. Jalaguier had already said that "the ecclesiastical doctrine of Protestantism as well as its dogmatic doctrine must reproduce fully the doctrine of the Bible; that is the condition for its power and its lasting quality, for that is the reason for its existence. Protestantism is 'Biblicism' or it is nothing; if it loses its foundation, it loses ground, and it is drifting toward Catholicism, or toward rationalism, or toward Illuminism."[50]

That is what the men of the nineteenth-century revival wanted.

REESTABLISHING THE AUTHORITY OF THE BIBLE

The first task demanding the attention of those who wish to reform the church is to reestablish the authority of the Word of God. Everyone seems to agree on this point. As we have seen, it was the foundation for the Reformers: *Verbum basis est* (the Word is the foundation)—*sola scriptura* (the Scripture alone).

Eric Fuchs, in his preface to "La vraie façon de reformer l'Eglise," sums up Calvin's position thus: "The real method to use in reforming the Christian Church is to take the Word of God seriously, cost what it may."[51] For Calvin the criterion of the true church is "conformity to the Scripture."[52] "The Church first constituted by the Apostles is a unique example of the true Church, which we must follow if we do not wish to greatly err and fail."[53]

THE WORD OF GOD IS THE CHURCH'S ONLY BASIS

Jalaguier contrasted Catholicism and Protestantism on the question of the Scripture-church relationship: "Catholicism places the Church first and approaches the Bible through her; Protestantism places the Bible before everything else and approaches the Church through the Bible, because for her, the Bible alone is the repository of the divine Word and the sovereign rule of faith."[54]

Among the present-day theologians, Barth was the first to insist on the importance of again giving heed to the Word. He tirelessly reminds us that apart from obedience to the Word of God there is no salvation for the church: "There could be no question of an ecclesiastical authority which would be other than the Word of God as testified in the Bible."[55]

He says, "In their austerity the Reformers took from us everything but the Bible."[56] And he maintains, "In all of the 'Churches' is not that which really separates us the same as that which divides a Biblical thought from a humanistic, non-Biblical thought?"[57]

Many theologians of our day affirm the necessity of renouncing all foundations other than the Bible, on which we have tried to build the churches in the course of the centuries.

RETURN TO THE BIBLICAL STANDARD

Emil Brunner writes:

> We cannot recognize the signs of the true Church of today in the light of the confessions of faith of the Reformers, but only in the light of the Bible.[58]
>
> The notion of the Church which is generally accepted in Protestant countries does not come from the New Testament alone, but also from the sudden excessive increase in church membership under Constantine in 312. That is why we must always ask ourselves what we must keep and what we must reject of the Constantinian heritage. We, the multitudinist churches, are we faithful to the Church of the New Testament? Can this form, which dates from the third and fourth centuries, still be justified? If so, in what measure? . . .[59] The authenticity of the Church, her message, and her teaching must be measured by the Biblical standard.[60]

ADAPT ONESELF TO THE PLAN AND WORD OF GOD

"It is precisely by constantly adapting herself to the plan and Word of God that the Church has true stability and true continuity," says Visser't Hooft. "There is a' truth for and a challenge to all churches in the words which appear in the constitutional documents of the Church of South India: 'The uniting churches acknowledge that the Church must always be ready to correct and reform herself in accordance with the teaching of those Scriptures as the Holy Spirit shall reveal it.' "[61]

But does not this dependence on the Holy Spirit risk opening the door to all the human interpretations? Listen to Visser't Hooft's precise details: "All appeals to the Spirit which seek to by-pass the historical record of the actual work of the Lord are therefore appeals to the spirit of man rather than to the Holy Spirit. . . .[62] The tragedy of a Church which does not give to the Bible the decisive place in its life is that . . . it becomes increasingly tempted to consider its existence as an aim in itself and thus loses the capacity for radical self-criticism and renewal of life."[63]

DILIGENTLY SEEK GREATER FAITHFULNESS TO THE WORD OF GOD

G. Casalis affirmed in his report to the plenary Assembly of French Protestantism in Montbéliard in 1960:

> We must constantly return to this: to preach is to be linked with the Truth, and through it to pledge oneself to a spiritual exercise which leads one to constantly strive to be more faithful to the Word, more in harmony with the Scripture. I do not hesitate to say that the first of the future

tasks for our churches is also their permanent task—to guard with jeaolus care the purity of their message. And here as elsewhere there are no special privileges, laymen as well as pastors in each parish, as well as in each council, are to be responsible for this basic task.[64]

"It is evident," states P. Courthial, "that we seldom find among men, even Churchmen, those who are willing to be unoriginal and to apply themselves to being faithful in heart, word, and deed to the revealed truth of God. The constant longing of men, since Adam's fatal error of unbelief, is to question the Word of God, to set themselves up as judges of it, and to deviate from it."[65]

THE AUTHORITY OF THE WORD OF GOD

It is on this point that people disagree and from this point that difficulties arise. To what extent are Protestant theologians—even those whom we have quoted—ready to identify God's Word with the biblical testimony as Professor A. Lecerf did? "One must maintain the identification of the Scripture in its entirety with God's Word."[66]

For what becomes of the authority of the Bible if it is separated from that of God's Word? Is it not in the attacks of higher criticism on the authenticity and inspiration of the Scripture that we see the origin of the crisis of the authority of the Bible in Protestantism today? It is carried to the point that certain men wonder what it is that still justifies the ancient "religion of the Book": "Is Protestantism justified by the authority of the Scripture, which one realizes more and more is scarcely more respected in our country than it is in many others?" asks de Senarclens.[67]

THE AUTHORITY OF THE BIBLE ACCORDING TO PRESENT-DAY
CATHOLIC THEOLOGIANS

Other theologians are engaged in giving us some lessons on this point, which is considered traditionally to be the distinctive criterion of Protestantism compared with Catholicism. At Vatican Council I courageous voices asking for a return to the Bible as authority had already been heard. In the midst of the council, Mgr. Strossmayer, bishop of Bosnia, arose and said,

> Let us return to the teaching of the apostles, since apart from that we have nothing but errors, darkness, and false traditions. Let us profit from our reason and intelligence and take the apostles and the prophets as our infallible teachers in all that concerns the question of all questions: "What must I do to be saved?" When that is achieved, we shall have established a firm and unshakeable foundation for our system of dogma on the durable and incorruptible rock of the divinely inspired Holy Scriptures. . . . Stop, venerable brethren, in the odious and absurd downward trend.

Save the Church from the disaster which threatens her, seeking in the Holy Scriptures alone the rule of faith which we must believe and profess.[68]

Here is what Küng, a recent writer, says:

But according to what *norm* shall action for the renewal of the Church be measured? . . . The norm to which we can keep looking, in all our deeds is Jesus Christ, the Lord of the Church, who speaks to the Church of every century in His Gospel, making His demands upon her.[69]

Neither opportunist modernism nor opportunist traditionalism, but fidelity to the Gospel of Jesus Christ is the right frame of mind for a renewal of the Church.[70]

Neither Catholics nor Protestants can consider themselves exempt from having to make a continuous effort to pattern themselves after the apostolic Church. Neither do appeals to Catholic tradition or to the Protestant Reformation free them from the obligation to embody the constantly new, which is the crucial factor, if one desires the designation "apostolic": namely, *essential agreement with the apostolic message.*[71]

Unity, holiness, and catholicity are the unity, holiness, and catholicity of the Church of Jesus Christ only if it is founded on the same grounds on which Jesus Christ willed to found His Church: It is the ground of the apostles. . . . It is only in the testimony of the apostles that we perceive the glorified Lord. This is why the attestation of the apostles occupies a unique, lasting—and unrepeatable—normative position within the Church and vis-à-vis the Church.[72]

Contrary to all, including the most solemn, teachings of the Church, it means that, according to the definition of the Vatican Council, Holy Scripture *alone* is God-inspired . . . God is its author.[73]

The Dominican father F. Refoulé wrote: "The ecumenical movement will progress, we think, only in the measure that Catholic and Protestant theologians have the courage to compare their respective theologies with the Scripture taken in its entirety, not excluding anything."[74]

Over against such a position which has been taken one can understand Barth's question: "Should we not decide to pray . . . to have a renewal *in our midst* . . . to listen to God's Word *in our midst* in a new way, and to speak of a new outpouring of the Holy Spirit, as does J. C. Blumhardt?"[75] Or, as Pastor Courthial writes: "The genuine movement of the Reformation opens the Word of God, leads back to the Word of God, causes us to flee from theological fancies as from the pest."[76]

One can only subscribe to all these declarations, no matter which side they come from, and wish that the churches from which these theologians come would follow the advice of those to whom they entrusted the task of watching over their condition. However, when one sees how far the present churches are from their models, one has a right to wonder if those who speak of submitting all the institutions and practices of the church to the biblical norm realize the extent of the challenge which the Word, whose authority they wish to reestablish, thrusts upon them. Are the churches of today ready to carry on the revolution which would be set in motion by putting these plans into practice?

RESTORATION OF THE CHURCH ACCORDING TO THE BIBLE

A SITUATION ANALOGOUS WITH THAT OF THE PRIMITIVE CHURCH

What does this reestablishment of the authority of the Scriptures and the abolition of all the foreign norms really signify for the church? Is it not, purely and simply, a return to the apostolic type of church, that is, to the church of professing believers? Undoubtedly no period of time since the fourth century has been more favorable for such a restoration of the apostolic church.

As the last strong defenses of Christendom collapse we find ourselves in a setting very much like that of the primitive church. "Our situation," writes Brunner, "is different from that of all the centuries of Christianity which precede us in that we find ourselves facing total secularism. . . . Our situation resembles that of the Church of the first three centuries, for opposite it also stood a world consciously and resolutely non-Christian. Today, like then, in spite of the differences, the situation is that of an essentially missionary Church in a very different sense from that of the Middle Ages or of the Reformation."[77]

Ninck adds, "If the Christians today form only a very small flock in a world alien to Christ, then our situation is analogous to that of the primitive Church."[78] And R. Mehl comments, "Our children and grandchildren will find themselves facing a situation like that of the primitive Church, obliged to confess their faith in a cultural and philosophical universe which was not at all ready to hear this message. It was at the price of an astonishing and powerful simplicity that they succeeded in making themselves heard."[79]

One of the principal objections to the reestablishing of churches similar to those we find in the New Testament was: "We are no longer in a missionary situation." This argument is no longer valid.

LET THE CHURCH BE THE CHURCH!

More than a century ago Monod said, "We complain that the Church of today has no hold on the masses, while it may be that what we lack to deeply move them is for the Church to again become what she professes to be, the Christian Church."[80] Is it in this sense that one must understand the theme initiated at the Oxford Conference: "Let the Church be the Church!"? "The essential duty of the Church and the greatest service that she can render to the world consists in this . . . in being a community of Christians," says Visser't Hooft.[81]

Or is it in the sense of the word of Barth: "It is possible today to make restorations, but no more reformations."[82] Or in the conclusion of the book, *Structures of the Church*, by the Catholic theologian Küng: "Today the task of theology should be to restore to the original structures the free play which the vicissitudes of time have thrown into the shadows and into oblivion."[83] That is, in any case, the opinion of Dr. Otto Riecker: "The life of the Church depends on one thing: her return to biblical principles."

Professor F. H. Littell says: "Instead of a permanent reformation, what we need is a permanent restitution [of the primitive order]."

PROGRESS OF THE CONCEPT OF THE CHURCH OF PROFESSING BELIEVERS

Circumstances themselves seem to impel churches to return to the type of church of the first centuries.

P. Lestringant: "In a general way, our churches have developed more or less distinctly toward the type of community which we are accustomed to call the Church of professing believers (The Free church)."[84]

A. Adam: "The present situation is characterized by the progress of the concept of the Free churches."[85]

E. Brunner: "The Free Churches are today numerically the strongest form of Protestantism."[86]

E. G. Léonard:

> The concept of the "Free churches" is being extended considerably in our day, and even in the Lutheran milieux this concept is represented by several small denominations, such as the Church of the Gospel of Christ, the pietist and the Lutheran Free Church, which in its concern for orthodoxy goes back in this matter to the primitive ideas of the Reformer. The Reformed churches began to half-open their doors to it by distinguishing their church members, some as simple parishioners and others as "responsible ones" signing a profession of faith; only they were admitted to participate in the directing of the communities. A more explicit manifestation of the same tendency causes them to gradually break away from infant baptism and to adopt the doctrine and practice of adult baptism on request and an explicit profession of faith. . . . This restricting of Protestantism to the Church of professing believers is a general phenomenon which affects all Christianity supported by a minority.[87]

F. H. Littell: "Recent historians are beginning to see that the traditional hostility to the pioneer Free Churchmen was more political and ecclesiastical than anything else."[88]

H. S. Venske:

"We find ourselves without any doubt at a broad turning-point in the history of the Church, going from the old style popular Church to the 'community church.' "[89]

CHURCHES OF MINORITY GROUPS

The church of tomorrow will be "a humble church . . . a church of the minority," says R. Mehl.[90]

According to Karl Barth, "It would be better for the evangelical Church if her numbers were reduced to one tenth or one hundredth part of her present size; she would then again become a light for all people, whereas her life is now being continually agitated and ravaged by endless kinds of those who . . . would like to find her or make her, openly or secretly, different from what she must be by virtue of her origin."[91]

The truth has always been served and disseminated by the few: Gideon's three hundred men, the seven thousand who had not bowed the knee to Baal, the three men in Babylon who remained faithful to the Lord. Again in the New Testament we find truth on the side of the minorities: twelve apostles, one hundred and twenty disciples, twelve converted in Ephesus, "some" at Athens. And, as we have already said, what were even the three thousand on the day of Pentecost when compared with the several hundreds of thousands of Jews who were in the city on that day? Were they not a mere handful over against an overwhelming majority?

"Those who are the true Church will never be the large number, but a small minority," says Barth.[92] The Bible affirms that "the Lord is never held back to work either through many or through few" (1 Sa 14:6). "Do not fear, little flock, for your Father is pleased to give you the kingdom" (Lk 12:32).

F. Godet claims, "The Church formed only an imperceptible minority of humanity, and that proportion between true believers and non-believers has remained constant in all times and places."[93] He further comments, "Jesus much preferred a small nucleus of men established in the faith and resolved to accept the renunciation which that entails, to these multitudes who were only apparently united to him."[94] And A. Vinet says, "All great things have had small beginnings."[95]

According to Agénor de Gasparin, "Without the men who have dared to stand alone against everyone, no progress would have been made: success excuses nothing; success proves nothing. In any case, it does not prove that justice has been done; success is not the finger of God."[96] What was true in the past is still true today. "The world lives and operates by a small number" says Albert Bessière.[97] "Accordingly, let us go out to Him outside the camp, bearing His reproach" (Heb 13:13).

A few committed Christians who are determined to realize God's plan with the help of the Holy Spirit would certainly do more than a great many councils, synods, and congresses. Would this not be the time to recall what Adolphe Monod wrote more than a century ago: "Wesley asked for only *ten true Methodists* to change the whole of England . . . nor would I, with ten true Protestants, despair of anything for the Reformed Church of France!" He also said, "Everywhere men are appealing for and expectantly waiting for the Church, a new Church."[98]

THE LAWS OF TRUTH

Are we in the church of Jesus Christ? The churches of the future will be churches of minority groups. But this minority will still have to be what God calls His "little flock." Being in the minority is not sufficient in itself to assure us we are in the plan of God, not any more than being scorned or persecuted suffices to win for us His approval. The little flock of Jesus Christ is composed of the good Shepherd's sheep who obey His voice.

Only that church which perseveres in the teaching of the apostles, in real communion of the brethren, in the breaking of bread as the Lord instituted it, and in prayers which conform to the will of God, remains a beneficiary of the promises of the Lord and of the help of the Holy Spirit. "Only the Church," says H. Venske, "but not the multitudinist Church, is a beneficiary of the promise of the Lord that "the powers of death [Hades] shall not prevail against it."[99] And Visser't Hooft comments,

> The promise that the gates of hell shall not overcome it is not given to every society which calls itself "Church." It is given only to the body which Jesus Christ calls "my Church." And the great question which every part of the Church or every church-body must ask itself with fear and trembling is therefore: "Are we truly in the Church of Jesus Christ?" . . . The real danger for every church is, therefore, not that it will be persecuted, but that it will assume that it is indeed the Church of Jesus Christ and will therefore live in a false security. Here again the history of the Church becomes relevant. Have we considered what it means that in the course of history great Christian Churches have been completely or almost completely wiped out?[100]

Calvin said that "every congregation which claims the name of Church must be brought to the test which God offers—the Scripture—as gold is tested by the touchstone."[101] Is this ecclesiastical organization to which we have belonged since our birth, perhaps, a true church of Jesus Christ, conforming to what the Bible presents to us under this definition? If the reply to this question must be in the negative, what should we do—sacrifice "the church" or sacrifice "the truth"?

The Christian who is in one of the large multitudinist systems must certainly wonder if he will not be more serviceable to God by sacrificing a part of the truth than he would be if he took too abrupt action. He could stay on, retaining the advantages and preserving his influence by making only a few compromises with error. Would he not be able to do more good by bringing the truth into his own milieu than by withdrawing from it? The temptation is subtle but not new. The Christian persecuted by Rome was required to sacrifice only a few grains of incense to the emperor in order to save his life; the Protestant of the sixteenth century, to attend mass in order to live in peace; the Anabaptists and their spiritual heirs, to renounce the baptism of believers in order to exchange their life as hunted animals for the bourgeois existence, perhaps even influential in the heart of an ecclesiastical organization. Why did they not make these "small" sacrifices?

Luther exclaimed: "Cursed are the love and unity gained at the risk of losing the Word of God." Calvin also found himself facing the compromisers, who skillfully tried to maintain their position and influence in the Roman Church. What does he say about them? "I well know what they think: it remains to be seen if by stepping one step backward they will advance three or four steps when the occasion arises. But from where will this hoped-for occasion suddenly come? I see them now leaving the main road, and I can only hope that by cutting across fields they will reach their destination; it is rather to be feared that God will judge their disloyalty by removing the part they think they have retained."[102]

The great temptation is to sacrifice a part of the truth for the sake of unity. This temptation, particularly strong now, is not new. All who have had a part in bringing to light the truths by which we live today have had to face it. Vinet warns us:

> To call for peace and fellowship against one's convictions and duty would be futile. Did our Master come to bring peace or the sword among men? Is not true peace, according to the word of the prophet, a fruit of justice, and is it justice to hold truth captive? Moreover, what peace and what communion can there be if these are based on ambiguity and dissimulation? And how much better and more charitable than such peace is not the holy war of light waged against darkness?
>
> In vain one would persuade himself that he can better serve the interest of the truth by sacrificing part of it in order to remain with his brethren

than by withdrawing from them in order to keep all of it. Perverse reasoning. . . . For to begin with, who can assure you that having sacrificed the truth on one point, you will not sacrifice it on all the others? When will you no longer find it necessary and expedient to make concessions? . . . You desire to serve your fellow-men by a slight dissimulation, but you are denying them the greatest of all services which you could render—that of teaching them that conscience is important—rather, that it is everything. . . .

Do not deceive yourselves; do not permit the multitude to dictate to you; God is greater than the multitude. Do not say to yourself: I am only a grain of sand; how can I resist this tempest of opinion which raises the dust, of which I am a part, and tosses it about in the air? Though an imperceptible grain of sand, you will carry the weight of a rock on this hurricane-swept ground, because you have all the truth. You have a surety who takes all responsibility for you. Stand upon His Word, and dare to be obedient, although all alone.[103]

TRUTH OR LOVE

Truth has priority rights over us if we claim to be disciples of the one who testifies to the truth (Jn 18:37), who has identified Himself with the truth (Jn 14:6), and who has promised His Spirit who "will guide you into all truth" (Jn 16:13). Do we wish to participate in the sin—and the judgment—of those who "through their wicked ways suppress the truth" (Ro 1:18)? "To suppress the truth," said Vinet, "is to suppress God Himself."[104] That is why "we must hold fast to the truth even though we stand alone."[105] And he affirms, "The duty of the one who possesses the truth is to give it out whether he has hope [of results] or not . . . no word of truth remains entirely without effect."[106]

The method today, it is true, is not particularly favorable to this proclamation of the truth. The hour is in dialogue with all the derivatives of Christianity, trying to discover particles of truth here and there. However, as Vinet said, "Of all the shreds of truth which cling to all the errors, one does not make truth. Truth is like the Lord's robe; it is seamless." In following the apostolic recommendation to speak the truth in love (Eph 4:15), love is stressed to the exclusion of speaking the truth and, as Vinet says, "Thus there is no tolerance for ideas."

"There is even less for principles," adds Francus, "and there is none for the institutions which pervert religious meaning. . . . It is a superior love which bluntly orders one to reveal his thought and to stand up and fight the sworn enemy of souls and to force him back into his last entrenchments . . . for there is no wrong which can be done to a soul comparable to the wrong of letting him believe that he is a Christian when he is not."[107]

Where would we be today without those men of the sixteenth century who dared, alone and against all others, to proclaim the inviolable rights of the truth? "You ask for gentleness and consideration," cried Luther, "I hear you. But does there exist any standard which is common to both a Christian and a hypocrite? . . . My opinion is that one should criticize everything, censure everything, deal the same way with everything, have respect for nothing, excuse nothing as long as Truth is not holding her head high on the public square, free, pure, and undisguised!"[108]

Practical Conclusions

The time has come to draw from these testimonies and experiences concrete lessons to determine our attitude and action. What, then, is the immediate task which demands our attention? Let us sum up what we have verified while examining the Word of God and the present situation:

1. The norm of the Christian is the Bible.
2. In the Bible we find only churches of professing believers.
3. The multitudinist churches are related to the Constantinian-Theodosian system of "Christendom."
4. The era of Christendom is ended.
5. The European churches which have, for the most part, remained faithful to the multitudinist system, are passing through a serious crisis while the American churches built on the principle of the free churches have increased in vigor over the past century.
6. Even in multitudinist churches the most clear-sighted leaders denounce the multitudinist system and call for a reformation and restoration of biblical-type churches.
7. In the twentieth century the church finds herself in conditions similar to those of the first century, that is, facing a non-Christian population and civilization.
8. All attempts to revive the multitudinist churches and to gradually transform them into churches of professing believers have failed.

So what practical course can we take to accomplish the will of God and restore to the church her true nature?

ACCEPT AND PRACTICE THE AUTHORITY OF THE WORD OF GOD

Since the foundation of all Christian life, individual and collective, is the Word of God, let us begin by *reestablishing His authority* over us and among us *in a practical manner*. In order to reestablish the authority of God's Word over us, we must begin by reading and studying it:

"Personal reading, study, and meditation on the Bible alone will be able to deliver us from the theological vogues which have been one of the plagues of Protestantism for the last two hundred years," says Courthial.[109] Let us read it as God's testament, that is, as the supreme expression of His will for us, by being ready to obey all that God will show us through it.

This Word enjoins us to shun the heretics. The heretic is literally "the one who chooses" among the biblical doctrines the ones which suit him and rejects the others. In this category the apostle Paul would have classed the theologians who declare unacceptable certain biblical truths and all those who do not persevere in all the teachings of the apostles. One must certainly avoid falling into narrow-mindedness and sectarianism, knowing that a total agreement on all doctrines is a utopian dream.[110]

However, one must be just as careful to beware of doctrinal latitudinarianism which would leave us at the mercy of all the seductions of the enemy. The Word of God orders us to avoid and shun those who teach false doctrines.[111] In his preface to the classical work on the multitudinist concept of the church, Dr. D. Félice wrote, "If the Church has the right, even the duty, to require a relatively real submission from the faithful, the member should have the right to withdraw from a Church in which he no longer receives the spiritual nourishment which he feels is necessary for his soul or in which his salvation would seem to be compromised, or which would appear to him to profess error rather than truth."[112]

That is talk which one scarcely hears any more today; however, truth always has the same rights, and error retains all of its seducing powers. Can we remain with impunity under the influence of a teaching which undermines the foundations of our faith and substitutes "another gospel" for the one which alone can save us? Unfortunately, experience proves the contrary, and the words of the great preacher Charles H. Spurgeon are just as true today: "A sincere believer's sure duty to men who profess to be Christians, even while they mutilate the Word and reject the foundations of the Gospel, is to 'come out from them and be separate from them.' Compromising with error will make the best of men powerless to act against it."

The idea that the Reformers would never have left the Roman Church if they had not been turned out was spread so widely that everyone finally believed it. Recently, in a lecture given in the cathedral of Geneva, Professor de Senarclens dared to destroy that myth: "For Calvin, the heretic or the schismatic is not the one who withdraws from the established Church, but rather, the one who deviates from the Gospel. He has no scruples about leaving a Church which he judges to be heretical and sectarian to join Christ. On the contrary, he declares that it is necessary for us to withdraw from them in order to draw near to Christ." (See Calvin's *Institutes* bk. 4: chap. 2, p. 6.)

Elsewhere he expresses much the same thought: "One must not fear," he writes, "that by withdrawing from participation in these sacrileges we are divorcing ourselves from the Church of God." (See Calvin's *Institutes* 4:2, 2.) When Calvin left the official church, his conscience was perfectly clear: "With regard to the objection they raised against me, that I separated myself from the Church, in that I feel no guilt," he wrote in a letter to Sadolet. He did it without reservation and long before they turned him out—and that "in order to rejoin the true Church, to draw near to Christ."[113]

It would be easy to show that Luther did not act otherwise. "The man who holds his doctrine to be true and certain," he wrote to Melanchthon, "cannot remain in the same sheepfold with the one who maintains an opposing doctrine." And Senarclens comments, "To divorce error is not a fault, but rather a duty of obedience."[114]

THE PRIORITY OF THE NEW BIRTH

The Bible presents the church to us as a society of converted, born-again believers. So it is by conversion and the new birth that we must begin if we wish to build the church—by our own conversion, perhaps, if we are not really born again; if not, all our religious and biblical knowledge—or theological—as well as all of our piety and all of our efforts will be in vain. "Appropriating salvation personally is the beginning of true Christianity and of the true church; each living believer must have a value of his own, as each stone has in a building," says Ecke.

If we are Christians, God asks us to testify of Jesus Christ and to boldly preach repentance and faith so as to bring others to the new birth. We can do it by the ministry of the Word, if God has entrusted us with that responsibility; we can also do it by the humble testimony to individuals, by the distribution of tracts, by lending books, inviting people to meetings, and by every other means inspired by our love for lost souls.[115]

Brunner says that "conversion to Christ is not a real possibility within the Constantinian Church situation, since there everyone is a baptized Christian. This is the reason conversion is hardly mentioned there. . . . The more the situation in Europe also is seen to be a missionary situation, the more will theology be forced to take seriously the biblical concept of conversion."[116] It is up to us to give real attention to these ideas of conversion and of the new birth.

REGROUP THE TRUE BELIEVERS

Wherever there are two or three Christians, there is a church. However large and old the religious congregation may be which is called the church, however venerable and imposing its edifices, however influential its leaders, it is where true believers, even only two or three, are assembled in the name of Christ that we have the true church. "The Church," said Luther, "is wherever the Holy Spirit gives faith to men and sanctifies them through it. Wherever you hear the Word of God, where you see it is believed, confessed and practiced, there—doubt it not—there must be a true church . . . a holy Christian people even if they are few in number."[117]

"These men of the sixteenth century," writes Barth, "were to seek and find the true church on the outside: outside of the walls of Jerusalem, apart from the ancient Church, from the Church with the completed past which, objecting to and relinquishing its Holy of Holies, could no longer be for them anything but the Church of the illusion or the deception, the Church of the Antichrist."[118]

If we have understood this truth, our task will be to work at regrouping the children of God in order that they may be mutually edified, exhorted, and encouraged. The new converts need this communion with their Christian brothers in order to grow. "The Church of Christ is, and will remain, the Body of Christ to which only the 'elect saints' belong, those who repent and believe with all their hearts," says Brunner. "It is especially from this concept, which one may call revolutionary but which is nevertheless fundamental and essential, that we must start in order to envisage the task of the Church at the present time."[119]

Join a church. If there is such a church in our locality to which, as a rule, only those who "repent and believe with all their heart" belong, our duty is to join them and aid them with our strength and the gifts which the Lord has given us for common edification. We also need all the ministries which God has bestowed on His body "to equip the saints for the task of ministering toward the building up of the body of Christ" (Eph 4:12).

Let us not imagine that we can grow harmoniously in the faith if we scorn God's plan and neglect the means of grace which He places at our disposal. Let us not seek the perfect or pure church; it does not exist here below. Let us not then let ourselves be stopped by some minor imperfection, by habits which seem strange to us, or by the presence of people who seem unattractive at first, so long as the foundation of the assembly as well as the essential doctrines are consistent with the Bible. If we join the church, we shall be able to help with our cooperation, and also, by our influence, to modify it in the direction which seems to us to come closer to conforming to the will of God.

Move closer to a church. If there is no community of believers existing where God has placed us, perhaps we should, before sinking into spiritual solitude or engaging in a pioneer work, ask ourselves if we should not consider changing residence so as to be closer to a living church of believers. Far from the hearth, the solitary brand dies out; it is not conforming to God's plan for a Christian to remain isolated; by baptizing us with His Spirit at the time of our new birth, God makes us members of the body of Christ—and a member is made to live in a body. Let us not be presumptuous and think that we shall succeed in keeping to the faith and growing in it; nor let us imagine that it will be easy to form a community of believers where we live, especially if we are new converts and have not experienced life in a church of believers. Let us not forget that it is God who designates each member's place in the body. Are we sure that He has called us to found and to organize a local group?

Opposition from Satan. Neither let us underestimate the efforts which the adversary will make to hinder the formation of a church conforming to God's plan. That is what he hates the most. A dead, formal church scarcely annoys him, but when a group of true believers is formed somewhere, when they begin to testify of Jesus Christ and to edify one another by getting their inspiration from the churches in the Bible, they can be sure of being the target of all the attacks of the enemy: insults, slander, contempt, threats—they will be spared nothing. Are we ready to face all the difficulties which from without will assail the group of believers, as well as all the dangers of disagreements and deviations which the adversary will not fail to incite within the group?

When the apostle Paul wrote to Timothy that the bishop of an assembly of believers was not to be a newly converted person, he gave, under the inspiration of the Holy Spirit, advice which wisdom and experience have many times confirmed. Paul prepared Christians—whether locally or in his missionary team—who would be entrusted with the responsibilities of church leadership. All who accept this heavy responsibility today should first have the opportunity to benefit from similar training in a living church, performing there the ministry which the newly formed assembly will entrust to them.

Establishing a church. If it is absolutely impossible for us to join a church of believers after our conversion, God knows it. To respond to an extraordinary situation, He can also give unusual qualifications and graces. If it is in His plan that a collective testimony be established where we live, He will definitely lead in that way, and we can go forward fearlessly, relying on His Word and trusting in His Spirit.

Let us begin humbly by witnessing to those about us and bringing them to become disciples of Jesus Christ. Two believers can begin to pray and meditate on the Word together. Perhaps for a long time it will remain a "church in a home," as were most of those in the book of Acts. God does not despise the day of small things. The more humble and modest the beginnings, the better the believers will escape the attacks of the adversary and the hatred of the enemies of the gospel. When we enter the church of Jesus Christ, we should quickly become accustomed to the idea that we have entered a minority group. According to Brunner,

> In his *Deutsche Messe,* Luther upheld this idea [of forming Christian cells and cultivating the life of the Christian community] and formulated some guide lines for it. Unfortunately, the official Church has always fought against the formation of these Christian cells, which they look upon as conventicles. We cannot indulge in the luxury of fighting this need nor of ignoring it. On the contrary, it is an urgent necessity. . . . In his *Smalkalde* articles, which constitute his only testament, Luther made this task explicit in the following instructions; *mutua conversatio et consolatio fratrum,*—a practical explanation of the Scripture with a sharing of experiences, mutual exhortation and brotherly consolation. In the reformed group, Wesley wanted something similar and put it into effect.[120]
>
> These groups are a realization of that idea which Luther never abandoned even if it was not possible for him to put it into practice.[121]

Permitting Jesus Christ to build His church. These small groups constitute the true local church of Jesus Christ. We need to become familiar with this idea which will enable us to see the promises of Jesus Christ realized in His church. He promised to give gifts to men (Eph 4:8), to grant to each of the believers "the evidence of the Spirit for the common welfare" (1 Co 12:7). We have the right to ask God to fulfill His promise. He will grant "to one person . . . a message of wisdom and to another the utterance of knowledge according to the same Spirit" (1 Co 12:8); others will perhaps receive a ministry of exhortation, of ruling (Ro 12:8), of evangelism, or perhaps even a gift of miracles. Is not the Spirit free to distribute His gifts "to each individual exactly as He pleases" (1 Co 12:11)?

The new birth and the gifts of the Holy Spirit are the two principal supports of the universal priesthood. In 1960, Pastor Casalis emphasized at Montbéliard "the necessity for finally taking seriously the great affirmation of the universal priesthood, and practicing it, which Luther so forcefully declared, and which our churches, prisoners that they were to idealistic schemas of Christendom, never truly translated into deeds."[122]

Nevertheless, the exercise of the universal priesthood, conforming to the example of the primitive church, can only be carried on where the local church is composed of believers who have received from God the gifts and callings for the edification of all. If God can work in this little group through consecrated men whom He uses as His instruments and His spokesmen, the work will prosper: souls, eager for truth and life, will be attracted; people will be born again; lives will be transformed; chains broken; wrongs redressed. Where the gospel is at work, visible changes are produced which cannot fail to attract the attention of those without and also of the adversary.[123]

Christians who enlist in the path of obedience for the whole will of God—including the one concerning the church—must reckon with the opposition of the world and of the ecclesiastical institutions. "The world is in the habit of calling those who do their utmost to spread the pure gospel among souls and thus obey God, heretics, seducers, impostors, scandal-mongers."[124]

The Scripture says, "In fact, all who want to live devotedly in Christ Jesus will be persecuted" (2 Ti 3:12). This law is still true, with this difference: that the most severe persecution comes most often from those who call themselves Christians. "It is not the hostility of the unbelieving world, but rather the false clerical, parsonic ecclesiasticism which has ever been the greatest enemy of the Christian message and of brotherhood rooted in Christ."[125]

The Anabaptists, Schwenckfeld, Lasco, Labadie, Spener and all those who tried to reestablish the apostolic church, experienced that most painfully. Unfortunately, it is often so even now. Slander, accusations of spiritual pride, or sectarianism will not be lacking. These are the decisive test of the sincerity and openness of mind of the true Christian members of multitudinist churches who ardently desire a reformation of the church. The "good church members," shaken in their tranquillity by the presence of living Christians, frequently react by a hardening of their "church conscience."[126] Pastor Venske writes:

> The multitudinist system has a long tradition behind it, ever since the time of Emperor Constantine. The Reformation did not bring to it any fundamental modification. It was not given to Luther to put into effect his good plans for forming the nucleus of a church of believers conscious of their call to evangelization. We drag on with what exists and care for it from one generation to another. Many sigh, but nobody believes that the situation can ever be changed.
>
> This is where we must take the first forward step. We must overcome this paralysis of thought. Luther, in any case, did not suffer from that paralysis; if he had, we would still be Roman Catholics.
>
> They should be able to expect us to be ready to joyously change our ideas.[127]

"We do not want a Lutheran theological renaissance which would only go back to the old phrases," says Walter Nigg, "but rather a religious revolution similar to Luther's which would prove its faithfulness to the Reformer by leaving the beaten path, by deviating from what he did. Only such an attitude will be able to arrest the disaster and change the course of the river."[128]

At the end of his book, *The Misunderstanding of the Church,* Brunner says:

> We must remain open to the possibility that it may be in the will of God to break the ancient framework of the Churches which contained the *Ekklesia,* or at least to create—as is happening in our days—new frameworks. . . . With or without the churches, if necessary even in opposition to them, God will cause the *Ekklesia* to become a real community of brothers. Whether the churches recognize this or, on the contrary, ignore it, will determine the question whether or not they have a future.[129]

Such affirmations are very encouraging—on the condition that they do not remain simple verbal declarations! Many believers in the heart of the historical churches share these aspirations; many of them think that it is time to "abandon all the forms of the institutional ghetto" in order to again find the authentic image of the *ekklesia* as God created it. Their longings are added to those of their brothers from the free churches who are also seeking, through many vicissitudes and imperfections, to bring to pass the will of God concerning the church.

In all churches and communities "those who seriously wish to be Christian," as Luther said, live side by side with those who, though seeking to benefit from the advantages of a religion, have not at all decided to accept the "yoke" and to "bear abuse for Him." In general, the gulf separating them is not apparent. On the other hand, the dividing line between free churches and multitudinist churches is itself often not very distinct.

Meanwhile, the ecumenical evolution, the reconciliation with Rome, the constitution of large ecclesiastical systems and, perhaps, the approach of more difficult times for Christians (see Rev 13:7, 15), will face each believer and each church with the need for taking a more definite position. As we approach "the end of time," the identification of Barth's "pseudo-Church" or Brunner's "illusion-Church" with the world will be completed. Then her true nature will be manifested and the differences between her and the *ekklesia* will clearly appear. Gradually, many illusions will disappear, and the eyes of many Christians will be opened. The line of separation between the true disciples and the nominal Christians, until then invisible, will be clearly seen. The comfortable peace of mind of those in the middle-of-the-road positions will be ended. People will have to come to a decision and choose: to follow the syncretic current which leads to Babylon, or else to return to the source, to the cross, and to the Jerusalem of the first church. "One or the other," as Kierkegaard tirelessly repeated. It is without doubt for such times as these that the Spirit of God makes the urgent call resound: "Come away from her [Babylon], My people, that you may not participate in her sins" (Rev 18:4). "We would have healed Babylon, but she is not healed. Forsake her. . . . Flee out of the midst of Babylon; let every man save his life!" (Jer 51:9, 6)!

On that day, certainly, in all the churches and assemblies, the believers who are "born of God" will understand that they will not be able to subsist and conquer except by uniting their efforts to construct the church *according to the plan of God*. What shall our practical attitude be today, in the light of this prospect? After having seen God's plan for the church, shall we continue to remain just on the fringe of the divine plan? Shall we be satisfied with intellectual adherence to the truth and with denouncing deviations? God is not satisfied with mere words or fruitless promises. He expects action from us (Mt 7:21; 23:3; Lk 6:46-48; 11:28; Ja 1:22; 1 Jn 2:3; 3:18). It is by the way we practice our convictions that we will be judged (Ro 2:2, 6, 13), and our degree of responsibility will be in proportion to our knowledge of the divine will (Lk 12:47-48). "If you *know* these teachings, blessed are you if you *practice* them" (Jn 13:17). "To the person who knows what is right to do and fails to do it, to him it is sin" (Ja 4:17). These principles are applicable both to our commitment to Christ and to our life in the church.

Even today, as in past centuries, Jesus Christ wishes to build His church. For that He needs living stones willing to be fashioned and used by Him —where and as He wishes. Are we willing to be such "stones"? After having recognized God's will, should we wait for others to have the same convictions we have, for the great masses to be awakened and for the organic structures to be transformed?

Monod said more than a century ago, "Happy are those who, ahead of their times in the Church, will gather together to do among themselves what they long in their hearts to see done in the Church! Blessed are those who will form a holy alliance to enter fully into the Christian life and who will know how to trust almighty God for the development of their nascent work, the God who, beginning with the twelve apostles, succeeded in establishing that Church in Jerusalem which you wish to reproduce in your midst."[130]

History has taught us that wherever the ideal of the apostolic church has been put into practice, it has rapidly gained ground. If we are faithful where the Lord has placed us, then perhaps we also shall see Monod's prophetic vision materialized:

Everywhere on the horizon I see rising up a people of God, a people few in number, but great in faith and love, who leave their old positions and stand ready for the Church of the coming days, a spiritual, brotherly, missionary Church. Oh! may the divine Spirit bring together upright and faithful souls who start out from all directions, gropingly seeking each other in the darkness, who may even struggle against each other for lack of knowing each other! May the holy army of the children of God band themselves together, not in the name of an indifferent system which deletes the essential doctrines of the Gospel, but in the name of a common faith which enables them to prevail over all that is secondary, human, and provincial![131]

Notes

1. The reformation of Sulze: see E. Sulze, *Die evang. Gemeinde.* Die Reform der evang. Landeskirchen nach den Grundsätzen des neueren Protestantismus dargestellt (1906).
2. G. Hilbert, *Ecclesiola in ecclesia*, p. 54.
3. Ibid., p. 65.
4. See A. Lüscher, *Wer glaubt, der flieht nicht*; and W. Ninck, *Die Christliche Gemeinde heute*, pp. 255-67.
5. Otto Riecker, *Erweckung heute*, pp. 54-57.
6. Ibid., p. 62.
7. G. Millon, *Combats pour l'Eglise*, p. 29.
8. See A. Kuen, *Que Tous soient Un*, pp. 47-79.
9. Emil Brunner, *The Misunderstanding of the Church*, p. 113; n. 2; p. 131.
10. John Calvin, *La Vraie Façon de Réformer l'Eglise*, p. 9.
11. Karl Barth, *Réflexions sur le IIe Concile du Vatican*, p. 30.
12. "Even a contemporary Catholic will be ashamed to read how through the political and financial traffic between the bishopric of Mainz and the Church of Peter, over indulgences, the apostolic Church was betrayed by all parties involved, just as earlier there had been a betrayal of the very *Spirit* of the apostles. . . . Even today, however, the Catholic Church will have to acknowledge culpability in this matter" (H. Küng, *Structures of the Church*, p. 107).
13. Calvin, p. 10.
14. "The Reformation in England sought to preserve as many elements of the medieval Church as seemed compatible with the elimination of the abuses of the Middle Ages" (Geddes MacGregor, *Corpus Christi*, p. 11).
"The young Anglican child is taught that to the question, 'Where was the Church of England before the Reformation?' the correct reply should be the counter-question, 'Where was your face before you washed it?'" (Leonard Hodgson, *The Doctrine of the Church as held and taught in the Church of England*, p. 7).
The Reformation is no longer an attempt to restore the primitive church but rather a cleaning up of the Roman Church. This is an argument which has had growing favor, especially in the present ecumenical perspective. See J. Courvoisier, "De la Réforme comme Principe critique du Protestantisme" in *Verbum Caro* (1953), pp. 11 ff. According to him, the whole Reformation wished to only be "a questioning *marginal note* within the context of the established Church" (p. 17).
15. MacGregor, p. 8.
16. Martin Luther, W. A. 6, 296.
17. Luther, W. A. 6, 407 ff.
18. K. Ecke, *Schwenckfeld*, p. 45.
19. The Silesian Reformer, Caspar Schwenckfeld, said of Luther: "Doctor Martin led us out of Egypt, across the Red Sea, and into the desert; there he left us, wandering about in the wilderness, all the while trying to persuade us that we were already in the promised land" (Schwenckfeld as quoted by Ecke, p. 34).

"In spite of real progress, in spite of the sincerity of the efforts, the Reformation of the XVIth century remained a 'Christendom,' containing within itself the world of the unconverted, associated with the world, opposed to the new reforms, and too often in favor of deserting Christ's plans. Therefore she is still to be reformed. . . . The Reformation did not know how to free the Church of Jesus Christ from the fundamental structures of 'Christendom' " (Millon, pp. 10, 24).

"Luther's work of renewal, which was so promising, stopped when only half completed" (O. S. von Bibra, introduction to Ecke's *Schwenckfeld*, p. 10).

"The Reformation restored the center of the Gospel but failed to restore the church to its believers' character" (H. S. Bender, *These Are My People*, p. 75). While certain Reformed (J. Courvoisier) and Lutheran (Vilmos Vajta) theologians are doing their utmost to show that the Reformers only wanted to purify the Roman Church from abuses while still remaining in the *Unam Sanctam catholicam*, Catholic theologians like Küng reproach them for not having finished what they began.

"Even Protestant [evangelical] theologians admit today that Luther (and hence other Reformers too) did not have St. Paul and the Scriptures behind them in all their declarations and demands, and were, to this extent, mistaken in particular points of their understanding of the Faith . . . nor can it be denied that the Reformation did not bring what Luther expected, a restoration of the Church on the pattern of primitive Christianity" (Küng, *The Council, Reform and Reunion*, pp. 74-75). "We have made these points only to shed a little light on the grave reasons why the Catholic Church rejected Luther and the Protestant Reformation," he concludes (p. 75). A jest? In any case it is cruel irony for the Protestant theologians!

20. John Robinson as quoted by E. H. Broadbent, *L'Eglise Ignorée*, p. 246.
21. G. Ischbeck, *John Nelson Darby*, p. 54.
22. Alexandre Vinet, *Liberté religieuse et Questions ecclésiastiques*, pp. 594, 636; and *Etudes sur la Littérature française du XIXe siècle*, 2:392.
23. Agénor de Gasparin, *Innocent III*, p. 192.
24. de Gasparin, *Les Ecoles du Doute et l'Ecole de la Foi*, p. 382.
25. Adolphe Monod, "Sermon sur la Vocation de l'Eglise" in *Sermons choisis*, p. 100.
26. Ibid., p. 83.
27. J. Izoulet, *La Métamorphose de l'Eglise*, p. 30, as quoted by Francus, p. 277.
28. W. A. Visser't Hooft, *Renouveau de l'Eglise*, p. 48.
29. Brunner, *Dogmatics*, 3:91.
30. J. Courvoisier, "De la Réforme comme principe critique du Protestantisme," *Verbum Caro* (1953), 3:23.
31. H. S. Venske, *Vollendete Reformation*, p. 90.
32. Ninck, p. 231.
33. Resolution of the study commission of the Ecumenical Council as quoted by Dilschneider in *Gefesselte Kirche*, p. 166.
34. Barth, *Foi et Vie* (1948), p. 495.
35. Barth, *L'Eglise*, p. 113.
36. Ibid., p. 127.
37. Küng, *The Council,* . . . , p. 9.
38. Pope Paul VI, address given at the opening of the second session of the Vatican Council.
39. Küng, *The Council,* . . . , p. 35.
40. Ibid., p. 97.
41. Roland de Pury, as quoted by J. de Senarclens, *La Réforme Hier et Aujourd'hui*, p. 10.
42. Senarclens, p. 12.
43. Barth, *Réflexions* . . . , pp. 21-22.
44. Senarclens, p. 18.
45. Barth, *L'Eglise*, p. 121.
46. Ibid., p. 162.
47. Rendtorff, *Die Taufe im Urchristentum im Lichte der neueren Forschung*, p. 55.
48. Gasparin, *Les Scoles du Doute* . . . , p. 383.
49. Visser't Hooft, *The Renewal of the Church*, p. 92.

50. P. Jalaguier, *De l'Eglise*, p. 358.
51. Eric Fuchs, preface to Calvin, *La vraie façon* . . . , p. 7.
52. See Calvin, *Institutes*, bk. 4, chap. 1, pp. 10-12.
53. Calvin, *Epistle to Sadolet*. "First, we protest that for the rule of our faith and religion we wish to follow Scripture alone without adding to it anything that has been invented by man's reasoning without the Word of God; and let us not claim to receive for our spiritual guidance any other doctrine than that which is taught us by this Word, without adding to it or subtracting from it, as the Lord commanded" (*1st Article of the Confession of Faith of 1537*).
54. Jalaguier, p. 265.
55. Barth, *L'Eglise*, p. 122. See also pp. 129, 149. If the Church is deprived of the authority of the Bible, what remains? "Pious smoke and all sorts of religious and moral odors" (Barth, *Die Schrift und die Kirche*, p. 17).
56. Barth, *Parole de Dieu et Parole humaine*, p. 140.
57. Barth, *Foi et Vie*, p. 494.
58. Brunner, *Les Eglises, les Groupes et l'Eglise de Jésus Christ*, p. 10.
59. Brunner, *Eglises et Groupes*, p. 39.
60. Ibid., p. 10.
61. Visser't Hooft, *The Renewal of the Church*, pp. 84-85.
62. Ibid., pp. 92-93.
63. Ibid., p. 94.
64. G. Casalis, *Rapport de la Xe Assemblée du Protestantisme*, p. 73.
65. P. Courthial, "Actualité et catholicité de la Réformation," *Revue réformée* 3(1962):15.
66. A. Lecerf, *Introduction à la Dogmatique réformée*, 2, chap. 4, pp. 153-59, as quoted by F. Gonin, *Alliance évangélique* (Oct. 1964), p. 7.
67. Senarclens, p. 10.
68. Mgr. Strossmayer, *Ein Bischof gegen die Unfehlbarkeit des Papstes*.
69. Küng, *The Council*, . . . , p. 56.
70. Ibid.
71. Küng, *Structures* . . . , p. 110.
72. Ibid.
73. Ibid., p. 118.
74. F. Refoulé, *Revue d'Histoire et de Philosophie religieuse* (1964), p. 470.
75. Barth, *Réflexions* . . . , pp. 28-29.
76. Courthial, p. 20.
77. Brunner, *Le Renouveau de l'Eglise*, p. 32.
78. Ninck, p. 162.
79. R. Mehl, "L'Eglise de l'Avenir," *Revue de l'Evangélisation*, no. 98 (1961), p. 482.
80. Monod, p. 96.
81. Visser't Hooft, *None Other Gods*, p. 70.
82. Barth, "Die Kirche—die lebendige Gemeinde des lebendigen Herrn Christus" in *Die Schrift* . . . , p. 43.
83. Küng, *Structures* . . . , p. 449.
84. P. Lestringant, "Les Membres de l'Eglise" in *Revue de Théologie et de Philosophie* (1939), p. 206.
85. A. Adam, article in *Religion in Geschichte und Gegenwart*, vol. 2, col. 1112.
86. Brunner, *Dogmatics*, 3:84.
87. E. G. Léonard, *Le Protestant français*, pp. 149-50.
88. F. H. Littell, *The Free Churcn*, p. 10.
89. Venske, p. 96.
90. Mehl, p. 483.
91. Barth, *L'Eglise*, p. 14.
92. Ibid., p. 62.
93. F. Godet, *Commentaire sur l'Evangile de Jean*, 2:58.
94. Ibid., p. 469.
95. Vinet, *Liberté religieuse*. . . .
96. de Gasparin, *Les Droits du Coeur*.
97. Albert Bessière *L'Evangile du Chef*, p. 44.
98. Monod, p. 100.

99. Venske, p. 91.
100. Visser't Hooft, *The Renewal* . . . , p. 69.
101. Calvin, *Institutes*, bk. 4, chap. 1, p. 11.
102. Calvin, *La Vraie Façon* . . . , p. 10.
103. Vinet, *Nouveaux Discours*, pp. 24-25, 28.
104. Vinet, *Essai sur la Manifestation des Convictions religieuses*, p. 115.
105. Ibid., p. 32.
106. Ibid., p. 45.
107. G. Francus, *Il n'y a pas de Protestants*, p. 11.
108. Luther as quoted by Francus, p. 9.
109. Courthial, p. 20.
110. See Kuen, pp. 75-78.
111. See 1 Ti 6:3-5; Gal 1:8-9; Ro 16:17-18; 2 Ti 3:5-6; Titus 3:10-11; 2 Jn 7-11.
112. Felice as quoted by Jalaguier, p. xx.
113. Senarclens, *De la Vraie Eglise, selon Calvin*, p. 29.
114. Ibid., p. 30.
115. See G. Verwer, *La Page Imprimée*; Wade C. Smith, *Come and See*; R. Torrey, *How to Lead Men to Christ*; Paget Wilkes, *The Dynamic of Christian Service*.
116. Brunner, *Dogmatics*, 3:276.
117. Luther, *Von Konzilien und Kirchen*, W. A. 50, 509-653.
118. Barth, *L'Eglise*, p. 4.
119. Brunner, *Le Renouveau de l'Eglise*.
120. Brunner, *La Situation de l'Eglise*, p. 21.
121. Brunner, *Eglises et Groupes*, p. 24.
122. Casalis, p. 98.
123. Klaas Sluys gives the account of the birth and development of a church of laymen right in the middle of Catholic territory. Without a pastor, this assembly grew and became established, after a few years numbering several hundred members. See his *Das Wunder von Boechout*. This Flemish experience is not the only one of its kind; one could give many examples, even in French-speaking countries.
124. This sentence was spoken more than four centuries ago by Nicolas Cop, vice-chancellor of the University of Paris, in his message at the reopening of the colleges after vacation (Nov. 1, 1533). Its real author was the young John Calvin, the rector's friend. Quoted by J. P. Benoît, *Dénominations et Sectes*, p. 7.
125. Brunner, *The Misunderstanding of the Church*, p. 117. The original is even much more assertive than indicated by the translation: "die falsche, klerikele, pfäffische Kirchlichkeit."
126. Read again how pastors Lüscher in *Wer glaubt der flieht nicht* and Riecker in *Erweckung heute* describe the consequences of the revival and the establishing of a group of true Christians within the framework of an official church. See also Van Zeijl, *Wenn Gottes Winde wehen*.
127. Venske, p. 97.
128. Walter Nigg as quoted by Dilschneider, p. 166.
129. Brunner, *The Misunderstanding* . . . , p. 118.
130. Monod, p. 98.
131. Ibid., p. 102.

For Further Reading

(Chapters 14-16)

Auftrag der Kirche in der Modernen Welt. Commemorative service on the 70th birthday of Emil Brunner.
Barth, K., Cullmann, O., Fuchs, E., Geiselmann, J. *Catholiques et Protestants*. Paris: du Seuil, 1963.
———. *Deliverance to the Captives*. New York: Harper, 1961.
Brunner, E. *Dogmatics*. Vol. 3.
———. *The Misunderstanding of the Church*. Philadelphia: Westminster, 1953.
———. *La Situation de l'Eglise et sa Mission Présente* (Ed. Labor—Je sers). Pamphlet: "Cause des déficits de l'église nationale et proposition de quelques remèdes."

Calvin, J. *Tracts and Treatises relating to the Reformation.* Vol. 1. Grand Rapids: Eerdmans, 1959.

Courthial, P. "Actualité et catholicité de la Réformation." *Revue Réformée* 13, no. 51 (3d trimester, 1962).

Courvoisier, J. "De la Réforme comme principe critique du protestantisme," in *Verbum Caro* (1953), pp. 11 ff.

Desbaumes, André. *L'Eglise—Communauté.* Lyon: rue Fénélon, 1946. Brochure.

Dilschneider, O. *Gefesselte Kirche* (Not und Verheissung). Stuttgart: Evang. Verlegswerk, 1953.

Ecclesia semper reformanda. Cahier spécial de Evang. Theol. 1952.

Flew, Newton. *The Catholicity of Protestantism.* London: Lutterworth, 1st ed. 1950, 2nd ed. 1951.

Foester, E. "Luthers Kirchenbegriff und die Kirchliche Krisis von heute." In *Zeitschrift für Theologie und Kirche* (1920).

Führ, E. "L'Eglise devient Diaspora." *Zeichen der Zeit,* no. 4 (April 1963). Shows by the New Testament what the role of the church is in a society which is mainly pagan.

Fürstenberg, Fr. "Formes de vie de l'Eglise et du monde." *Zweitwende,* No. 4 (April 1963). Problem of the re-formation of the church.

Küng, Hans. *The Council, Reform and Reunion.* New York: Sheed & Ward, 1961.

Litell, Franklin H. *The Free Church.* Boston: Beacon, 1957.

Mehl, R. "L'évolution de l'ecclésiologie dans la pensée du mouvement oecuménique." *Revue d'Historie et de Philosophie religieuse,* Nos. 2-3 (1962).

Morrison, C. C. *The Unfinished Reformation.* 1953.

Nagel, G. *Der grosse Kampf.* Bonn: Schergens. A contribution which throws light on the question: Church or Assembly of Believers.

Neill, S. *The Unfinished Task.* London: 1957.

Newbigin, Lesslie. *Is Christ Divided?* Grand Rapids: Eerdmans, 1961.

———. *Trinitarian Faith and Today's Mission.* Richmond, Va.: John Knox, 1964.

———. *A Faith for This One World.* London: SCM Press, Ltd., 1961. See chap. 1, "The End of Christendom and the Rise of a World Civilization," pp. 9-29 and chap. 5, "The Pattern of the Christian Mission to the Nations," pp. 106-26.

Ninck, W. *Christliche Gemeinde heute.*

Riecker, Otto. *Erweckung heute und ihre Botschaft an uns.* Brockhaus, 1958.

Schultz, H. J. *Kritik an der Kirche.* Kreuz-Verlag, Stuttgart und Walter-Verlag, Olten und Freiburgi. Br. A series of radio messages in which Protestant and Catholic laymen and theologians submit the church of today to criticism.

Senarclens, J. De. *La Réforme hier et aujourd'hui.* Geneva: Labor et Fides, 1964.

———. *Héritiers de la Réformation.* 2:210-44. L'Eglise. Geneva: Labor et Fides.

Venske, Herbert. *Vollendete Reformation.* Wuppertal: Vg. Brockhaus, 1958. From the State Church to the Living Assembly.

Vinay, Tuillio. "Les Eglises minoritaires et le service des autres." *Etudes théologiues et religieuses,* No. 3 (1963).

Visser't Hooft, W. A. *Le Renouveau de l'Eglise.* Geneva: Labor et Fides.

Vogel, H. "Die permanente Reformation der Kirche." *Junge Kirche* 19 (1956): 589 ff.

Wölber, Hans Otto. *Religion ohne Entscheidung.* Göttingen: Vandenhoeck.

See also the articles by Rev. Heiko Oberman on "Réforme, prédication et *ex opere operato,*" by O. Cullmann on "Ecriture et Tradition" and of Barth on "L'Eglise."

Selected Reading List

For lists of works devoted to various questions relative to the church, consult the bibliographies in the following works:

Hirsch, E. *Geschichte der neueren evang. Theologie.* Vol. 5, pp. 145-231.
———. *Religion in Geschicte und Gegenwart.* Vol 3, pp. 1303-4.
Kittel, Gerhard and Friedrich, G., eds. *Theological Dictionary of the New Testament.* 4 vols.
———. *L'Eglise dans la Bible.* Pp. 169-202.
Linton, Olof. *Das Problem der Urkirche in der neueren Forschung.* Pp. 14-32.
MacGregor, Geddes. *Corpus Christi.* Pp. 277-91.
Valeske, Ulrich. *Votum Ecclesiae.* Vol. 2.
A Catholic work which gives several thousand books and articles devoted to this problem and written by Protestant, Orthodox, and Catholic writers in German, French and English.

Books Written from the Point of View of Churches of Professing Believers

I. Biblical Studies

Chafer, Lewis S. *Major Bible Themes.* Grand Rapids: Zondervan, 1926.
Hammond, T. C. *In Understanding Be Men.* London: Inter-Varsity, n.d. See Part 6: "The Corporate Life of the Christian," pp. 160-87, and a list of evangelical English works on the church, p. 167.
Nicole, Albert. *La Notion biblique de l'Eglise et nos Devoirs actuels.* P. 36.
Pache, René. l'Eglise in *Notes sur les Actes des Apôtres,* pp. 69-76. 3d ed. Ed. Emmaus, 1964.
———. *The Person and Work of the Holy Spirit.* Chicago: Moody, 1960. See "The Holy Spirit and the Church."
Rienecker, Fritz. *Die Herrlichkeit der Gemeinde Jesu nach dem Epheserbrief.* Wuppertal: Brockhaus, 1951.
———. *Praktischer Handkommentar zum Epheserbrief,* pp. 439 ff. "Die Ekklesia nach dem N. T. unter Berücksichtigung des Epheserbriefs." Neumunster i. Holstein: E. Ihlhoff, 1934.
Saillens, R. *Le Mystère de la Foi,* "Le mystère de l'Eglise" Ed. Institut Biblique de Nogent.
Stibbs, Alan. *God's Church.* Stibbs is Anglican, but he shows how under the old covenant as well as the new covenant the church was composed of only true believers.

II. Authors Belonging to the Following Groups

A. Assembly of the Brethren

Ferguson, F. *L'Eglise de Dieu*. Argenteuil, 1950.
Goodman, George. *Principles of Gathering*. London: Pickering & Inglis.
Hoste, W. *Israel, the Church and Christendom*. Ritchie Kilmarnock, s.d.
——. *The True Church*. "What is it? Who compose it? 70 testimonies from different lands." London: Pickering & Inglis.
Lang, G. H. *The Churches of God*.
Mac Donald. *The Church and the Churches*.
Perret, Paul. *Nos Eglises dissidentes*. Nyon: "Je Sème," 1966.
Sauer, E. *Gott, Menschheit und Ewigkeit*. Brockhaus, 1955.
——. *The Triumph of the Crucified*. Grand Rapids: Eerdmans, 1951.
Short, Rendle. *The Open Brethren*.
Squire, S. *L'Eglise ou la Maison de Dieu*.
Vine, W. E. *Divine Headships of the Bible*. London: Pickering & Inglis.
Watson, J. B. *The Church: A Symposium of Principles and Practice*. London: Pickering & Inglis, 1951. Collaboration containing 26 studies on the principal questions concerning the life of the church by the most qualified representatives of the Assembly of the Brethren in England.

B. Darbyist Assemblies

Darby, J. N. *L'Eglise selon la Parole* and *L'Eglise*, 2 studies.
Mackintosh, C. H. *L'Assemblée de Dieu ou la pleine suffisance du nom de Jésus*
Prod'hom Frédéric. *Qu'est-ce aujourd'hui qu'une Assemblée de Dieu?*
Prod'hom, Samuel. *Réunis en "Assemblée"*.
P. S. *L'Assemblée de Dieu*.
E. L. *L'Eglise, corps de Christ et le Témoignage*.
A. G. *L'Assemblée de Dieu*. Valence, 1949.
Le Messager évangélique. (Vevey). Periodical.
Hütet die Herde Gottes die bei euch ist. Periodical.

C. Baptist Churches

Clifford, P. R. *The Christian Life*. London: Carey Kingsgate, 1954. A book about baptism and church membership.
Cook, Henry. *What Baptists Stand For*.
Dana, H. E. *Christ's Ecclesia*. The New Testament Church. Sunday School Board of the Southern Baptist Convention.
Dubarry, R. *Pour faire connaissance avec un idéal d'église* Nimes; 9 rue des Bénédictins.
Haynes, D. C. *The Baptist Denomination*.
Itty, Edmond. *Servitude et Grandeur de la Religion*. "Qu'est-ce qu'un Chrétien?" Paris, 1948.
Payne, E. A. *The Fellowship of Believers*. 2d ed. London: Kingsgate, 1952.
Robinson, H. Wheeler. *Baptist Principles*.
Schneider, Johannes. *Die Gemeinde nach dem Neuen Testament*. Kassel: Oncken, 1955.

D. Churches of Christ

Brownlow, Leroy. *Why I am a member of the Church of Christ.*
Gogdill, Roy E. *The New Testament Church.* Fayette, Ala.: Marion David.

E. Free Churches

L'Union des Eglises libres de France.
L'Union des Églises évangéliques libres de France (1849-1949). Cahors: Couselant, 1949.
Gasparin, A. de. *L'Eglise selon l'Evangile.* Paris: Calman-Lévy, 1879. 2 vols.
Pressensé, E. de. *Discours religieux.* Part 1: "L'Eglise et ses moyens de Grace."
Vinet, A. *Questions ecclésiastiques.* Lausanne: Payot, vol. 1, 1945; vol. 2, 1946. "Qu'est-ce qu'une église?"

F. Mennonite Churches

Detailed history of the Mennonite Churches. Montbéliard, 1914.
Bender, Harold S. *These Are My People.* "The nature of the Church and its Discipleship according to the New Testament."
Estep, William R. *The Anabaptist Story.* Nashville: Broadman, 1963.
Hillerbrand, H. J. *A Bibliography of Anabaptism, 1520-1630.* Elkhart, Ind.: Institute of Mennonite Studies, 1962.
The Mennonite Quarterly Review.
Williams, G. H., *The Radical Reformation.*

G. Methodist Churches

Roux, T. *L'Oeuvre d'une Société centenaire* (1813-1913).
———. *Le Methodisme en France.* 1914.

H. Pentecostal Churches

Dallière, L. *D'Aplomb sur la Parole de Dieu.* Valence, 1932.
Hofer, E. A. *Eglise où es-tu?*

I. Others (interdenominational organizations for evangelization)

Boemerle, T. *Die Gemeine und ihre Glieder.* Reutlingen: A. Fuhr.
Clasen, P. A. "Ekklesiologie," *Der Salutismus.* Iena, 1913.
Foster, H. *The Reality of God's House.* London: A Witness and a Testimony.
Grubb, Norman. *The Liberating Secret.* Chrn. Life.
Nee, Watchman. *The Normal Christian Church Life.*
———. *What Shall This Man Do?* London: Victory, 1961. Pp. 86, 138.
Salvation Army. *Principes et Méthodes de l'Armée du Salut.* Librairie Altis, 1938.
Sparks, T. Austin. "The House of God" in *The School of Christ.* London: A Witness and a Testimony.
———. *God's Spiritual House.* London: A Witness and a Testimony.
———. *The Centrality and the Universality of the Cross.* "The Cross and the Church," chaps. 5 and 6. London: A Witness and a Testimony.

——. *The Stewardship of the Mystery.* 2 vols. London: A Witness and a Testimony. Available from M.O.R.E., P. O. Box 68505, Indianapolis, Ind.

Torrey, R. A. *Practical and Perplexing Questions Answered.* "Meaning of the Church—Conditions of entrance". Chicago: Moody, n.d.

THEOLOGICAL WORKS

I. Studies of the Church in the New Testament

Dietrich, S. de. "The Mystery of the Church." In *God's Unfolding Purpose.* Philadelphia: Westminster, 1960.

Howard, W. F. *The Church in the New Testament.* Edinburgh: The Expository Times, 1950-1951. Theological research on the church in the New Testament in the last decades.

Koehnlein, H. "La notion de l'Eglise chez l'apôtre Paul" in the *Revue d'Histoire et de Philosophie religieuses* 17 (1937): 377.

Leenhardt, Franz J. *Two Biblical Faiths: Protestant and Catholic.*

——. *Etudes sur l'Eglise dans le Nouveau Testament.* See especially chap. 3: "Eglise et Corps de Christ" and chap. 4: "L'Organisation de l'Eglise Primitive."

Menoud, P. *La Vie de l'Eglise Naissante,* Cahiers Théologiques de l'actualité protestante, Delachaux et Niestlé, 1952. Commentary on Acts 2:42, starting with the biblical concept of church members, those who "one day took the decisive step of placing their faith in Christ," p. 8.

Spoerri, T. *Der Gemeindegedanken im ersten Petrusbrief.* A contribution on the concept of the structure of the early church. (Neutest. Forschung. 2 Reihe, 2 Heft, Gütersloh: C. Bertelsmann, 1925)

Valeske, U. *Votum ecclesiae,* 2: 5-8, and 8-10, "Eglise Primitive."

II. Theological Studies

A. Individual Works

Barth, Karl. *Church Dogmatics.*

——. *Community, Church and State.* Gloucester, Mass.: Peter Smith.

——. *German Church Conflict.* Richmond, Va.: John Knox, 1965.

——. *Credo.* New York: Scribner, 1962.

Boeni, G. *Le Problème de l'Eglise.* Lausanne: Payot. Research on the concept of the church in Christian antiquity.

Bonhoeffer, Dietrich. *Sanctorum communio.*

——. *Communion of the Saints.* New York: Harper, 1964.

——. *Life Together.* New York: Harper, 1954.

Brunner, Emil. *Dogmatics.* Vol. 3.

——. *Les Eglises, les Groupes et l'Eglise de Jésus-Christ.*

——. *Le Renouveau de l'Eglise.*

——. *Zwischen den Zeiten.* "Theologie und Kirche."

Brunner, Peter. *Evang. Akademie de Tützing.* No. 12 on the nature of the church.

Cullmann, O. *Christology of the New Testament.* Rev. ed. Philadelphia: Westminster, 1964.

——. *Early Christian Worship.* Naperville, Ill.: Allenson.

Dahl, Nils Alstrup. *Das Volk Gottes.* An investigation of the church conscious-
ness in early Christendom.
Flew, R. Newton. *Jesus and His Church.* Naperville, Ill.: Allenson, 1943.
Goguel, Maurice. *The Birth of Christianity.* New York: Humanities, 1953.
Liberal.
Hildebrandt, Walter. *Das Gemeindeprinzip der christlichen Kirche.* The doc-
trine of the church as the basic concept of the church.
Jacobs, Manfred. *Die Evangelische Lehre von der Kirche.* "Sources on the
study of confessions." Anthology of the most important texts by Reformers
and representative theologians of different Protestant schools, with a brief
introduction on the evolution of the concept of the church in Protestantism.
Critical notes and bibliographies.
Morrison, Charles Clayton. *What Is Christianity?* Chicago: Will Clark, 1940.
Lectures given at Yale University in 1939.
Nelson, J. R. *The Realm of Redemption.*
Nygren, A. *This Is the Church.*
Schmidt, K. L. *The Church.* London: Adam and C. Black, 1957. Bible key
words from Gerhard Kittel's *Theological Dictionary of the New Testament.*
Simon, Marcel. *Les Premiers Chrétiens.* Paris: PUF, 1952. "Que sais-je?"

B. Collective Works

Origine et Nature de l'Eglise. Paris: Professors of the Faculty of Theology of
Paris, 1939.
Le Problème de l'Eglise. University Press of France, 1947. Liberal.
La Sainte Eglise Universelle. Ecumenical. Florovsky, G., Leenhardt, F. L.,
Prenter, R., Richardson, A., Spicq, C. Cahiers théologiques de l'actualité
protestante, Delachaux et Niestlé, 1948.
Die Kirche im Neuen Testament. Berlin, 1930. Articles by A. Lang and
G. Wobbermin, on "The Scriptural Concept of the Church," and W. Zoell-
ner, on "The Church according to Ephesians."

C. For various Protestant concepts of the church, see U. Valeske's *Votum
ecclesiae,* 2: 27-32 (172 titles), pp. 35-43 (76 titles).

D. Works of General Interest

Boegner, Marc. *Qu'est-ce que l'Eglise?* Paris: "Je sers," 1931. Series of lectures
given in the Reformed Church of Passy in 1931.
Désordre de l'Homme et Dessein de Dieu, pp. 95-109: "L'Eglise, congrégation
vivante de Jésus-Christ, le Seigneur vivant." Neuchâtel: Delachaux & Niestlé,
1949.
Newbigin, Lesslie. *L'Eglise, Peuple des croyants, Corps de Christ, Temple de
l'Esprit.*
Pury, Roland de. *La Maison de Dieu.* Protestantism of today.
Visser't Hooft, W. A. *Misère et Grandeur de l'Eglise.*

III. The Church as Seen by Confessional Churches

A. Lutheran point of view

Blanc, R. *Etudes évangéliques,* "Quelques indications pour une ecclésiologie
luthérienne." Aix, 1963. No. 2.

Kinder, E. *Der evang. Glaube und die Kirche*. Fundamentals of the Evangelical Lutheran concept of the church. Berlin: Luth. Verlagshaus, 1960.

Koeberle, Adolf. *Die Seele der Christentums*. 3d ed. "Die Gemeinschaft der Heiligen," pp. 133-55. Berlin: Furche, 1932.

———. *Quest for Holiness*. Minneapolis: Augsburg.

Mayer, F. E. *The Religious Bodies of America*. St. Louis: Concordia, 1961. How the Lutherans of the Missouri Synod look upon the other churches.

Mueller, J. T. *Christian Dogmatics*. See "The doctrine of the Church." St. Louis: Concordia, 1934.

Prenter, Regin. *Creation and Redemption*, "The Church of the Word and Faith." Philadelphia: Fortress, 1967.

Schlinck, E. *The Nature of the Church*.

———. *Theology of the Lutheran Confession*. Philadelphia: Fortress, 1961.

Schnepel, Erich. *Briefe aus dem Berliner Osten*, "Die Wirklichkeit Jesu und seiner Gemeinde." Berlin: Furche, 1937.

Thimme, L. *Kirche, Sekte und Gemeinschaftsbewegung*, Bahn in Schwerin: Fried, 1925).

Waitz, E. *Das Wesen der evangelischen Kirche*. Hanover, 1913.

Wehrung, G. *Kirche nach evangelischen Verständnis*.

A Book concerning the Church (*Ein Buch von der Kirche*. Written in collaboration with Swedish theologians. By Gustaf Aulen, Anton Fridrichsen, Anders Nygren, Hjalmar Linderoth, Ragnar Bring. Göttingen: Vanderhoek & Ruprecht, 1951.

B. Reformed viewpoint

Allis, Oswald T. *Prophecy and the Church*. Philadelphia: Presbyterian and Reformed, 1945. Chap. 3: "The Kingdom and the Church"; chap. 4: "Paul's Doctrine of the Church."

Cadier, J. *Man God Mastered: John Calvin*. Grand Rapids: Eerdmans.

Calvin, J. *Le Catéchisme*, followed by the Confession of Faith of La Rochelle. Paris: "Je sers," 1934.

———. *Le Mystère de l'Eglise*. Based on *Ephesians*. Foi et Vie, 1948.

Jalaguier, Paul. *De l'Eglise*. Multitudinist point of view.

Mac Gregor, Geddes. *Corpus Christi*. The nature of the church according to the Reformed tradition.

———. *Coming Reformation*. Philadelphia: Westminster, 1960.

Senarclens, J. de. *De la Vraie Eglise, selon Calvin*.

C. Independent Evangelical Reformed churches

Les Eglises réformées évangéliques ont-elles fait leur temps? 1951.

D. Anglican point of view

Allen, Tom. *The Face of My Parish*.

Lyall, Leslie T. and Newbigin, Lesslie. *The Church Local and Universal*. London: World Dominion.

Richardson, Alan. *La Saint Eglise Universelle*, "Une interprétation anglicane de l'Eglise." Neuchâtel: Delachaux, 1948.

———. *Religion in Contemporary Debate*. Philadelphia: Westminster.

E. Orthodox point of view

Clement, Olivier. *Qu'est-ce que l'Eglise orthodoxe?* Paris: Ecumenical Center Enotikon, 1961. Yearbook of the Orthodox Church of France. For a bibliography concerning the Eastern Churches see the *Bulletin du Centre protestant d'Etudes et de Documentation.* New series No. 86 (Jan. 1964). See also Valeske, *Votum ecclesiae,* vol. 2.

Florovsky, R. P. G. *La Sainte Eglise Universelle,* "Le Corps du Christ vivant." Neuchâtel: Delachaux & Niestlé, 1948.

F. Catholic point of view

Bardy, G. *La Théologie de l'Eglise de Saint Clément de Rome à Saint Irénée.*
———. *De Saint Irénée au Concile de Nicée.* Coll. Unam Sanctam. Paris: Cerf, 1947.
Cerfaux, L. *The Church in the Theology of Saint Paul.*
Chirat, H. *L'Assemblée chrétienne à l'âge apostolique.* Paris: Cerf, 1949.
Congar, Père Y. *Mystery of the Church.* New York: Helicon, 1960.
———. *Tradition and Traditions in the Church.* New York: Macmillan.
Courtois, Abbé A. *Nos Frères, les premiers Chrétiens.* Paris: Editions ouvrières, 1938.
Goosens, W. *L'Eglise, corps du Christ d'après Saint Paul.*
Küng, Hans. *The Structures of the Church.*
Prunel, Mgr. Louis. *L'Eglise.* 23d ed. Paris: Beauchesne, 1932.
Schnackenburg, R. *The Church in the New Testament.*
Valeske, U. *Votum ecclesiae,* 2: 20-26 (230 titles). Critique of the Catholic viewpoint by Protestants, p. 27 (21 books).
For the recent evolution in Catholic ecclesiology read in *La Revue Réformée* nos. 64-65 (1965/4-1966/1) the article by Vittorio Subilia entitled "L'Ecclésiologie de Vatican II."

Bibliography

Adam, A. Article in *Geschichte und Gegenwart*. Vol. 2.

Adam, Karl. *Le vrai Visage du Catholicisme*. Paris: 1934.

Aland, K. *Did the Early Church Baptize Infants?* Trans. G. R. Beasley-Murray. Philadelphia: Westminster, 1963. Trans. of *Die Sauglingstaufe im Neuen Testament und in der alten Kirche*.

Albert, A. *Les Fondements de l'Eglise d'après Calvin*.

Alexander. *Pentecôtisme ou Christianisme*.

Allen, Tom. *The Face of My Parish*.

Allo, E. B. *Saint Paul: Seconde épitre aux Corinthiens*. Etudes bibliques. Paris: Gabalda, 1956.

Amyot, François. *Vocabulaire de Théologie biblique*.

Andrews, H. T. *Lectures on the Church and the Sacraments*.

Anrich, G. *Martin Bucer*. Strasbourg: K. J. Trübner, 1914.

Ansbacher evangelischer Ratschlag. Sept. 30, 1524.

The Anti-Nicene Fathers. Buffalo: Chrn. Lit. Co., 1886.

Antomarchi, A. *Rome face á l'Evangile*.

Antonin, M. *Union des Eglises évang. libres de France*.

Arnold, Gottfried. *Unparteiische Kirchen—und Ketzerhistorie von Anfang des N.T. bis auf das Jahr 1688*.

Asmussen, H. "Grundsätzliche Erwägungen zur Volkskirche." *Junge Kirche* (1935), pp. 288 ff., and (1939), p. 134.

Aubigné, J. H. Merle d'. *L'Autorité des Ecritures*.

Auftrag der Kirche in der Modernen Welt. Commemorative service on the 70th birthday of Emil Brunner.

"Autour du renouveau de l'ecclésiologie." *La Vie intellectuelle* 51(1939):9.

Babut, E. C. *Priscillien et le Priscillianisme*. Paris: H. Champion, 1909.

Baillie, John. *Baptism and Conversion*. New York: Scribner, 1963.

———. *What Is Christian Civilization?* New York: Scribner, 1945.

Barclay, William. *And Jesus Said*. Edinburgh: Church of Scotland Youth Committee, 1960.

———. *New Testament Wordbook*. London: SCM, 1955.

Bardy, Canon G. *La Théologie de l'Eglise de Saint Clément de Rome à Saint Irénée*. Paris: Editions du Cerf, 1947.

Barnes, Albert. *Critical and Exegetical Commentary*.

———. *Notes, explanatory and practical, on the New Testament*. New York: Harper, 1834-51.

———. *Notes on the Acts*.

Barth, Karl. Article in *Alliance évang.* Oct. 1964.
———. *Church Dogmatics.* Trans. and edited by G. W. Bromiley. Edinburgh: T. & T. Clark, 1961.
———. *Les Communautés chrétiennes dans la Tourmente.* Neuchâtel: Delachaux, 1943.
———. *La Confession de Foi de l'Eglise.* Neuchâtel: Delachaux & Niestlé, 1946.
———. *Connaître Dieu et le servir.* Neuchâtel-Paris: Delachaux & Niestlé, 1945.
———. *Deliverance to the Captives.* London: SCM, 1961.
———. *L'Eglise.* Geneva: Labor et Fides, 1965.
———. *Esquisse d'une Dogmatique.*
———. *Parole de Dieu et Parole humaine.* Eng. trans: *The Word of God and the Word of Man.* New York: Harper, 1957.
———. *Réflexions sur le IIe Concile du Vatican.* Geneva: Labor et Fides, 1963.
———. *Die Schrift und die Kirche.* Zollikon-Zurich: Evangelischer, 1947.
———. *The Teaching of the Church Regarding Baptism.* London: SCM, 1948.
———. "Volkskirche, Freikirche, Bekennende Kirche." *Evangelische Theol.* 3 (1936):411-22.
Barth, Karl; Cullmann, O.; Fuchs, E.; Geiselmann, J. *Catholiques et Protestants.* Paris: du Seuil, 1963.
Barth, Markus. *Die Taufe—ein Sakrament?* Zollikon-Zürich: Evangelischer, 1951.
Battifol, Mgr. *Dicto. cath.*
Baumgarten, M. *Zwölf Kirchengeschichtliche Vorträge.*
Beasley-Murray, G. R. *Baptism in the New Testament.* London: Macmillan-Scott, 1962.
Belarmin, Cardinal. *Symbolie.*
Bellamy, J. Article in *Dictionaire de Théologie catholique.* Devacant-Mangenot. Fasc. X, pp. 176-66.
Bellardi, W. *Die Geschichte der "christlichen Gemeinschaft in Strassburg."* Leipzig: Heinsius, 1934.
Bender, Harold S. *Conrad Grebel, 1498-1526, the Founder of the Swiss Brethren.* Goshen, Ind.: Mennonite Historical Society, Goshen College, 1950.
———. *Das Täuferische Leitbild.*
———. *These Are My People.* Scottdale, Pa.: Herald, 1962.
———. *La Vision Anabaptiste.*
Benoît, A. *Le Baptême chrétien au 11e Siècle.* Paris: U. France, 1953.
Benoît, Jean-Daniel. *Calvin et le Baptême des Enfants.*
Benoît, J. P. *Dénominations et Sectes.* Les Bergers et les Mages, 1965.
Bergmann, Gerhard. *Die Aufgabe des Volkes Gottes heute.*
Bergmann, V. G. *Alarm um die Bibel.* 2d ed. Gladbeck, 1963.
Berguer, G. *Traité de Psychologie de la Religion.* Lausanne: Paylot, 1946.
Bernouilli, M. *Vocabulaire biblique.* Neuchâtel: Delachaux & Niestlé, 1954.
Bessière, Albert. *L'Evangile du Chef.*
Besson, J. *Histoire du Pentecôtisme en Allemagne.*
Besson, Mgr. *L'Eglise et la Royaume de Dieu.*
Blanke, F. "Täufertum und Reformation" in G. F. Hershberger, *The Recovery of the Anabaptist Vision.* Scottdale, Pa.: Herald, 1957.
———. *Brüder in Christo.* Zürich: Zwingli, 1955. Eng. trans.: *Brothers in Christ.* Scottdale, Pa.: Herald, 1961.

Blocher, J. *Le Catholicisme.*
Boegner, Marc. *Le Problème de l'Eglise.* Paris: PUF.
Boehmer, Julius, ed. *Martin Luthers Werke.* Deutsche Verlags Anstalt.
Boehmer, Heinrich. *Der junge Luther.* Eng. trans.: *Martin Luther: Road to Reformation.* New York: Meridian Books, 1946.
Bonhoeffer, Dietrich. *The Cost of Discipleship.* London: SCM, 1948.
———. *Temptation.* New York: Macmillan, 1955.
———. *Sanctorum communio.* Munich: C. Kaiser, 1954.
Bonnard, P. Article in *Vocabulaire biblique.*
Bonnet, J. L. *Le Nouveau Testament de notre Seigneur Jésus-Christ expliqué.* Vol. 1. Lausanne: Bridel, 1892-99.
———. *N. T. annoté.*
Bost, A. *Dict. d'Hist. ecclés.*
Boudou, P. Adrien. *Actes des Apôtres.* Verbum Salutis.
Boulenger, Canon. *Apologétique.*
A Brief History of the International Fellowship of Evangelical Students. Lausanne: IFES.
Broadbent, E. H. *The Pilgrim Church.* London: Pickering & Inglis, 1935.
———. *L'Eglise Ignorée.*
Bruce, F. F. *The Dawn of Christianity.* London: Paternoster, 1951.
———. *The Growing Day.* London: Paternoster, 1951.
———. *Light in the West.* London: Paternoster, 1952.
Brunner, Emil. *Cause des déficits de l'église nationale et proposition de quelques remédes.* Pamphlet.
———. "Die christliche Nicht-Kirche-Bewegung in Japan." *Evang. Théologie,* 1949, pp. 147-55.
———. *The Divine-Human Encounter.* Philadelphia: Westminster, 1943. Trans. of *Warheit als Begegnung.*
———. *Dogmatics.* Vol. 3. Philadelphia: Westminster, 1962.
———. *Eglise et Groupes.*
———. "Eglise et Révélation." *Revue de Théologie et de Philosophie,* Jan.-Mar. 1930, p. 7.
———. *Les Eglises, les Groupes et l'Eglise de Jésus Christ.* Geneva: Labor et Fides, 1937.
———. *Le Malentendu de l'Eglise.*
———. *The Misunderstanding of the Church.* Philadelphia: Westminster, 1953.
———. *Der Mittler.* Tübingen, 1930.
———. *Le Renouveau de l'Eglise.* Geneva: Labor et Fides, 1935.
———. *La Situation de l'Eglise.* Paris: Labor—Je sers.
———. *Unser Glaube.* Bern: Gotthelft, 1935. Eng. trans.: *Our Faith.* New York: Scribner, 1936.
Bruston, V. *La Discipline ecclésiastique réformée dans la Pensée de Calvin.* Lézan: Comité d'entente évangélique.
Burghard. "Volkskirche, Freikirche." *Das Evangelische Deutschland,* 1936, pp. 11-13.
Busch, H. *Melanchthons Kirchenbegriff.* Bonn, 1918.
Busch, W. "Selbstmord der Kirche." In *Licht und Leben-Ruf zur Entscheidung.*
Cadier, Jean. *L'Apôtre Pierre est-il le Chef de l'Eglise?*
Cadonau, Pastor. *Gott hilft.*

——. Studium und Zeugnis. No. 2. N.P., 1957.
Calvin, J. Confession de Foi des Eglises réformées de France. N.p., 1555.
——. Confession de Foi des Pays-Bas.
——. Disc. ecclés.
——. Ecrit sur les Conciles.
——. Epistle to Sadolet.
——. Epître à Sadolet. 3 vols. Paris: "Je sers," 1934.
——. Institutes. Philadelphia: Presbyterian Bd. of Pubns., 1911. In French: Institution. Paris: Belles Lettres, 1937.
——. La Vraie Façon de Réformer l'Eglise. Geneva: Labor et Fides, 1957.
——. Tracts and Treatises Relating to the Reformation. Vol. 1. Grand Rapids: Eerdmans, 1959.
Campbell, J. Y. "The Origin and Meaning of the Christian Use of the Word Ekklesia." Journal of Theological Studies, 1948, pp. 133 ff.
Casalis, G. Rapport de la Xᵉ Assemblée du Protestantisme.
Catéchisme luthérien. Strasbourg, 1932.
Cell, G. C. The Rediscovery of John Wesley. New York: Holt, 1935.
Cerfaux, Mgr. L. La Théologie de l'Eglise suivant Saint Paul. Eng. trans.: The Church in the Theology of Saint Paul. New York: Herder & Herder.
Chemnitz, Martin. Loci Theologici. P. Leyser, 1690.
Christiani, Canon. Catholiques, Protestants, Frères quand-même.
Church of Zürich. Dienst der Kirche in unserer Zeit. Zürich, 1966.
Clavier, H. "Brèves remarques sur les commentaires patristique de Matt. 16:18." In Studia Patristica I. Berlin: Akademie, 1957.
Confession de foi de l'Association des églises evangéliques baptistes.
Congar, Père Y. Jalons pour une Théologie du Laïcat, 1953.
Cook, Henry. What Baptists Stand For. London: Kingsgate, 1947.
Correll, E. H. "Harold S. Bender und die täuferische Forschung." In Das Täufertum.
Couleru, J. R. Le Baptême selon la Parole.
Courthial, P. "Actualité et catholicité de la Réformation." Revue réformée 13, no. 51 (1962).
Courvoisier, J. La Notion d'Eglise chez Bucer. Alcan, 1933.
——. "De la Réforme comme Principe critique du Protestantisme." Verbum Caro 3 (1953): 11 ff.
Cullmann, O. Le Baptême des Enfants et la Doctrine biblique du Baptême. Neuchâtel: Delachaux & Niestlé, 1948.
——. The Earliest Christian Confessions. London: Lutterworth, 1949.
——. Königsherrschaft Christi und Kirche im Neuen Testament. Zürich, 1941. Eng. trans.: The Early Church. Philadelphia: Westminster, 1956.
——. Peter: Disciple—Apostle—Martyr. Philadelphia: Westminster, 1953.
——. La Royauté du Christ et l'Eglise dans le Nouveau Testament.
——. La Tradition. Neuchâtel-Paris: Delachaux & Niestlé, 1953.
Cremer, H. "Taufe, Wiedergeburt und Kindertaufe." In Kraft des Heiligen Geistes, 3d ed. Gütersloh, 1917.
Dahl, Nils Alstrup. Das Volk Gottes. Oslo: Jakob Dybwad, 1941.
Dallmeyer, H. Erfahrungen in der Pfingstbewung.
——. Sonderbare Heilige in Kassel.
——. Die Zungenbewegung. Lagenthal: Pflug, n.d.

Davidson, F.; Stibbs, A. M.; and Kevan, E. F. *New Bible Commentary*. Grand Rapids: Eerdmans, 1953.

Davies, J. G. *Daily Life of Early Christians*. Boston: Little, Brown, 1953.

Deissmann, G. A. *Licht vom Osten*. Eng. trans.: *Light from the Ancient East*. New York: Hodder & Stoughton, 1910.

Desbaumes, André. *L'Eglise—Communauté*. Lyon: rue Fénélon, 1946. Brochure.

Dibelius, Otto. *Das Jahrhundert der Kirche*. Berlin, 1926.

———. *Die werdende Kirche*. Berlin, 1938.

Dictionnaire d'Archéologie chrétiene. Vol. 1.

Dienst der Kirche in unserer Zeit. Zürich: Zwingli, 1966.

Dilschneider, O. *Gefesselte Kirche*. Stuttgart: Verlagswerk, 1953.

Dinkler, Erich. Articles in *Religion in Geschichte und Gegenwart*. Vols. 4 & 6.

Dix, Dom Gregory. *The Shape of the Liturgy*. 2d ed. Westminster (London): Dacre, 1954.

———. *The Theology of Confirmation in Relation to Baptism*. Westminster (London): Dacre, 1946.

Dodd, C. H. *The Apostolic Preaching and Its Developments*. London: Hodder & Stoughton, 1936.

———. *The Parables of the Kingdom*. London: Nisbet, 1935.

Doellinger, Canon J. J. I. von. *La Papauté et son Origine au Moyen-Age*. Paris, 1904.

———. *Lettres et Déclarations au sujet des Décrets du Vatican*. Paris, 1893.

———. *Les Origines de la Papauté*.

Doene, M. "Was heisst Volkskirche?" *Theologia Militans* 1 (1935).

Drews, Paul. "Entsprach das Staatskirchentum dem Ideale Luthers?" In *Zeitschrift für Theologie und Kirche*. N.p., 1908.

Drobnitzky, W. "Die ewige Kirche." *Eine heilige Kirche*, no. 17 (1935), p. 285.

Drummond, Henry. *Natural Law in the Spiritual World*. New York: J. Pott, 1890.

Duchesne, Mgr. Louis. *The Early History of the Christian Church*. New York: Longmans, Green, 1913-24.

Durand, A. *Verbum salutis*. Paris, 1948.

Durand-Pallot. *Baptême, Confirmation, Saint-Cène*.

Ecclesia semper reformanda. Cahier spécial de Evang. Theol. 1952.

Ecke, K. *Schwenckfeld, Luther, und der Gedanke einer apostolischen Reformation*. Berlin, 1931.

Eicher, Erich von. *Flugfeuer fremden Geistes*. Gnadauer, n.d.

———. *Heiliger Geist, Menschengeist, Schwarmgeist*. Wuppertal: Brockhaus, 1964.

Farner, O. *Zwinglis Bedeutung für die Gegenwart*. N.p., 1919.

Fathers of the Church. 42 vols. New York: Scribner, 1854.

Faye, E. de. *Esquisse de la Pensée d'Origène*. Paris: Leroux, 1925.

———. *Vie, Oeuvre et Pensée d'Origène*. Paris: Leroux, 1923, 1927.

Fèbvre, L. *Un Destin: Martin Luther*. Paris: PUF, 1945.

Feine, D. *Realenzyklopädie für prot. Theologie und Kirche*. Bk. 19.

Finney, Charles G. "Christ, the Husband of the Church." In *Lectures to Professing Christians*. New York: Revell, 1879.

Flemington, W. F. *The New Testament Doctrine of Baptism.* London: SPCK, 1948.

Flew, R. Newton, *The Catholicity of Protestantism.* London: Lutterworth, 1st ed., 1950; 2d ed., 1951.

Foester, E. "Luthers Kirchenbegriff und die Kirchliche Krisis von heute." *Zeitschrift für Theologie und Kirche* (1920), pp. 103 ff.

Forsyth, P. T. *The Church and the Sacraments.* 2d ed. London: Independent Press, 1947.

Foucart, G. *Les Mystères d'Eleusis.* Paris, 1914.

Francus, G. *Il n'y a pas de Protestants.*

Friedrich, J. *Geschichte des Vatikanischen konzils.* Bonn, 1877.

Führ, E. "L'Eglise devient Diaspora." *Zeichen der Zeit,* no. 4 (Apr. 1963). The author shows by the New Testament what the role of the church is in a mainly pagan society.

Fürstenberg, Fr. "Formes de vie de l'Eglise et du monde." *Zeitwende,* no. 4 (Apr. 1963). Problem of the reformation of the church.

Gabus, J. P. *Centre prot. études et doc.* Nos. 83, 84.

Gasparin, Agénor de. *Les Droits du Coeur.*

———. *Les Ecoles du Doute et l'Ecole de la Foi.*

———. *Innocent III.*

———. *Paganisme et Christianisme.*

Geppert, W. *Die Pfingstbewegung.* Lagenthal: Sonnenweg, n.d.

Glage, N. *Volkskirche oder Freikirche?* N.p., 1935.

Gloege, G. *Reich Gottes und Kirche im N.T.* Gütersloh, 1929.

———. "Volkskirche, Freikirche oder Bekennende Kirche." *Reformation oder Restauration,* 1935, p. 50.

Göbel, Max. *Geschichte des christlichen Lebens in der rheinisch wesph. Kirche.* Koblenz, 1848.

Godet, F. *Commentaire sur I Cor.*

———. *Commentaire sur l'Evangile de Jean.* Vol. 2.

———. *Etudes bibliques sur l'Ancien Testament.* Ed. Ligue pour la lecture de la Bible.

Goguel, M. *The Primitive Church.* New York: Macmillan, 1964.

———. *Le Problème de l'Eglise.*

Gonin, F. Article in *Alliance évangélique,* Oct. 1964, p. 7.

Goosens, Werner. *L'Eglise, corps du Christ d'après Saint Paul.* 2d ed. Paris: Gabalda, 1949.

Gore, Charles. *The Holy Spirit and the Church.* London: J. Murray, 1924.

Graham, Billy. *World Aflame.* New York: Doubleday, 1965.

Griffith, Gwilym O. *Pocket History of the Baptist Movement.* London: Kingsgate, n.d.

Grundmann, H. *Religiöse Bewegungen im Mittelalter.*

Grundmann, S. "Kirchenverfassung." In *Religion in Geschichte und Gegenwart,* vol. 3.

"Gustachten des Evang. Theol. Fak. der Univers. Tübingen über: Fragen der Taufordnung."

Guiton, W. H. *Le Mouvement de Pentecôte.* Paris: Bons Semeurs, n.d.

Haas. *Grand Catéchisme.*

Haddal, I. *John Wesley.* New York: Abingdon, 1961.
Hadorn, William. *Die Reformation in der deutschen Schweiz.* Leipzig, 1923.
Halldane. *De l'authenticité et de la divine inspiration des Saintes Ecritures.* Toulouse, 1910.
——. *Dieu a parlé.* Voix de l'Evangile, 1965.
Haller, J. *Das Papsttum.* Stuttgart, 1950.
Hallesby, O. *Why I Am a Christian.* Minneapolis: Augsburg, 1930.
Halphen. *Etudes critiques sur l'Histoire de Charlemagne.* Alcan, n.d.
Harder, Günther. "Die Bedeutung der Kirchengliedschaft im Kirchenkampf." *Evangelische Theologie,* 1960, pp. 70 ff.
Harnack, A. von. *Die Mission und Ausbreitung des christentums in den ersten drei Jahrhunderten.* Vol. 1. Leipzig: Hinrichs, 1902.
——. *Das Wesen des Christentums.* Gütersloh: Bertelsmann, 1903.
——. *What Is Christianity?* New York: Putnam, 1901.
Hauterives. *Dict. des Racines européennes.* Larousse, n.d.
Heggelbacher, Othmar. *Die christliche Taufe als Rechtsakt nach dem Zeugnis der frühen Christenheit.* Freiburg, Coll Paradosis. Schweiz, 1953.
Hegler, Alfred. *Geist und Schrift bei S. Frank.* Freiburg, 1892.
Heim, Karl. *Die Gemeinde des Auferstandenen.* Munich, 1949.
——. *Ich gedenke der vorigen Tage.*
Heitmüller, F. *Die Krisis der Gemeinschaftsbewegung.* Hamburg: Christl. Gemeinschaftsbuchhandlung, 1931.
——. *Taufe und Abendmahl bei Paulus.* N.p., 1903.
Heppe, H. *Geschichte des Pietismus in der reform. Kirche.*
Herdt, René. "Détresse et espoir de l'Eglise." *Foi et Vie,* no. 1 (1939), pp. 1-25.
Hering, J. *Comm. 2 Cor.* Neuchâtel: Delachaux-Niestlé, 1958.
Hershberger, G. F. *The Recovery of the Anabaptist Vision.* Scottdale, Pa.: Herald, 1957.
Heyer, Henri. *L'Eglise de Genève.* Geneva, 1909.
Hilbert, G. *Ecclesiola in ecclesia.* A. Deichertsche Verlagsbuchhandlung. 2d ed. Leipzig-Erlangen: W. Scholl, 1924.
——. *Volkskirche und Bekenntniskirche.* N.p., 1919.
——. *Volksmission und innere Mission.* N.p., 1917.
——. *Wie kommen wir zu lebendigen Gemeinden,* N.P., 1922.
Hildebrandt, Walter. *Das Gemeindeprinzip der christlichen Kirche.* Zürich: Zwingli, 1951.
Hirsch, E. *Geschichte der neueren evang. Theologie.* Vol. 5. Güterloher: Verlagshaus Gerd. Mohn, 1960.
——. *Hilfsbuch zum Studium der Dogmatik.*
——. *Zum Verstandnis Schweinckfelds.*
Hobhouse, Walter. *The Church and the World in Idea and History.* London: Macmillan, 1910.
Hodgson, Leonard. *The Doctrine of the Church as Held and Taught in the Church of England.* London: Oxford, 1948.
Hoeckendijk, J. Christian. *Die Zukunft der Kirche und die Kirche der Zukunft.* Kreuz-V., n.d.
Hofer, E. A. *Eglise où es-tu?* St-Etienne du Rouvray, Seine Maritime: Sentinelle, 1964.

Holl, K. "Die Entstehung von Luthers Kirchenbegriff." In *Gesammelte Aug-sätze*, 1:288 ff.

———. *Erganzungsheft.*

———. *Festschrift.*

———. *Luther und das landesherrliche Kirchenregiment.*

———. *Ouvres complètes.*

Hübner, F. *Weltreich und Gottesreich in Prophetie und Erfüllung.* Stuttgart: Hänssler, 1958.

Hundeshagen, K. B. *Beiträge zur Kirchenverfassungsgeschichte und Kirchen politik.* Vol. 1. N.p., 1864.

Indo-germanisches etymologisches Wörterbuch. Bern-München: Francke, 1959.

Information Bulletin of the National Council of Churches (Dec. 1945).

Iremonger, F. A. *William Temple.* New York: Oxford U., 1948.

Ischbeck, G. *John Nelson Darby.* Lausanne: Vie et Liberté, 1937.

Isely, Gustave. *Chrétiens, Sectaires et Mécréants.* Geneva: Labor et Fides, n.d.

Izoulet, J. *La Métamorphose de l'Eglise.*

Jacobs, Manfred. *Die Evangelische Lehre von der Kirche.* Lüneburg: Heiland, 1962.

Jalaguier, Paul. *De l'Eglise.* Paris: Fischbacher, 1899.

Jamieson, R.; Fausset, A. R.; and Brown, D. *A Commentary Critical and Explanatory on the Old and New Testaments.*

Jeremias, Joachim. *Die Kindertaufe in den ersten vier Jahrhunderten.* Göttingen: Vandenhoek & Ruprecht, 1958.

Jetter, W. *Die Taufe beim jungen Luther.* Tübingen, 1954.

Johansson, Dean Nils. "Wer gehört zur urchrislichen Kirche?" In *Ein Buch von der Kirche.* Göttingen, 1951.

Judge, E. A. *The Social Pattern of Christian Groups in the First Century.* London: Tyndale, 1960.

Kähler, Martin. *Die Sakramente als Gnadenmittel.*

———. *Zur Bibelfrage.* N.p., 1907.

Keller, A. *Church and State on the European Continent.* London: Epworth, 1936.

Kellerhals, E. *Bekehrung und Wiedergeburt.* Brochure.

Kettler, F. H. Article in *Religion in Geschichte und Gegenwart*, vol. 6.

Kierkegaard, Søren. *L'Instant.*

Kittel, G. and Friedrich, G., eds. *Theol. Worterbuch zum N.T.* 4 vols. Stuttgart, 1938. Eng. trans: *Theological Dictionary of the New Testament.* Grand Rapids: Eerdmans, 1964-69.

———. *L'Eglise dans la Bible.* Studia-Desclée: Coll. Studia de Brouwer, 1962.

Köhler, Walter. "Enstehung der reformatio ecclesiarum Hassiae 1526." *Deutsche Zeitschrift für Kirchenrecht* 16 (1906): 217.

———. *Jubiläumsband 1519-1919.*

———. *Zwinglis Werke.* Leipzig, 1927.

Kolde, T. "Luthers Gedanken von der Ecclesiola in Ecclesia." *Zeitschrift für Kirchengeschichte*, 1892, pp. 554-55.

Kostlin, Julius. *Luthers Theologie in ihrer Geschichtlichen Entwicklung und in ihrem inneren Zusammenhang.*

———. *Martin Luther, sein Leben und seine Schriften.*

Krahn, Cornelius. *Der Gemeindebegriff des Menno Simons im Rahmen seines Lebens und seiner Theologie.* Karlsruhe: H. Schneider, n.d.

Krajewski, E. *Leben und Sterben der zürcher Täuferführers Felix Mantz.* Kassel: Oncken, 1957.

Kuen, A. *Que Tous Soient Un.* Brussells: Litt. biblique, n.d.

Küng, Hans. *The Council, Reform and Reunion.* New York: Sheed & Ward, 1961.

———. *The Structures of the Church.* Notre Dame, Ind.: U. Notre Dame, 1968.

Lamorte, A. *Réflexions à propos des doctrines de la prédestination et du Baptême chez Calvin.* Paris: Libr. prot., 1959.

Lang, H. G. *The Churches of God.* 1928. Reprint. London: Paternoster, 1959.

Latourette, Kenneth S. "A Historian Looks Ahead: The Future of Christianity in the Light of Its Past." In *Church History.* N.p., 1946.

———. *A History of the Expansion of Christianity.* Vol. 4. New York: Harper, 1945.

Lecerf, A. *Introduction à la Dogmatique réformée.* Vol. 2. Paris, 1938.

Lecomte, P. "Rapport sur le Membre d'Eglise." *Verbum Caro*, 1958, p. 185.

Leenhardt, Franz J. *Catholicisme romain et Protestantisme.* Geneva: Labor et Fides, 1957. Eng ed.: *Two Biblical Faiths: Protestant and Catholic.* Philadelphia: Westminster, 1964.

———. *Etudes sur l'Eglise dans le Nouveau Testament.* Geneva: U. Geneva Faculty of Theology, 1940.

———. *L'Eglise et le Royaume de Dieu.* Geneva: Labor et Fides, n.d.

Legault, A. Article in *L'Eglise dans la Bible.* Desclée, 1962.

Lelièvre, Mathieu. *Wesley, sa Vie et son Oeuvre.* Paris, 1922.

Lemaître, A. *Foi et Vérité.*

Léonard, E. G. *Histoire générale du Protestantisme Français.* Vol. 1.

———. *Le Protestant Français.* Paris: PUF, 1955.

———. "Le Protestantisme entre l'Eglise de Multitude et l'Eglise de Professants." *Revue réformée* 1 (1953): 8.

Lestringant, P. "Les Membres de l'Eglise." *Revue de Théologie et de Philosophie*, 1939.

Lettre pastorale du Synode de l'Eglise Réformée des Pays-Bas. Les Berges et les Mages.

Lewis, Edwin. *The Ministry and the Sacraments.*

Lichtenberger, F. Article in *Encyclopédie des Sciences religieuses*, vol. 4.

Liermann, H. Article in *Religion in Geschichte und Gegenwart*, vol. 3.

Linton, Olof. *Das Problem der Urkirche in der neueren Forschung.* Uppsala: Almqvist-Wirksells, 1932.

Littell, Franklin H. *The Free Church.* Boston: Starr King, 1957.

Lobstein, Paul. "Essai d'une Apologie du Baptême des Enfants." In *Par le Christ à Dieu.*

Löhe, Wilhelm. "Drei Bücher von der Kirchen." *Gesammelte Werke* 5 (1954): 116.

Lortz, J. *Die Reformation in Deutschland.* 4th ed. Freiburg: Herder, n.d.

Lovsky, F. Article in *Foi et Vie*, 1950.

Lüscher, A. L. *Laodizäa die Christuslose Endkirche.* N.p., 1939.

———. *Der Triumph der Hl. Geister über das Selbst.* Switzerland: Langenthal.

———. *Wer glaubt der flieht nicht.*

Luther, Martin. *An den christlichen Adel.*
——. *Ad librum . . . Ambrosis Catharini.*
——. "Artikles de Smalkalde." In *Die Bekenntnis-Schriften.* 1537.
——. *Artikel gegen Satans Schule.* W. A. 30, 2.
——. *Commentary on Matthew.*
——. *Corpus Reformatorum.*
——. *De la Captivité babylonienne de l'Eglise.* 1520. W. A. 6, 560, 33.
——. *Disputat. Acta.* July 5, 1519.
——. *Hauspostville.*
——. *Kurzes Bekenntnis vom heiligen Sakrament.* 1544.
——. *The Large Catechism.*
——. *Livres symboliques.* Paris, 1946.
——. *Oeuvres de Luther.* Geneva, 1962.
——. *Schriften zur Neuordnung der Gemeinde, des Gottesdienstes und der Lehre.*
——. *Sermon John 6 to 8.* 1531. W. A. 33, 365, 21.
——. *Smalkalder Artikel.* 1537.
——. *Vom Papsttum zu Rom.* 1520.
——. *Von Konzilien und Kirchen.* 1539.
——. *Wider die Schwarmgeister.*
——. *Wider Hans Worst.* 1541.
MacGregor, Geddes. *Corpus Christi.* Philadelphia: Westminster, 1958.
Maron, G. Article in *Religion in Geschichte und Gegenwart*, vol. 5.
Marx, J. *Lehrbuch der Kirchengeschichte.* Trier, 1908.
Maurer, V. W. "Franz Lambert von Avigon und das Verfassungsideal der Reformatio ecclesiarum Hassiae." In *Zeitschrift für Kirchengeschichte* 11:209 ff., and bibliography.
Maurer, Will. "Kirche und Geschichte nach Luthers Dictata super Psalterium." In *Lutherforschung heute.* Berlin: Luth. Verlagshaus, 1958.
McIntyre, Alasdair. *Diskussion zu Robinsons Gott ist anders.* Munich: C. Kaiser.
Mehl. R. "L'Eglise de l'Avenir." *Revue de l'Evangélisation*, no. 98 (1961), p. 472.
——. "L'évolution de l'ecclésiologie dans la pensée du mouvement oecuménique," *Revue d'Histoire et de Philosophie religieuse*, no. 2, 3 (1962).
——. Article in *Verbum Caro*, 1958.
Melanchthon. *Loci praecipiu theologici* (1559). In *Works of Melanchton*, ed. Stupperich, vol. 2.
Menegoz, E. "Le Baptême des Enfants d'après les Principes de la Théologie paulinienne." *Revue chrét*, 1884.
Mennonitisches Lexikon. Vol. 2. Hege-Neff, n.d.
Menoud, P. "Eglise." In *Vocabulaire biblique.* Neuchâtel: Delachaux-Niestlé.
Mertz, G. "Volkskirche, Bekenntniskirche oder Volkstumskirche." *Junge Kirche*, 1934, pp. 784-90.
Michel, Otto. *Das Zeugnis des N.T. von der Gemeinde.* Göttinger: Vandenhoek-Ruprecht, 1941.
Millon, G. "Ecriture sainte et Tradition en Cahier," *Le Vent Souffle*, no. 2-3, p. 53.
——. *Combats pour l'Eglise.*

Minear, Paul S. *Images of the Church in the New Testament*. Philadelphia: Westminster, 1960.

Mollard, Abbé. Article in *Revue Esprit*, Dec. 1961.

Monod, Adolphe. "Sermons sur la Vocation de l'Eglise." In *Sermons choisis*, ed. du Centenaire. Paris: Fischbacher, 1902.

Moore, J. A. *Der starke Jörg*. Kassel: Oncken, 1955.

Moreton. *Rome et l'Eglise.*

Morrison, Charles Clayton. *The Unfinished Reformation*. New York: Harper, 1953.

Morton, Ralph T. and Gibbs, Mark. *God's Frozen People*. Philadelphia: Westminster, 1965.

Mott, J. *Liberating the Lay Forces of Christianity*. New York, 1932.

Müller, Gerhard. "Ecclesiologie und Kirchenkritik beim jungen Luther." *Neue Zeitschrift für systematische Theologie und Religionsphilosophie* 1 (1965): 100-28.

Mueller, J. T. *La Doctrine chrétienne.*

———. *Christian Dogmatics.*

Müller, Karl. *Kirchengeschichte.*

———. *Kirche, Gemeinde und Obrigkeit.*

Muralt, L. von and Schmid, W., eds. *Quellen zur Geschichte der Täufer in der Schweiz* 1, no. 14 (1952).

Murray, Iain. *The Reformation of the Church*. London: Banner of Truth, 1965.

Nagel, G. *Der gross Kampf*. Bonn: Schergens, n.d. A contribution which throws light on the question: church or assembly of believers?

Naunin. "Die Kirchenordnungen des Johannes Lasci." *Deutsche Zeitschrift für Kirchenrecht* 19 (1909):24 ff., 196 ff., 348 ff.

Nee, Watchman. *The Normal Christian Church Life*. Washington, D. C.: International Students, 1962.

Neff, G. *Geschichte der täufgesinnten Gemeinden.*

Neill, S. C. *The Unfinished Task*. London: Edinburgh House, 1957.

Nelson, J. R. *The Realm of Redemption*. London: Epworth, 1951.

Newbigin, Lesslie. *L. E'glise*. Neuchâtel: Delachaux & Niestlé, 1958. Eng. trans.: *A Reunion of the Church*. London: SCM, 1948.

———. *A Faith for This One World?* London: SCM, 1961. See chap. 1: "The End of Christendom and the Rise of a World Civilization," pp. 9-29, and chap. 5: "The Pattern of the Christian Mission to the Nations," pp. 106-26.

———. *Is Christ Divided?* Grand Rapids: Eerdmans, 1961.

———. *Trinitarian Faith and Today's Mission*. Richmond: John Knox, 1963.

———. *L'Universalisme de la Foi chrétienne*. Geneva: Labor et Fides, n.d.

Nicole, Albert. *La Notion biblique de l'Eglise et nos Devoirs actuels*. Nogent: Institut Biblique, 1929.

Nicole, J. M. "Calvin, Homme de la Bible." *Revue de Théologie et d'Action évangélique*, Oct. 1943, pp. 310-27.

Niebuhr, H. Richard. *The Kingdom of God in America*. Chicago, 1937.

Ninck, Werner. *Die Christliche Gemeinde heute.*

Nisbet. *L'Evangile ne dit pas cela.*

Odeberg, A. F. "Der neuzeitliche Individualismus und der Kirchengedanke im N.T." In *Ein Buch von der Kirche*. Göttingen, 1951.

Oulette, L. Article in *L'Eglise dan la Bible*. Desclée, 1962.

Paradis, Abbé Hubert. Article in *L'Eglise dan la Bible*. Desclée, 1962.

Pascal, Blaise. *Les Opuscules*. Paris: Hachette, n.d.

Pelikan, Jaroslav. "Die Kirche nach Luthers Genesis Vorlesung." In *Lutherforschung heute*. Berlin: Luth. Verlagshaus, 1958.

Plachte. *Die Wiederentdeckung der Kirche*. Göttingen, 1940.

Pourrat. *La Spiritualité chrétienne*.

Prenter, Regin. "L'Eglise d'après la Confession d'Augsbourg." In *La Sainte Eglise universelle*.

———. *Schopfung und Erlösung*.

Pury, Roland de. *La Maison de Dieu*. Neuchâtel: Delachaux & Niestlé, 1946.

Pressensé, E. de. *Discours religieux*. Paris: ch. Meyrueis, 1859.

Quenstedt. *Theologia didactice-polemica* 4 (1961): 478.

Ramsey, A. M. *The Doctrine of Confirmation Theology* 48 (1954): 201.

Ramseyer, J. P. *Histoire des Baptistes*.

———. *Vocabulaire biblique*.

Refoulé, F. *Revue d'Histoire et de Philosophie religieuse*, 1964.

Rendtorff. *Die Taufe im Urchristentum im Lichte der neueren Forschung*. Leipzig, 1905.

Renouvier, C. *Philosophie analytique de l'Histoire*.

Rican, Rudolf. *Die Böhmischen Brüder*. Berlin: Union, 1961.

Richter, J. "Volkskirche oder Freikirche?" *Christliche Welt* 51 (1937): cols. 723-26.

———. "Volkskirche oder Kirche der Auserwählten." *Die christliche Welt* 51 (1937): cols. 460-67.

Riecker, Otto. *Erweckung heute und ihre Botschaft an uns*. Wuppertal: Brockhaus, 1958.

Rienecker, Fritz. *Biblische Kritik am Pietismus*. Offenbach, 1952.

———. *Stellungsnahme zu Bultmanns Entmythologisierung*. Wuppertal: Brockhaus.

Ritchie, J. *The Tabernacle in the Wilderness*. New York: Gospel Publishing House, 1895.

Ritschl, Albrecht. "Luthers Anschauungen von der Unsichtbarkeit u. Sichbarkeit des Kirche." *Th. St. u. K.*, 1900, pp. 416 ff.

———. "Taufertum." In *Geschichte des Pietismus*. Bonn, 1880.

Robinson, H. Wheeler. *Baptist Principles*. London: Kingsgate.

Roth, F. *Augsburgs Reformations Geschichte*. Munich, 1901.

Rousseau, G. *Le drame anabaptiste*.

Roy, A. *Union des Eglises évangéliques libres de France*.

Sambin, J. *Hist. du Concile oecuménique et général du Vatican*.

Samouélian, S. *Aperçu historique des Eglise de Professants*. Nîmes: Dépôt des publications méthodistes, 1958.

Schaeffer, Francis A. *Néo-modernisme ou christianisme*. Maison de la Bible.

Schaff, Philip. *Church and State in the United States*. New York: Putnam, 1888.

———. *History of the Apostolic Church*. 3 vols. New York: Scribner, 1854.

Scheel, O. *Zum urchristlichen Kirchen—und Verfassungsproblem*.

Scheuerl. "Die geistliche und die rechtliche Kirche." In *Sammlung Kirchenrechtlicher Abhandlungen*. Erlanger, 1872.

Schindelin, F. *Es begann in der Ewigkeit.* Gladbeck, n.d.

Schlatter, A. *Der Evangelist Matthäus.* Stuttgart, 1929.

Schleiermacher, Friedrich. *The Christian Faith.* Edinburgh: T. & T. Clark, 1928. Trans. from *Der Christliche Glaube,* 1821.

Das Schleitheimer Täuferbekenntnis 1527. Thaygen, Switzerland: Augustin, 1951.

Schlink, M. B. *Und keiner wollte es glauben.* Wuppertal: Brockhaus, 1965.

Schmidt, K. L. *Die Kirche des Urchristentums.*

———. "Ekklesia." In *Theol. Worterbuch zum N. T.* ed G. Kittel and G. Friedrich. Stuttgart, 1938. Eng. trans.: *Theological Dictionary of the N.T.* 4 vols. Grand Rapids: Eerdmans, 1964-67.

———. "Kaleo." In *Theol. Worterbuch zum N.T.* Stuttgart, 1938.

Schmitt, Jakob. *Die Gnade bricht durch.* 3d ed. Basel-Giessen: Brunnen, 1957.

Schnackenburg, R. *Die Kirche im N.T.* Freiburg: Herber, 1961. Eng. trans.: *The Church in the New Testament.* New York: Herder & Herder, n.d.

Schneider, Johannes. *Taufe und Gemeinde im N.T.* Kassel: Oncken, 1956.

Schnepel, E. *Jesus im Römerreich.*

Schoen, Christian. *Christianus Irenicus.* Frankfurt, 1722.

Schultz, H. J. "Christentum incognito?" In *Kritik an der Kirche.* Stuttgart: Kreuz. A series of radio messages in which Protestant and Catholic laymen and theologians submit the church of today to criticism.

Schwenckfeld, Kaspar. *Ungelöste Fragen der Reformationzeit.* Gütersloh: Bertelsmann, 1952. Abridged edition reedited under the title, *Fortsetzung der Reformation.* Memmingen: Missions-verlag für urchristliche Botschaft, n.d.

Secrétan, Louis. *Baptême des Croyants ou Baptême des Enfants.*

———. *Philosophie de la Liberté.*

Senarclens, J. de. *De la Vraie Eglise, selon Calvin.* Geneva: Labor et Fides, 1965.

———. "L'Eglise," *Héritiers de la Reformation.* Vol. 2. Geneva: Labor et Fides, n.d.

———. *La Réforme hier et aujourd'hui.* Geneva: Labor et Fides, 1964.

Simon, Dean M. *Les Premiers Chrétiens.* Paris: PUF, 1952.

Sluys, Klass. *Das Wunder von Boechout.* Giessen-Basel: Brunnen, 1963.

Smith, Wade C. *New Testament Evangelism "Come and See"—"Go and Tell."* Richmond: Onward, 1930.

Snaith. Article in *The Methodist Recorder,* June 17, 1948.

Sohm, R. *Kirchenrecht.* Vols. 1, 2. Leipzig, 1892.

Sondheimer, F. *Die wahre Taufe.* Kassel: Oncken, 1951.

Stauffer, R. *Le Premier Concile du Vatican.*

Stephan, Raoul. *L'Epopée huguenote.*

Stibbs, Alan. *God's Church.* 2d ed. London: Inter-Varsity, 1963.

Stier, R. *Discours du Seigneur.* Vol. 2.

Stoll, C. *Kirchenzucht.*

Stork, T. *The Life of Luther.* Philadelphia: Lindsay & Blakiston, 1854.

Strack-Billerbeck. *Kommentar zum Matthäus-Ev.*

———. *Kommentar zum N.T. aus Talmud und Midrasch.* Vol. 1.

Strohl, H. *La Pensée de la Réforme.*

Strossmayer, Mgr. *Ein Bischof gegen die Unfehlbarkeit des Papstes.* Munich, n.d.

Sulze, E. *Die evang. Gemeinde.* 1891.

Taylor. *Sayings of the Jewish Fathers.*

Thornton, L. S. *The Common Life in the Body of Christ.* Westminster (London): Dacre, 1946.

Thurneysen, E. "Die Frage nach der Kirche." *Zwischen den Zeiten* 4 (1926).

Torrance, T. F. *The Doctrine of Grace in the Apostolic Fathers.* Edinburgh: Oliver & Boyd, 1948.

Torrey, R. *How to Bring Men to Christ.* Chicago: Revell, 1893.

Tournier, P. *De la Solitude à la Communauté.* Neuchâtel: Delachaux-Niestlé.

Troeltsch, E. *Kirchliches Amt und geistliche Vollmacht in den drei ersten Jahrh.* N.d., 1953.

———. *Die Soziallehren der christl. Kirchen und Gruppen.* Tübingen, 1919.

Trotter, Lilias. *Parables of the Cross.*

Utchimura, K. *Wie ich Christ wurde.* Stuttgart: Gundert, 1923.

Valeske, Ulrich. *Votum ecclesiae.* Vol. 2. Munich: Claudius, 1962.

Valloton, P. *Christ et la Foi.*

Van Zeijl. *Wenn Gottes Winde wehen.*

Venske, Herbert. *Vollendete Reformation.* Wupperthal: Brockhaus, 1958. From the state church to the living assembly.

Verghese, Paul. "Vocation des Eglises à un service renouvelé." In *Report of Nyborg III.*

Verwer, G. *La Page Imprimée.*

Vinay, Tuillio. "Les Eglises minoritaires et le service des autres." *Etudes théologiques et religieuses,* no. 3 (1963).

Vinet, Alexandre. *Discours sur quelques sujets religieux.* Lausanne: Payot, 1929.

———. *L'Education, la Famille et la Société.* N.p., 1855.

———. *Etudes sur la Littérature française du XIXᵉ siècle.* Vol. 2.

———. *Hist. de la Littérature française au XIXᵉ Siècle.* Vol. 3.

———. *Liberté religieuse et Questions ecclésiastiques.*

Vischer, Wilhelm. *Die evangelische Gemeindeordnung.*

Visser't Hooft, W. A. *Misère et Grandeur de l'Eglise.* Geneva: Labor et Fides, 1943.

———. *None Other Gods.* New York: Harper, 1937.

———. *The Renewal of the Church.* London: SCM, 1956.

———. *Le Renouveau de L'Eglise.* Geneva: Labor et Fides, 1956.

Vogel, H. "Die permanente Reformation der Kirche." *Junge Kirche* 19 (1956): 589 ff.

Warns, S. *Baptism, Studies in the Original Christian Baptism.* London: Paternoster, 1957.

Wedel, Theodore. *The Coming Great Church.* New York: Macmillan, 1945.

Wehrung, G. *Kirche nach evangelischen Verständnis.* Güterloh: C. Bertelsmann, 1945.

Westin, Gunnar. *Geschichte des Freikirchentums.* Kassel: Oncken, n.d.

What Is Christian Hope in the Christian Century? Report for the Evanston conference of the WCC. Neuchâtel: Delachaux-Niestlé, 1946.

White, F. H. *Christian Baptism*. London: Partridge, n.d.

Wilkenhauser. *Die Kirche als der mystische Leib Christi nach dem Apostel Paulus*. Münster, 1937.

Wilkes, A. Paget. *The Dynamic of Service*. Kansas City, Mo.: Beacon Hill, 1944.

Williams, George Hunten. *The Radical Reformation*. Philadelphia: Westminster, 1962.

Williams, N. P. *Ideas of the Fall and Original Sin*.

Windisch, H. "Zum Problem der Kindertaufe im Urchristentum." ZNW 28 (1929): 118 ff.

Winford, St. *The New Testament Teaching on Baptism*.

Wittacker, E. C. Article in *Theology* 59 (1956): 104.

Wölber, Hans Otto. *Religion ohne Entscheidung*. Gottingen: Vandenhoeck, n.d.

Wolff, H. W. *Neue Liebe zur alten Kirche*. Gütersloh, 1947.

Workman. *Foi et Constitution*.

Yoder, J. H. *Täufertum und Reformation in der Schweiz*. Karlsruhe: Schneider, 1962.

Zoellner, W. "Die Kirche nach dem Epheserbrief?" In *Die Kirche im N.T.* Berlin, 1930.

Index